Chinese politics and society

Chinese politics and society: An introduction

Flemming Christiansen and Shirin M. Rai

 Prentice Hall
Harvester Wheatsheaf

London New York Toronto Sydney Tokyo Singapore
Madrid Mexico City Munich

First published 1996 by
Prentice Hall Europe
Campus 400, Maylands Avenue
Hemel Hempstead
Hertfordshire, HP2 7EZ
A division of
Simon & Schuster International Group

Typeset in 10/12pt Sabon
by Keyword Publishing Services, Barking

Printed and bound in Great Britain by
T.J. Press (Padstow) Ltd

Library of Congress Cataloging in Publication Data

Christiansen, Flemming, 1954–
    Chinese politics and society : an introduction / by Flemming
Christiansen and Shirin M. Rai.
      p.   cm.
    Includes bibliographical references and index.
    ISBN 0-13-354656-X (alk. paper)
    1. China—Politics and government—1949– 2. China—Economic
conditions—1949– 3. China—Economic policy—1949– 4. China—
Social conditions—1949– I. Rai, Shirin. II. Title.
JQ1502.C466 1996
951.05—dc20   95–51538
                                                                                                      CIP

British Library Cataloguing in Publication Data

A catalogue record for this book is available from
the British Library

ISBN 0-13-354656-X

---

1 2 3 4 5   00 99 98 97 96

Contents

List of tables, boxes and figures

Tables

Boxes

Figures

Preface

As we approach the end of the twentieth century China is poised for dramatic growth, which builds upon the changes it has experienced in the twentieth century. Its economic reforms have laid the foundations for significant growth of its influence in the global political economy, as well as the international political system. With a fifth of the world's population, and arguably the fastest growing economy in the world, China is already a world power. Add to this 'new rich' status China's ancient history, its cultural sophistication and its military might, and we can begin to understand why it has caught the imagination of so many over the years, and continues to do so.

If the world's perception of China is changing in light of its recent economic success, the Chinese too are re-evaluating their position in the world. China has seen many changes in the twentieth century. It has moved from a position where its elites were able to create in the Chinese imagination a central place for China – *Zhongguo*, the Middle Kingdom – to one where the country was called the 'sick man of Asia' and the Chinese were helpless to challenge the carving up of their country. The certainties of the Middle Kingdom gave way to an unpredictable 'opening up' of China.

'Opening up' has been an important political theme in modern Chinese history, and also runs throughout this book. We argue that the Chinese have both initiated and repulsed contact with the outside world. They have both rejected and accepted, both fought against and compromised with, the outside influences, ideas and pressures. 'Opening up' has brought China humiliation as well as opportunities, and China has learnt from one and benefited from the other.

The twentieth century saw one of the most dramatic revolutions and a rejuvenation of the country's pride when the communists marched into Beijing and declared the founding of the People's Republic of China on 1 October 1949. The Chinese people had stood up, declared Mao Zedong. China started on a new journey halfway through the century, a journey that was to take it on a tortuous road with many diversions before China could reach the goal it had set itself – to be powerful again in the community of nations. No longer the Middle Kingdom, it has nevertheless gained a central place in the world system.

There have been costs attached to this success. Violence has marked Chinese history in the twentieth century. Violence of social and economic exploitation, of political chaos, oppression and rebellion, and violence to the demographic and ecological balance in the country. Violence has marked not only the end of the *ancien régime* in China, but its new beginnings as well. The contemporary Chinese state is a product of the violent revolution that is the twentieth century in China.

While historically central to the political organization in China, state power in socialist China is perhaps the most powerful that the country has experienced. In its control of the political, economic and surveillance infrastructures, the Chinese state is enormously powerful. This control has not always been uniform, or even secure; the state, while centralized, has always experienced subversion of its authority in a *de facto* if not a politically overt way. The economic reforms have made China more prosperous, but they have not realized social harmony – widening social cleavages and persisting political violence are symptoms of more fundamental issues of population growth, competition for resources and the upsetting of the ecological balance. If the problem that the twentieth century posed for China was one of economic development, in the next century China faces the task of reorganizing its authority structures to accommodate the new actors and pressures that economic success has brought with it.

The political transformations during the twentieth century stand at the centre of our explorations in this book. In order to capture the broad field of scholarly approaches to Chinese politics, the Introduction (Chapter 1) highlights the most important models and conceptual frameworks.

The issue of ideology is often discussed in connection with Chinese politics. Instead of isolating the discussion of 'ideology' from the political developments, this book seeks to integrate the discussion of ideology with the real events in Chinese economy and politics. This is in accordance with the authors' views that ideology represents a rationalization of political behaviour, and is not an independent motive force in history.

Part I examines the context within which Chinese politics is set, including the historical roots of the Chinese Revolution, the revolutionary movement from its inception, and the ideological and philosophical foundations on which the Chinese Communists built the socialist state.

Part II lays out the political structures of post-1949 China in Chapter 5, its political practices and processes in Chapter 6, and its military and foreign policy in Chapters 7 and 8.

Part III is an examination of the political economy of China; Part IV discusses China's social concerns and the policies it has pursued in regard to addressing the issues of ecology and demography (Chapter 11), gender relations (Chapter 12) and ethnic and regional autonomy (Chapter 13).

Finally in the Conclusions (Chapter 14), we project the lines of China's development into the future, gauging where the dynamics of Chinese politics might lead the country in the twenty-first century.

Basic facts about China

State

The official name of the Chinese state is *The People's Republic of China*. The capital of China is Beijing (Peking); in the 1920s to the 1940s Beijing was called Beiping (Pei-p'ing), while the capital of the Chinese Republic was established in Nanjing (Nanking) and Chongqing (Chungking). Since 1949 the nationalist government in Taiwan has established its capital in Taibei (Taipei), and refers to itself as the 'Republic of China' or ROC. The official flag of the People's Republic of China is a red banner which shows five stars in the upper left corner. The national emblem shows the Gate of the Heavenly Peace (Tiananmen) and five stars in a circle of grain with a cogwheel and draping of red cloth in the lower part of the perimeter. The national day is 1 October, the day on which the establishment of the People's Republic was declared in 1949.

Administrative division

China is divided into 31 provincial-level jurisdictions, of which three (Beijing, Tianjin and Shanghai) are cities directly under central government control, 23 are provinces (including Taiwan) and five are autonomous regions. China also claims sovereignty over the colonies Hong Kong (under British rule) and Macau (under Portuguese rule); the former will revert to Chinese administration in 1997, and the latter in 1999. Taiwan Province and a number of islands on the coast of Fujian Province (Jinmen and Mazu) are controlled by the nationalist government in Taibei.

Cities

China has 570 cities (at the end of 1993), of which 10 have more than 2 million inhabitants, 22 have between 1 and 2 million inhabitants and 36 have between 500,000 and 1 million inhabitants.

Territory

The Chinese land territory is estimated to be 9,600,000 km². One-third of the territory consists of mountains, and more than one-quarter of plateaus. Only about 40 per cent of the territory is in altitudes lower than 1,000 m, and only one-quarter below 500 m. More than one-quarter is above 3,000 m altitude. Only 10–15 per cent of the land territory is arable, and another 13 per cent is dedicated to forests. About 40 per cent of the territory is characterized as 'prairies'. China's major river systems are the Changjiang (Yangtze River) (6,300 km); the Huanghe (Yellow River) (5,464 km); the Songhua Jiang (Sungari River) (2,300 km); the Zhujiang (Pearl River) (2,214 km) and the Liaohe, Haihe and Huaihe rivers (each about 1,000 km).

China's population

In 1993 the population size was 1,185,170,000. According to the official statement on the population census in 1990 it was 1,130,510,638, excluding the People's Liberation Army, Taiwan, Jinmen, Mazu, Hong Kong and Macau; if these are included, the total population was 1,160,044,618 in 1990.

Nationality and citizenship

Chinese citizenship follows the principle of *jus sanguinis*, so that persons borne by Chinese citizens are Chinese; this means that Chinese persons holding foreign passports, Taiwanese passports, as well as Hong Kong and Macau travel documents, are considered to be Chinese. However, for these categories of people (i.e. overseas Chinese, Hong Kong, Macau and Taiwanese compatriots), the Chinese authorities have special legislation and administrative procedures. China does not accept dual nationality, and so does not issue Chinese passports to Chinese who have assumed a foreign citizenship. Chinese citizenship is extended to persons of all 56 officially recognized nationalities in China.

Economy

The Chinese economy ranks among the 10 largest economies in the world in absolute terms; some observers even claim that it is the third-largest economy, if world-market prices are used to measure the domestic economy. In per capita terms, the Chinese economy still belongs in the low-income group. The Chinese economy is one of the fastest growing economies in the world, with growth rates of the gross domestic product of above 13 per cent in 1992 and 1993, and sustained growth rates over a decade approaching 10 per cent. In the early 1990s, 21 per cent of the gross national product was created in agriculture, 52 per cent in industry and 27 per cent in the service sectors.

Currency

The Chinese currency is *renminbi* (literally 'people's currency'), often referred to as RMB or *yuan*. The *renminbi* is not (yet) convertible, but the currency bank of the state, the Bank of China, plans to make it convertible in the latter part of the 1990s.

Some practical notes

Chinese transcription

The transcription of Chinese words and names since the end of the 1970s has followed an international standard, which adopts the Hanyu Pinyin transcription from the Chinese mainland. Most books and periodicals presently adopt this transcription, and we also stick to it here. However, if you read older books and articles (or English texts produced in Taiwan) about China, you are likely to come across the Wade–Giles transcription, which was used for personal names and for ordinary words. A different postal transcription was used for place names. In official English language publications from the mainland before 1979, a modified version of Wade–Giles was used.

Except for the personal names Sun Yat-sen and Chiang Kai-shek, and the geographical name Hong Kong, all other names in this book are in Hanyu Pinyin.

Some examples of differences in transcription are given here. **Hanyu Pinyin; Wade–Giles; modified Wade–Giles**: Mao Zedong, Mao Tse-tung, Mao Tsetung; Jiang Qing, Chiang Ch'ing, Chiang Ching; Song Qingling, Soong Ch'ing-ling, Soong Chingling; Liu Shaoqi, Liu Shao-ch'i, Liu Shaochi; Deng Xiaoping, Teng Hsiao-p'ing, Teng Hsiaoping; Chen Boda, Ch'en Po-ta, Chen Pota. **Hanyu Pinyin, Postal**: Beijing, Peking; Guangzhou, Canton; Xianggang, Hong Kong; Tianjin, Tientsin; Xi'an, Sian; Sichuan, Sechwan; Chongqing, Chungking; Guizhou, Kweichow; Suzhou, Soochow.

Chinese names

The names of all Han Chinese have the family name first and the personal name last: MAO Zedong, LIU Shaoqi and DENG Xiaoping can be referred to as Chairman Mao, President Liu and Vice-Premier Deng, for example. The usage 'comrade Xiaoping' is often seen in internal party documents, and indicates that high-level party cadres can address each other by forename. Most Chinese surnames are monosyllabic, and the majority of forenames have two syllables, like the names mentioned above. JIANG Qing and KANG Sheng have monosyllabic forenames.

Chinese measures etc.

Reading books and articles about China, you may come across the following measures: jin (500 g, sometimes referred to as a *catty*); mu (667 m², one-fifteenth of a hectare or one-sixth of an acre, sometimes written *mou*). The Chinese currency is *renminbi*, or RMB for short; it is often referred to as *yuan*. In the early and mid-1990s the exchange rate was approximately 13 yuan to one pound British sterling or between six and eight yuan to one American dollar.

Terminology

The terminology used in this book to describe the Chinese political system is kept as simple as possible, and special expressions are explained in context. The index indicates where a term is defined or its meaning discussed most thoroughly. The term used in this book for the administrative level *diqu* between province and county is 'district'; some other books on Chinese politics use the term 'prefecture'. Please note that political and administrative terminology is often obscured in translations (e.g. *Beijing Review*, Xinhua News Agency bulletins, Summary of World Broadcast and Foreign Broadcast Information Service (FBIS)), and that it is advisable to corroborate translations of source material before drawing conclusions.

About Further Reading sections

There are sections of further reading bibliographies after each chapter, which aim at giving you an opportunity to read additional works in commonly accessible books and journals. These lists are not exhaustive, and you will profit from looking up other literature in the full bibliography at the end of the book. This book is meant to be a gateway to the issues and debates that deserve your further exploration in other descriptive works and sources.

Study aids and sources for Chinese politics

Kenneth Lieberthal has compiled the *Research Guide to Central Meetings in China* (Vol 1: 1976; Vol 2: 1989) which is recommended if you need to verify a state or party meeting or find a reference to a political decision. Foreign Languages Press in Beijing has published a *Who's Who in China. Current Leaders*; use of the latest edition of this or similar works may be helpful to identify or verify Chinese leaders and their careers. Since the early 1970s the German monthly *China Aktuell* has provided detailed English-language listings of leadership changes and activities in China, as well as other exact information. In each issue the British journal *China Quarterly* summarizes political developments in a Chronicle, which is of great importance for those who need to know the political highlights of a period. *Beijing Review* (formerly *Peking Review*) is an official journal of the Chinese government and prints major policy documents in English translation. *Issues and Studies* from Taiwan occasionally gives English translations of political documents from the mainland. Some documents can be found in Schurmann and Schell (eds), *Communist China: Revolutionary Reconstruction and International Confrontation 1949–66* (1977).

List of abbreviations and acronyms

CCP   Chinese Communist Party
Comintern   Communist International
CPPCC   Chinese People's Political Consultative Conference
FBIS   Foreign Broadcast Information Service
KMT   Guomindang (Kuo Min Tang, the Nationalist Party)
NPC   National People's Congress
PLA   People's Liberation Army
PRC   People's Republic of China
ROC   Republic of China
UN   United Nations

List of Chinese characters

Anhui 安徽
Bai Hua 白桦
baihua (vernacular) 白话
bao gan dao hu (household responsibility system) 包干到户
Beihai 北海
Beijing 北京
Cantonese (Guangdonghua) 广东话
Changjiang (Yangtze River) 长江
changnei shiye (unemployment in the factories) 厂内失业
Changsha 长沙
Changzhou 常州
Chen Duxiu 陈独秀
Chen Junsheng 陈俊生
Chen Muhua 陈慕华
Chen Yonggui 陈永贵
Chengming (Zhengming, monthly) 争鸣杂志
chengshi jumin hukou (urban resident household) 城市居民户口
Chiang Kai-shek (Jiang Jieshi) 蒋介石
chiku (suffer, "eat bitterness") 吃苦
Chongqing 重庆
Cixi (Empress Dowager) 慈禧
cun (village) 村
daiye renshi (people awaiting job allocation) 待业人士
Dalian 大连
danwei (work unit) 单位
Deng Xiaoping 邓小平
Deng Yingchao 邓颖超
Dianchi Lake 滇池
difang (locality) 地方
diqu (district, prefecture) 地区
Duan Qirui 段祺瑞
fan gui (foreign devil) 番鬼
Fang Lizhi 方励之
Fenghuang County 凤凰县
Foshan 佛山
Fujian 福建
Fuzhou 福州

Gan (dialect) 赣
Gaoming 高明
geming weiyuanhui (revolutionary committee) 革命委员会
gengzhe you qitian (land to the tillers) 耕者有其田
geti jingji (individual economy) 个体经济
geti qiye (individual enterprise) 个体企业
getihu (individual entrepreneur) 个体户
gongshe (commune) 公社
gongzuo danwei (work unit) 工作单位
Guangxu (dynastic period) 光绪
Guangzhou 广州
guanxi (relationship) 关系
Guomindang 国民党
Hai Rui 海瑞
Haihe 海河
Hakka (Kejia) 客家
Han (nationality) 汉
Hangzhou 杭州
Hankou 汉口
Heshan 鹤山
Hong Kong (Xianggang) 香港
Hong Xiuquan 洪秀全
Hu Qiaomu 胡乔木
Hu Shi 胡适
Hu Yaobang 胡耀邦
Hua Guofeng 华国锋
Huaihe 淮河
Huanghe (Yellow River) 黄河
Huangpu River 黄浦江
Huimin (Moslem) 回民
Hunan 湖南
huodong (movement) 活动
Jiang Qing 江青
Jiang Zemin 江泽民
Jiangmen 江门
Jiangsu 江苏
Jiangxi 江西
jihua danlie shi (direct planning city) 计划单列市
jin (weight measure) 斤
Jinggang Shan 井岗山
jingji tequ (special economic zone) 经济特区
Jinmen 金门
Kaifa Xibei (Open Up the North West) 开发西北
Kang Keqing 康克清

Kang Youwei 康有为
Kongzi (Confucius) 孔子
laodong fuwu gongsi (labour service enterprise) 劳动服务公司
laodong youhua (labour optimalization) 劳动优化
Lei Feng 雷锋
Li Lisan 李立三
Li Peng 李鹏
Liang Qichao 梁启超
Lianyungang 连云港
Liaohe 辽河
Lin Zexu 林则徐
Liu Shaoqi 刘少奇
Lizu (ethnic minority) 黎族
Lu Shan Mountain 庐山
Luhua 绿化
Luoding 罗定
Ma Yinchu 马寅初
Macau (Aomen) 澳门
Manchu (Manzu) 满族
Mao Zedong 毛泽东
Mazu 马祖
Minbeihua (dialect) 闽北话
Minnanhua (dialect) 闽南话
mu (land measure) 亩
Nanhai 南海
Nanjing 南京
Nantong 南通
neihang (insiders, professionals) 内行
Nian (rebellion) 念
Ningbo 宁波
nongye hukou (agricultural household) 农业户口
Peng Dehuai 彭德怀
Peng Pai 彭湃
pingjun diquan (equal right to the land) 平均地权
Pu Yi 溥仪
Pudong New Area 浦东新区
Qianlong (dynstic period) 乾隆
Qing (dynasty) 清
Qingdao 青岛
Qinghua University 清华大学
Qingming (festival) 清明
Qinhuangdao 秦皇岛
Qu Qiubai 瞿秋白
qunzhong (masses) 群众

renminbi 人民币
Ruijin 瑞金
Shaanxi 陕西
shangfang (lodge complaints) 上访
Shanghai 上海
Shenzhen 深圳
Sichuan 四川
Song Qingling 宋庆玲
Songhua Jiang (Sungari River) 松花江
Su Shaozhi 苏绍智
Subei (northern Jiangsu) 苏北
Sun Yat-sen (Sun Zhongshan) 孙中山（逸仙）
Suzhou 苏州
Taibei 台北
Taihu Lake 太湖
Taiping 太平
Taishan 台山
Taishanhua (dialect) 台山话
Taiwan 台湾
tian ming (mandate of heaven) 天命
Tiananmen 天安门
Tianjin 天津
tiaotiao, kuaikuai (branches and areas) 条条块块
Tigaiwei (System Reform Commission) 体改委
Tong Wen Guan 同文馆
Tongmenghui (United League) 同盟会
waihang (outsiders, politicians) 外行
Wan Li 万里
Wang Dan 王丹
Wang Hongwen 王洪文
Wang Juntao 王军涛
Wang Ming 王明
Wang Ruoshui 王若水
Wang Ruowang 王若旺
Wei Guoqing 韦国清
Wei Jingsheng 魏京生
Wenzhou 温州
Wu dialect 吴语
Wu Guixian 吴桂贤
wu lun (five relationships) 五论
Wuchang 武昌
Wuhan 武汉
Wuxi 无锡
Wuyi 五邑

xiafang (send to the countryside) 下放
xiafang qingnian (rusticated youths) 下放青年
Xiamen 夏门
Xiang (dialect) 湘
xiang (township) 乡
xiangzhen qiye (rural enterprise) 乡镇企业
xiao jiti qiye (small collectives) 小集体企业
Xikang 西康
xingzhengcun (administrative village) 行政村
Xingzhonghui (Revive China Society) 兴中会
Xinhui 新会
Xinjiang Autonomous Region 新疆
xitong (system) 系统
Yan Jiaqi 严家其
Yan'an 延安
Yang Baibing 杨白冰
Yang Shangkun 杨尚昆
Yantai 烟台
Yao Wenyuan 姚文元
Yao Yilin 姚依林
Ye Jianying 叶剑英
Ye Qun 叶群
yi gong dai zhen (work for compensation in kind) 以工代赈
yijia (negotiated price) 议价
yuan 元
Yuan Shikai 袁世凯
Yue dialect 粤语
yundong (movement) 运动
Zhang Chunqiao 张春桥
Zhang Jian 张謇
Zhanjiang 湛江
Zhao Ziyang 赵紫阳
Zhaoqing 肇庆
zheng-feng (rectification campaign) 整风
Zhongguo (China, litt.: Middle Kingdom) 中国
Zhongguo Funu 中国妇女
Zhongguo Funu Bao 中国妇女报
Zhongshan 中山
zhou (district) 州
Zhou Enlai 周恩来
Zhu De 朱德
Zhu Rongji 朱熔基
Zhuhai 珠海
Zhujiang (Pearl River) 珠江

Map of the People's Republic of China

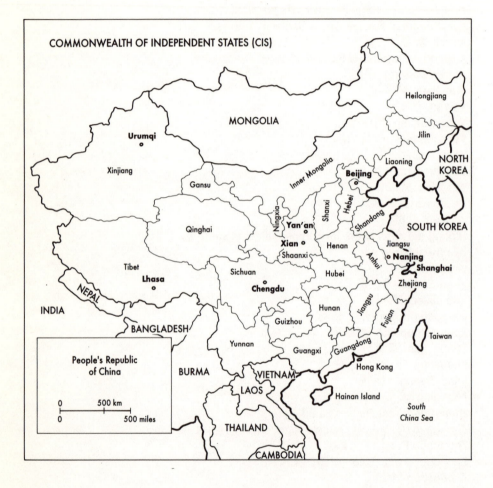

1 Introduction: Approaches to the study of Chinese politics

Where do we get our ideas and perceptions of Chinese politics from? This chapter aims to give a *tour d'horizon* of the commonest views of Chinese politics as they have appeared in the scholarly literature. We neither attempt to be exhaustive nor selectively prescriptive in our discussion.

THEORIES AND CONCEPTS: SHIFTING VIEWS OF CHINA

It is the conviction of the authors of this book that critical understanding can only be achieved when we know our tools, the analytical concepts we employ when we seek to comprehend the reality of Chinese politics. To achieve this, we will in the following sections of this chapter introduce some of the most important concepts, models and theories that have been used to explain Chinese political reality.

Our 'Chinese' problem in the West is that China in the minds of people, strongly supported by philosophers, writers and political propagandists (from the Jesuits and Leibnitz to Jean-Paul Sartre), has oscillated between utopia and the dungeons of hell, and between being a great civilization or a socialist alternative that works and being 'the sick man of Asia' or a repressive communist regime. The deficiencies of Europe could easily be contrasted with the civilized order of the Chinese empire, supported by tall stories and travellers' tales. The deplorable situation in the Soviet Union, in most Third World countries and even in Europe could be juxtaposed with the Chinese miracle, a socially just paradise freed of all exploitation and corruption, supported by visitors' accounts of the people's communes. The racially 'superior' Christian Westerner was, in the nineteenth century and far into the twentieth century, reassured by the fact that he was not one of those suffering, heathen 'Chinamen', and in current times Western democracy claimed a similar moral edge above the Chinese political system. We must push these stereotypes aside in order to understand China.

The images of China depicted above do not reflect the general standard of Western research on Chinese politics. On the contrary, most studies of Chinese politics are cautious, well researched, and normally based on profound knowledge of the country and its main language. However, when we – as non-Chinese – study Chinese politics, we are discussing a political culture with an historical and cultural background different from our own. Our intellectual and political categories, our historical and cultural foundations, and our definitions of ourselves and our environment are those of foreign countries sharing a common cultural background different from that existing in China. Our 'discovering' of China is influenced by all these factors. The expectations and value patterns underlying most political science approaches may prove to be very limited when we attempt to understand countries like China, with which these expectations and values are not shared. This dilemma is fundamental. On the one hand, we need a functional and understandable frame of reference when we examine China; on the other hand, our understanding will be unsatisfactory if we impose our cultural prejudices on China. We cannot hope to solve the dilemma, but we can try to keep it in mind. At a more practical level, the literature and the selection of material with which we are presented as students of Chinese politics invariably pledges itself to different approaches and conceptualizations which shift over time. The understanding of China in Western literature, therefore, is an important interface for our own understanding of China. It is important that we distinguish between different concepts and approaches, that we let them come out into the open, and that we weigh them against each other.

TOTALITARIANISM

Doak A. Barnett was one of the most influential observers of Chinese politics (Barnett, 1964). His view of China was based on the totalitarian model. Barnett's main effort was to analyze how the centralized power of the Chinese Communist Party (CCP) was exercised, how a small handful of leaders were able to maintain control of this vast country. His analysis had as its fundamental hypothesis that China was *totalitarian*.

The totalitarian model was used to describe societies which are totally controlled by one political force, i.e. dictatorships and other autocratic regimes which exert power through coercive means, *but which are also characterized by an ideological core*. The model was used to classify repressive political systems (Italy under Fascism; Germany under National Socialist rule; the Soviet Union under Stalin) in the 1950s and well into the 1960s.

Friedrich and Brzezinski in their book *Totalitarian Dictatorship and Autocracy*, first published in 1956, described the main characteristics of a totalitarian state as: (a) an official ideology for everyone to follow; (b) a mass party headed by a charismatic leader; (c) terroristic police control; (d) a state monopoly on communication; (e) a state monopoly on the possession of arms; and (f) a centrally directed and controlled economy. The political agenda underlying this approach was to juxtapose, quite unfavourably, the Stalinist Soviet Union (which was compared to the Third Reich) and Western democracies (Box 1.1).

Box 1.1 *Totalitarianism*

Totalitarianism was a child of the Cold War. The hostile climate towards the Soviet Union in the post Second World War period gave credibility to the image of communism as an evil, repressive ideology maintaining an authoritarian regime equal to the nazi and fascist states in the 1930s. The Korean War in the early 1950s, where the Chinese Liberation Army fought with great success against the UN forces led by the United States, helped create a negative picture of the People's Republic which was maintained by the totalitarian model used to analyze Chinese politics.

Barnett's description of the Chinese leadership reflects a similar approach. In his book *Communist China: The Early Years 1949–55*, he wrote:

> The leaders of the Chinese Communist Party (CCP) form a tightly knit brotherhood of experienced, competent, devoted, tough revolutionaries. At the top are the members of the Central Committee, who hold key posts in the government and army, as well as in the Party itself, throughout the country. They decide policy and supervise its execution. The fate of China, for the foreseeable future, is largely in their hands. (Barnett, 1964: 6)

When Barnett wrote this, Mao Zedong was 'still the undisputed leader of the Party' (Barnett, 1964: 7). Barnett's description of the Chinese system portrays a virtually unrestricted power of the central Party leadership. The structure of the Party, with its network of cells, its strict code of obedience, and its organizational hierarchy, was seen as symptomatic of a 'totalitarian' authority tightly controlling every aspect of Chinese society. The influence of the members of the Central Committee, wrote Barnett, 'is omnipresent, and their decision-making power is well-nigh omnipotent' (Barnett, 1964: 8).

Popular versions of the totalitarianism model

Totalitarianism as a model in the study of Chinese politics came to occupy an important position in popular ideas about China and especially in journalism. In reportage, the clear-cut image of a monolithic, repressive state with unlimited power to suppress its citizens is very attractive for the simplicity of the argument. The term 'totalitarianism' is also often used to refer to individual characteristics of the political system. The use of terror and physical coercion during long periods since 1949, the personality cult of Chairman Mao Zedong, the political intervention in the economy, the rigid exegesis of the official ideology (Marxism–Leninism–Mao-Zedong-Thought), and militaristic traits of social organization, are all *crucial elements* of a totalitarian system, and they were certainly prominent features of the People's Republic over long periods.

However, the totalitarian model was, in the wider perspective, not very satisfactory as a framework for the analysis of Chinese politics. It implied that there was a high degree of power concentration in one person, and that the political system was effective in maintaining central control. The reality, however, seemed to be more complex. The collective leadership seemed not to agree on fundamental ideological and political issues, control from the centre appeared to be less rigid, with the provinces asserting ranging levels of autonomy. While Doak A. Barnett recognized such anomalies within the totalitarian model, he was able to accommodate them within his analysis. However, the model appeared to be fundamentally flawed to those who identified the continuous existence of competing groups or elites within the Chinese leadership. The totalitarian model was soon replaced in favour of analytical frameworks which could offer clearer explanations of Chinese political life.

Four main areas of attention in studies on Chinese politics have been factionalism, interest groups, complex bureaucracies and political economy/class analysis. Under these headings a large number of overlapping models and approaches can be identified.

FACTIONALISM AND ELITE CONFLICT

The importance of personal leadership in China and the disagreements that were perceived to exist among the Chinese leaders led to the development of factionalism models. The most well-known analysis of leadership conflict in terms of factions, providing a coherent model for the analysis of Chinese politics, is Andrew Nathan's 'A Factionalism Model for CCP Politics' (1973). A faction is, according to Nathan, based on clientelist ties, i.e. a maze of individual, personalized ties between a leader and his political supporters (Box 1.2).

Box 1.2   *Clientelism in the factionalism model*
Nathan's definition of clientelist ties includes seven features. A clientelist tie is:

1. a relationship between two people;
2. a relationship which the partners cultivate with specially selected members of their social networks;
3. based on constant exchange of gifts and services;
4. based on inequality and dissimilarity between the partners;
5. characterized by well-understood, but rarely explicit, rights and obligations between the partners;
6. terminated at will by either partner; and
7. not exclusive – either member is free to establish other simultaneous ties.

Clientelism in this context should not be understood as *guanxi*.

A leader of a faction may, in his turn, be the supporter of the leader of another faction. Factions are flexible and do not rely on strong formal organization:

> The members need never meet, although they may do so. The members' activities in disparate locations and institutions can be coordinated through individual communications with the leader. Indeed, in routine political situations, regularized coordination can be dispensed with entirely, since the faction as a whole can rely on the members' loyalty to the leader to insure that each member works to the faction's benefit. Thus, the faction is capable of the greatest flexibility in seizing political opportunities and in engaging in a general political strategy on the basis of scattered positions throughout a political system or an organization. (Nathan, 1973: 42)

The limitations of factions are the level of communication (and exchange of goods and services) possible between a leader and his supporters, and the number of leaders at different levels that can be involved without distorting the flow of information and the coordination of political action.

The disagreements within the Chinese leadership over core policy issues down through the 1950s and 1960s led political scientists to look for factions working against each other. In the most simple explanation, leader personalities would join together in mutually supportive, albeit shifting alliances.

The model carries some weight since it reflects fundamental traits of the Chinese leadership, especially until the 1978 reforms started. The ruling elite in China consisted basically of those Party leaders who had joined the Long March, and who had gained political posts in the Yan'an period and kept high political office after 1949. Some of the ruling elite had divergent backgrounds. Their relative influence in the leadership originated in their capacity to control segments of the bureaucracy or the military, and especially through their personal links to each other. The system was not based on friendship or representation, but on patron–client relationships. The emergence within the leadership of contending political factions was based on this type of personal tie.

However, such an explanation presumes that the formation of factions occurs amongst a small elite of peers. Therefore, politics, according to the factionalism model, would appear to be conducted in a sphere separated from the social reality of the country, and the actions of leaders would not be analyzed in terms of their response to socio-economic developments. The intra-elite dynamics of the factionalism model present the main protagonists centre-stage, postulate that all action emanates from their collective will, and relegate other social and economic dynamics to the backstage.

CLIENTELISM

Clientelism, as it has developed into a model of analysis in understanding Chinese politics, has built upon the factionalist and elite models but has also gone beyond these. As seen above, the factionalism and elite models confine themselves to analyzing elite-level politics. The focus is on how various groups of those in power or with access to power interact with each other, and influence policy. While both the factionalism and the clientelism models have centred patron–client relationships in the study of politics in China, the emphasis of the two models is different. In the words of one of the foremost exponents of the clientelist model, Jean Oi, clientelism can be seen as 'a type of elite-mass linkage through which both the state and the party exercise control at the local level and individuals participate in the political system' (Oi, 1989: 7). The difference between the two models is thus clear. The clientelist model seeks to examine not only the patron–client relationship that exists among the elites of the country, and how that effects policy formation, but also how patron–client relationships affect the interaction between the state elites and the citizens, and how that effects policy implementation. The emphasis is less on formal structures and institutions of power and participation, and more on the informal, personal relationships as means of participation in politics. The focus shifts from the group to the individual as the political actor. This is an important shift because it allows us to see individual citizens as agents in a highly centralized political system like China's; they can be regarded as more than just passive objects of state policy. In this context, it is not necessary to stop at proving the ineffectiveness of formal institutions, but to begin at that point and to see how it is through the process of implementation of policy rather than policy formation that individuals forge strategies for maximizing their interests. It also encourages us to look beyond the structures to the operations of power where institutions are not the only referents in politics.

Clientelism in the village and the factory

Two texts that have been influential in explaining the clientelist model and using it to study Chinese politics are Jean Oi's *State and Peasant in Contemporary China* (1989) and Andrew Walder's *Communist Neo-Traditionalism* (1986). Oi's book examines the relationship of the Chinese peasant with the communist state in terms of struggle over the division of harvest. Walder's work features the urban work unit and focuses on two characteristics of industrial relations in communist China: 'organized dependence' and 'principled particularism'. Organized dependence refers to the monopolistic controls that the Party/state, through factory leadership, has over the workforce. This is established through the non-market character of the production unit, and through the Party's political monopoly. Principled particularism describes how the factory leadership exercises that power by establishing and maintaining a relationship of patronage with individual workers, and thus builds up a network of loyal activists who also become sources of envy and dissension within the workforce, further exacerbating the control of the factory leaders. However, the individual worker in relationship with the leaders is not simply a tool in the hands of the management. To retain a place on the workforce he or she must take into account the expectations and needs of the workers and negotiate with the leaders accordingly. The very effectiveness of loyal supporters depends, says Walder, on this mediation. If the fruits of patronage are in excess of common acceptance, or if the client-worker is insensitive to the demands of the workforce, it is unlikely that he or she will retain their position for very long (Walder, 1986: 102–6). Walder further points out that the workers themselves, by a conscious withdrawal of efficiency, can directly participate in opposition to the demands put upon them by the leaders (Walder, 1986: 238–40).

Oi examines how the peasants in the Chinese commune dealt with the demands for grain by the central state. Because of the special relationship that the Chinese communists formed with the peasants during the revolution, Stalinist policies of procurement were not open to them. The Chinese party-state much preferred to negotiate with the peasants through the local cadres – the team and brigade leaders – even if it meant less than total procurement of grain (Oi, 1989: 229). This meant that the local cadres became mediators between the centre and the peasants. Patronage flowed from the fact that the cadres were able to negotiate with the centre better deals for procurement of their commune. They also colluded with the peasants in withholding grain from the state in the safety of the patron–client relations they themselves were part of. This informal system of politics 'circumvented the contradictions inadvertently created by the formal political and economic systems' of communist China (Oi, 1989: 229). While the post-Mao reforms have reduced the power of the cadres and therefore that of the patron–client relationships in the village, the partial nature of the reforms means, says Oi, that it is the nature of the power of the cadres that has changed not so much its content. The need for various forms of licence and control over the distribution of key inputs allows these cadres to continue to service the patron–client relationships established (Oi, 1989: 231–2).

Authority and clientelism

While the scope of the two studies is different, both argue the case of clientelism convincingly. The major features of the model that emerge are: first, that under a communist system it is not risk-minimizing that leads to patron–client relationships being established, but interest-maximizing (Oi, 1989: 9). It is not struggle for subsistence that underlies clientelism, but a fear of erosion of existing benefits and security. Second, they argue that in the absence of 'formal channels for meaningful participation and interest articulation . . . individuals regularly pursue their interests using informal networks built upon personal ties' (Oi, 1989: 8). These ties cannot be regarded as 'deviant' or even 'corrupt' because, within the logic of the system, they are rational strategies arising from the constraints that the state tries to impose. From the clientelist perspective, the elites and the non-elites develop a relationship in which authority is exercised through patronage rather than simply through formal sources of power. This leads to a focus on how authority is exercised in a centralized state system, rather than arguments about *how much* authority the state has. Third, the clientelist model is very conscious of the enormous power and influence that the local-level cadres have in a patron–client situation. This power is exercised not simply in the service of the central state, but in their own interest too. Indeed, Oi fears that the local cadres have the 'potential' of becoming a 'new class' in Djilas's terms (Oi, 1989: 231). This acts as a constraint upon the central state that can result in friction within the system. Fourth, this model holds that opposition to state policy takes the shape of *informal* action by *individuals* who try to maximize their interest. Opposition is thus covert and cloaked in compliance. This lessens the predictability of opposition and increases its effectiveness in a system which does not countenance open group opposition, as in a multi-party political system. It therefore does not present a totalizing picture of the political system. However, both Oi and Walder are clear about the power of the state. The informal nature of opposition underscores this fact; Oi goes so far as to write: 'When the state chose to apply its controls and where work teams were sent in those instances when the state chose to make an example of an indiscretion, the state was impressively effective and every bit as awesome as the totalitarian model would predict' (Oi, 1989: 229). In conclusion, the clientelist model, while acknowledging and building in a space for individual action through patron–client relationships, is also very conscious that 'without organization, amorphous social action is limited in its effectiveness: it represents "friction" in the system, not political initiative' (Walder, 1986: 240).

Criticism of the clientelist model

Clientelism, though a very sophisticated model of analysis, has its critics. It is noted that while clientelism does take us beyond the totalitarian model of the state, its focus does not shift significantly enough: 'the narrowness of his [Walder's] focus on state power gives an artificial slant to his paradigm similar to that of the earlier paradigm of totalitarianism' (Womack, 1991: 314). Second, it has been argued that the group is forgotten in the clientelist model. The focus of the enquiry is the individual in an atomized society, rather than any form of collective. Collective action, resistance or participation finds no place in this model. Both the major studies that form the basis of this model have been non-elite studies based on production units. Can the relationships established at the elite level mirror the relationships established in the context of the work unit? If we regard clientelism as not rooted in the work unit, does it not become very difficult to distinguish from a very generalized approach to patronage that exists in all political systems, irrespective of levels of institutionalized politics? It has also been argued that the clientelist model continues to present a 'pathological' approach to power in its preoccupation with uncovering latent and overt exercise of total power (Womack, 1991: 320). Finally, say the critics, clientelism does not take into account the changing economic and political reality of the country and therefore minimizes the impact of variables like changes in the levels of scarcity, the operations of the market and the intervention of ideology.

THE CLASS STRUGGLE APPROACH

If totalitarianism was in part a product of the Cold War and the fear of the spread of communism, the class struggle approach which emerged in the 1970s has to be examined in the context of the student revolt of 1968 and the rise of the critical Left in Europe and the United States. This approach was rooted in Marxism and emphasized the importance of relations of production in characterizing any socio-economic system. Many scholars who felt disillusioned with the Soviet Union's invasion of Czechoslovakia, its attempts to build relations with the United States and its talk of 'peaceful co-existence' used the class struggle approach to criticize the Soviet Union. Among the most prominent of these scholars were Charles Bettelheim from France, Paul M. Sweezy of the United States and Joan Robinson of Great Britain. Bettelheim was perhaps the most influential of the class struggle theorists. He situated himself in what came to be known as the structuralist school of thought and was inspired by the French philosopher Louis Althusser. The structuralist school has been characterized by the building of 'grand theories', an attack upon positivism and its preoccupation with empirical data. Science depended, according to this school, on the creation and validation of theories within their own logic and context. It is interesting to note here that though Bettelheim was very influential in casting the debates around China, and particularly the Cultural Revolution, he himself was not a sinologist. His visits to China were short, and his observation of the lived reality of the people of the country necessarily limited. Despite this, his theory of transitional societies made a tremendous impact on the study of Chinese politics in the late 1960s and early 1970s.

Double alienation

Bettelheim argued that ownership and control were two separate concepts and should be treated as such when judging whether a society in transition from capitalism was moving towards socialism or not. In the Soviet Union, Bettelheim contended, social ownership of the means of production through the state had led to the alienation of the state from the proletariat. There were no adequate means of controlling the bureaucracy of the state that *in effect* had taken possession of the state-owned enterprises. The state bureaucracy in effect performed the functions of the capitalists without even taking the risk that the capitalists took. They made all the decisions about how to produce, how much to produce, and about the price of the product that was produced. They determined not only the workers' wages but also their work practices. The proletariat in whose name the revolution was made remained equally distant – or alienated – from decision making as under capitalism. A second form of alienation that Bettelheim was concerned about was the alienation of production units from each other. There seemed to him to be little or no cooperation between factories as managers remained concerned with their immediate material problems, and tried to resolve them by whatever means they could even if it adversely affected others. This system of production Bettelheim maintained was one of 'double alienation' that Marx had made the central feature of capitalism in his *Economic and Philosophical Manuscripts of 1844*. Bettelheim called the Soviet bureaucracy 'state bourgeoisie', and the Soviet system 'state capitalism'. The interests of the 'state bourgeoisie' and the workers, therefore, were opposed to each other and it was through a continuing class struggle that the workers would be able to reassert their control over the means of production. Bettelheim saw the alternative to 'state capitalism' in the continuous control through mass participation of the state bureaucracy; this he found on his trip to China during the period of the Cultural Revolution. In the Preface to his book *Cultural Revolution and Industrial Organization in China* Bettelheim wrote, '[The Cultural Revolution] "discovered" . . . an essential form of the class struggle for the construction of socialism' (Bettelheim, 1974: 10).

Two-line struggle – class struggle

The 'two-line struggle' between Mao Zedong's 'mass line' politics and Liu Shaoqi's more bureaucratic functioning characterized the class struggle in China. The resolution of this struggle in favour of Mao would take China on to the road to socialism. The means by which this struggle would be carried on would be new practices of workers' control over management of their work units. Bettelheim saw 'class struggle' in the General Knitwear Factory in Beijing taking the form of struggle between newly formed workers' management teams and manager–cadre controls (Bettelheim, 1974: 22). The efforts of the workers to regain control over their work and the products of their work were, Bettelheim pointed out, backed by the 'revolutionary' sections of the Communist Party. The purification of the ranks of the Party that formed part of the two-line struggle during the Cultural Revolution was crucial if the struggle of the workers was to succeed. This was accomplished both by campaigns to study the works of Mao, and by subjecting Party cadres to mass criticism to help modify their relationship with the workers (Bettelheim, 1974: 38). This alliance between revolutionary workers and Party cadres was further strengthened by the inclusion into the factory committees of members of the People's Liberation Army. While Bettelheim saw the management teams as evolving in their organization, he pointed out that the aim of all such teams was the same: 'to develop organizational structures affording the greatest possibilities for the masses to participate in running the factories and to make their weight felt' (Bettelheim, 1974: 43). Bettelheim was convinced these management teams would also set standards for 'socialist cooperation', as the workers who lived close to the factories would be concerned about the wider environment of their workplaces. He gave examples of cooperation of factory management teams to control pollution and treatment of waste products to illustrate his point (Bettelheim, 1974: 66). Bettelheim further pointed out that these achievements in worker participation and a different approach to production were neither spontaneous, nor a mechanistic result of the level of productive forces existing in China. They were the result of the constant class struggle that was being waged in the country during the Cultural Revolution, which he felt should be 'viewed as a stage in the struggle between the proletarian line of the Chinese Communist Party and the bourgeois line' (Bettelheim, 1974: 105).

Class struggle model versus reality

Perhaps the single most important reason for the decline of the class struggle model in the mid-1970s was its complete variance with the empirical data that was released by the post-Mao Chinese regime. The darker side of the Cultural Revolution revealed not the triumph of workers' management but the manipulation and coercion of workers and Party members by contending groups in the CCP leadership that led to great injustices, corruption and even terror (Box 1.3).

Box 1.3   *Was the Cultural Revolution that bad?*

The information initially provided in the Chinese media to disclose the consequences of the Cultural Revolution at the end of the 1970s and in the early 1980s was mainly supplied by the section of the Communist Party leadership which was opposed to the Cultural Revolution and had suffered greatly during it. However, the evidence from many less partisan sources confirm the view that the Cultural Revolution caused economic stagnation and generated severe social injustices.

The problem of obtaining empirical information is great in China since foreigners had (and still have) limited and selective access to information, and because the public media are centrally controlled. Propaganda during the Cultural Revolution was replaced in the 1980s by propaganda against the Cultural Revolution. However, the greater access in the 1980s and 1990s to travel and to research in China, as well as the greater individual freedom of Chinese citizens to express their views, mean that it is possible to corroborate present propaganda claims on the Cultural Revolution and to establish that many Western observers were led to have distorted views of Chinese development. Second, and linked to the problem of data, was the question of perception. Bettelheim seemed to take on the entire baggage of Maoist rhetoric – also couched in class struggle language – without being at all critical. It seemed, especially in the context of the reappraisal of the Cultural Revolution, that Bettelheim had been unable to see reality for the rhetoric. The influence of this approach was further diminished as structuralism lost ground to the various post-structuralist theories that emerged during the late 1970s and the 1980s with a growing attack on 'grand theories'. The world seemed too complex in its economic arrangements and political alliances for sweeping generalizations to make sense.

Other Marxist approaches

While the Marxists of the class struggle approach regard the economic organization of China almost exclusively in terms of one class exploiting another, other writers use the political economy approach to examine the functioning of the country from a wider angle.

Non-orthodox Marxists consider the organization of production and ownership structures to be the most important explanatory factors for social and political development. While the *ownership* of the means of production in a narrow sense seems not to lead to class formation (landowner/peasant or capitalist/proletarian) in socialist China, the access to and control of means of production are still of dominant importance. The differences of ownership existing between the countryside and the cities, the differences between collective and state ownership, the differences between public (state and collective) ownership and various forms of private, semi-private and cooperative ownership, as well as the changes occurring in the ownership situation, in themselves form an interesting topic for study.

After the beginning of the 1980s, very empirical political economy research of China gained importance. Based on comparatively good access to reliable information, it was propelled forward by the sudden demise of the people's commune system, which had come to be regarded as the most stable organization in the Chinese economy and the very safeguard against run-of-the-mill Third World poverty, injustice and class division. What can be summarized as the political economy approach has resulted in a great abundance of analyses of Chinese rural society in the 1980s, and some studies of urban society.

INTEREST GROUPS MODEL

As with totalitarianism, the interest group approach had its origin in the study of Soviet politics, especially in an article by Gordon Skilling (1966). It arose out of the awareness that the diversity between functional and occupational groups in socialist societies – as anywhere else – generated different outlooks, interests and preferences. An interest group would be defined as an 'aggregate of persons who possess certain common characteristics and share certain attitudes and values on public issues, and who adopt distinct positions on these issues and make definite claims on those in authority'. The concept of 'Interest groups' is very useful since it focuses on the differences between people and the degree to which they assert specific interests and seek to influence the political establishment. In this way it becomes possible to identify real and potential cleavages in the 'monolithic' state. The fundamental importance of the interest group approach, accordingly, was that it recognized the heterogeneous organization of society. This approach was considered valid in the Chinese political context, as for example discussed in a volume edited by David Goodman (1984). Broad occupational groups could be understood to have different interests, like workers, cadres, peasants and, intellectuals, but also people sharing very specific functional tasks were seen to share common interests, e.g. cadres in charge of personnel management under the *nomenclatura*, or party secretaries (Box 1.4). Ethnic and religious groups, as well as linguistic groups, are other examples of interest groups.

Box 1.4 *Nomenclatura*

The nomenclatura (originally a Latin word, but borrowed through Russian into English; in Chinese referred to as *renshi zhidu*) is the Party personnel administration and control with posts. The Chinese Communist Party has a number of lists of posts within the state and Party hierarchies, the holders of which must be vetted by appropriate Party branches. The top-level appointments and elections roughly down to vice-minister level and vice-provincial-governor level must be sanctioned by the Political Bureau. Lower-level posts must be sanctioned by a Party branch at a higher level of authority. For a detailed study, see Burns (1989).

Problems of definition

Since Skilling's working definition of interest groups is relatively loose (note that an interest group need not be internally organized – it is an 'aggregate of persons', not a group – and its constituent members may share characteristics and act similarly without knowing each other or even understanding their own actions as expressions of interest) the concept of interest groups has generated some problems. There have been disagreements about the definition (what constitutes a real interest group?) and the rather loose application of the concept to people sharing any characteristic (e.g. is it relevant to claim that provincial first Party secretaries constitute an interest group?).

It is difficult to establish what an interest group is and why it is relevant to look at a specific 'aggregate of persons'. It is, for example, doubtful whether persons sharing common characteristics (e.g. first Party secretaries) and attitudes (the resolution to make specific types of decisions in favour of their respective provinces) constitute an interest group if they *are* at the centre of decision making. They do not make claims on those in power, they are among those in power, or rather they are integrated in the policy-making process to a degree where their shared characteristics and interests as a 'group' become secondary to the differences in provincial interest they represent and the bargaining positions they take. However, it is useful to regard school teachers sharing social, educational, occupational, professional characteristics, and some fundamental attitudes, as an interest group. Their claims 'on those in power' spring directly from their social and professional characteristics.

Interest groups are limited as a concept. Most professional and functional groups overlap formal, organizational structures of the state, and it may be more useful to look at these rather than the groups. If, for example, we look at the military officers, the workers, the managers of large state enterprises and the intellectuals, these may be better understood in terms of the corporate interest of the institutions they belong to. This pushes the perspective away from the interest groups and in the direction of institutional structures. We will introduce this viewpoint under the discussion of 'complex bureaucracies' below.

Interest groups and civil society

The interest group approach is more useful if it is combined with the idea of a 'civil society'. Civil society is the sphere of political action outside the realm of direct state intervention or domination (but within parameters of indirect state regulation in laws and constitutions) which creates the space for the aggregation of political interest. Broadly defined, civil society includes both formal and informal social networks – non-governmental organizations, economic interests operating free of state control, free media and even public houses and cafés, etc. Within civil society, interest groups have clear features as active political organizations. In Chinese society, there have been great obstacles to achieving a civil society. The dominant public ownership structures and the organization of the workforce within public frameworks make the evolution of organized interest groups representing aggregate political interest extremely difficult, if not impossible. The social organization of the workplace (work unit, *danwei*) as a society *en miniature*, e.g. as described in Walder (1986), imposes severe limitations on the creation of links across the formal structures of state organization, let alone the formulation of an aggregated political interest outside state control. Until the 1980s the emergence of a civil society in rural China, with its domination of collective structures and relatively closed communities, did not seem to be a possibility either.

Interest groups and economic interests

During the reform era which began in 1978, structures of economic management have changed. There are presently many private entrepreneurs and workers in the private sector. Large parts of the collective and state-owned sectors have become relatively independent in day-to-day management. The fact that 'market forces' are increasingly important for the exchange of goods has led to renewed interest in the concept of interest groups and civil society. According to this reasoning, the increasingly independent economic decision making leads to a greater scope for political interest articulation by groups of people who tend to *share common characteristics and attitudes*, who are relatively *independent of official state structures*, and who *have a certain degree of power, economic resources and social status which enables them to assert themselves*. The assumption is that these groups will not merely pander to the authority of those in power, but will claim political rights, seek to organize themselves in independent political organizations cross-cutting official boundaries of authority, formulate political platforms and programmes and seek to influence decision making so as to include their own interests. Such a development of civil society might eventually lead to democratization of the political system.

THE STATE/CIVIL SOCIETY DICHOTOMY

As mentioned earlier, civil society is the sphere of political action outside the control of the state where political interest is aggregated. This definition raises several questions: (a) to what extent is political interest in China aggregated in fora which are independent of the state (and the CCP); and (b) is it possible to identify a division line between the level or sphere of political action which belongs to the state and that which does not (thereby constituting society)?

The clearest answer is that there do not exist in China political parties which have not subscribed to the leading role of the Chinese Communist Party. It is claimed that there exist illegal political organizations demanding democracy, but, if that is the case, they are not allowed to aggregate political interest and they do not have a status in which they can influence public opinion or participate in policy making. There do exist some semi-independent organizations (academic, religious and professional associations) which have a limited scope of action, and which are ultimately controlled by the Party and the state. There also exist secret societies, brotherhoods and sects which are mostly criminal organizations of a traditional character. Do they form civil society?

It may be useful to reserve the term 'civil society' to the sphere of political action, independent of the state, which actually has the power, social standing and legal status to enable it to assert itself by influencing policy making in a sensible way. In that sense, there *does not* exist a civil society in China.

Fragmented society

The lack of civil society can be ascribed to the fragmentation of society in work units and *xitongs* (literally translated 'systems', i.e. vertically organized institutional structures like the army, the ministries and the mass organizations) in the cities and in relatively closed village communities in the countryside, which frustrate most inclinations towards political alignment along social and economic cleavages that transcend village or work-unit boundaries. With the growing economic and political independence of work units (which have during the post-1978 reforms become accountable for their profits and losses, and which increasingly rely on horizontal, market-oriented links) and the emergence of private enterprise, it is likely that a different type of 'civil society' could arise. This field of political action would be an arena for aggregating political interest between corporate bodies (private and public enterprises, and institutions, i.e. work units) outside the direct intervention of central state organs (see Yang, 1989: 37–38 for an elucidation of this point). This would not fundamentally impinge on the strong cohesive forces within the work units.

There are several perspectives which must be examined in this connection: (a) the assertion that economic liberalism leads to pluralism and democracy; (b) the idea that there exists an identifiable state/society or state/civil-society dichotomy; and (c) that social, ethnic, cultural, religious and economic cleavages are actually accentuated by the devolution of the economy and the evolution of pluralist decision making.

THE CASE FOR POLITICAL PLURALISM

Liberal theorists often argue that there is an almost automatic link between the 'free market' and 'democracy'. Without one, the other will not work. The Chinese dissident Wei Jingsheng carried forward this view in his article about the 'The Fifth Modernization' in 1979, claiming that the reforms contemplated by the leadership (the Four Modernizations) could only be realized if full-blown liberal democracy was introduced (Box 1.5). Similar views hold sway in more

---

Box 1.5 *The Fifth Modernization*

The dissident Wei Jingsheng's ideas on democracy as the 'Fifth Modernization' were expressed in several articles published during the first months of 1979, and they had a wide impact both in China and abroad. The 'Four Modernizations' (in agriculture, industry, defence, and science and technology) as proposed and heavily propagated by the leadership under Chairman Hua Guofeng since winter 1976/1977 could only be accomplished if a fifth modernization were to be added: democracy (see, e.g. Wei, 1979). Wei Jingsheng also attacked the new leadership under Deng Xiaoping as a 'dictatorship', and was later jailed for 15 years for divulging state secrets to a foreign journalist.

popular debates on Chinese reforms. However, looking at the current political science literature on China, this opinion is not very prominent.

Most Western studies of China seem to agree that the devolution and privatization in the Chinese economy has not led in the direction of democracy. In spite of the fact that popular demands for democracy have gained impetus since the reforms started in 1978, there has not as yet emerged an independent civil society, and democratic institutions (as defined by Western observers) have not developed (Box 1.6).

Box 1.6 *People's democracy*

The Chinese communists claim that China is a *people's democracy*, and that its political institutions represent a type of democracy that is more advanced than the bourgeois–liberal democracy in the West, which is an instrument of the 'dictatorship of the bourgeoisie'. The people's democracy means that it is democratic for the people, but exerts dictatorship over the enemies of the people; it is thus identical to the 'dictatorship of the people'.

It is, however, generally accepted that the reforms have led to more independence from the Party and the central authorities – politically, socially and economically – and that it is easier to pursue individual, economic interest now than before the reforms started. The developing private sector, which according to official statistics encompassed approximately 7 or 8 million urban people in 1990, as well as greater independence for, and competition between, enterprises owned by the state, mean that the political system must process a multitude of diverging views on policy matters, brought forward by groups, parts of the bureaucracy or enterprises. This diversity has changed the performance of the political system in a pluralist direction, so that it is more capable of accommodating conflicting interests and solving the concomitant problems.

To Western observers, accordingly, it is obvious that a certain 'market liberalization' and a derived social and economic stratification has taken place in the 1980s and the beginning of the 1990s. However, this situation has not led to democracy. In the debates about this, the coexistence of a liberal market and authoritarian structures of political management in China has been compared to the situation in South Korea, Taiwan and Hong Kong; it is referred to as 'neo-authoritarianism'.

The impact of other cleavages

The division of the population by various types of cleavages is generally considered to be important for the development of democratic structures. In

China the reforms have brought this aspect to the fore. The accentuation of social, ethnic, cultural, religious and economic cleavages during the reform process is a trend which has been observed empirically. It is obvious that privatization and greater economic autonomy contribute to the widening of social and economic gaps. Greater local responsibility has among other things led to a decline in the state's function as a redistributor of wealth. The difference between poor and rich villages and enterprises has therefore increased. The social differentiation between families has also widened, due to economic, social and traditional factors. The decrease in direct state control entails more freedom to engage in activities that were banned in the 1950s to the 1970s, e.g. folk religious ceremonies. Religious freedom ensured by the 1982 Constitution is explicitly limited to officially recognized activities by authoritative religious organizations (temples and churches), excluding a wide range of 'superstitious' activities. However, the new freedom has brought about an upsurge in religious activity, and thereby differentiation among people. Ethnic differences are great in China with its 56 recognized ethnic minority groups. The Han (Chinese) nationality dominates, however, constituting between 93 and 95 per cent of the total population. The history of the People's Republic since 1949 has witnessed continuous ethnic conflicts, most due to clashes between Han Chinese cadres and ethnic groups. Some conflicts, like the Tibetan and Xinjiang conflicts, include various contentious aspects (Han chauvinism or racism, foreign policy issues, religion, socio-economic backwardness, cultural differences, etc.). Given the small size of the Chinese national minorities and their regional containment, there is little to argue that they form a strong element in a civil society. The reforms, however, have widened the particular interests of the national minorities by enlarging their autonomy, by allowing border trade along all borders, and by condoning various forms of cross-country trade. The Uighurs, for example, took up informal trade in money in China's largest cities. Insofar as ethnic minorities have been active in these respects, they have increasingly been regarded with hostility by other groups.

Apart from the ethnic conflicts there is a general problem of language and regional origin in China. Prejudice between various groups of dialect speakers is prevalent, e.g. between Hakka (Kejia) and Cantonese (Guangdonghua) and between speakers of dialects from northern Jiangsu (Subei) and Shanghainese speakers in Shanghai. Linguistic cleavages have always existed and form the basis of social prejudice. The greater mobility of the population during the 1980s has led more unskilled people from regions speaking other dialects to enter the large cities (including Shanghai and Guangzhou). Such groups of migrants form an 'underclass', but they do not form the basis of 'civil society', being marginalized and lacking resources.

Interest groups and civil society arguments give a potentially interesting framework for discussing Chinese political structures and fields of conflict in a society which appears to be much more heterogeneous than the totalitarian model acknowledges.

COMPLEX BUREAUCRACIES MODEL

The complex bureaucracies model focuses our attention on the processes through which decisions are arrived at and policies are implemented. This model, which was first developed by Graham Allison in discussing the Cuban missile crisis, assumes that political leaders at all levels of the bureaucratic hierarchy bargain with each other in order to reach a consensus that is translated into policy. Each organization tries to extend its own influence, guard and/or expand its own resources, and preserve its own interests to the best possible extent. For this, the representatives of each organization form alliances, and participate in a bargaining process that has little to do with the grand plans of national development or ideological advancement.

The complex bureaucracies model is attractive not only because it explains the present, but also because it draws upon historical precedent. China's bureaucratic system, after all, is the oldest in the world. Further, the way China's economy developed under the communist regime has strengthened that bureaucratic political structure enormously. The entire Chinese socio-economic system is based upon the idea of the work unit (*danwei*). These work units have developed a sense of self-sufficiency that almost bespeaks a seige mentality of the revolutionary period. Such an approach to social and economic organization allowed institutions to regard themselves as 'independent' and in a distinct relationship with the political bureaucracies of the area. The heads of these organizations thus became responsible not only for the efficient running of the organization but also for the general welfare of their workforce. This included looking after their material and non-material interests outside of the workplace – providing housing, cheap transport, shopping facilities, etc. Such arrangements were common not only in the countryside communes, but also in the urban factories and other institutions like hospitals and universities.

The way bargaining works in this model is very complex. At the macro-level the central bureaucracy bargains with the local bureaucracy to define a policy. However, the representatives of the local political bureaucracy have to have carried out elaborate bargaining before defining their own position with those below them. There is a prolonged period of negotiation and consensus building that goes on before the policy is formulated. At the point of implementation this process goes on in the reverse. At each level the representatives of organizations fight their own corner to get the best possible deal for their own members. Recently, there have been many in-depth studies of the policy-making processes in China that have taken this approach, the most important being those by Lampton (1987) and Lieberthal and Oksenberg (1988). In their version of the model, they focus on the fragmented nature of state power and the decision-making processes, while asserting that the system is authoritarian or non-democratic. The many players in the politics game do not constitute a democratic deliberation process. They call the model 'fragmented authoritarianism'.

Political dynamics

The complex bureaucracies approach explains politics in terms of how institutions work and how decisions are made. The focus is on how different authorities seek to consolidate themselves or expand in terms of budgetary allocation, jurisdiction, scope of powers and authority. The cement linking together power centres in a complex bureaucracy consists of codes of conduct, formal and informal bargaining structures, and a shared value and ranking system. By examining the Chinese institutions, their procedures, and their relative power it is possible to gain a valuable understanding of how the political system functions. The advantages of this view are that: (a) political processes are seen as dynamic, with their own inertia; rather than being based on erratic decisions by whimsical leaders, they follow set practices and frameworks within which conflicting interests are weighed against each other; (b) sudden shifts in the political life may influence but not, in the short term, radically change the bureaucratic practices; this explains the relative continuity of the Chinese political system *vis-à-vis* the great political upheavals in China; (c) it is generally confirmed by the high degree of bureaucratic organization in China (which has been necessary for the management of the planned economy); and (d) it fits well in the historical perspective with China as one of the oldest and most profusely bureaucratic states in world history.

While this approach does have the enormous advantage of explaining politics in terms of the actual working of institutions of a highly organized society, it tends to focus primarily on formal organizations. The different ways in which people try to influence or oppose policies, and the informal networks of power and influence, are subsumed under the ambit of organizations which are not always representative of actual politics. While the bureaucratic model is useful in understanding the formal networks of power and how they work, we have to look elsewhere for an understanding of the informal processes of politics.

Changes in the bureaucratic structures have taken place since 1949, most markedly the shift to radicalism during the Cultural Revolution and the regularization and consolidation in the 1980s. In the study of Chinese politics these changes in the frameworks for policy making are of great importance, so they will be discussed at length in this book.

THE CULTURALIST APPROACH

In the study of Chinese politics, there exists a widespread view that China is a case apart, a political system which is rooted in its own past, and therefore cannot be perceived of in Western terms. This view has given rise to a number of strategies for dealing with China's particularity. These have been very influential and have generated some mystique about China.

While we want to subscribe to the fundamental point that Chinese politics cannot in a simple and straightforward way be subjected to scrutiny, using a crude set of Euro-centric analytical tools, we want to point to some problems of the culturalist discourse which make it problematic. The culturalist approach is based on general assumptions about China's political and cultural past, sometimes extending 4,000 years back in history. It is assumed that in various ways the historical events and the structures of thought in the past determine the present.

The link between the past and the present in the culturalist approaches is not always clear; it is sometimes understood as a received frame of mind, an inherited psycho-sociological disposition of the people to accept or support specific forms of governance. The Chinese are, for example, considered to be more willing than other nations to subject themselves to tyrannical rule because they are brought up in a Confucianist world view which emphasizes obedience *vis-à-vis* higher authority.

Sometimes it is thought the present-day government follows dynamically from a long history of rule, the fundamental structures of which have been transformed into more recent forms. These engrained rules of governance are based on a strong state, ruled by an emperor and a large bureaucratic class, tolerating no independent sources of political power, and interpreting the world through an ideological–moral framework – Confucianism. Modern rule, it is held, corresponds to this fundamental pattern, substituting Mao for the emperor, the Party cadres for the bureaucrats, and Mao-Zedong-Thought for Confucianism. Yet other times, culturalism implies that modern-day politicians mirror themselves in history and gain their inspiration for political action in the classics; Mao Zedong is a prime example of this, seeking inspiration in the great masters and often referring to the classical heritage, being in constant dialogue and disagreement with themes hidden deep in the Chinese past. Hence, Chinese political discourse forms a consistent reference to the cultural heritage, and can only be understood through the lenses of history.

These three types of culturalism have formed the basis of many inspiring and erudite analyses of Chinese politics in historical light, with Lucien Pye and Tang Tsou as eminent examples of this school of political science.

The writing of modern-day politics in the perspective of historical experience presents us with a number of fundamental methodological problems, which the culturalists have been unable to solve. The first point is the combination of generalization and eclecticism in analyzing long perspectives of history. Drastic generalizations are made, whereby the circumstances and contexts of history are lost for the argument; at the same time, in order to make comparisons, details are drawn from the huge body of history, severing them from their context and roots. The culturalists make generalizations and choose detailed evidence in historical retrospective: (a) they have a case to prove about the roots of a modern phenomenon; (b) they are likely to be influenced by moral values of their own age and place in the world; and (c) they use evidence from a largely officially sanctioned body of classical historiography and ideology; the major

Chinese histories were commissioned by dynastic leaders, and under all circumstances were written by scholar-bureaucrats.

The problem of historiography is a real (but not insurmountable) problem for historians, but comparisons in the culturalist school are not fully equipped to cope with the source problem and the problems of postulating similarity between historical data which are torn out of their historical context.

Masterly sweeping statements may lead to a sense of continuity through the millennia, as for example a statement by Pye (1991):

> In the contemporary world, Mao Zedong, Deng Xiaoping, and Chiang Kai-shek, though acting far more civilly than the dynastic emperors, all tended to blend ruling and reigning, to intervene in the details of governing at one moment and then to pull back into aloof isolation for prolonged periods. Mao, much like an emperor, depended on his bureaucracy, yet he felt compelled to clash with it and to distrust its most professional members. To be sure, the tradition of castigating bureaucratic behaviour is as old as bureaucratic tradition itself. But in China, unlike the West, it was a tradition which came from above, from the court itself, and not from below.

Brash and sweeping comparisons, summarizing millennia in a single subordinated clause, and huge, vaguely defined parts of the world in three words, may give one the confidence of overview and secure knowledge, but in reality makes one blind to important differences and details. The parallels between today's politics and events decades or centuries ago do not explain causality, they only postulate similarity. The question 'why was Mao's relation to the "bureaucrats" whimsical?' cannot be answered by 'because that was what the emperors in the past were'.

Culturalist approaches are still very common, and generally not very useful for an understanding of Chinese politics.

CONFUCIANISM AND CHINESE POLITICAL CULTURE

The most popular and least credible variety of the culturalist approaches preaches that Chinese politics are determined by the heritage of Confucianism. The idea is that Confucianism is a code of governance, a statecraft, which has melted into communist rule. At the most basic level of argument it is possible to find superficial similarities between an abstract textbook version of Confucianism and perceived autocratic practices in China today.

Confucius, or Kongzi, was an itinerant sage who lived in the fifth century before Christ. His main contribution was that he discussed statecraft with rulers of the time. The records of his dialogues have been transmitted, and through history have had an immense influence on Chinese culture as the ideological backbone of the bureaucrat-scholar class. They have been interpreted and reinterpreted, and have been the core of imperial examinations. They have split off into 'small traditions', popular rules of life, and have had profound influence on family and clan life in pre-modern China.

The fundamentals of Confucianism are centred around hierarchical structures of authority. The moral obligation was to submit to the will of the superior, be it the emperor, the scholar-bureaucrat, the father, the husband, the elder son or the elder brother. The person who had authority had the moral obligation to be just and reasonable. Prosperity and progress were only possible when these rules of obligation were kept.

At a very abstract level of argument it is possible to claim parallels between Confucianism and communism, with just as much validity as if one says that modern European democracies are inspired by Socrates and Plato or Jesus Christ. It is evident that even if one could argue that such a parallel is *true*, it is likely to be of very little value for a real understanding of the political system in China today.

CONCLUSIONS

The purpose of this chapter has been to familiarize the reader with the various approaches to Chinese politics. None of the approaches described above can be called comprehensive in their explanations of Chinese politics. However, all have contributed to our understanding of what has been happening in China. These approaches are themselves as much the products of their time as they are important in explaining the times in which we view China. The totalitarian model seems extremely partial, and simplistic to us today, but in the political climate of the Cold War the appeal of this approach was clearly significant. In the post-structuralist intellectual environment in which we work today, it is not difficult to understand why the focus of attention has shifted from model building and universalist explanations of political systems to more micro-level studies of a country's politics. These various approaches have also been circumscribed by or have benefited from the political climate within China. Greater or lesser access to information, to archives, and to people in China has affected the levels of sophistication achieved by various approaches. The class struggle model, therefore, suffered not only from a problem of 'grand theory', but also from very limited availability of information. The use that any information is put to is an important question, but access to material has an important impact on any research. Today, scholars working on Chinese politics have far greater resources and access to China than ever before. This has greatly enhanced the quality of research on China. Clientelism, the state/civil society dichotomy, the political economy approach – all of these have made significant contributions to recent debates regarding China. All these approaches present sophisticated, well-resourced and well-researched works explaining the complex and evolving political reality in today's China.

The view from the outside

One thing that all the above approaches to Chinese politics share is that they have emerged in the West; they are explanations from the outside. Here it is important to note that the relationship between the West and the East rests on an imbalance of power in the international political and economic system. Concepts and meanings are made significant and validated in this context of power. What is desirable and what is unacceptable is constructed and debated in this context. The way scholars approach China is also affected by this power hierarchy. What do the Chinese themselves think of their own system? How do they make sense of the changing reality of China? The Chinese have been the objects of many studies on China; what do they feel as subjects participating in the analysis of their own political reality? Some work has reflected Chinese voices (Chen, 1984; Su, 1988; Bachman and Yang, 1991), but largely China continues to be defined from outside its own boundaries. Can we, however, take the stance that those on the outside can never understand Chinese reality? Such is not our position. Our purpose in bringing up this question is only to point to the partiality of even the most sophisticated analytical tools that are used to approach China.

Most of the theories, models or concepts mentioned in this chapter are useful avenues to a better understanding of Chinese reality. All of them have specific shortcomings. They focus on different aspects of Chinese politics, and they give different weight to different empirical data. All approaches to Chinese politics are reductionist; they try to examine a small number of explanatory variables to create clarity of the whole. The factionalist model, for example, reduces its scope of interest to a very limited pantheon of leaders, while disregarding or treating as subsidiary the formal social or political structures. The complex bureaucracy model – not considering individual leaders as the focus of analysis, but looking at formal structures for policy making – is at advantage, since it can follow the continuity and change of policies over a long period.

FURTHER READING

There are very few works that deal critically with methods and approaches to Chinese politics in a comprehensive and comparative way. One excellent, but dated, exception is Oksenberg (1969: 155–215). Further reading in the works mentioned in this chapter is encouraged.

PART I
The making of modern China

Part I of this book is devoted to uncovering the underlying economic and political grid upon which contemporary China is situated. Without an understanding of how an ancient culture and a stable political system and economy encountered, confronted and adjusted to the demands made upon it, we cannot explain the incremental changes that have made China a modern nation-state of today. In any country the process of change is difficult and overlaid with historical movements; in China this echoing of the past into the present and the future seems very exaggerated and clear. This might have something to do with the stability of China's political system, its relative cultural cohesion, or the sophistication of its economy, or a combination of all these. The self-confidence of the Chinese emperors was great. Perhaps the changes, when they became imperative, were therefore exceedingly painful and slow, violent and untidy.

In this part of the book we set out the history of modern China in two chapters. The first begins with the 'opening up' of China (which is a recurrent theme in the book), charts the decline of the Chinese economy and political system, and also its renewal through examining the impact of the Opium Wars, the Hundred Days Reforms, the 1911 Revolution, the period of warlordism, and the May Fourth Movement of 1919 which became a watershed in the history of modern China. The second chapter is a history of the rise of the communist movement in China and traces the course of the Chinese Communist Party from obscurity to power in 1949. Of necessity these are broadbrush chapters, but will familiarize the reader with the backdrop of the communist revolution. The final chapter in this part of the book addresses the theme of transition. The Chinese communists, from being a movement, had taken the reins of government; the transition was not easy.

2   A history of the Chinese Revolution

This chapter examines the traditions that go into forming the Chinese world view today. 'Opening up' as a central concept explaining political changes in China in the nineteenth and twentieth century is examined as a means of refuting the simple culturalist explanations of Chinese politics. 'Opening up', which underpins the relationship between China and the West, is examined in the light of the impact of the two forces on each other. The chapter concludes by tracing the growth of modern political movements in China – the 1911 Revolution and the May Fourth Movement – that laid the basis of the modern Chinese nation-state.

THE 'OPENING UP' OF CHINA

China has grown from being regarded as the 'sick man of Asia' into one of the most powerful economic and political nations in the world. In its modernization programme the Chinese leadership has been able to draw upon a rich tradition of political and philosophical discourse and experience. China's view of the world, of its position within a world system, and the Confucianist traditions of rulership, have all affected the processes of creation of the modern nation-state, though these have not been the only sources of inspiration for Chinese leaders. Other sources have been Western ideologies of liberalism, Marxism and modern nationalism, but these have been creatively interpreted and applied to the Chinese conditions. The evolving economic relations within China and its relations with Western capitalism have also impacted upon the Chinese state and politics. China in the historical context is a China that has experimented with the new, but has remained conscious of its past; it has 'opened up' to the outside, while retaining a sense of its traditions and its place in the world.

Modern Chinese history has been the history of its self-definition *vis-à-vis* the rest of the world, especially the West. It has been the history of 'opening up', and of coming to terms with the consequences of 'opening up'. This 'opening up' has sometimes been achieved by the changing perceptions of, and initiatives by, the Chinese elites, and sometimes because of external pressures. The external pressures have been especially important in the late Qing period of the late eighteenth and nineteenth centuries, though traditions of cosmopolitanism have existed in China, expressed in the activities of travellers, traders and explorers. The most serious problem for the Chinese ruling elites has been how to manage change that has resulted from the 'opening up' of the country, and its economic and cultural boundaries. The history of management of change in China provides us with an interesting perspective on Chinese politics today. We find that the difference between the 'opening up' of the mid-1880s and the 1980s is the relative strengths of the Chinese state. The latter took place with a strong, self-confident, powerful Chinese state at the helm, while the former led to significant erosion of Chinese sovereignty. This erosion of sovereign power fuelled much of the political activity that we discuss in this chapter. It also affected the way in which the Chinese state regarded 'opening up' as a political issue.

China as the Middle Kingdom

'Opening up' has had important repercussions in Chinese politics, because for long periods China remained locked within its own boundaries, jealous of its cultural organization, apprehensive of breaches of confidentiality and cultural cohesion, and convinced of its centrality in the group of nations that it looked out on to. In modern Chinese history we see a return to this isolation during the period of the Cultural Revolution (see Chapter 9). The political perceptions of the Chinese elites before the seventeenth century, and particularly the eighteenth century, were based upon viewing China as the Middle Kingdom (*zhongguo*). This was an important concept, myth and reality rolled into one as far as the Chinese self-definition is concerned.

The Middle Kingdom was not difficult to construct in the imagination of the Chinese people, especially that of the elites. Ninety-four per cent of the Chinese population is of the Han race, shares the same written language and accepts a common national identity, even while retaining strong regional and local loyalties. The imperial age in China (221 BC to AD 1911) saw significant Chinese contributions to most areas of knowledge, technology, trade, and governance which reinforced the centrality of Chinese civilization in the imagination of the Chinese people and its elites (see Box 2.1).

The Chinese elites were able to organize countrywide both state functioning and economic activity. Development of printing and shipbuilding helped communications across the Middle Kingdom, while the sophisticated and meritocratic civil service ensured implementation of policies, and growing periods of political stability (see Loewe, 1990).

Principles of the Chinese state

A culturalist explanation of the political stability of the Middle Kingdom would give central place not so much to state organization, but to the Confucian philosophy or ethics which were 'designed to uphold the dignity of man and to

---

Box 2.1 *The Qian Long Emperor's mandate to King George III (1793)*

Yesterday your Ambassador petitioned my Ministers to memorialize me regarding your trade with China ... Hitherto, all European nations, including your own country's barbarian merchants, have carried on their trade with our Celestial Empire at Guangzhou although our Celestial Empire possesses all things in prolific abundance and lacks no product within its own borders. There was therefore no need to import the manufactures of outside barbarians in exchange for our own produce. But as the tea, silk, and porcelain which the Celestial Empire produces are absolute necessities to European nations and to yourselves, we have permitted as a signal mark of favour that foreign *hongs* (Chinese business associations) should be established at Canton, so that your wants might be supplied ...

But your Ambassador has now put forward new requests which completely fail to recognize the Throne's principle to 'treat strangers from afar with indulgence', and to exercise a pacifying control over barbarian tribes, the world over ... I do not forget the lonely remoteness of your island, cut off from the world by intervening wastes of sea ... But the demands presented by your Embassy are not only a contravention of dynastic tradition, but would be utterly unproductive ... Do not say that you were not warned in due time! Tremblingly obey and show no negligence!

(Source: Schurmann and Schell, 1967: 103–7)

---

establish the ideal social relationships which would ensure such a result' (Loewe, 1990: 103). The underlying principles of the Confucian discourse emphasized relations between things rather than their individual characteristics. In this tradition, hierarchies were established in society that were characterized by *wu lun* (five relationships), i.e. relations between the emperor and his subjects, father and son, husband and wife, elder brother and younger brother, and friend and friend – all of which were based on moral obligations. As such, personal example as a means of education in public values was favoured above codes of conduct and punishment enshrined in law. The role of law in society was to secure harmony in society not to ensure individual rights. Arbitration was the central principle of law, not judgement. Social hierarchies and personal qualities were the bulwarks against social change, even though change was considered unavoidable and recurrent in a cycle of birth, growth and decay.

While the Confucian tradition is important to our understanding of the hegemonic discourse on governance in imperial China, this does not presuppose that the subversion of this discourse did not routinely take place, by both the state elites and other groups and classes in the country. The history of ethnic conflict, changes in productive and class relations, and peasant uprising bespeaks the need for a more complex understanding of Chinese state politics. For example, the concept of the 'mandate of heaven', which is linked to the Confucian tradition, has been regarded as crucial to the stability of the Chinese state. The acceptance of change as a philosophical principle of governance implied a fundamental divergence between the Chinese and the European traditions of governance. To accept cyclical change implied the negation of the principle of the 'divine right to rule'. The 'mandate of heaven' (*tian ming*) was granted not in perpetuity but for as long as the emperor was able to fulfil his obligations to his subjects. Most of these obligations arose from the needs of the Chinese economy. Its geography – in particular its rivers – ensured that state investment and regulation were needed to overcome obstacles to a prosperous and stable political economy which included not only agricultural production, but also significant internal trade, and increasing overseas trade. Once the emperor reneged on his duties, peasant rebellions were inevitable, as was the passing of the 'mandate of heaven' to the one who was able to take on the obligations of governing, together with its power. However, we find that the mandate principle legitimized the change of rulership without jeopardizing the authority of the emperor (Fitzgerald, 1952: 14–15). It did not ensure a smooth transfer of power from one dynasty to another.

While Confucianism provided a hegemonic discourse of power within the Chinese polity, the power of the emperor also rested on political stability that could be ensured only through loyal administration. Taxes had to be collected, rebellions put down, and people administered. As early as AD 518 in the Sui dynasty period, the Palace Examinations were instituted to select personnel for the civil service. The principle of meritocracy and mobility was thus enshrined in social practice through the route of political governance. However, the value of the examinations as a judge of the quality of would-be officials was undermined by the emphasis laid on conformity, rather than independence, dogma rather than innovation. Further, the examinations required a significant investment in time and resources, which few from the poorer sections of the population could afford. Favouritism through family and clan connections (*guanxi*) also undermined the openness of the system (see Needham (1970) on 'bureaucratic feudalism'). However, the civil service did give to China an administrative unity, and, perhaps more significantly, the idea of mobility which secured the loyalty of the bureaucratic elites.

All these characteristics of the state created what Jack Gray has called 'habits of mind' which gave China a stability that was not necessarily linked to the successful functioning of its political institutions (Gray, 1990: 19). However, by the eighteenth century these political institutions were increasingly malperforming as corruption set in at every level.

THE WEST LOOKING EAST

The nineteenth century saw the 'opening up' of China to the West in the context of the spread of capitalism and imperialism. While the Chinese, as already mentioned, had a rich tradition of trade and scholarly exchanges with other countries of the East, its contact with the West had been limited until the seventeenth century. What we see emerging during the unfolding of this relationship with the West is a complex picture. There were those within the Chinese political elites who were convinced for the need to modernize China's governing apparatus, as well as its defences, and who looked outward for inspiration. There were also sections of the elites who were opposed to the patterns of governance in China and wanted to explore Western philosophical traditions to provide alternatives or supplements to traditions of opposition to state power in China. Away from this debate, prizing China open was simply necessary for the Western powers.

China was, and always has been, too important a country to ignore. In geopolitical, demographic and economic terms it has presented the West with both opportunity and challenge. Whether it was the forced entry into China by the European imperialist powers at the beginning of the seventeenth century, or the gradual American-led wooing of China into the international fold after the Cultural Revolution, the Chinese markets have mattered too much to the West to leave the country alone for long. The fascination with China, though driven by its economic potential, has been more than that. The cultural claims of the Chinese state, its history, and its political institutions have also fed into the construction of China, created by the West and inscribed into its own imagination, that first validated and then challenged the myth of the Middle Kingdom. Based on the partial experience of coastal cities of south China like Shanghai and Guangzhou, the Western scholars found a rich seam to mine in the culturalist tradition. As the Western powers forced themselves upon a weakening Chinese state, the 'treaty-port' culture of these cities became symbolic of China's weakness. This was then extrapolated onto the entire canvas of China, without any consideration of the contested relationship between rural and urban, provincial and metropolitan China.

Orientalism and the Chinese puzzle

In his book *Orientalism* (1995), Edward Said argues that the European construction of the Orient was essential to its self-definition, as it provided Europe with its most significant 'cultural contestant'. This project entailed bringing about a consensus concerning the nature of the Orient that has spanned many generations in both time and space. While Said's focus is the Middle East, and the colonies of European powers, the Orient encompassed the Far East and China as well. So as recently as 1990 we find a series of titles such as *The Pride that was China, The Wonder that was India, The Splendour that was Egypt,*

The Greatness that was Babylon and *The Majesty that was Islam* (published by Sidgwick & Jackson). These titles suggest two things to the reader: the acknowledgement of a past which becomes a comment on the present. It indicates a rich but exhausted culture in need of rejuvenation. The role of Europe in this context was then made clear: the revitalization of these decaying cultures by injection of industrialization and trade on the one hand, and the infusion of individualism and liberalism on the other. Such a discourse therefore was an important means of justifying colonialism, or, as in the case of China, imperialist intervention. Orientalism is, however, a discourse that affects Chinese scholarship even today, as the Sidgwick & Jackson series suggests. The construction of Chinese people – all 800 million of them – during the Second World War and the Cold War as the 'blue ants' or the 'yellow peril', generalizations about the Chinese character as subservient because of the tradition of emperor worship, or the Chinese as 'natural traders' in the post-Mao era, all point to the contemporary relevance of Said's concern.

Europe and pre-revolutionary China

In the seventeeth century there occurred a shift in the balance of power between the Middle Kingdom and the European colonial powers. Once the English boats had shot their way into China and opened up trade in 1637, the weakness of the Chinese state could not be masked behind the pomp of the Celestial Court. The China that the European powers forced their way into was a China approaching crisis, which was reached by the intrusion of Western capitalism. An important question in this context is whether, given its vibrant internal and external trade, China could have undertaken the project of economic modernization without external intervention? Could the political crisis that China experienced during the twentieth century have been avoided through economic modernization? The answers to these questions are important for our understanding of China at the threshold of change in the twentieth century, as they have important resonances for China's economic strategy in the post-Mao era.

THE CHINESE ECONOMY UNDER THE QING DYNASTY

Economic explanations of the decline of the Chinese state predominate. The argument is that the Chinese state was unable (or even unwilling) to 'modernize' and was therefore holding up Chinese development. Further, that while imperialism brought much social and political pain to China, it also had a 'regenerative' role which was primarily in pushing willy nilly a 'backward' China down the road of modernization (see Marx, 1968; Fairbank, 1987). There are historians and political analysts of the Chinese Revolution who find the economic explanation insufficient (Gray, 1990; Sckocpol, 1979) and point to China's vibrant economy. They regard the decline of the Chinese empire as a result of a set of conjunctive factors of which the economy was one. What did the Chinese economy look like in the seventeenth to the nineteenth centuries?

Agriculture and peasant lives

The Chinese economy under the Qing dynasty was an agrarian economy. It was not a feudal economy in the sense of European feudalism with its seigneurs and tenants. Land ownership was widespread, and landlordism was defined by local conditions rather than by a centralized system of land distribution. As early as the fifteenth century, a free market in land had developed, making for a predominance of independent producers in China's agricultural system. There was, however, a significant minority of tenant farmers who worked for landlords. The number of tenants rose and fell with economic cycles. Though Chinese peasants were not subsistence farmers, the margin of surplus they produced was small and bad weather and natural disasters could easily force them into debt. The rates of interest were high and unregulated which meant that it was almost impossible to repay their debt, and dispossession of land inevitably followed (see Gray, 1990). If the rates of interest were high, the burdens of taxation were onerous. Taxes were collected by officials who had to meet a quota, after which they could keep the rest for themselves and their establishment (Fairbank, 1987: 43).

As the officials were not salaried civil servants, the tendency to squeeze the maximum out of the peasants was hard to resist for most officials. Candidates for official posts as a matter of routine activated patron–client relations to gain office, and to remain in office; the interests of the peasants ranked far below those of the scholar-bureaucrat officialdom. In the Qing dynasty period China saw a tremendous increase in population: from 65–80 million in 1400 to around 400 million by the mid-nineteenth century (Sckocpol, 1989: 74). With no new land available – partly due to the deteriorating land:person ratio, and partly because the Manchus restricted Chinese migration to the north, as well as overseas – population pressure became an important issue for the Chinese economy, as well as its political life. They feared the swamping of their native Manchuria on the one hand (a fear that has been proved right in the post-revolutionary China) and concentration of political dissent in overseas locations (also borne out by later events) (see Fitzgerald, 1970: 20). Finally, with the advent of Western powers, and importing of manufactured goods, the peasants lost out on an important traditional income from village handicrafts. There was no concurrent expansion of modern industry in China due to the attractiveness of land investment by rural elites, who could, unlike their Western counterparts, use land as collateral. Western tariff restrictions also discouraged varied investment for industrial growth, and the weakness of the Chinese political elites did not allow them to counter these pressures strongly enough to prevent the loss of the village handicraft income, which was a grievous blow to the peasant economy in China.

Trade, industry and urbanization

China had a vibrant internal trade network both in food and handicrafts, and in manufactured goods. Such commerce was aided by China's extensive network of navigable waterways that were partly natural, such as the Yangtze River, and partly constructed, like the Grand Canal that linked the Yangtze and the Yellow rivers and extended from Hangzhou almost to Beijing. There was significant trade within provinces, regions, and towns and villages. The manufacture of goods was organized at different levels. At the village level handicraft production, especially of cloth, was important, as was the cultivation and sale of mulberries for silk production; these were family based. There is also some evidence of large-scale production, with up to 100 people working under one roof in Guangzhou, together with the existence of a 'putting-out' system (Gray, 1990: 12). Chinese manufacturing and trade also benefited from a sophisticated guild system set up to facilitate merchants' activities (Fairbank, 1987: 57). Guilds were financed by entrance fees. They took on the regulation of commerce, in place of the local government, and provided dormitories for merchants passing though; they also served the community in a variety of ways – building roads and bridges, taking care of the water supplies, and even building and running schools. At their zenith they indicated the strength of the Chinese merchant class.

While there was a tremendous growth in Chinese commerce, it is disputed whether or not it succeeded in breaking the stranglehold of governmental interference in the form of licensing of commercial monopolies (see Fairbank, 1987; Gray, 1990). The role of the government remained primarily one of collecting taxes rather than combining that with organizing the industrial and commercial infrastructure. However, there was a growing monetization of the economy which was essential for the growth of capitalism, as well as new forms of banking in China's commercial centres like Shanxi and Ningbo.

All these features of the Chinese economy allowed Chinese communists to make the claim that China was moving towards capitalism and industrialization, and that this historical process was disrupted by the intrusion of imperialism. Historians like Gray, while acknowledging the growth of commercial capitalism and noting the significance of the changing patterns of production and monetary organization, point to the Chinese political institutions as the main culprits in China's slow movement towards a modern economy (1990: 15). Other China scholars like Fairbank emphasize the 'regenerative' role of imperialism in the modernization of China, while also noting the internal pressures that were facing a political system which was increasingly falling behind a growing economy (1987: 47, 62).

THE CAUSES OF THE POLITICAL DECLINE OF THE QING DYNASTY

The fact that the Chinese political system was not able to absorb the changes that were being introduced by a vibrant and growing economy on the one hand, and foreign encroachment on the other, points to the growing malaise in the government that was to prove critical in the process of socio-economic change in China. This change led to the disintegration of the Chinese empire, the transformation of its economic system, political institutions and culture, and to military humiliation at the hands of both internal and external forces of opposition which traumatized the Chinese elites and people for a long time to come. Perhaps the one event that symbolizes the humiliation of traditional, imperial China at the hands of the 'foreign devils' (*fan gui*) is the infamous Opium War.

The Opium War and the imperialist encroachment

The Opium War (1839–1842) was a clash between an *ancien régime* and a new, self-confident imperialist power, and the victory of the latter led to the collapse of the former. By the 1830s the imports from China to Great Britain were so great that they were draining the coffers of Britain. Opium, grown and taxed in India, provided a way out of the trade imbalance that Britain found itself suffering from. As the opium trade grew (1,000 chests in 1799; 3,210 in 1816; 40,000 in 1838) the Chinese society and economy began to feel the consequences of not only the drug, but also the power of the new imperialism. When Imperial Commissioner Lin Zexu was sent to Guangzhou to cut off the trade, the consequence was the Opium War which resulted in the Treaty of Nanjing in 1842 (this included the cession of Hong Kong by China to Great Britain) which began the system of unequal treaties which was not abolished until 1943.

The Opium War also saw the coining of the term 'gunboat diplomacy' to describe the relationship that developed between the weakening Chinese state and the imperialist commercial interests. Between the Opium War and the Anglo-French Chinese wars of 1858–1860, which led to the occupation and burning of Beijing, a pattern was set which allowed the imperialist powers to set up 'spheres of influence', open up new ports for trade, and establish the principle of extraterritoriality whereby they had jurisdiction over their citizens on Chinese soil. Other features of the various treaties that the Chinese government had to sign after the Treaty of Nanjing allowed foreign powers to press for a 'most favoured nation' treatment in trade, a right to send missionaries anywhere in China, a right to establish factories in the treaty ports and get tax immunity for articles made by them, and a right to station troops in the legation areas of the Chinese capital. Most important perhaps were provisions whereby the Chinese government was unable to adjust its tariff rates, administer customs and appropriate customs revenues on the one hand, while facing enormous bills for forced indemnity payments after wars with the imperialist powers on the other. After the Opium War the Chinese government had to pay US$21 million. Together with extraterritoriality, these last two provisions meant not only an enormous economic burden on the Chinese economy, but also they became symbolic of the helplessness of the Chinese regime before the irresistible forces of imperialist encroachent. From the splendid isolation of the Celestial Empire, China was being forced into a state of abject surrender to foreign powers. Defeat in the Sino-Japanese War of 1894 epitomized this surrender.

Decline of the Manchus

While the Opium War and the consequent 'opening up' of China symbolized Chinese weakness *vis-à-vis* the growing power of industrial capitalism, the internal decay which allowed this to happen had many different causes. Indeed, one could argue that the Qing dynasty got an extended lease to rule from the interventions of the imperialist powers and without that intervention would have been overthrown as their Mandate of Heaven ran out. By the mid-nineteenth century a combination of factors – an increasing population, deteriorating economic infrastructure, limited revenue from taxation (taxes had been fixed in 'perpetuity' in 1759), and the growing demands of the military due to increasing rebellions – found the government in the red. One way of raising finances, among the many, that the Qing regime devised, was the selling of office to the highest bidder. The implications for corruption of the government, for efficiency and for legitimacy are obvious. These in turn fed into the growing anger of the people against what they saw as a depraved court symbolized by the powerful eunuchs who came to wield tremendous influence in the palace, especially under the Dowager Cixi. As the Taiping, Mohamaden, and Nian rebellions show, domestic peace was a thing of the past, and the mounting bills of keeping the borders of the empire policed further fuelled resentment as taxation rose and correspondingly so did levels of repression of dissent (Box 2.2).

Repression, however, was not the only strategy that a beleaguered regime employed to contain the haemorrhaging of its authority and power. A mixture of resistance, reconciliation and reform was tried out. Two attempts were made by the regime to confront the issues of socio-economic and political decline of the country. The first was the Self-Strengthening Movement. This initiative saw a combination of attempts at restoring China's political and social institutions, and a slow cautious programme of modernization of its military and financial systems. The first modest reforms included the establishment of a foreign office in Beijing, a language school for diplomats, and in 1861 the creation of a small modernized military force (bannermen). However, these initial reforms fell foul of increasingly bitter internecine feuds for influence in the imperial court. The watchwords for this period of reform were 'Chinese learning as essence,

Box 2.2 *Hong Xiuquan: Leader of the Taipings*

Hong Xiuquan was born in 1814 in Guangdong in a family of peasant proprietors. He became a school teacher after his family could no longer support his schooling. He, like most bright young men in China, studied for the provincial examination for the civil service. Given the rigidities of the system on the one hand, and the creative ability of Hong, it is not surprising that he failed in all his four attempts to pass the examinations. A mental breakdown followed and during this time he saw a vision that converted him to a modified version of Christianity. In this vision, full of angels and beautiful maidens, Hong was ordered by an old man – God – to drive out evil from the land. He was adopted by God as his second son – a younger brother to Jesus Christ. Hong, and his associates, began to destroy idols in the local temples, and were dismissed for their efforts to proselytize the word of God. The minority Hakka tribe accepted Hong's faith, lending the anti-Manchu element to the movement, which led to a full scale attack on the God-Worshippers by the end of 1850. The rebels seem to have been prepared, and declared the establishment of the Taiping Tianguo – the Heavenly Kingdom of Transcendent Peace – on 11 January 1851. Hong's kingdom was a theocracy, and all laws drew their inspiration from Hong's revelations: all property belonged to God/State, all surplus to the treasury while the people were paid for their labour by rations, and supervised in the villages by a sergeant who was administrator, policeman and preacher all rolled into one. The Christian beliefs of Hong did not get him the support of western Christian missionaries, who declared his claims to being the second son of God as blasphemous. During the period between 1851–1853 the Taipings, as they were called, launched two great expeditions designed to conquer China – one north to Beijing and the other west to Sichuan. The battles were bitter and the opposition fierce. By 1856 the Taipings controlled the lower Yangtze, but by this time the Kingdom was becoming less credible, with Hong's sanity coming into doubt as he withdrew from the affairs of the state resulting in growing suspicions among his lieutenants. The end of the Kingdom soon followed in 1864 with the seige of the seat of the Heavenly Kingdom at Nanjing, and the death of Hong from either poisoning or disease. The end was as violent as the ascendency of the Taipings – a hundred thousand Taipings died at Nanjing rather than surrender. Their religion died with them, leaving behind only a folklore which valorised their puritanism and their courage, and their opposition to Manchu authority which gave inspiration to many nationalists, including it is said, Mao Zedong.

(Source: Gray, 1990: 55–76)

Western learning for practical use'. This slogan has deep resonances in modern Chinese history and politics as it has come to symbolize the Chinese elites' response to pressure from the Western powers. We will come across this phrase again, much later, in the period of communist rule, and indeed in the context of post-Mao reforms (Chapter 6).

The first attempts at reform were started in 1898 and, though very limited, were followed by a more comprehensive programme that came to be known as the Hundred Days Reforms.

The Hundred Days Reforms

If the Treaty of Nanjing had established an unequal relationship between the Chinese state and the Western powers, the Treaty of Shimonoseki that was signed after the Chinese defeat in the Sino-Japanese War of 1894–1895, completed the humiliation. The result was an intellectual and elite response to the now evident decline of the Manchus. The two leading scholars associated with this response were Kang Youwei and Liang Qichao. They argued that Confucius was a reformer whose vision could be realized in a context of renewal of Chinese social and political life. They influenced the young Guangxu Emperor to pass a sweeping set of reforms in 1898. These included the modernization of the traditional examination system for the civil service, the elimination of sinecures and the creation of a system of modern education. These were to lay the basis for an eventual system of constitutional monarchy.

The impact of the reformist strategy

While the reformers suffered a defeat at the hands of the conservative faction in the court, the reforms themselves survived in part. Their implementation was taken up by the provincial officials, creating regional bases of power and influence that were to contribute to the rise of warlordism in Chinese politics soon after the 1911 Revolution.

The partial implementation of reforms created their own stresses and strains. First, the industrial manufacturers were not happy with the nature of the protection that they were given. They were at a disadvantage in competing with the Western powers and looked to the state for support, which did not materialize because of the bankruptcy of the Manchu dynasty. This growing and yet frustrated bourgeoisie would play an important part in the 1911 Revolution. Second, the merchants and traders were also becoming increasingly unhappy. At the time, China was the only formally independent nation where its own merchants payed higher taxes than their foreign counterparts. This was especially true for merchants who traded in Chinese goods rather than in Western imports.

Third, the peasantry was becoming restive too. The neglect of the irrigation system and of the river dykes, growing exploitation by the landlords and corruption of the gentry class, and natural disasters in the north of the country all led to increased dissaffection. The burden on the peasantry increased enormously with the imposition of huge indemnities on China by Japan in the

Treaty of Shimonoseki and by the Western powers after the Boxer Rebellion of 1900. The secret societies found willing recruits among the peasantry, and the anti-Manchu feeling ran high. Fourth, the military was a divided force, and the Hundred Days Reforms exacerbated these divisions. The younger, more radical military commanders wanted to modernize the army and realized that this could be done only through a state that was itself modern. The corruption and decay of the Manchu bannermen and their opposition to any project of reforming the army angered the young officers.

Further, new social groups were beginning to stir. The Chinese students and urban youth (who would play a crucial role in Chinese politics from now on) were greatly influenced by the ideas of reformers like Kang Youwei and Liang Qichao. Educated women began to participate in public life and helped open fundamental issues for the Chinese society as well as polity. Finally, institutional reforms introduced by the Manchu court after the Hundred Days Reforms also generated opposition. In particular, the abolition of the numerical balance between Chinese and Manchu officials led to disaffection in the bureaucracy, and the setting up of a constitutional government at the national and provincial levels in 1909, but with only a consultative role, made these into centres of opposition. A nationalist agenda began to take shape that distinguished itself from the traditions of isolation of the Celestial Empire on the one hand, and the abject humiliation and surrender to the foreigners on the other.

This nationalist agenda had two aspects to it: it was anti-Manchu and it was anti-imperialist. It based itself on an opposition to both absolutism and foreign domination. In the first instance, anti-Manchu feeling became the focal point for both these aspects – the Manchus were absolutists as well as foreigners. However, different oppositional groups interpreted nationalism differently. The secret societies for example chose to emphasize the anti-foreign aspect, while the intelligentsia focused more on the ills of absolutism. This was particularly the case as the intellectual elites in China came into contact with ideas that had their origin in Western capitalism: representation, accountability, individual rights, and the relationship between citizen and the state. These contributed to an alternative vision of China.

All these factors combined to organize opposition in the form of modern political parties that would play a crucial role in the revolutionary transformation of China.

THE SUCCESSORS TO THE CELESTIAL EMPIRE: THE 1911 REVOLUTION

Sun Yat-sen led a revolution that has been called 'enormously ambitious and proudly unrealistic' (Wright, 1968). Sun had organized the Xingzhonghui (Revive China Society) in 1895, inspired by the Hundred Days Reforms. It had two aims: to expel the Manchus and to establish republican government in

China. Sun tried to capture Guangzhou, failed, and fled to Japan, where in 1905 he founded the Tongmenghui (United League). Its first recruits were Chinese students in Tokyo, and its charter included equal rights for citizens and a republican goverment in China. By 1911 the Tongmenghui had branches in south China, and had participated in the growing agitation about the national-ization of the railways by the Manchus which contradicted the railways 'rights recovery' movement against foreign rail companies based in the provinces.

Regionalism therefore played a crucial part in the revolution at this stage. There were subversive activities led by the Tongmenghui in the Wuchang garrison in Hubei. When a powder keg exploded accidentally, two soldiers who belong to the banned Tongmenghui organization were arrested. This led to a mutiny by young officers which, with the support of the Tongmenghui, spread to barracks across south China, and in the end became the catalyst that triggered the overthrow of the Manchus. The movement was, however, only partially responsible for the fall of the dynasty. Military satraps played an important role in the whole affair, especially Yuan Shikai who became the power broker between the dynasty and the revolution.

Yuan, as the 'Northern Viceroy' or the most powerful governor of the country, was strongly opposed to the revolution. He had in part been responsible for the failure of the Hundred Days Reforms when he betrayed the reform faction and joined the Dowager Empress. When the revolutionaries set up a Provisional government in Nanjing, led by the Provisional President Sun Yat-sen, Yuan dispatched soldiers to quell the revolution. However, the Provisional government (through one of its members, Zhang Jian) negotiated a deal with Yuan, by which he would be appointed the first president of the republic on the condition that he included the revolutionaries in his Republican government. Yuan then forced concessions from the Manchus by insisting that revolutionary groups be legalized, and he be given the full command of the army. The Manchu court had to agree and many provinces declared their independence from the Manchus and gave allegiance to the Republican government in Hankou. In December 1911 it was decided in a meeting between Tongmenghui officials and the representatives of Yuan that the latter would become China's first president upon the abdication of the Manchu dynasty. The revolution had become a reality, or had it?

Sun departed for Japan, and the Tongmenghui won 269 of the 596 seats in the national Senate elected in 1913. However, Yuan did not want to share power. Supported by the Western powers, who were suspicious of the anti-imperialist rhetoric of Tongmenghui, the Senate was dissolved in 1913 and the Tongmenghui was delegitimized. Yuan became a dictator, and in 1915 crowned himself emperor! To forestall foreign opposition Yuan agreed to accept the infamous Twenty One Demands put forward by Japan, and signed agreements with Great Britain and Russia recognizing their special interests in Tibet and Outer Mongolia, respectively. Sun Yat-sen also reorganized during this period the Tongmenghui into the Guomindang (Kuo Min Tang, normally abbreviated

KMT) in July 1914. He also organized the Chinese Revolutionary Army of which he was generalissimo, and set out to militarily reverse Yuan's monarchial arrangement. Sun was able to mobilize support from several provinces like Yunnan, Guangxi and Shandong. Yuan retreated in face of this opposition, and his political demise was followed by his death on 6 June 1916.

Several factors led to the failure of the 1911 Revolution in its immediate sense. The revolutionary leadership, especially Sun Yat-sen, succeeded in inspiring the Chinese people to support a break with political tradition, but could not provide either a political or an intellectual viable alternative to dynastic rule. This was because the leadership was unable to resolve the reformist–republican feud within the movement. The reformists, inspired by Liang Qichao, insisted that a dynastic overthrow would lead to political chaos and therefore that China needed a reformed monarchy which represented a strong authority at the centre. The republicans would have none of what they saw as half-measures and saw the monarchy as representing all that was weak and corrupt in Chinese political life. Further, and equally important, there was no class or organized elite which could be the recognized support base of the government – the emergent bourgeoisie was too weak, the landed gentry too corrupt and discredited, and the military too divided and isolated from the people. The Tongmenghui also did not mobilize a wider political base, which the Chinese Communist Party successfully did much later. A lack of a specific political constituency was also reflected in the eclectic putting together of a political programme and philosophy. Sun's Three People's Principles, which included nationalism, democracy and people's livelihood, were at their best a means of capturing people's imagination but not easily translatable into either policy or political institutions, especially as Sun himself did not fully grasp the implications of power relations then dominant in China.

While the 1911 Revolution failed to transform itself into a government and state, it did represent a break with tradition and a point of departure for China that laid the foundation for further changes. It delegitimized dynastic rule for example. One of the important reasons for Yuan's eventual isolation was that his becoming emperor was seen as a betrayal of the revolution. Anti-imperialism became a modern oppositional ideology into which the Communist Party would tap for support. Modernization of China became the project of every regime after the revolution. This modernization would include not only the political institutions of China but also equally importantly its economic base and its social framework. With the Tongmenghui, political parties became actors on the Chinese political stage for the first time. Other parties followed, e.g. Liang Qichao's Progressive Party and of course the Chinese Communist Party. With political parties we also see the emergence of the published media: in particular, newspapers which became vehicles for informing and mobilizing the urban educated public opinion. Newspapers played an increasingly important role in Chinese political life, especially during the next important phase in the life of revolutionary China – the May Fourth Movement.

THE MAY FOURTH MOVEMENT: FROM REPUBLICANISM TO SOCIALISM

Yuan Shikai died in 1916, and with him gone China lost any sense of central authority. The government led by President Duan Qirui was characterized by weakness, lethargy and a purposelessness which did not allow it to withstand Western political bullying, or read the changing mood of the Chinese people. The acceptance by the Duan Qirui government of the provisions of the Treaty of Versailles, which handed over the German concessions in Shandong to the Japanese to appease a growing Eastern power and to lure it into the League of Nations, was seen by young radicals as an affront to Chinese pride. The outrage felt by the urban masses in China – especially the increasingly vocal intelligentsia – spilled onto the streets of Beijing when 3,000 people marched against the treaty and the Chinese government on 4 May 1919. While led by the students of Beijing University, the march also attracted some merchants and workers, giving it a wider political and social base. Ten youths were arrested, prompting a boycott of Japanese goods, and a run on the banks contributed to a sense of crisis which forced the government into a retreat; it refused to sign the Treaty of Versailles. The May Fourth Movement had commenced (Chow, 1960).

The New Culture Movement

The political movement developed in the context of the growing vigour of the New Culture Movement in Beijing. The movement had started in 1916 with the publication of the journal *New Youth* which was edited by Chen Duxiu (later the chairman of the Chinese Communist Party). This movement emphasized experiments with language, enlarging the accessibility of ideas to the common person, critically examining Western ideas, as well as Chinese history, in order to regenerate Chinese culture from within (Box 2.3).

Box 2.3   *Hu Shi on the New Culture Movement, 9 April 1917*

The Chinese classical style was already a dead language two thousand years ago ... [The] system of literary examinations prolonged the life of the dead classical style ... But the vernacular of the populace could not be suppressed.

The conscious advocacy of vernacular literature began only with the literary revolution movement since 1916. In two respects this movement is different from the movements for vernacular newspapers and alphabetization. First, there is no distinction between 'us' and 'them' in this movement. The vernacular style is not a bone fit only to feed the underdog, but a treasure which the people of the entire country should appreciate. Secondly, this movement honestly attacks the authority of the classical style, and regards it as 'dead literature'.

[Source: Teng and Fairbank, 1981: 355–6]

The centre of the movement was Tong Wen Guan (the language school of diplomats) at Beijing University, whose president, Cai Yuanpei, became one of the leading lights of the movement. Under his encouragement, young, enthusiastic and radical literary critics, historians and writers flourished. Many were 'returned' students whose sojourns abroad made them eager to introduce reform into a declining regime. The two most famous were Chen Duxiu himself, who preached 'science and democracy' and attacked Confucianism, and Hu Shi, a liberal critic influenced by John Dewey, the American educationalist and philosopher. Hu was at the forefront of attempts at simplifying the Chinese language and encouraging vernacular literature. If the 1911 Revolution had successfully delegitimized the monarchy in China, the May Fourth Movement, as it came to be called, succeeded in diminishing the intellectual predominance of Confucianism, which became one of the many competing ideologies in Chinese public life after this point. Other ideologies that made their mark on Chinese intellectual life during this movement were liberalism, anarchism, and socialism, all rooted in the Western philosophical and historical traditions.

Socialism in fact was the 'big idea' of the May Fourth Movement, which has led the CCP to claim the movement as its own. The Chinese intellectuals were disillusioned by Western liberal ideas in the aftermath of the First World War and the compromises made in the Treaty of Versailles. One response to this perceived betrayal was neo-traditionalism, the other was socialism which attracted a generation of Chinese youth that was to provide the leadership of revolutionary change throughout the 1930s and 1940s including Mao Zedong. The impact of the Russian Revolution, and the establishment of a socialist Soviet state, enthused young people to study the philosophy that inspired the Russian socialists. Translated Marxist texts made their appearance as part of the new literature of the political as well as the cultural movement. Li Dazhao, professor of history and the librarian of the Beijing University library and the first Chinese Marxist theorist, became the leader of a group of socialists, Mao Zedong among them, and the founder of the Chinese Communist Party in 1921.

New social classes became politically active during this phase of Chinese history. In urban China we see the maturing of the Chinese middle classes – the bourgeoisie and the intelligentsia – as political actors, as well as of the Chinese working class.

The Chinese middle classes

The Chinese bourgeoisie, which had gone through a period of accelerated development after the fall of the Manchu dynasty, came into its own between 1917 and 1923, a period which has been called the 'golden age of Chinese capitalism' (Bergere and Chesneaux, 1983). The growth of Chinese capitalism followed a similar trajectory to the development of a national, indigenous capitalist class in many other colonized nations. The First World War allowed the indigenous capitalist classes to take advantage of the vacuum in production as the factories of the colonial states were mobilized to fulfil war commitments. Bankers and industrialists began to take over from the merchants. This allowed the Chinese communists to make the distinction between the national (industrial) and the comprador (merchant) bourgeoisie when they sought a united front of classes to fight against foreign aggression, first in 1922 and then later in 1941 (see Chapter 3). The former were welcomed into the United Front, the latter were kept out. The expansion of the industrial bourgeoisie lasted throughout the war and, with the breaking of the bureaucratic stranglehold of the mandarins, allowed its interests to be recognized by political leaderships during this period. Where it failed was in translating this recognition into political power. Neither the Tongmenghui (and later the KMT), nor of course the CCP had their social roots in this class; both sought to mobilize it for their own projects of transformation.

The Chinese bourgeoisie for its part became one of the important sources of finance for both parties. This class was strongest in the coastal industrial base of China, and there it did become a dominant political force. During the warlord period (see pages 46–47) the merchants of Guangzhou refused to let their city be drawn into the fray, and tried to bribe the troops of Chen Xiru to leave the city and let the northern forces take over in the interests of political stability. During the inter-war years the capitalist class grew mature, and started articulating its interests not only informally through political networks, but also through organizations and publications such as the Shanghai General Chamber of Commerce, and the *Shanghai Bankers' Weekly* and the *China Cotton Journal*. The growing strength of the bourgeoisie during the inter-war period was also reflected in the acceleration of urban developments which became centres for the working class movement which grew in tandem with the industrial bourgeoisie.

The working class

The May Fourth Movement also marked the growing strength of the working class movement in China's urban centres. Despite the miniscule numbers of industrial workers, their strategic positioning in the cities gave them political clout, and helped them to become an important force in the Chinese political context by 1925 (see Chesneaux, 1968). Between 1919 and 1921 a wave of strikes was organized by the Chinese working classes, and were to some extent successful. They also indicated the growing organization of the working class as spontaneous strikes gave way to organized action. The May Fourth Movement gave a nationalist focus to the political activity of the working class movement, and allowed for a brief moment in history a convergence of interests of the capitalists and the workers. This was reflected in what have been called 'semi-proletarian' (Chesneaux, 1968) organizations such as the Society for Promotion of Industry, the General Society of Chinese Trade Unions, the All-China Society for Industrial Advance, and by the end of 1919 the establishment of the Chinese Labour Federation.

One of the aims of these organizations was to develop small-scale industry as part of the campaign launched soon after the May Fourth Movement to encourage import substitution. These organizations also worked at promoting welfare projects for workers, such as hospitals, savings banks and a benefit system. This approach to working class organization, combining articulation of class interests with welfare, continued after the establishment of a socialist state in China when the trade unions became organizationally linked to the Chinese Communist Party. Because of the weak class basis of these associations they failed to organize a strong working class movement but were successful in introducing the idea of proletarian organization and mobilization. May Day celebrations in Shanghai for example started at this time. With the establishment of the Chinese Communist Party there was a fusion of the labour movement and the revolutionary nationalist movement. The Marxist emphasis on the revolutionary role of the proletariat provided the theoretical basis for the alliance, which was cemented by the setting up of trade unions, and publications like the *World of Labour*. As the communist movement spread it gained a firm footing in other working class centres like Guangzhou. The growing confidence of the working class movement can be seen in the great wave of strikes that were organized by the communist-led trade unions between 1922 and 1923. This contributed to the formation of the first United Front (see Chapter 3) between the Chinese Communist Party and the KMT under the leadership of Sun Yat-sen. The labour trade unions also attempted to form an alliance with the growing number of peasant organizations that were formed during the 1920s in response to increased exploitation and nationalist fervour. However, the internal doctrinal differences within the CCP did not allow this alliance to realize its potential at this stage. With a spate of strikes in 1925, and the growing influence of the CCP in the United Front, the trade unions showed a growing maturity and strength. This was recognized by Sun Yat-sen who proposed a National Convention to review China's political strategy and prospects and in which trade unions were also to participate. With the death of Sun in 1925, the convention was also dispersed. However, the period following the May Fourth Movement was a watershed in the history of the Chinese labour movement and introduced an organized working class as a political actor in Chinese politics.

The May Fourth Movement was essentially an urban intellectual movement and yet its impact on the trajectory of modern Chinese history has been significant. First was its 'cultural iconoclasm' which dethroned Confucianism and introduced many streams of Western philosophy to Chinese audiences. The clash of ideologies that occurred during this movement allowed the spread of ideas of pragmatism, liberalism, and most important, socialism. Second, its origins focused on anti-imperialism – The way in which the Western powers disregarded the Wilsonian ideals of national self-determination and abolition of secret diplomacy crystallized the opposition to Western imperialism in China. The form that the movement took – of intellectual debate on the one hand, and a conscious expansion of the infrastructure of cultural and political dissemination on the other – laid the basis for a modern political system. While the May Fourth Movement can be called the first mass movement in modern Chinese history, its significance was arguably greater in the intellectual leadership that it provided through a relatively small group of individuals who were set to make their mark on the Chinese political scene in the years to come.

Women's participation

One of the important breakthroughs during the May Fourth Movement was the participation of women in the New Culture as well as the political movements of the time. There emerged a growing number of young, middle class, educated women who put the 'woman question' on the Chinese political map at this time. They wanted women to be equal partners in building a new China, and they spoke out against the patriarchal oppression of Chinese women. As educated women they were articulate and confident and put their case across strongly in the various journals of the time. Many women also left China to join the growing exile community of Chinese students in Japan and Europe. During this period, we also witness the remarkable phenomenon of many educated women committing suicide as a protest against the subordinate position of women in Chinese society. This particular form of protest moved Mao Zedong to write an open 'Letter to Miss Zhao' in 1921 in which he invited Chinese women to join the Communist Party and help overthrow feudalism and imperialism which, he claimed, were the major sources of women's oppression in China. Nationalism and socialism both claimed women's participation as part of their agendas.

WARLORDISM AND POLITICAL DECLINE: THE 1920s

While the long-term impact of the May Fourth Movement was significant in modern Chinese history, it was unable to do more than provide a critique of the Chinese situation. Meanwhile, the domestic situation in China deteriorated rapidly after the death of Yuan Shikai. Without even a semblance of a strong central authority the country slid into general upheaval that was called 'warlordism'. This period, which began in 1916, lasted through much of the 1920s and left a lasting imprint on Chinese political understandings, and underscored the traditional importance of centralized authority in China. 'Warlordism' has been resurrected, in the arguments about current Chinese reforms, by Chinese and Western scholars who fear that without the Chinese Communist Party's centralized authority China might slide into a second phase of warlordism and consequent economic and political decay.

The roots of warlordism lie not in militarism but in the failure of political institutionalization after the overthrowing of the Manchus and the declaration of a republic. The lack of effective institutions of governance was a result of a combination of factors: Yuan's intervention, Sun's compromise, economic decline and political impotence exacerbated by the pressures of the Treaty Powers in China, and failure of the republican movement to create a social base for mobilizing its political resources. In such a context the military strength of the warlords was countered by the military might of the state in a political situation that none of the engaged parties could capitalize on (Sheridan, 1975).

While the various warlords involved in the carving up of China during this period varied in ability, class and social attitudes, and consequently presided over sometimes radically different regimes, they nevertheless all contributed to a time of increased exploitation and even terror for the people of China. Militarism made great demands on the public coffers which were soon emptied and then replenished through a series of extremely oppressive measures. Taxes were imposed on an astonishing array of things, and worthless and 'unbacked' currency was published and people were forced to accept it (which meant straightforward expropriation). The need for funds meant that the warlords encouraged the growing of cash crops and none was as lucrative as opium, leading to increased social demoralization on the one hand and famine on the other as resources were diverted away from the production of food crops. Political instability and economic bankruptcy also meant a gross neglect of public infrastructure, especially of flood control measures and the system of food distribution – leading to famine and generalized hardship. As the warlord armies moved from one area to another, and as individual warlord fiefs expanded and contracted, the result was undisciplined soldiers preying on the peasantry. Looting and rape were common, as was the use of terror in dealing with opposition, and forced conscription of young peasants into ill-equipped and untrained armies.

The result of this unfolding tragedy for the lives of the Chinese people was a growing attraction of nationalism as a means of ensuring political stability. Both the KMT and the CCP benefited from this craving for peace. However, warlordism also introduced militarism into Chinese politics. The warlords had to be subdued by force; therefore better armies than their's were needed. The setting up of military academies by the nationalist KMT are evidence of this growing militarization of Chinese politics. The significance of warlordism as a motivating force in Chinese politics has been disputed. While some China scholars have maintained that this period left an indelible mark on the importance of the military in Chinese politics which continued into the communist period (Pye, 1971), others have pointed to the failure of warlordism as demonstrating that military power alone is inadequate for long-term political power in China (Sheridan, 1975). Perhaps the significance of warlordism beyond its immediate impact on the lives of millions of Chinese lies in its political symbolism. It came to suggest the political impotence of China, and also the importance of a strong central government and institutions if China was to revive its belief in itself and to rebuild its social and economic infrastructure.

CONCLUSIONS

By 1920, Chinese society and politics had been transformed. The influx of the Western economic and political power had shaken the self-belief of the Chinese elites and contributed to the fall of the Qing dynasty. However, the 'opening up' of China – due both to initiatives of the Chinese leaders and to the insistence of Western powers – also led to the introduction of new ideas of nationalism, republicanism, and socialism, and the reworking of Confucian traditions to explain contemporary political projects (Box 2.4).

Box 2.4 *Liang Qichao on China's future 1922*

The revolution of 1911 and the abdication of the Manchu Emperor have great political significance ... Hereafter there will be really no Manchus in the world. This amounts to our absorbing all the eastern barbarian tribes ... [and] concludes a great stage in the expansion of the Chinese race ...

In the realm of learning and thought, ... there has been considerable progress, and ... a way of great progress has been opened for the future. In this the most vital turning point is the abolition of the civil service examination system ... During the last fifty years the Chinese gradually have realized their own insufficiency. This little consciousness, on the one hand is the cause of the progress of learning; and, on the other, it may be counted as the result of the progress of learning.

In the first period our mechanical articles were first realized to be insufficient. This realization gradually started after the Opium War ... [1861–1874]. In the second period [1894–1918] there was a feeling of insufficiency concerning our [political and social] institutions. After the defeat by Japan ... wondered why the great and grand China should have declined to such a degree, and discovered that all was due to her bad political system ... In the third period [1919–1922] there was a feeling that the foundations of our culture were insufficient ... By degrees there has grown up a demand for a reawakening of the whole psychology ... We may grudgingly grant that all other things have progressed in the last fifty years; only government, I am afraid, has entirely retrogressed ...

I feel that China during the last fifty years has been like a silkworm becoming a moth, or a snake removing its skin. These are naturally very difficult and painful processes ... after we have undergone the unavoidably difficult and painful process, the future will be another world ...

(Source: Teng and Fairbank, 1981: 267–74)

The growth of not only new social classes, but also social and political movements, saw China engaged in the task of both economic and political reconstruction. The era of the Celestial Empire was well and truly past, but the country itself was in flux. This flux was to bedevil China for another 30 years before revolutionary transformation would translate into political stability. The period between the Hundred Days Reforms and the May Fourth Movement laid the foundation of contemporary China by framing the central questions that were answered by the communist revolution – how does a country like China, with its ancient traditions and deeply embedded patterns of rulership, manage the change that was needed to modernize its economy and its polity, while building on the particularity of the Chinese situation?

FURTHER READING

For information about imperial Chinese social and political systems, see Bergere and Chesneux (1977). Gray (1990) provides a detailed historical overview of the Chinese Revolution and a chronology of events that would be useful; see Chapters 2, 3, 5 and 6. Fairbank (1987) has a good account of the social and economic conditions prevailing in China in the eighteenth and nineteenth centuries; see Chapters 4, 5, 6 and 9. Fitzgerald (1952) gives a predictably Western oriented but detailed account of Chinese society before the revolution; see Chapters 1 and 2.

Fitzgerald (1970) makes a culturalist argument, among others, about Chinese perceptions of their place in the world. Loewe (1990) gives an interesting account of the concept of the Middle Kingdom (Chapters 6, 8 and 9). Said's (1995) *Orientalism* is a classic work exploring the relation between the colonizing West and the construction of the colonized 'Orient'. Schifrin's *Sun Yat-sen* (1968) is a most comprehensive biography of the nationalist leader.

Read Chapters 2 and 3 of Sckocpol (1979) for an informative account of social and economic changes in China in the nineteenth and twentieth centuries. Wright (1968) provides a perceptive account of the events leading up to the 1911 Revolution. A good selection of documents covering the developments discussed in this chapter are contained in two volumes by Teng and Fairbank (1981) and Schurmann and Schell (1967).

3 The making of the communist revolution: A brief history

This chapter examines the course of the Chinese communist revolution. Two major themes of the revolution – nationalism and socialism – are discussed. We argue that the Chinese communist leadership was able to synthesize the two ideologies and place them in the particular social and political context of China. We discuss the role of the various classes, political elites and the leaders of political movements to assess the making of the communist revolution.

THE CHINESE COMMUNIST PARTY AND THE CHINESE REVOLUTION

In the last chapter we charted the course of China's political transition from a traditional monarchy to a modern republic. We noted that this was an incomplete transition, and that it posed new and fundamental political and social issues without providing the answers. While representing a break with the past, this period of transition also built upon the experience of history. One of the primary ideas of this period was nationalism as a means of rejuvenating China's political system and society. The other was that of socialism as a means of harnessing the energies of people and fighting inequality among nations. Both these ideas were to shape the next four decades of Chinese politics leading to the establishment of the People's Republic of China as we now know it.

Any study of contemporary Chinese politics is incomplete without understanding the origins of the movement that led to the establishment of the communist state. There are two reasons for this: first, it is believed that the Chinese Revolution succeeded in establishing a socialist state because the Chinese Communist Party was able to address the particular conditions prevailing in China at the time – the revolution embodied the sinification of Marxism carried out by the CCP, under the leadership of Mao Zedong. This affected not only the outcome of the revolution but the post-revolutionary reconstruction and institution building. Second, the strategy and tactics employed by the CCP during the period of the revolution – guerrilla warfare, for example, and the building of united fronts with various parties and classes – were carried forward into the period of economic and political reconstruction.

The debates between Mao Zedong and his rival Liu Shaoqi, for example, resonate with allusions to the revolutionary period. The revolution is also, of course, the foundation upon which the edifice of the Chinese state was built. For all these reasons, this chapter will briefly relate the evolution of the Chinese revolutionary movement from its inception to its victory in 1949. We will tease out the continuing themes outlined above, and tell the story of the revolution which inspired millions, and succeeded at the cost of millions of lives.

Several different elements contributed to the triumph of the CCP in 1949: the impact of the republican revolution, the destruction of political institutions and stability during the period of warlordism, the symbolic and economic impact of the presence of imperialist powers in China, and the growing nationalism of the Chinese urban elites, the relations between the International Communist Movement and the Chinese communists, and the mobilization of the Chinese peasantry into political and social movement by the CCP. All these discrete elements were meshed together in a complex but rich tapestry that reflected the sophistication, creativity, vision and also opportunism of the Chinese communist leadership.

Marxism or nationalism?

What role did the doctrine of Marxism play in the success of the Chinese Revolution, and how far did the sinification of Marxism diverge from the core tenets of Marxism? Chalmers Johnson (1971) has asserted that the Chinese Revolution was really a nationalist not a socialist revolution. Johnson argued that the success of the revolution was built upon a recognition by the CCP that it must mobilize the peasantry on a manifesto of anti-imperialism, nationalism and basic land reform in order to succeed. Mao Zedong, as the chairman of the CCP, has been given credit for this policy. He pursued a primarily nationalist agenda which was successful in bringing the CCP to power. We will examine Johnson's thesis in the light of events making up the revolutionary struggle. However, the focus will not simply be on the making of the revolution; we shall uncover the ideological and political base that was laid during the revolutionary movement: in particular, the theory of mass line, and new democracy, which shaped the structures and political processes of the new Chinese state. As Samuel Huntington has written, 'A complete revolution involves . . . the creation and institutionalization of a new political order' (Sckocpol, 1979: 163).

The three stages of revolution

The history of the rise and success of the CCP can be studied in three different stages. These can be called the stages of departure, manoeuvre and arrival (Chatterjee, 1986). The first stage – of departure – lasted from 1921 to 1927 and can be seen as the orthodox phase. This was a period of urban mobilization, trade union activity and the First United Front with the KMT. In this period the

Communist International (Comintern) exerted predominant influence on the CCP. It ended with the Shanghai Massacre of 12 April 1927. The second phase of CCP revolutionary history lasted from 1927 to 1934 and marked the beginning of deviation from orthodoxy, and the eventual sinification of Marxism itself becoming an orthodoxy accepted by all factions of the Party. It was symbolized by the beginning of the Long March, perhaps the most celebrated event in the official CCP revolutionary history. The final phase – that of the CCP embracing nationalism, the Second United Front with the KMT and establishment of the Yan'an revolutionary base, the anti-Japanese war, and finally the civil war leading to the communist victory – lasted from 1935 to 1949.

THE MOMENT OF DEPARTURE: ORTHODOX BEGINNINGS, 1921–1927

The Chinese Communist Party was founded in May 1921, in Shanghai, with Chen Duxiu as its first general secretary. Mao Zedong was one of the 12 founding members of the CCP, all of whom were essentially revolutionary intellectuals inspired by the social and political ferment in China, rather than representatives of the working classes of the country. The total membership numbered 57, and the impact of the organization, on Chinese politics in its formative years, was negligible. The first opportunity of making inroads into national politics came in 1924 when Sun Yat-sen invited them to join the KMT which was being reorganized with Soviet help. The merger with the KMT allowed the CCP to operate much more openly, particularly among the recruits of the Whampoa military academy of the KMT.

The Chinese Communist Party was, like all Leninist communist parties, a cadre-based, hierarchical party, with clear lines of command and a committed, and disciplined band of members who soon took advantage of the new political situation to increase the membership of the CCP to 10,000 by late 1925, and 58,000 by the spring of 1927.

Lenin, the Comintern and the Chinese communists

In the age of 'post-communism' it is difficult to recreate for the reader a picture of the centralized network of international communist parties that was functional between 1917 and 1953. The Moscow-based and Soviet-controlled Comintern wielded influence over practically all communist parties the world over. These parties were greatly dependent on the Comintern for financial and material support, and theoretical and political direction. The key elements of policy advocated by the Comintern for the establishment of communist parties during this period were inspired by Lenin's writing on *Imperialism, the Highest Stage of Capitalism* where he argued the following points to justify his position that Russia was ripe for a socialist (rather than a bourgeois nationalist) revolution:

1. The European working classes had been 'corrupted' by the inflows of capital from the colonies to the imperialist centres.
2. This meant that advanced European states could not be the sites of socialist revolutions led by the working classes as predicted by Marx; Russia as the 'weak link' in the capitalist/imperialist chain, and thus least able to bribe its working class, would therefore be the site of the first socialist revolution.
3. As a socialist state, and believing in the concept of socialist internationalism, Russia's task was to encourage the breakdown of the imperialist system by supporting national liberation struggles in the colonies. This would lead to the independence of colonies peoples on the one hand, and the re-radicalization of the European working classes on the other (as the colonial centres could no longer afford to bribe them).
4. As a consequence, the role of the communist parties in the colonies was to support the main nationalist parties in their struggle for independence.

As a result of this analysis KMT was identified by the Comintern as the major nationalist party in Chinese politics with support in all major classes – the bourgeoisie, the petty bourgeoisie, the workers and the peasants. This was the first orthodoxy. This analysis of the KMT led to a fundamental error for which the CCP paid dearly. The CCP underestimated the danger represented by Chiang Kai-shek, who became leader of the KMT after the death of Sun Yat-sen in 1925. This danger was not simply that of an ambitious leader wanting to subdue potentially competing political organizations, but originated in the deep class-based ideological divisions between the two parties, which soon became irreconcilable.

The vanguard of the working class

In this period the CCP organized the urban working classes in the cities. This was in keeping with the second orthodoxy of the Comintern – a Marxist view of communist parties as vanguards of the working class. This orthodoxy led the CCP and the Comintern to commit a second vital mistake. It underestimated the revolutionary capacity of the poor peasants. As we have seen in Chapter 2, the industrial working class in China was very small, concentrated on the south-eastern coast, heavily dependent on Western investments, and with strong links with the countryside which militated against easy unionization. The traditional guilds that organized most of the artisans (as opposed to the industrial working class) included both the employees and the employers. Secret societies were involved in recruiting, making provisions for and keeping discipline among workers. These societies were formidable barriers to unionization, as was the huge and growing group of migrants workers. The first trade union led by the

CCP was set up in Shanghai in 1920 – the Shanghai Mechanics Union. Labour journals, workers' schools and the first formal structures of a wider trade union network (Committee for the Worker's Movement) were also set up. By 1922 the CCP was able to organize the first national trade union congress with 162 delegates. Perhaps the high point of the workers' mobilization by the CCP and its political impact was the May Thirtieth Incident in 1925. The shooting of 12 workers in the British Concession in Shanghai led to an unprecedented national strike in which both the nationalists and the communists participated. The incident linked the growth of the Chinese workers' movement clearly to an anti-imperialist and nationalist agenda which accelerated the growth of the trade union movement. However, when the workers' organized against Chinese employers the results were not as favourable. The links between the KMT and the Chinese bourgeoisie were strong, and the political will to support trade union action against them consequently low, as was evident in the suppression of the Beijing–Hankou rail strike of 1924 when the union members were massacred when they went on strike (Gray, 1990: 219).

If the May Thirtieth Incident was the high point of the urban mobilization then the breaking up of the First United Front in 1927 was the one event that signalled the failure of the urban-based strategy of the CCP.

The Shanghai Massacre

With the death of Sun Yat-sen and his replacement by his brother-in-law Chiang Kai-shek, the KMT and CCP entered a new phase of inter-party relations which was to deeply affect the course of Chinese politics in the years to come. Chiang was a military man, and a shrewed politician. He first neutralized the right-wing of his party with the support of the communists, and then turned on the Left in the *Zhongshan* gunboat incident in January 1926. The CCP was unable to respond to the growing constraints imposed on it within the KMT because of the Comintern's insistence that the United Front be kept alive. Indeed, Chiang persuaded Comintern officials to support his Northern Expedition to unite northern China with the now more or less unified south. Though both Borodin, the chief Comintern negotiator, and the CCP recognized the dangers involved in supporting a war effort which could only lead to increased influence of the military wing (opposed to the communists) in the KMT, the command from Moscow was clear – the United Front had to be maintained. During this period, workers' militancy was on the rise after the May Thirtieth Incident. In Shanghai this militancy led to widespread strikes as the Northern Expedition of Chiang Kai-shek advanced. On 27 March Chiang entered the city unopposed by any foreign powers or the local warlords. The success of the Northern Expedition strengthened Chiang's hand. He gained politically as the leader who could unite China and defeat the warlords. He also gained militarily as the surrendering troops and commanders of the warlords he defeated joined the Nationalist Army, increasing Chiang's power.

The communists were pledged to the abolition of foreign concessions but Chiang gave them an assurance of safety, and insisted that the Nationalist Army alone should have the responsibility of protecting them. The rift between the Left and Chiang widened, especially when army officers tried to disarm the unions. On 12 April 1927 Chiang finally ended the charade of the United Front and turned on the communists. His troops and members of various secret societies launched an attack on unions, CCP cadres and workers in Shanghai. Thousands were massacred, and the CCP was nearly obliterated in the city, and driven underground. The Comintern strategy lay in tatters but there was no reassessment in Moscow. On the contrary, attempts were made to seek reconciliation with Chiang, which ended only when the left wing of the KMT broke away and formed the Wuhan coalition which the CCP then joined. Neither of the two orthodoxies mentioned above were discarded. The alliance with the 'national bourgeoisie' continued through the links with the Wuhan coalition and any involvement with the growing peasant unrest – charted by Mao Zedong during 1926 in his 'Report on an Investigation of the Peasant Movement in Hunan' – was denied (see Mao [1927]). The CCP denounced the 'excesses' of the peasants in Central China who were on a warpath against the landlords and refusing to pay rents. Even at this price the class divisions between the CCP and the KMT were too great to let the United Front survive, and in July the Wuhan coalition expelled the CCP from its ranks, and the Comintern representative, Borodin, had to flee Wuhan, while Chen Duxiu – who had predicted the betrayal by Chiang – was removed from the post of secretary general. He was succeeded by Qu Qiubai, with Li Lisan as an influencial member of the CCP Central Committee. The First United Front was truly dead and buried. Despite there being seeds of alternative political strategy present among the leadership of the CCP, it would be another tortuous 8 years before the two orthodoxies would meet the same fate.

THE PERIOD OF MANOEUVRE: DEVIATIONS AND COMPROMISES, 1927–1935

This is a confused, violent, sometimes seemingly purposeless phase. However, it was through defeats during this phase that the communists learnt lessons that would lead to their eventual success. The two main lessons learnt by the CCP from this period were, first, the importance of peasantry as a revolutionary force in China, and, second, the need for harnessing their agenda of socio-economic reform to the demands of nationalism. It took the CCP 8 years to learn these lessons, hindered as it was at every step by the Comintern, but it learnt them well. The value of pragmatism, some would say conservatism, that the CCP learnt during this phase not only took it to eventual victory in 1949, but also laid the basis of the first period of economic and political reconstruction in the People's Republic. The costs of learning these lessons, however, were high. Tens of thousands died in the course of this period of manoeuvring for power.

Jinggang Shan and the making of peasant revolution

After the Shanghai Massacre and the rout of the CCP from coastal cities, the party was in disarray. The White Terror unleashed by Chiang led to the brutal suppression of most political activity. An alternative strategy was needed, though, as we have seen, it was not forthcoming from the CCP leadership because of Comintern dictates. While the CCP was pursuing the policy of urban-based political work, Mao had been witness to the growing radicalization of the peasantry in Hunan in 1926. This was partly the consequence of growing oppression and desperation in the countryside, and partly the result of an initiative by a CCP member, Peng Pai, who started organizing peasant associations in 1924. Mao wrote the 'Report on an Investigation of the Peasant Movement in Hunan' which was published in March 1927 (see Mao [1927]), but got no response from the leadership (Box 3.1).

Box 3.1 *Peasants as revolutionaries*

The present upsurge of the peasant movement is a colossal event. In a very short time, in China's central, southern, and northern provinces, several hundred million peasants will rise like a mighty storm, like a hurricane, a force so swift and violent that no power, however great, will be able to hold it back ... There are three alternatives. To march at their head and lead them? To trail behind them, gesticulating and criticizing? Or to stand in their way and oppose them?

(Source: Mao [1927])

After the Shanghai Massacre, Mao returned to his home province of Hunan, collected a band of peasants and intellectuals and led an attack upon the city of Changsha. This came to be known as the Autumn Uprising. While this was easily put down, it has been celebrated in official CCP history as the turning point for the political direction of the party – away from the cities. After the defeat at Changsha, Mao and his band of activists plunged into the Jinggang Shan (Jinggang Mountains) on the border between the Hunan and Jiangxi provinces. There, in October 1927 the first rural base area was established, and the beginnings of a guerrilla strategy worked out. Jinggang Shan became the magnet attracting other revolutionary groups and gradually the Red Army took shape under the military command of Mao, Zhu De, and Peng Dehuai, all major figures in post-liberation China. The three elements of Mao's winning strategy were beginning to take shape at this point:

1. to establish a base area within which the CCP could establish uncontested authority;
2. to build a Red Army which could defend the integrity of the base area; and

3. to mobilize the peasants in the base area by carrying out agrarian reform, recruiting them into the Party, army and local government and building credible mass organizations.

While the Jinggang Shan experiment clearly indicated a peasant-based strategy, the CCP was officially still wedded to the 'proletarianization' of the party. The Sixth Congress of the CCP, which was held outside Moscow in June 1928, charged the Party leadership, by this time headed by Li Lisan, to bring more workers into the Party, to strengthen the Party's central leadership, and to ensure that while a programme of land reform was advocated in the base areas, the Party did not get involved in the administration of things but rather concentrated on ideological education of the peasants. These were contradictory and sometimes difficult demands, especially given the factionalism within the Party, and the lack of communication channels between the centre and the increasing number of rural revolutionary groups setting up business in the Chinese hinterland.

The Chinese communists in Jinggang Shan were able to establish the first 'soviet' in southern Jiangxi, with Ruijin as its capital, by November 1931. This was largely because of the preoccupation of the nationalist armies with the remnants of the warlord threat. The reputation of the Red Army under the leadership of Zhu De and Mao Zedong was growing, and the land redistribution was winning the CCP converts among the peasantry. By 1933 it was clear to the CCP central leadership that it was impossible for the CCP to organize in the 'white' urban areas, and under the leadership of Wang Ming and the '28 Bolsheviks', who had replaced Li Lisan in 1930, the politburo moved to Jiangxi Soviet. This could have been considered an admission of political defeat by the central leadership on the question of class basis of the Chinese communist movement. This was not the case. Throughout the period of their stay in Jiangxi Soviet, the 28 Bolsheviks continued to press for an urban-based strategy for the CCP.

Mass line and good cadres

While these ideological battles were being fought, the deeper strategy Mao was to follow after the Long March was also taking shape during this period. The most important element of this strategy was Mao's formulation of the mass line. In the initial stage, this meant simply to 'combat bureaucratism' or 'commandism'. By 1933 the conceptualization of mass line included the education of the masses and the leaders, open channels of communications between the two groups, the elimination of bad habits and poor style of functioning and continuing consultation between the masses and the leaders, and for justice not only to be done but to be seen to be done (Box 3.2).

This conceptualization of mass line remained relevant to Chinese politics under Mao right up until his death in 1976, and was especially important during

---

Box 3.2 *Mass line*

[A]ll correct leadership is necessarily 'from the masses, to the masses'. This means: take the ideas of the masses (scattered and unsystematic ideas) and concentrate them (through study turn them into concentrated and systematic ideas), then go to the masses and propagate and explain these ideas until the masses embrace them as their own ... And so on, over and over again in an endless spiral ...

(Source: Mao [1943a]: 120)

---

the period of the Cultural Revolution (1966–1969). The problem was that this understanding of mass line depended very much on informal education and networks of consultation. The element of accountability of leaders to the masses was dealt with by talking of improving the *style* of cadre functioning. All this placed a great deal of emphasis on individual cadres being 'good', and too little on institution building and rules of accountability. For example, the way this translated into the judicial system was not through the development of a system of independent judiciary and the rule of law, but by public hearings that were meant both to encourage people's participation in the process and to educate them. While one might argue that the context in which this concept evolved had a lot to do with its limitations, the fact that it came to be canonized in the Maoist period meant that it remained essentially unchallenged as a non-institutionalized system of governance. Chinese politics remained extremely personalized and therefore dependent on the vagaries of individual leaders' formulation and commitment to any consultation with the people (Rai, 1991: Chapter 1). Not much of that happened, as we shall see in the chapters to follow. However, at a time when corruption was rife in nationalist China, and violence marked the rule in areas controlled by the warlords, mass-line politics advocated by Mao seemed both appropriate for peasant mobilization, as well as desirable to the masses who were given respect, even if largely in rhetoric, for the first time in living memory.

Socio-economic radicalism

The Jiangxi Soviet was more than just a site for the ideological battles within the CCP. A radical programme of economic and social change was carried out. Land was redistributed, taxation reorganized, and changes made to the economic structures by introducing the first cooperatives and mutual aid teams. The Red Army's participation in production was emphasized, and women were mobilized into production on a large scale, and to a lesser extent into the army. In order to mobilize women their social and personal position was reviewed and a Marriage Law was passed in December 1931 which gave women the right to property, to marry by choice, to divorce and to cohabit without marriage. These policies were, however, not without problems – most of which arose from the factionalism within the Party. Under the influence of the Comintern (which was itself divided between Stalin and Bukharin) the 28 Bolsheviks decided that land redistribution must include not only the landlords but also the rich peasants. Mao on the other hand, did not see the rich peasants as exploiters, though he agreed that they had the potential to become so. His understanding of the rich peasants equated them with the national bourgeoisie of the urban areas, especially as he was aware of their productive capacity so needed by the Soviet areas at the time. Mao was, however, overruled, and a 'land investigation' campaign was launched in 1933 to determine ownership of land, and to 'accelerate the struggle against the rich peasants'; this became a campaign of Red Terror against the landlords and rich peasants by 1934, when the Soviet collapsed.

These were radical policies, and their impact on the relations between the leaders and the masses, and between the CCP and the peasants, was not entirely positive. While the attractions of these policies to the poor peasants were obvious, the patron–client relations in the villages meant that even their support was not easily forthcoming. The rich peasants were alienated by the land policies, and the Marriage Law created a sense of panic not only among the male peasants, but also among the local CCP cadres who were themselves predominantly male, embedded in rural social relations, and suspicious of this challenge to gender relations in rural China.

Military strategy

If the social and economic policies were areas of contention between the two factions of the CCP, so was the military strategy to be pursued. Based on the experience of the Jinggang Shan period, and the establishment of the Jiangxi Soviet, Mao had formulated his military strategy. This was based on his analysis of 'the concrete conditions' prevailing in China at the time, and had four points of departure:

1. that China was a vast, semi-colonial country and very unevenly developed;
2. that the strength of the enemy – the KMT and the imperialist powers – was considerable;
3. that the Red Army was small and weak; and
4. that there was a strong leadership of the CCP allowing the military tactics to be wedded to political strategy and class analysis.

Mao came to believe that all these factors meant that the Chinese Revolution would be a 'protracted' one, and not a military–political putsch like the one that catapulted the Bolsheviks into power in Russia.

The military strategy that was appropriate under these conditions had certain key elements: (a) mobile warfare rather than a war of position; (b) active and passive defence; (c) strategic retreat; (d) counter-offensive; (e) concentrating forces to overwhelm the enemy and; (f) war of quick decision. However, for Mao, this strategy could work only if the Red Army operated in a political context. He emphasized this political element in the task of education that he gave not to only the Party but also to the army. In terms of military strategy Mao wanted to be able, when necessary, to trade 'space' (land/territory) for 'time' (to mobilize, regroup) which in turn had to be converted into political 'will'. This last was the key element in Mao's strategy, which we will see being employed by Mao in his economic and political policies in the post-1949 context – during the Great Leap Forward (1958–1960) and the Cultural Revolution (1966–1969). Political will was for Mao the force that moved mountains and overcame the objective constraints of a particular situation. The main elements of his military strategy were summarized by him in two slogans: 'Political power grows out of the barrel of a gun' underlined the importance of the correct military strategy and 'the Party commands the gun and the gun must never command the Party' emphasized the balance of power between the political and the military wings of the communist movement. The predominance of the political wing (as defined by the Party) was thus crucial to success as far as Mao was concerned (see Chapter 7).

However, the Japanese invasion of Shanghai in January 1932 once again made the Wang Ming leadership look to the cities as the bases of eventual revolution. Anti-imperialism was a potent factor in the cities, but not as yet in the countryside. The Red Army, based in the countryside, was the sole weapon that the CCP had, and was to be used to 'win a preliminary victory in one or more provinces', stated a Party resolution of 9 January 1932. The task before the Red Army was to consolidate its power, coordinate its action and concentrate on attacking provincial cities. To do this the Red Army needed to be proactive not reactive to the attacks by the enemy, as Mao had wanted it to be. Positional warfare, not guerrilla tactics were to be pursued, and the Red Army trained accordingly. To implement this new strategy a new leadership was required, and so in August 1932 Zhou Enlai was made the political commissar of the Red Army instead of Mao.

The divisions within the CCP and the resulting policy decisions in both the socio-economic and the military spheres contributed significantly to the destruction of the Jiangxi Soviet in 1934. Chiang Kai-shek had mounted four 'Extermination Campaigns' against the base but failed. However, in 1934 he launched the fifth campaign of encirclement, together with a stiff economic blockade. This deprived the guerrillas of their best weapon – mobility – already under attack from the 28 Bolsheviks. The other essential element in a guerrilla's armoury – peasant support – was also blunted by this time because of the radical policies being pursued under the leadership of the 28 Bolsheviks. The communists had only two alternatives – to accept the unequal challenge of positional warfare, or to flee. They tried the first, but failed, and so on the night of 15 October 1934 they began the strategic retreat of the Red Army which would end in its eventual victory 15 years later.

The Long March

The Long March is perhaps the most celebrated event in the Chinese revolutionary history – a symbol of victory over adversity, of courage, and of new beginnings for the communists. During the Cultural Revolution young Red Guards went on the trail of the original Long Marchers to be inspired by the revolutionary history of the CCP, as the radical wing of the Party led by Mao claimed the Long March for its own. This, however, is a view from hindsight. At the time it happened, the Long March was neither heroic nor victorious – it was simply a retreat forced upon the CCP forces by the success of the Fifth Extermination Campaign led by Chiang Kai-shek's forces, and the radical policies pursued by the CCP and the factionalism within the Party. Estimates vary as to the casualties, but only one in ten of the 60,000 who embarked on this (mis-)adventure reached Yan'an to set up the third soviet, which would remain the base of the communists till their victory in 1949. The magnitude of the casualties, the epic nature of the march, and the change of leadership of the CCP – though it did not end the factionalism within the Party – with Mao finally installed as the general secretary at the Zunyi Conference on 6–8 January 1935, all led to the canonization of the Long March (Box 3.3).

The end of the Long March, which took the Red Army from Jiangxi to Guizhou in the west, through home territories of Chinese minorities, and north to Shaanxi Province, saw the establishment of the third revolutionary base at Yan'an. It was here, under extraordinary pressures that the CCP under the leadership of Mao formulated the strategy of revolution that came to be known as the Yan'an Way (Selden, 1971). This was a strategy based on the principles of nationalism, the united front of all nationalist classes and parties, moderate

---

Box 3.3   *The Long March*

The Red Army fears not the trials of the Long March,
Holding light ten thousand crags and torrents.
The Five Ridges wind like gentle ripples
And the majestic Wumeng roll by, globules of clay.
Warm the steep cliffs lapped by the waters of Golden Sand,
Cold the iron chains spanning the Tatu River.
Minshan's thousand li of snow joyously crossed,
The three Armies march on, each face glowing.

(Mao Zedong, October 1935)

socio-economic reforms, voluntarism that could be employed to overcome objective constraints, and a belief in the validity of a peasant-based
socialism. This last was to result not only in continued feuding within the
Party, but also the eventual schism between the Soviet Union and China
under Mao.

Japanese imperialism and the Second United Front

It is arguable whether the Red Army could have survived and set up base in
Yan'an if the Japanese had not extended their activities in China with the setting
up of a puppet regime in Inner Mongolia in 1935. In 1936 Japan signed the
Anti-Comintern Pact and adopted a policy of unrestrained expansion in China.
The Japanese forces pursued their aims with a determination and brutality that
made national sovereignty the most important issue for all the political parties
in China. The Long March, and the pursuit of the Red Army by the Nationalist
Army under Chiang has to be seen in this light. The march was not only symbolic
of communist victory over huge odds, it also became the symbol of Chinese
fighting Chinese while the Japanese made huge inroads into the country. The
CCP exploited this growing unease, especially amongst the nationalist
intelligentsia in the cities. The Soviet Union demanded that the CCP enter a
Second United Front and concentrate on a nationalist alliance against the
Japanese rather than a class alliance against Chiang. Matters came to a head
when Chiang's general, Zhang Xueliang, refused to participate in further
pursuing the CCP, and seized Chiang when the latter went to Xi'an. Zhang then
proclaimed a United Front with the CCP against the Japanese, and released all
political prisoners.

The debate within the CCP about what to do with Chiang was fierce with
Mao opposing his release, and others insisting that the nationalist mood would
not tolerate anything else. The background of this debate was of course the
betrayal of the First United Front by Chiang. However, in the end Chiang was
released and Mao pressed the CCP's advantage in securing not simply an anti-
Japanese coalition with the Guomindang, but also an opportunity for expansion
of the CCP. This was perhaps the moment of arrival for the CCP.

THE MOMENT OF ARRIVAL: MAOISM AND THE YAN'AN
WAY, 1935–1949

The Second United Front was a tremendous publicity coup and political
breather for the CCP – they projected themselves as mature nationalists, willing
to put ideological differences and recent political enmity behind them when
China was under threat; they also became major political players from being
'communist bandits' on the run. The nationalists, on the other hand, suffered a
decline in prestige – the Japanese were attacking and winning in the coastal belt

of China which was the nationalist stronghold. Chiang's reluctance to join the United Front made him seem petulant, irresponsible, and careless with China's future. The corruption, hyperinflation and military defeats made even the United States question the legitimacy of the nationalist regime. In contrast, the honesty, discipline and courage of the communists took on greater value. In the end, however, neither the nationalists not the communists defeated the Japanese; that was a result of the general war effort of the Western powers, and, finally, the bombing of Hiroshima. The Japanese invasion of China was, however, important to the mobilization of forces within China which proved more beneficial to the communists than any other single event.

The collapse of the Japanese threat, the respite gained by the CCP through the Second United Front, and the demoralization and corruption of the nationalist regime all contributed to the victory of the Red Army in the civil war that followed the Japanese surrender. The Nationalist Army fled to Taiwan and the People's Republic of China came into being on 1 October 1949.

Marxism, nationalism and Maoism

A strong case has been made for rejecting the CCP's claim to being a Marxist party on grounds that 'The Party leaders did not really begin to study Marxism until the late 1930s in Yan'an, and what they studied was the Marxism of Stalin' (Ladany, 1988: 5). Most Marxist texts did not appear in Chinese translation until the 1930s and 1940s. As we have seen, what drew intellectuals and others to the CCP was an anger against China's decline, and a resolve to create a new (not necessarily socialist) China. Nationalism, rather than Marxism, was the starting point for the Chinese communists. It is important to acknowledge that, however it was constructed, Marxism, especially in its Leninist version, played an important part in the success of the CCP by giving it a cohesion, a purpose, and a framework within which to organize (Sckocpol, 1979).

'Maoism' can perhaps be seen as an amalgam of a rather impressionistic Marxism, classical Chinese philosophy, and a pragmatism that allowed Mao tremendous flexibility in evolving strategy and tactics during the revolutionary period. At another level, Maoism became a way to legitimize, within the Marxist framework, policies actually pursued by the CCP under certain political and military constraints. In this section (instead of yet again addressing the the tired old question, 'was Mao a Marxist?') we will explore Maoism in its own terms as a political response to prevalent Chinese reality between 1930 and 1940. Three elements of Maoism will be considered to reflect on how appropriate was Mao's response to the crisis in China – nationalism, voluntarism, and conflict resolution. The first and the last of these point to Mao's pragmatism, the second to his idealism; all three were essential to his success, and all contributed to the eventual downfall of Maoism as an ideology.

Nationalism

As we have seen in Chapter 2, resistance to the Western powers, and then to the Qing dynasty, had as its starting point the perception of decline of the Chinese civilization. Intellectuals flocked to Sun Yat-sen's fold, not in pursuit of political equality or economic justice, but to ensure that China regained its rightful place in the community of nations. We have also seen how the CCP emerged out of this nationalist response – the May Fourth Movement was the starting point of political activism for a whole tranche of Chinese communist leadership. Mao Zedong was of course part of this group of young, idealistic intellectuals who jumped into the political fray in order to revive China's fortunes. So it can be no surprise that nationalism was perhaps the most important tenet of the Maoist canon. Nationalism also received the support of the communist movement internationally, especially after Stalin's ousting of Trotsky from the leadership of the Bolshevik Party. Lenin had already acknowledged the revolutionary force of nationalism, however circuituously, when discussing 'Imperialism the highest stage of capitalism', but when Stalin came up with the theory of 'socialism in one country', nationalism found a firm footing in communist political discourse. The final element in the emergence of nationalism as a primary ideological and mobilizational feature of Maoism was of course the invasion of China by Japan, a country not too long ago a dependency of China and now a leading world economic and military power threatening China's very existence.

Linked to the question of nationalism is also the question of peasant participation in the Chinese Revolution. While nationalism had some resonance in the official Comintern discourse, the peasantry never gained legitimacy as a leading revolutionary class. And yet, in China the nationalist revolution, as conceived of and carried out by Mao and his faction within the CCP, depended on the peasantry, which in turn was mobilized in defence of land and nation. The question that has exercised many China scholars has been whether the peasants were primarily attracted to the CCP because of it social radicalism, or its nationalism. Chalmers Johnson (1971) has argued that the communist revolution succeeded because the CCP was able to mobilize peasant resistance to the Japanese in the context of the Second World War. This nationalism, according to Johnson, was different from the nationalism of the intelligentsia – a 'nationalism of despair' – and made a direct connection between survival and defeating the Japanese. Once the CCP could portray itself as the primary force of opposition to Japan, it could count upon the loyalty of the peasantry in China. Our study of the lessons that the CCP drew from its failure in the Jiangxi Soviet experiment seems to support this analysis. Other scholars, while conceding the importance of Johnson's insights, have pointed to a combination of factors that led to the massive peasant support for the CCP. Bianco (1971), for example, points to the impact of war on the economy – hyperinflation and, scarcity – but also to social and political decay – corruption and brutality in everyday life – as causes of the revolution. The war allowed people to witness the disintegration of the Nationalists under Chiang, not only through military defeat, but also through massive incompetence, unbridled corruption, and in the end a failure of courage brought about by a lack of vision – the vacuum of ideology. As Gray has pointed out, 'to look at nationalism and revolution as two mutually exclusive kinds of appeal is false, not only for China but for much of the Third World' (1990: 274).

Nationalism became one of the core values of the Chinese Revolution and of Maoism, and if compromises were needed in order to support the cause of nationalism, Mao was prepared to make them. An interesting example of the compromises made is the issue of gender relations. In Jiangxi Soviet the CCP tried to refashion gender relations in line with its belief in equality between sexes. It introduced laws that would, if implemented, lead to a fundamental refashioning of gender relations – giving rights to property and permitting 'free marriage' to women for the first time. The radicalism of these changes perturbed not only the male heads of peasant households in the Soviet, but even the male Party cadres who were primarily responsible for their implementation. In Yan'an, however, while there was no retraction of the laws regarding gender relations, the rhetoric was 'realistic', and the more radical women members of the Party were disciplined if they attempted to rock the boat. Another lesson the CCP learnt was how to build alliances in the name of nationalism. The rich peasants, targeted for land acquisition in Jiangxi Soviet, were eventually left alone, and even wooed, in Yan'an.

The Rectification Campaign of 1941–1944, which repudiated factionalism within the Party, brought the Party back into line, as a disciplined organization with a common nationalist and ideological framework. The nationalist revolution could not be jeopardized by ideological orthodoxy, nor by factionalism. This disciplining of the Party also fitted in with Mao's growing confidence as a *national* leader and emphasized the 'sinification of Marxism' that he saw as his unique theoretical and practical contribution to the cause of communist revolution:

> [T]he sinification of Marxism . . . must be understood and solved by the whole party without delay. We must put an end to writing eight-legged essays on foreign models; there must be less repeating of empty and abstract refrains; we must discard our dogmatism and replace it with a new and vital Chinese style and manner, pleasing to the eye and to the ear of the Chinese people. (Mao [1938])

The main task of the Chinese Revolution, Mao wrote in 1939, was 'to carry out a national revolution to overthrow foreign imperialist oppression and a democratic revolution to overthrow feudal landlord oppression, the primary and foremost task being the national revolution to overthrow imperialism'.

Voluntarism

The second element of Maoism is its voluntarism. This is perhaps the clearest deviation from all accepted interpretations of Marxism and even Leninism – the transcending in theory of bounds of objective constraints. Historical material-ism, and the structural, even positivistic, analysis that went with it was, while being rhetorically endorsed, negated in Maoist political practice. There are two strands to this voluntarism: the first of overcoming objective constraints, and the second of making the political voluntarism central to the making and the analysis of revolution. Voluntarism legitimized the actuality of Chinese revolutionary practice; the Chinese communists had come to power against all odds on the basis of political mobilization and organization that had overcome all barriers to power. China's backwardness in this context becomes not a handicap but an advantage, its poverty a spur to activism, its vastness important to communist strategy, and its 'semi-colonial' status leading to anti-imperialist struggles that would bring down the structures of not only colonialism but also dependent capitalism.

Maoism encapsulated a belief that socialism is a product not only of the struggles between the working class and the bourgeoisie in a socio-economic context of developed capitalism, but also of the struggles of the masses against imperialism. A further belief was that socialism rests not only on the development of material productive forces but also on the creation of a political will among the masses, who themselves, though 'poor and blank', were the best material to draw the most beautiful pictures on. The paintbrush was of course in the hands of the Communist Party, its cadres, and its leadership.

Voluntarism was never allowed to compromise the issue of leadership of the Communist Party (Box 3.4). When we examined the concept of 'mass line' we saw how the emphasis remained on inculcating the 'right attitude' into people and cadres, rather than institutionalizing procedures of consultation and accountability. Voluntarism, similarly, was used by Mao as an instrument of mobilization rather than as a check upon the role and the power of the Party. Political will was of no use unless harnessed to an organization which functioned with discipline, and a long-term strategy overseen by a leadership that was able to translate its ideological position into policies ensuring victory.

Box 3.4   *Voluntarism*

Today, two big mountains lie like a dead weight on the Chinese people. One is imperialism, the other is feudalism. The Chinese Communist Party has long made up its mind to dig them up. We must persevere and work unceasingly, and we, too, will touch God's heart. Our God is not other than the masses of the Chinese people. If they stand up and dig together with us, why can't these two mountains be cleared away?

(Source: Mao [1945]: 272)

The unassailable position of the CCP thus was not to be threatened by the mobilization of political will; it became one of the primary instruments for carrying out the will of the Party.

Conflict resolution

As a movement of resistance and opposition, and, eventually, as the party that would wield power, the CCP needed a strategy for resolving social and political conflict. In order to do that the CCP needed an understanding of what constituted a contradiction: what were its key elements and how to go about handling these contradictions? While the nationalist struggle was the primary contradiction facing China, it was not the only one. The major contradictions that the Maoist leadership encountered were between factions within the CCP, between different classes and, between various interest groups. 'On Contradiction' is the primary theoretical piece written by Mao [1937b] which addresses this issue of conflict resolution. Mao believed that contradictions are ever present in any society, and that 'the law of the unity of opposites' is the 'fundamental law of thought'. The concept of contradiction was, for Mao, not a static one:

> True, the productive forces, practice, and the economic foundations generally manifest themselves as the leading and decisive factors . . . But in certain circumstances, such aspects as the relations of production, theory and the superstructure in turn manifest themselves as the leading and decisive factors . . .
> (Mao [1937b])

Political ideas and movements thus could be as important, and at times more so, than changes in the economic base as a catalyst for change. A deep understanding of Chinese social relations also allowed Mao to move away from the polarities of class contradictions evident in the writings of Marx (Schram, 1987: 842). Mao emphasizes not only the importance of contradictions, but also the shifting hierarchy of contradictions – 'principal contradiction' – and the complexity of each individual contradiction – 'principal aspect of contradiction'. Such an analysis allowed Mao a political flexibility in the formation of factional and class alliances which was critical to his success.

Finally, Mao, inspired by Lenin, emphasized that 'Antagonism and contradiction are not at all one and the same. Under socialism, the first will disappear, the second will remain' (Mao [1937b]: 71). Mao developed this theme theoretically in a 1957 article 'On the Correct Handling of Contradictions Among the People' (Mao [1957]). Dealing with antagonistic and non-antagonistic contradictions requires different procedures, skills and frameworks. Mao's theory of contradiction can also be read as an incipient theory of interests within the broad Marxist framework which allowed him to synthesize the concepts of class and interests. This was important to the politics of the Second United Front when the contradiction between the Chinese nation and imperialism was defined as an antagonistic contradiction, as was the contradiction between the landlords and the peasants. On the other hand the conflict between the rich peasants and the poor, and the 'national bourgeoisie' and the working class, was characterized as non-antagonistic and therefore as one among the 'people', which required not the annihilation of the enemy, but compromise and resolution.

The logic of 'primary contradiction', however, has a darker side to it. In insisting that the resolution of all other contradictions must be subordinated to addressing the 'main contradiction', Mao endorsed a hierarchy of interests defined by the Party leadership. The intolerance shown to dissenters from this prescribed hierarchy was great, as evidenced for example in the Rectification Campaign and more theoretically in Mao's *Yan'an Lectures on Art and Literature* [1942]. Issues of gender, ethnicity and individual freedom of expression once subordinated to the grand project of nationalist (later socialist and then communist) revolution never moved up the ladder of priorities. Further, once characterized as the enemy, there remained no room for manoeuvre for those involved – annihilation seemed the only logical recourse. This conflation of normative and descriptive analysis was to plague Chinese political practice throughout the Maoist period.

CONCLUSIONS

In the making of the Chinese Revolution we have seen a particular conjunction of circumstances – social and economic change in the Chinese society, Western imperialist intervention and the Second World War; ideologies – nationalism and socialism; political opportunities – the Shanghai Massacre, the Second United Front; and a leadership able to synthesize and take advantage of all these. While it is clear in our sketch (Box 3.5) of the revolutionary movement that the CCP was far from being a supine instrument of a particular leader, and that factionalism was endemic among its leaders until the 1940s, we have also seen the important role played by Mao Zedong in contributing not only to the military successes of the movement, but more importantly, to the eventual direction of the Chinese Revolution. Mao's successful synthesis of nationalism and socialism, class politics and alliance politics, and his insistence upon making the Chinese conditions central to any social analysis were responsible in large part for the CCP's success. There is a distinctiveness to the Chinese Revolution which is undeniable, both in its scale and the time it took to come to fruition. The Chinese Revolution, in harnessing nationalism to social revolution, provided a model for other Third World revolutionaries, even though nowhere was such a revolution made again.

If the Chinese Revolution was a 'protracted' affair, the reconstruction of the Chinese economy and society was no less so. The twists and turns of China's development strategy are even more tortuous, painful and complex than its

Box 3.5 *Chronology*

1921	Chinese Communist Party founded
30 May 1922	May Thirtieth Incident
March 1927	'Report of an Investigation into the Peasant Movement in Hunan' by Mao is published
12 April 1927	Shanghai Massacre
October 1927	Establishment of the Jinggang Shan 'base area'
November 1931	Establishment of the Jiangxi Soviet, with Ruijin as its 'capital'
August 1932	Mao replaced by Zhou Enlai as the political commissar of the Red Army
15 October 1934	The Long March begins
6–8 January 1935	Zunyi Conference – Mao installed as general secretary of the Party
1935	Xi'an Incident
1941–1944	Rectification Campaign
1 October 1949	People's Republic of China founded

strategy of making a revolution. The transformation of a movement into a state, of a revolutionary leadership into government, always poses new dilemmas. The next chapter examines the period of transition and coalition politics pursued by the Chinese leadership in the process of economic reconstruction of the country.

FURTHER READING

There are certain articles written by Mao that should be read:

1. 'Report on an Investigation of the Peasant Movement in Hunan' [1927]. This is the clearest exposition of Mao's position on the role of the peasantry in the Chinese Revolution.
2. 'Problems of Strategy in China's Revolutionary War' [1936] and 'Problems of Strategy in Guerrilla War Against Japan' [1938] for Mao's exposition of guerrilla tactics in the context of a movement of socio-economic transformation led by the CCP.
3. 'On Practice' [1937a] and 'On Contradiction' [1937b] are perhaps Mao's most creative contributions to Marxist–Leninist theory, and are crucial to understanding his analysis of China's political situation.
4. 'The Chinese Revolution and the Chinese Communist Party' [1939] gives a clearly argued case for the particularity of the Chinese revolutionary situation.

Other useful texts include: Wright (1968), Guillermaz (1972) and Johnson (1971) for the thesis on nationalism and the Chinese Revolution; and Bianco (1971) for an alternative perspective. Harold Isaac's (1961) gives a largely Trotskyite critique of the Maoist vision of the Chinese Revolution and Snow's *Red Star Over China* (1937) is a wonderfully easy, sympathetic read of the period leading up to the Yan'an base. More recent useful references include books by Ladany (1988), Gray (1990) and Hartford and Goldstein (1989).

4   Problems of transition

The most important issue before the Chinese Communist Party when it assumed state power was how to plan the gradual transition towards socialism. The core was the policy of New Democracy which Mao Zedong formulated in the early 1940s. In this chapter, we will follow the theme of shifting ideas of transition through to the end of the 1980s.

THE NEW DEMOCRATIC REVOLUTION

The idea of the New Democratic Revolution originated in theoretical and ideological debates in China and the Soviet Union, and played a prominent role in shaping the policies of the Chinese Communist Party in the 1940s and well into the 1950s.

There were three major issues which had to be dealt with in making a strategy of transition. The first issue was to make the Chinese Revolution fit within the Marxist–Leninist theory of revolution and to explain it within the wider framework of communism. The second issue was how to define a successful political strategy for state building in both the shorter and the longer terms. The third issue was how to transform the economy and society after the assumption of power. The three issues were linked together in one web, and we will treat them as such in the following presentation.

As long as the CCP was an opposition movement in the margins, with limited territorial dominance and in a situation of constant warfare, these problems were not of much importance. However, around 1940 the assumption of power became a possibility, and the CCP had to set out its political aims clearly. This was essential to instil purpose into the struggle of the revolutionaries and to give direction to cadres of the CCP. And it was essential in order to obtain broader support for the revolutionary struggle. The policy for transition which took shape during the early 1940s can best be summed up in the term 'New Democracy'.

NEW DEMOCRACY

The new strategy was formulated by Mao Zedong in several works, including 'On New Democracy' (Mao [1940]). The thrust of the argument was that the

Chinese 'old democratic revolution', the bourgeois revolution of 1911, had failed and that a successful 'new democratic revolution', under the leadership of the Chinese communists, must include both the proletariat and the bourgeoisie. The prospects for a world revolution had, argued Mao, changed due to the First World War and the October Revolution in Russia in 1917. Globally speaking, the anti-imperialist national bourgeoisie in countries like China now depended on the cooperation of the proletariat and the existing socialist states − like the Soviet Union − in order to succeed.

The Chinese bourgeoisie had failed to attain the aims of the 1911 Revolution. The aspirations of the small Chinese bourgeoisie in 1911 had been to: (a) rid China of the Manchu dynasty; (b) abolish feudal land rights; and (c) free China of foreign domination and unfair market competition from foreign powers. The revolutionaries only achieved the abdication of the infant emperor and the establishment of a shaky republican government, which had to rely on the gentry (big landowners-cum-bureaucrats) for political power, and was weak in relation to foreign powers in the treaty ports and on the international arena (e.g. during the peace negotiations in Versailles in 1919). The failure of the bourgeois revolution was, accordingly, mainly blamed on the interference from the imperialist powers. The Chinese bourgeoisie had no other choice than to link up with other anti-imperialist forces to achieve its aim of national independence.

According to Mao's analysis, China, due to the imperialist aggression and foreign intervention, had been unable to rid itself of the feudal system, and had additionally become semi-colonized. This semi-colonial, semi-feudal society's revolution, therefore, had to be part of the world revolution, and had to rely on the leadership of the proletariat.

The crucial change, according to Mao, occurred during the May Fourth Movement in 1919, when the Chinese bourgeoisie stood up as an anti-imperialist force and joined the proletariat's anti-imperialist slogans.

This means that the Chinese Revolution had a dual character: on the one hand it was a nationalist, anti-feudal, anti-imperialist, bourgeois revolution and on the other a proletarian revolution aimed at setting up a socialist state.

In Mao's formulation, New Democracy consisted of two stages, one of which was the fundamental accomplishment of the aspirations of the bourgeois or 'old democratic' revolution, and a second stage which was to realize the socialist revolution.

Dialectical materialism

The ideas and strategies of the New Democratic Revolution were formulated within the framework of the Maoist version of *dialectical materialism*.

Dialectical materialism in Mao Zedong's version was formulated in 'On Practice' and 'On Contradiction' in 1937 (Mao [1937a, b]). As we have explained in Chapter 3, in these two texts Mao argued that the main notion of dialectical materialism is that all phenomena are composed of contradictions. The contradictions are either main contradictions or subsidiary contradictions. In order for the contradictions to be resolved, it is essential to identify and resolve the main contradiction first: in the Chinese Revolution this contradiction was between the Chinese people and its enemies.

Marxism normally sees social development in terms of class struggle. The notion of contradiction between the Chinese people and its enemies was indirectly based on class analysis. It was assumed that certain classes were likely to be opposed to the New Democratic Revolution and that other classes would be disposed to it: the feudal landlords were supposed to be against and the Chinese bourgeoisie were supposed to be for the revolution. The inclination of the bourgeoisie for the revolution had two reasons: (1) that it was deprived of space for growth because the Chinese governments were unable to resist the domination of imperialism; and (2) the objectives of the Chinese revolution were defined in terms of New Democracy (and not a socialist revolution) – objectives which largely coincided with their economic interests as a class. The definition of friend and foe of the people was thus, in its initial meaning, an economic category of relationship to the means of production.

Using class analysis to define friends and enemies of the revolution, however, is not unproblematic. In its consequence, this strategic endeavour turned into its opposite; class was defined subjectively by gauging an individual's acceptance of the revolution. If one professed allegiance to the revolution, one must belong to the bourgeoisie or another progressive class; if one was a capitalist expressing doubts about core elements of the revolution, one was ranked as belonging to the feudal forces, or to the 'comprador bourgeoisie', acting on behalf of the imperialist powers. Such analysis had important repercussions for China's subsequent social and political development.

During the first stage of the New Democratic Revolution, the struggle was between those who represented imperialism and feudalism on the one hand and those who favoured the Chinese Revolution on the other. Yet, the strategic definition of the friends and enemies of the revolution shifted over time. An important example of the strategic regrouping of friends and foes was that the contradiction between the Chinese Communist Party and the Guomindang was 'suspended' between 1937 and 1945 during the Second United Front, where both parties fought on the same side against the Japanese invaders. Strategically, the enemy was the Japanese. After 1945, the Chinese Communist Party reinstated its contradiction with the Guomindang. The communists strategically designated the leaders of the nationalists as the 'Guomindang reactionaries', whose political aims were opposed to those of the Chinese bourgeoisie. Hence, the communists cooperated with the Guomindang Revolutionary Committee and other organizations which professed to fight for bourgeois interests.

Based on this class and strategic political analysis the economic policy of first stage of the New Democracy was aimed at nationalizing all large enterprises (e.g. banks, railways and airline companies) which could not be operated by private persons, but not confiscating other private assets. In the event, the large assets were considered to be state owned anyway or owned by Guomindang bureaucrats. Shifting the class analysis, so that owners of large amenities were by definition bureaucrat-capitalists, and adding bureaucrat-capitalism to the ranks of the enemies of the Chinese people, was easily done during the 1940s.

Rural reform in the first stage of the New Democratic Revolution was to follow the (rather ambiguous and vague) policies put forward by Sun Yat-sen, namely to give the 'land to the tillers' (*gengzhe you qi tian*) and to ensure 'equal right to the land' (*pingjun diquan*). This was to be carried out through wide ranging land reforms. It must be noted here that Guomindang rural policy, and especially land policy, during the late 1920s and early 1930s, was radical, aiming at curbing the rights of large landowners. However, the Guomindang Land Law of 1930 and other progressive policies were never carried out because the Guomindang leadership joined in an alliance with great landlords in order to gain political support and in order not to endanger their mechanisms for maintaining fiscal incomes from the countryside. The land reform, in other words, was very close to Guomindang ideology and Guomindang left-wing policies. The main difference in policy between the two parties was that the communists stressed political struggle against landlords as a method of achieving land reform, while the nationalists sought to induce change through administrative intervention and tax policies.

In economic terms it follows that the New Democratic policies in the first stage were aimed at creating a capitalist small-producer economy in the rural areas and an urban capitalist economy in which the state controlled large, monopolitic amenities.

In terms of political power, New Democracy was aimed at a broad class alliance of shared political power, in which the communists played a predominant role. The intention in the formulations of 1940–1941 was to continue the coalition of the Anti-Japanese War for a long time, but soon the hostility between the communists and the nationalists excluded the latter from the coalition.

Until 1949 Mao Zedong did not specify which instruments were to be used to uphold the coalition and to share political power. New Democracy and the principles of dialectical materialism thus formed a flexible framework for dealing with the complex strategical issues in the 1940s.

POLITICAL COALITION AS A TOOL FOR TRANSITION

New Democracy involved the establishment of a new state structure, in which there was a degree of power sharing between the bourgeoisie and the communists. The structures of the state, as we shall see in Chapter 5, were centred around a state-founding coalition of those parties, organizations and individuals who rallied behind the New Democratic Revolution, and who accepted the leading role of the Chinese Communist Party in the revolution. A dozen or so political parties, associations and societies (which could broadly be characterized as 'bourgeois') subscribed to the conditions and took part in the state-founding coalition.

These organizations were given a nominal status in the political system, and they eased the emergence of new state structures, supplying members for political and administrative functions. Their function was mainly to serve as an organ for *co-optation* of groups outside the Communist Party; by nominally sharing power and acclaiming political decisions, they constituted a way of imposing political consent upon society. At the symbolical level they gave a legitimacy to the new state which was broader than that of the Chinese Communist Party.

There was, however, no room for independent political influence or genuine opposition from the bourgeois parties and organizations, and while they continued to have formal functions throughout the 1950s and until the start of the Cultural Revolution, their role declined rapidly after 1949. In 1979, after the reform policies started, they were again given official recognition, but little political power. It should be noted, however, that some protagonists from these parties and organizations do have very high social prestige, and are in some cases appointed to high office in the state, act as consultants and policy advisers to the State Council or ministries, or perform tasks as heads of charitable organizations and non-governmental organizations of various kinds.

In summary, political coalition to govern transition mainly provided legitimation and channels for co-optation of social groups, and yielded little real political authority for the bourgeoisie in the new state.

THE LOGIC OF TRANSITION: THE SOCIALIST TRANSFORMATION

With the New Democracy, the communists had an eminently flexible instrument for defining and redefining strategies. With the victory in 1949 of the revolution and the rallying of a broad coalition behind the constitutional structures of the new state, as well as behind the initial legislation (on land reform, the status of women, and the position of workers), the Chinese communist authorities set out to realize the first stage of new democracy, appropriating foreign and 'bureaucrat-capitalist' assets, carrying out land reform, and clamping down on feudal and immoral practices.

In the mid-1950s, when this had been basically achieved, the communists, pressed on by Mao Zedong, started considering how to realize the second (socialist) phase of the New Democratic Revolution. This meant turning against the erstwhile allies of the Chinese bourgeoisie. This is how Mao discussed the problem in 1957:

In our country, the contradiction between the working class and the national bourgeoisie comes under the category of contradictions among the people. By and large, the class struggle between the two is a class struggle within the ranks of the people, because the Chinese national bourgeoisie has a dual character. In the period of the bourgeois-democratic revolution, it had both a revolutionary and a conciliationist side to its character. In the period of the socialist revolution, exploitation of the working class for profit constitutes one side of the character of the national bourgeoisie, while its support of the Constitution and its willingness to accept socialist transformation constitute the other . . . The contradiction between the national bourgeoisie and the working class is one between exploiter and exploited, and is by nature antagonistic. *But in the concrete conditions of China, this antagonistic contradiction between the two classes, if properly handled, can be transformed into a non-antagonistic one and be resolved by peaceful methods.* (Mao [1957] [italics added])

During the Socialist Transformation, the assets belonging to the national bourgeoisie were gradually bought from them by the state, and in many cases the national capitalists were employed by the state as directors in the enterprises that had once been theirs. However, their position was, in broad terms, not easy, and they often had to concede to very tough conditions in order to be able to hold on to some wealth and reasonable employment. During the Cultural Revolution, their situation worsened, and many had their fortunes (mainly non-productive assets like bank deposits, houses, jewellery, etc.) confiscated; in 1979, their ownership was in many cases restored, or (part) compensation for losses was paid, and the confiscation was termed an aberration.

The second stage of the New Democratic Revolution was aimed at transferring the ownership of the means of production into public ownership, either as 'ownership by the whole people', that is ownership where the organs of the state manage the ownership on behalf of all citizens, or 'Ownership by the labouring masses', i.e. that is where the workers own their means of production as a collective. Both forms were actually instituted in the mid-1950s and became the only legal forms of ownership.

In Marxist theory, once the ownership of the means of production had been transformed the basis for class division ceased to exist: no class was able to exploit another class any more.

The differences in affluence and living conditions which continued to exist under socialism, it was held, could be regulated and gradually disappear – they were not expressions of any antagonistic contradiction.

THE CULTURAL REVOLUTION: PERVERTED TRANSITION?

New Democracy, one could say, was fundamentally changed when the Socialist Transformation began, and it started to be fundamentally challenged during the Great Leap Forward in 1957. In this period the 'second stage' of the New Democratic Revolution took place, eliminating the role of the bourgeoisie.

In order to fully appreciate the complexity of the ideological reasoning, we will briefly look at the Cultural Revolution (for a detailed discussion, see Chapter 6). The Cultural Revolution shifted the perspective away from economic classes in a strict sense, and was concerned with the contradiction between leaders who wanted to 'restore capitalism' and leaders who wanted to realize communism.

The Great Proletarian Cultural Revolution, which was initiated by Mao Zedong in the mid-1960s, sprang from a political disagreement in the leadership over the direction of development. While Mao Zedong was in favour of radical policies which aimed at rapid realization of the communist ideals (i.e. promoting development by populistic, voluntaristic methods), his opponents in the party leadership (Liu Shaoqi and Deng Xiaoping) favoured a more gradual approach, which was to ensure congruity between economic development and the social and political structures. This inner-party disagreement (called two-line struggle) during the Cultural Revolution was turned by Mao into the main contradiction facing China in its second stage of transition, that is from New Democracy to advanced socialism:

> Chairman Mao points out . . . 'Those representatives of the bourgeoisie who have sneaked into the Party, the government, the army and various spheres of culture are a bunch of counter-revolutionary revisionists. Once conditions are ripe, they will seize political power and turn the dictatorship of the proletariat into a dictatorship of the bourgeoise'. We must thoroughly criticise and repudiate these counter-revolutionary revisionists, clear them out and seize them from the power of leadership which they have usurped. 'Our struggle against them can be nothing but a life-and-death struggle'.
>
> This means that the principal contradiction we must resolve in the great proletarian cultural revolution is the *contradiction between the proletariat and the handful of Party people in authority taking the capitalist road*. This contradiction is an antagonistic one, a contradiction between the enemy and ourselves. The general orientation of the struggle in this revolution is precisely the resolving of this principal contradiction by directing the spearhead of the struggle against the handful of Party people in authority taking the capitalist road. (Editorial Departments of Hongqi and Renmin Ribao, 1967: 49 [italics added])

While the objective basis for the existence of class differences (private ownership) had disappeared, Mao and the radicals held that a protracted policy of economic development was tantamount to wanting to restore capitalism. Liu Shaoqi and Deng Xiaoping (referred to as the capitalist roaders) were to be the object of the struggle during the Cultural Revolution. The radical line sought to create a seamless ideological continuation of the class struggle theme. The antagonistic classes, during the Cultural Revolution, were regarded as being represented by those people in the leadership who allegedly wanted to betray the revolution and restore capitalism.

THE POST-MAO LEADERSHIP

The post-Mao leadership has legitimized the strategies of the reform policy (which have been pursued since 1978) by referring back to the logic of the New Democratic Revolution.

According to the reform leadership, the Cultural Revolution was an aberration from the politics of New Democracy. The Cultural Revolution, it is claimed, sought to jump ahead of development and realize communism before the material conditions for this were present. They claim that the first stage of the New Democratic Revolution is completed, and that the present stage is that of the socialist revolution. They divide this stage into primary and secondary stages and argue that China at the moment, and for a relatively long time, will be in the primary stage of socialism.

The main contradiction in the 'primary stage of socialism' is not class struggle, but is set between China's relative economic backwardness and the Chinese people's aspirations for a material and spiritual civilization:

China is now in the primary stage of socialism. There are two aspects to this thesis. First, the Chinese society is already a socialist society. We must persevere in socialism and never deviate from it. Second, China's socialist society is still in the primary stage. We must proceed from this reality and not jump over this stage. Under the specific historical conditions of contemporary China, to believe that the Chinese people cannot take the socialist road without going through the state of fully developed capitalism is to take a mechanistic position on the question of the development of revolution, and it is the major cognitive root of Rightism. On the other hand, to believe that it is possible to jump over the primary stage of socialism, in which the productive forces are to be highly developed, is to take a utopian position on this question, and that is the major root of Left mistakes.... [P]recisely because our socialism has emerged from the womb of a semi-colonial, semi-feudal society, with the productive forces lagging far behind those of the developed capitalist countries, we are destined to go though a very long primary stage [of socialism]. During this stage we shall accomplish industrialization and the commercialization, socialization and modernization of production, which many other countries have achieved under capitalism.

[F]or a long time we relegated the task of expanding the productive forces to a position of secondary importance and continued to 'take class struggle as the key link' after the socialist transformation was basically completed. Many things which fettered the growth of the productive forces and which were not inherently socialist, or were only applicable under certain particular conditions, were regarded as 'socialist principles' to be adhered to. Conversely, many things which, under socialist conditions, were favourable to the growth of the productive forces and to the commercialization, socialization and modernization of production were dubbed 'restoration of capitalism' to be opposed. As a consequence, a structure of ownership evolved in which undue emphasis was placed on a single form of ownership, and a rigid economic structure took shape, along with a corresponding political structure based on over-concentration [*sic*!] of power. All this seriously hampered the development of the productive forces and of the socialist commodity economy. . . . [T]he specific stage China must necessarily go through while building socialism under conditions of backward productive forces and an underdeveloped commodity economy . . . will [last] at least 100 years from the 1950s, when the socialist transformation of private ownership of the means of production was basically completed, to the time when socialist modernization will have been in the main accomplished, and all these years belong to the primary stage of socialism. This stage is different from both the transitional period, in which the socialist economic basis was not yet laid, and the stage in which socialist modernization will have been achieved. *The principal contradiction we face during the present stage is the contradiction between the growing material and cultural needs of the people and backward production.* Class struggle will continue to exist within certain limits for a long time to come, but it is no longer the principal contradiction. *To resolve the principal contradiction of the present stage we must vigorously expand the commodity economy, raise labour productivity, gradually achieve the modernisation of industry, agriculture, national defence, and science and technology and, to this end, reform such aspects of the relations of production and of the superstructure as are incompatible with the growth of the productive forces.* (Zhao, 1987 [italics added])

The theoretical foundations for dealing with the problem of transition change under the particular circumstances. However, it is worth noting that the underlying structures of the argument, the whole discourse of transition, follows the same basic rules as they did more than 50 years ago, when 'On New Democracy' was written (Mao [1940]).

This emphasizes the need for a new coalition of forces for China's economic development, a coalition which includes private entrepreneurs and traders. Harking back to the principles of transition in New Democracy also provides the CCP leadership with a legitimacy based on continuity. Current policies can thus be presented as having a pedigree within the communist system and discourse.

CONCLUSIONS

China was a semi-feudal, semi-colonial society, which was unable to achieve national independence and development under a bourgeoise leadership, and so had to rely on a coalition of the bourgeoisie and the communists to gain national independence.

Gaining state power had to be based on a coalition of forces, and it was of the greatest importance that the members of the coalition were reassured; the Communist Party from the very beginning was adamant that it had the leadership of the revolution. While the communists promised a measure of power sharing for an unspecified time, they did not indicate the formal structures for power sharing and they redefined the 'enemies of the people' at will.

The communists wanted the economic transition to be smooth, and were able to gain vivid support from most of China's national capitalists by adopting transitional policies which were much in line with their ideals. Within 6 years, however, the targets had been redefined, and the national bourgeoisie must now submit to the communist request for state control with, and ownership of, their enterprises.

These concrete policies were set in a context which made it easy to change them and to reformulate the targets. Both the Cultural Revolution and the post-Mao reforms bear testimony to this.

Transitions in China have not been managed uniformly well: they have been dependent on the dominant political leadership's approach to coalition building. Even major strategic coalitions between the CCP and other political forces in China have not enjoyed long-term stability, largely because of the essentially political nature of these coalitions. The economic basis of current coalition building in China during the economic reforms, however, might provide a greater stability to the current coalition of socio-political forces.

FURTHER READING

The core works to consult are 'On New Democracy' (Mao [1940]) and 'On Practice', and 'On Contradiction' (Mao [1937a, b]).

PART II
Politics

Part II of this book is composed of four chapters that examine the different features of the Chinese political systems. This part of the book sets out the main features of the political structures and practices that frame Chinese society and economy. The securing of power in 1949 had been a 'protracted' affair for the CCP. However, what lay ahead was perhaps even more difficult to accomplish. The Chinese communist leadership had to make a nation and a state out of a country that had been devastated by war, whose political institutions were in tatters, and with its economy destroyed. China needed to secure its threatened borders, and it needed to realign, formalize and institutionalize its political practices. Were the institutions that were established, the political processes that were allowed, and the structures of surveillance and security that were set up, adequate for the needs of China? The current phase in Chinese political life is one of the many transitions that a modernizing China has made in the last century. We examine how successful this last transition has been in the light of the earlier experience.

Chapter 5 discusses the constitutional arrangements of political power, the setting up of political institutions and their functioning. Chapter 6 assesses the processes of mobilization of the Chinese people and how these have been subverted, and whether China is moving towards a more open polity. Chapter 7 examines the metamorphosis of an amateur army into a professional military and the tensions that this has brought about, and Chapter 8 situates a changing China in a changing world.

5   The Chinese state and political institutions

This chapter describes how the state institutions of the People's Republic of China were established. The first part is mainly about the formal divisions of power in China's constitution. In the second part, the issue of power and the political organization are discussed thoroughly.

INTRODUCTION: CHINESE POLITICS

One may ask what the relevance is of a close examination of the Chinese political constitution; it is a common opinion that it is not adhered to anyway. However, it is useful to explore how the political system legitimizes itself through establishing formal procedures and institutions. The political constitution of any country establishes a framework, which is modified and used by its political actors. To understand the power relations of and political activities in China, we have to examine the formal grid of rules within which politics is (normally) conducted.

In Chinese politics this gap between formal structures of governance and the real distribution of political power is of dynamic importance. One must see the two in their relationship and understand how the Chinese constitution is wider and more complex than the written constitution may indicate. Of special importance are the situations where the formal structures for political conflict solution are inadequate, and where the political system is thrown into crises like the Great Proletarian Cultural Revolution and the succession struggles after Mao Zedong.

The Chinese Communist Party is the centre of political power in China, and the Communist Party is *de facto* controlled by a 'supreme leader', or 'peremptory arbiter' (like Mao Zedong and Deng Xiaoping). The functions of the leader are part of the complex political order of China, and should not be taken to represent a confirmation of totalitarian explanations.

In China, like in other socialist states, the written constitution is a declaration of general political aims, and it establishes a legitimation of party power. In that sense it is an extension of the party programme. The status of the written constitution is ambiguous, since it both bestows legitimate authority on the leadership and stipulates ideals to be achieved, while at the same time it does not effectively limit the behaviour of the leadership. The *written* constitution, therefore, should be seen as an element in a broader structure of the *political* constitution.

CHINA'S POLITICAL CONSTITUTION

The new Chinese state under communist leadership was established on 1 October 1949. The new Chinese political constitution embodied the principles of New Democracy, which Mao had first formulated in 1940. The new masters of the country were not just the Chinese Communist Party, but a coalition of progressive forces, who had pledged themselves to fight feudalism, imperialism and bureaucratic capitalism.

The Chinese Communist Party had prepared for the founding of the new state by convening a meeting of outstanding communist and non-communist Chinese individuals, political parties and pro-revolutionary organizations in the Chinese People's Political Consultative Conference (CPPCC). This symbolically represented the united front against feudalism, imperialism and bureaucratic capitalism. It was the CPPCC which established the People's Republic of China (PRC) by imposing a set of laws in late September 1949. The People's Republic of China was subsequently proclaimed by the Chairman of the CCP, Mao Zedong, on 1 October 1949 from the rostrum in Tiananmen.

Constitutionally, the establishment of the PRC was significant in its clear break with the past. The new state did not inherit institutions of the previous regime, and it did not legitimate itself by claiming succession according to the established constitution. Systemic change based on institutional succession is constitutionally very different from the 'clean break' strategy adopted by the Chinese Communist Party. In justifying the new political constitution, all previous regimes including the Guomindang, which fled to Taiwan, were ignored. However, in terms of ideology, the CCP claimed to be the heir of 'the great revolutionary Sun Yat-sen, the leader of the Revolution of 1911'.

To sum up, the fundamental structures of China's political constitution are conditioned by the ways in which the Chinese Communist Party sought to legitimize its accession to power: (a) the formal distinction between party and state; (b) the institution of an appointed state-founding assembly in the form of the People's Consultative Conference; (c) the formalized leadership of the Chinese Communist Party in the new state; and (d) the formalization of historical development as a struggle against feudalism, imperialism and bureaucratic capitalism.

THE BASIC PROVISIONS OF THE POLITICAL CONSTITUTION AGREED BY THE UNITED FRONT

It was essential for the CCP to rally all groups of the Chinese people behind the People's Republic of China, and so the party co-opted existing organizations and influential personalities into the Chinese People's Political Consultative Conference. This became the first formal legislature of the PRC, under the dominant leadership of the CCP.

At its first plenary session on 29 September 1949, the CPPCC passed the following:

- the Common Programme of the Chinese People's Political Consultative Conference;
- the Organic Law of the Chinese People's Political Consultative Conference;
- the Organic Law of the Central People's Government of the People's Republic of China; and
- the Declaration of the First Plenary Session of the Chinese People's Political Consultative Conference.

These summed up the fundamental and formal rules for political activity in the new state, each reflecting a different perspective. The Common Programme prescribed the fundamental principles of statehood and sovereignty, and obliged the Central People's Government to pursue the aims of New Democracy. The Organic Law of the CPPCC indicated the membership and tasks of the CPPCC, while the Organic Law of the Central People's Government described the procedures for forming the new government of the state. The Declaration simply declared the founding of the PRC.

The form of government was described as the 'people's democratic dictatorship led by the working class, based on the alliance of workers and peasants, and uniting all democratic classes and all nationalities in China'.

The people's democratic dictatorship

By limiting the objectives of the 'people's democratic dictatorship' to abolishing feudalism, imperialism and bureaucratic capitalism, the communists were able to rally the Chinese middle classes and the peasants behind them (Box 5.1). Abolishing 'feudalism' meant to dispossess landowners with holdings larger than the area they could cultivate with the use of their own family labour, as well as to break up land owned by large clans, monasteries, etc., and to give the land as property to former tenants and landless peasants. It also included the equal rights of women and men, doing away with 'the feudal system which holds women in bondage'.

The fight against imperialism meant to do away with all foreign prerogatives in China, mainly by expelling foreign powers from territorial concessions in China and by fully restoring Chinese jurisdiction over foreigners in China. All rights bestowed on foreigners by unequal treaties were abolished. The most important implication, however, was that the PRC did not 'inherit' any international commitments, and that recognition of the PRC must be unconditional and not subject to renegotiation of old treaties, restoration of confiscated foreign assets or guarantees of any sort.

Box 5.1   *The people's democratic dictatorship*

The notion of the people's democratic dictatorship originated in the First United Front in 1923 between the communists and the nationalists, which the CCP entered into at the behest of the Executive Committee of the Communist International. Since the Chinese Communist Party was too small and did not represent large strata in the population, and – even more important – since the class structure and the material conditions for a communist revolution had not become a reality, the strategy was to seek an alliance with the bourgeois classes to accomplish a 'democratic revolution' first. This meant that the initial objective could not be the institution of the 'dictatorship of the proletariat', but would have to be the 'people's democratic dictatorship', uniting the anti-feudalist and anti-imperialist groups and strata in Chinese society. Later, bureaucratic capitalism was added to the list of evils that the 'people's democratic dictatorship' must suppress; this referred to the large monopolies and concessions which a conglomerate of capitalists and nationalist government officials had hoarded under the protection of the Guomindang.

The nationalization of bureaucratic capitalist assets was the third aspect. Property left behind by the fleeing Guomindang officials was confiscated and put into the possession of the people's state.

The institution of the state was based on the concept of 'people's democratic dictatorship' which was a coalition of social classes that supported the socialist revolution. It was a dictatorship in that: 'Feudal landlords, bureaucratic capitalists and reactionary elements in general, after they have been disarmed and have had their special powers abolished, shall, in addition, be deprived of their political rights in accordance with law for a necessary period'. It was democratic in allowing the people to formally participate in the politics of the country through various institutions: 'The people's congresses and the people's governments of all levels are the organs for the exercise of state power by the people' (Common Programme of the Chinese People's Political Consultative Conference). The Common Programme foresaw the establishment of an All-China People's Congress elected by universal franchise, which would be the legislature of the state.

Democratic centralism according to the Common Programme

The Common Programme also instituted democratic centralism, laid down with the following formulation, which is the most precise and succinct description of democratic centralism:

> The People's Congresses shall be responsible and accountable to the people; the People's Government Councils shall be responsible and accountable to the People's Congresses. Within the People's Congresses and within the People's Government

Councils, the minority shall abide by the decisions of the majority; the appointment of the People's Governments of each level shall be ratified by the People's Government of the higher level; the People's Governments of the lower levels shall obey the People's Governments of the higher level and all local People's Governments throughout the country shall obey the Central People's Government. (Common Programme of the Chinese People's Political Consultative Conference)

This statement is essential for the understanding of future Chinese constitutional development. The overriding principle of democratic centralism meant that a three-tier legislature, similar to the system in the Soviet Union, was established. Local elected bodies (People's Congresses) delegated a number of participants to the next level of People's Congresses, which again delegated participants to an even higher level of People's Congresses, ending in the National People's Congress. A majority vote was decisive at each level, but could be superseded by a majority vote at a higher level. Hence, no level of People's Congresses, except the National People's Congress, was to have full decision-making autonomy within its jurisdiction.

The People's Congresses were, in the formulation of the Common Programme, to be accountable to the people, yet it was not specified whether this was in the form of the electorate or in an abstract sense. Likewise, the People's Governments (to be elected by the People's Congresses), were to be bound by higher-level decision making, and so were not to have any significant autonomy *vis-à-vis* the Central People's Government.

Hence the legislative and executive systems provided for in the Common Programme were designed to create a strong concentration of power and to allow for a popular co-optation in policy making. Members and delegates in the People's Congresses would act in unison according to the decisions made in the Central People's Government.

The CPPCC in these decisions from 1949 defined narrow rules for the future structure of the legislature. The CPPCC was to remain the legislature until the first National People's Congress (NPC) was convened. Once the NPC was convened, the CPPCC would continue to exist mainly as a deliberative body with the right to submit proposals to the NPC and the Central People's Government.

According to the Organic Law of the CPPCC, group membership was open to all organizations which agreed to the principles laid down in the preamble of the Organic Law, and it was also open, on invitation, to individuals.

Between plenary sessions which were to be held each year, the CPPCC would be represented by an elected National Committee for carrying out day-to-day business. Local Committees could be set up in large cities and provinces, as well as other important areas. Unlike the NPC, the CPPCC did not include a system of delegation among various levels of jurisdiction.

It was the task of the National People's Congress to decide on a written Constitution (Box 5.2).

Box 5.2 *The scope of the political constitution in the PRC*

It may be difficult to define the elements that represent the political constitution in China. It is obvious that it includes more than the *written* constitution, but what else? There are many possible ways of defining the scope of the political constitution, so we encourage the reader to arrive at her or his own opinions about this: However, we suggest, pragmatically and heuristically, that the following items are essential parts of it:

- the CPPCC and the NPC, as well as the legal frameworks that govern their functions in the four documents from the CPPCC in 1949, the written Constitution (*Xianfa*) and the Electoral Law (*Xuanjufa*);
- the local legislatures (people's congresses), as well as sub-state political bodies (including villagers' committees);
- the formal relationship between the Chinese Communist Party and the state organs;
- in view of the special role accorded to the Chinese Communist Party, the formal structures of power within the Party, including the Party Constitution;
- the rights of the individual as they are formalized in state law;
- legitimation of the political system and historical exegesis.

THE CONSTITUTIONAL FRAMEWORK, 1949–1965

The CPPCC functioned as a provisional legislature between 1949 and the First Session of the National People's Congress in September 1954, and thereafter became a deliberative body.

The two most important pieces of legislation passed by the CPPCC were the Marriage Law, which codified women's rights as equals to men, and which was a major step in the abolition of 'feudalism', and the Land Reform Law which divided the land equitably among the peasants and abolished the landlord class, which was considered to epitomize 'feudal relations of production'.

On 20 September 1954, the Constitution of the People's Republic of China was adopted by the National People's Congress. The Constitution stated in its preamble that it was based in the Common Programme of the CPPCC and that it constituted a continuation of that programme. In terms of ideological significance, it represented the stage after the victory of the revolution over feudalism, imperialism and bureaucratic capitalism, when China entered the phase of socialist transformation (Box 5.3).

So the new Constitution was aimed at enabling the transition to a socialist economy, while at the same time reassuring the state-founding coalition. However, with the new written Constitution in 1953, the operation of the state

---

Box 5.3   *The socialist transformation*

The main achievement in the years 1949–1953 had been the abolition of the landlord class in the countryside through an elaborate land reform and 'class struggle'. The counter-revolutionary forces had been suppressed and the national economy had been stabilized. Ownership of the means of production was predominantly private, the land reform having instituted agriculture as a smallholder economy, capitalist enterprises were largely untouched (but regulated more vigorously by the state), and only assets controlled by the Guomindang cliques were confiscated by the new state.

The aim of the socialist transformation was to turn this private, smallholder, capitalist economy into a socialist economy, dominated by public-ownership forms.

---

shifted from the united front in the form of the CPPCC to an elected legislature in the form of the NPC.

The National People's Congress

The organization of the NPC has from the very outset been based on a hierarchy of congresses (Figure 5.1): at the basic level the local People's Congresses, elected by general suffrage; various intermediate levels of People's Congresses, each of which were composed of delegates from lower levels of People's Congresses; and the National People's Congress, which was composed of delegates from provinces, autonomous regions, cities directly under state administration (i.e. Beijing, Tianjin and Shanghai), the armed forces and Chinese who were resident abroad.

The selection of deputies to the National People's Congress was carried out by the Standing Committee of the National People's Congress, a body elected by the National People's Congress. This may seem odd, but the idea was that not only the various provincial-level juridictions and the People's Liberation Army must be equitably represented, but that all major groups in Chinese society must be represented in certain proportions. Proportional representation is therefore given to peasants, workers, intellectuals and soldiers, women, national minorities, as well as the 'democratic parties' (i.e. United Front organizations). Provincial levels of People's Congresses are urged by the Standing Committe of the NPC to comply with specific quotas relating to the social status, nationality and gender of the delegates. City and county levels ensure a similar composition of the provincial People's Congresses and so forth. This ensures that not all delegates are Han-Chinese, male, octogenarian factory directors and headmasters.

The electoral system was structured so that the vote of four peasants (at local

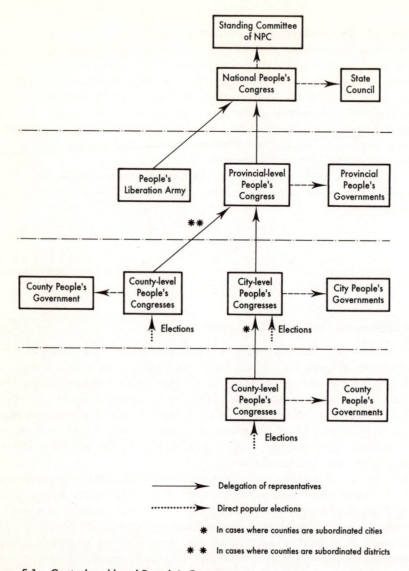

Figure 5.1 *Central and local People's Congresses*

level elections) had the same weight as the vote of one urban dweller. For the representation to the provincial-level People's Congresses, the peasant vote was only worth one-fifth of an urban vote, and for delegation to the National People's Congress the proportion was one to eight. Due to the separate election of delegates from the People's Liberation Army, the real 'peasant delegation' (mainly local officials in rural areas, and, only rarely, practising farmers) to the

National People's Congress was only one-tenth of all delegates (while the peasants constituted around 80 per cent of the population). The aim of this arrangement was to ensure representation of all groups in Chinese society. It was felt that the workers represented intrinsically more progressive forces in society than peasants, and that they therefore should have a much higher proportion of the seats than the peasants.

Functions of the National People's Congress

The role of the National People's Congress, according to the 1954 Constitution, was to pass legislation (amend the Constitution and enact laws) and to elect the executives of the state (chairman and vice-chairman of the PRC), as well as the two independent branches of the judicial system: the president of the Supreme People's Court and the chief procurator of the Supreme People's Procuracurate.[1]

The prime minister, and the National Defence Council members were all proposed by the president of the PRC, and decided by the NPC.

The NPC also decided on the national economic plan, examined and approved the state budget and the financial report, and ratified boundaries of provincial-level jurisdictions.

Limitations to NPC power

In theory, the role accorded to the NPC was, therefore, to act in ways similar to the legislature in a liberal democracy with checks and balances between the three independent powers of the state, where the power is biased towards the legislature. However, the following aspects mean that the NPC cannot be regarded as a liberal-democratic institution:

- the indirect electoral or delegation system, by which representation was achieved through at least three levels of electoral colleges (local-level People's Congresses);
- the corporatist structure of representation, by which delegates were supposed to represent predefined ideal-type societal interests and were selected not because of their views and opinions, but rather because of their personal attributes;
- the explicit adherence to the principle of democratic centralism.

The NPC was not able to amend the written Constitution independently: its formal power to formulate, enact and amend the Constitution, as well as its power to act as a legislature were derived from the Common Programme of the

---

[1] Roughly corresponding to: (a) the courts of justice; and (b) the attorney-general/crown prosecution service in the English-speaking world.

CPPCC. It would not be possible to change the written Constitution in ways which transcended the limitations set by the CPPCC, e.g. the adherence to the democratic centralism.

This limitation on the NPC implies a structure of power dispersal at the formal level, which impedes change of the constitutional structure of the country. As will be discussed later, power dispersal at the formal level of the political system is an important aspect of consolidating party power in the political system.

The NPC was elected for 4 years and was only in session for a short period each year. The Standing Committee of the NPC (elected by the NPC) would conduct the day-to-day business, and had very wide powers to represent the NPC. The core of NPC power was in effect concentrated in the Standing Committee, which controlled the (s)election of delegates and convened the NPC, and which had censuring powers *vis-à-vis* the executive (State Council) and the two branches of the judiciary (Supreme People's Court and the Supreme People's Procuracurate), as well as provincial-level authorities. While the Standing Committee could not remove the heads of the branches of the judiciary, the premier or the chairman of the People's Republic (the president), it could remove and appoint vice-premiers, ministers, etc., and it could annul unconstitutional decisions by the State Council and could revise or annul inappropriate decisions by provincial-level governments.

The central government

The central government of the People's Republic of China was the State Council, consisting of the premier, the vice-premiers, the ministers, the heads of commissions and the secretary-general, and its structure was determined by a separate law (Figure 5.2). The State Council proposed bills to the NPC and reported to the NPC on the work of the government, on the implementation of the national economic plan and on the state budget.

The State Council was in formal terms not a strong executive according to the written Constitution of the 1950s; it was not established independently of the legislature, but elected by it, and it could be censured by the NPC and/or its Standing Committee.

The Chinese Communist Party

The most important part of the Chinese political constitution was related to the role of the Chinese Communist Party, which was written into the Common Programme of the CPPCC and the Preamble of the Constitution of the People's Republic of China, as the leader of the revolution and of the people's democratic united front.

The formal structures of the state enabled the Chinese Communist Party to

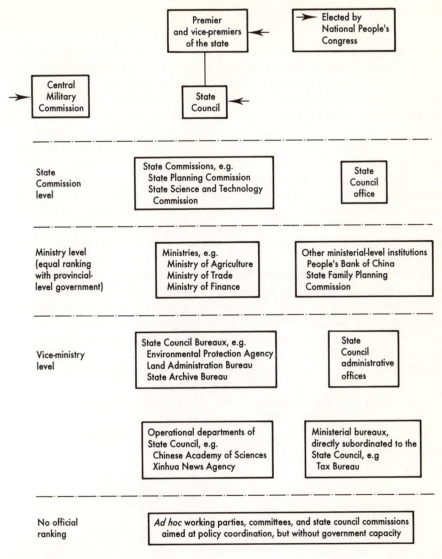

Figure 5.2 *Central government*

exert control over the country by managing elections and appointments to core posts. The Chinese Communist Party could base its power on broad co-optation of popular support for its policies; this was mainly due to:

● the functional division of roles in the Standing Committee of the NPC and the State Council, as well as the CPPCC;

- the principles of indirect delegation; and
- democratic centralism.

At the same time, the functional division of tasks and power dispersal within the state structure prevented or retarded the emergence of constitutional changes which were not initiated and carried out by the Party. A strong, directly elected legislature or a directly elected president appointing his/her own government would have been able to challenge Party control. Similarly, a strong NPC, unchallenged by the CPPCC and its own Standing Committee, or a powerful, formally independent executive, could hypothetically have developed a dynamic of its own which would be difficult for the Chinese Communist Party to control.

The Chinese Communist Party in the mid-1950s was a large mass organization (Table 5.1). While the Party had performed multifarious tasks between the 1920s and 1949 (as a small fighting unit, a subversive, tightly knit organization, the spine of the administration and a mass Party in liberated areas, the rallying point of anti-nationalist opposition and as the general staff of huge armies, especially in the 1940s), the tasks in the 1950s were very different.

The Party was to become, in its own understanding, the instrument of the people's democracy or the people's dictatorship in the state-building process. In its understanding, the Party must maintain close links with the 'masses' (*qunzhong*) of the people, and must be the core political structure in the new state. The Party saw itself as the vanguard of the working class and set itself the aim of achieving socialism and communism in China. It saw Marxism–Leninism as the guiding theory for achieving this end.

Table 5.1   *The membership of the Chinese Communist Party 1921–1995*

Year	No. of members	Year	No. of members
1921	53	1945	1,210,000
1922	195	1956	10,730,000
1923	432	1973	28,000,000
1925	950	1977	35,000,000
1927	57,900	1982	39,650,000
1928	40,000	1995	55,000,000

Organizational structure of the CCP

The Party, in order to control the state, sought to organize itself as the dominant political structure in the country. It would establish primary Party organizations in towns and townships, factories and mines, residential areas, etc. Large primary Party organizations could establish primary Party committees, and could, where relevant, establish branches (e.g. based on work, production or residence). Above the level of the primary Party organizations, the structures of the Party were based on the the administrative divisions of the country.

According to the 1956 Constitution of the CCP, the authority structure of the Party was to be based on geographical or industrial principles. This allowed the Party to supervise and control the constituent parts of the country closely. Another effect is that Party organization comes to be associated with the corporate interest of the area or the enterprise.

The Party adheres to democractic centralism, and is hierarchically organized. The inner-Party command structures are aimed at creating uniformity of action and ensuring that central decisions are followed. The Party constitution especially seeks to avoid factionalism or regional disobedience within the Party ranks. Disciplinary action can be taken against disobedient Party members. Members are allowed to criticize decisions within the Party, but have to carry them out without hesitation as soon as they have been made. Local Party organizations have the authority to make decisions on local matters, but have to carry out central decisions which supersede their own.

The highest authority of the CCP is the National Party Congress, which is convened by the Central Committee once every five years, though during the Mao period it convened infrequently. The Central Committee is elected for 5 years by the National Party Congress. The Central Committee is in charge of directing the work of the Party when the National Party Congress is not in session; most importantly: 'The Central Committee guides the work of the central state organs and people's organizations of a national character through leading Party members' groups within them'.

The Central Committee convenes at least twice a year in plenary sessions by the Political Bureau of the Central Committee. The Political Bureau of the Central Committee is elected by the plenary session of the Central Committee, which also elects the Standing Committee of the Political Bureau, the Secretariat, as well as the chairman and vice-chairmen of the Central Committee. The latter are concurrently chairmen and vice-chairmen of the Political Bureau. The Political Bureau and its Standing Committee exercise the powers and functions of the Central Committee when the Central Committee is not in session.

Hence the formal linkage between the state and the Party, according to the 1956 Party Constitution, is the control of the day-to-day state management through leadership Party groups. Each state organization, large enterprise, etc., will have a Party group consisting of Party members who are appointed into the leadership of the state organ or enterprise.

The main structure of control, however, is the fact that different levels of public appointments must be vetted by a higher level of Party authority. Appointments to central state and Party functions, for example, must be decided by the Central Committee. This Party control with appointments is normally referred to as the nomenclatura.

The democratic parties

The Chinese political system includes a number of small political parties which are formally, albeit not actually, independent of the Chinese Communist Party. These nine parties are part of the United Front. The most famous of these parties is the Revolutionary Committee of the Guomindang, an organization set up in 1947–1948 by members of the Guomindang from various radical factions of the Guomindang, who promoted democracy and nationalism and protested against the dictatorial regime of Chiang Kai-shek. Other parties include the Chinese Democratic Alliance, the Association for Promotion of Democracy and, the Third of September Society, the latter of which was established in commemoration of victory in the Anti-Japanese War on 3 September 1945.

The membership of the small democratic parties is rather limited, and is mainly from among intellectuals. The democratic parties suffered strongly under the Cultural Revolution, but were given their former status back after 1978. This means that they have been able to, on a limited scale, recruit younger members. The parties are strongly bound by the Chinese Communist Party, whose policies they support.

Some of the parties have supplied persons to fill leadership posts in the state apparatus; some of their members are consultants to government bodies, so they are included in the political structures both at national level and at local level in large cities. Apart from delegates to the Chinese People's Political Consultative Conference, there are also members from small democratic parties in the National People's Congress.

Citizens and the state

The written Constitution includes a Bill of Rights, including the standard freedoms and rights, as well as the entitlements to work, the right to rest and leisure, the right to education, and the right to gender equality. The duties enumerated in the written Constitution of 1954 were to abide by the Constitution, laws and work discipline; respect and protect public property; pay taxes according to the law; and perform military service according to the law.

The interpretation of the rights and freedoms, of course, were more important than the fact that they were formulated in the written Constitution. The atmosphere of anti-feudal repression and the strides to rid China of counter-revolutionaries in the 1950s meant that freedom of speech, assembly, press, association, procession and demonstration was limited by the degree to which these acts were considered acceptable by the leadership. If stamped counter-revolutionary, the wrath of the people's dictatorship could legally be executed towards the citizen. The freedom of the person meant that nobody could be arrested without a decision by a people's court or the sanction of the people's procuracurate. However, non-arrest detention was instituted early on to circumvent the constitutional formulation, and various forms of disciplinary action within work units were designed, which infringed the rights of the person. A culture of autocratic infringements on personal freedom was wilfully established by the Chinese Communist Party early in the People's Republic with the purpose of 'crushing' 'counter-revolutionaries', 'feudal forces', 'imperialist spies', etc.

From the end of the 1950s, the freedom of residence was *de facto* abolished by law through the household registration system which fixed the residence of all citizens and prevented migration. Change of residence was limited to state employees changing their place of work, and in the countryside for women marrying into a different village. The citizenship of Chinese citizens was therefore indirect: they belonged to society by belonging to a locality of residence. Different rights were accorded to peasants and urban residents. The 'agricultural household registration' (*nongye hukou*) signified membership of a rural collective, while the 'urban resident household registration' (*chengshi jumin hukou*) gave rights to food rations, goods at reduced prices, etc.

As a further aspect of citizenship it is important to notice the emergence of the work-unit system (*gongzuo danwei*) in urban China. The place of work became the universe of life for all urban Chinese: It not only provided lifelong employment, but also pensions, social security, leisure, training and provision for children, and even education and political rights (the party organization and the polling district for the local People's Congress). The citizenship or urban citizens was, hence, mediated by membership of the *danwei*.

Members of the Chinese Communist Party are normally not subject to criminal prosecution under the state system, but instead to disciplinary action within the Party. In reality this means that the Party in each case decides whether a Party member can be prosecuted under criminal law.

The lines of control in the political constitution of China as they emerged during the 1950s were essential for the later evolution of the political constitution, and also determined the way in which power alliances in the political life of China could develop.

THE COLLAPSE OF THE FORMAL CONSTITUTION, 1965–1978

With the Cultural Revolution in 1965, the normal functions of the political constitution became obsolete. In terms of ideology this was justified with an extension of the revolution to attack powerholders within the Chinese Communist Party who sought to restore capitalism and feudalism or who dithered in the revolutionary struggle. This meant that existing political structures and formal restrictions on political power were disregarded.

The core of the Party hierarchy and central state functions continued to exist, but without clear command lines and with drastic shifts in the personnel due to campaigns purging the ranks of officials.

The system was, in fact, attacked by various factions of rebels, deriving their legitimacy directly from Chairman Mao and drawing on the works of Mao-Zedong-Thought for inspiration. Mao Zedong became the 'red star in our hearts', who authorized the young to rebel against the political system, 'bombarding the headquarters'.

Political structures of the Cultural Revolution

The authority to carry out the Cultural Revolution was derived from decisions in the Political Bureau and the Central Committee. Most importantly, the Central Committee appointed a special committee for waging the Great Proletarian Cultural Revolution. The initial phases of the Cultural Revolution thus took place within a legitimate framework of decision making. In the event, however, those who benefited from the Cultural Revolution were able to exclude opponents from leadership decision making, and were able to oust them from their Party and state posts altogether.

During the Cultural Revolution the non-central organs of the state and the Party collapsed into one structure, the revolutionary committees, and no distinction was made between state and Party in practical administration.

The period 1965–1970 illustrated the fundamental problems of the Chinese political system. The formal dispersal of power over many institutions and the concentration of power according to democratic centralism created a situation where one person could assume dictatorial power and prevent the formal structures of authority from functioning.

The 1969 Party Constitution

In 1969, the Chinese Communist Party convened its Ninth National Congress, which was the first step on the way back to a formalized constitutional and administrative life of the state. The new Constitution of the Chinese Communist Party in 1969 was radically different from the Party's 1956 Constitution.

In rough terms, it maintained the fundamental structures of the Party, but with less elaborate definitions of how authority within the Party was distributed. It explicitly subsumed the political organs of the state under Party control, an aspect which had been more implicit in the 1956 Party Constitution. Most importantly, it placed Chairman Mao explicitly as the leader of the Party and named Lin Biao as his successor. The 1969 Party Constitution also reiterated the theme of the Cultural Revolution, which was to act against powerholders who took the capitalist road, etc.

A main clue to the radical nature of the Party Constitution was that it referred to the Communist Party as the 'political party of the Chinese proletariat', thus narrowing the scope of inclusion, and emphasizing the struggle against the bourgeoisie. The implication was that the united-front theme of New Democracy had been removed from the fundamental thinking of the Party.

The 1969 Party Constitution, in fact, reinstated the Party as a coherent political institution with a strong discipline, which did not tolerate independent power centres within and outside its ranks (thus doing away with the practice of the Cultural Revolution), but it confirmed the most fervent proponents of the Cultural Revolution as the leaders of the Party, and declared that the Party would be responsible for achieving the goals of the revolution. Symbolically, the Party embraced Mao Zedong and claimed the same intimate relationship with the 'broad masses of the people' as he had claimed during the Cultural Revolution.

While the 1969 Constitution included an indication of a separation of state and Party authority, the state structures were still directly politicized by the Party, and local governments and leaderships were still termed 'revolutionary committees' (*geming weiyuanhui*), and in most cases did not represent an independent state structure. The ambiguity of state vs Party authority continued to exist down through the 1970s, right up until the new Party Constitution in 1982.

In the 1970s the political structures, practices and re-emerging administrative routines were volatile and subject to fierce power struggles. The Party Constitution was changed twice, in 1973 and 1977, each time with slight changes only. The most important aspect was the removal of Lin Biao from the constitution in 1973, following the Lin Biao incident (Box 5.4).

Box 5.4   *The Lin Biao Incident*

Lin Biao, who had been one of the most prominent politicians in China during the Cultural Revolution, and had even been 'designated successor' to Chairman Mao, disappeared from the political scene in 1971 under mysterious circumstances. It is generally believed that he and his entourage died in an air crash in the Mongolian People's Republic during a flight to the Soviet Union. According to materials leaked by the Chinese government and information circulated within the CCP, Lin Biao had plotted to kill Mao Zedong with the aim of gaining power. His plan for the *coup d'état*, coded '571', was discovered by the other members of the leadership, but Lin Biao was able to escape arrest because he managed to commandeer a plane from the air force. The crash in Mongolia was an accident. There are other versions of this story, but they all focus on a severe conflict between Mao and Lin. It is speculated that Lin Biao was fiercely opposed to the opening of political contacts with the United States of America, which Mao had proposed.

The criticism of Lin Biao was carried out in the large-scale campaign for the Criticism of Lin Biao and Confucius which dominated the early 1970s. It was claimed that this former Cultural Revolutionary politician harboured the secret wish to restore feudalism, an aim he wanted to realize by usurping state power.

The re-emerging state

The state constitution was also changed twice in the 1970s, in 1975 and 1978. Both these constitutions indicated that the Party dominated the state, and that the Party was 'the core leadership of the Chinese people'.

The 1975 Constitution

The Constitution of 1975 in very brief formulations reintroduced the core features of the Constitution of the 1950s, with the sole exception that the post of president of the state was abolished. The most important aspect of the 1975 Constitution was that it sanctioned the two elements which were to become the cornerstones of the economic reforms in the 1980s. It legalized individual small-scale urban enterprises and it allowed peasants to till so-called 'private plots' for their own consumption. These two items were, at the time (in the mid-1970s), attacked as 'capitalist tails' by the radicals in the CCP. This, albeit limited, scope for private enterprise ensured the latent existence of a non-planned economy during the 1970s.

The 1978 Constitution

The 1978 Constitution was largely a refinement of the brief 1975 Constitution. Most importantly, it set clearer rules for the local levels of people's congresses and governments (termed 'revolutionary committees'). According to the 1978 Constitution, revolutionary committees were the executive organs of the local People's Congresses and at the same time local branches of central government. This clarified the ambiguous role of revolutionary committees, since the end of the 1960s, as dual Party-and-state organs. They were formally separated from their Party identity in the 1978 Constitution, and they were to be elected by the local People's Congresses. While the 1978 Constitution did not differ much from the 1975 Constitution, it did more clearly reinstate the formal distinctions between Party and state, which had prevailed in the Constitution of the 1950s.

Although the 1978 Constitution came prior to the power-exchange between Hua Guofeng and Deng Xiaoping in December 1978, which led into the reform era, it did represent clear steps in the direction of a more regularized political structure. The electoral law of 1979 made provisions for the election of People's Congresses at all levels.

BACK TO FORMALITY: CONSTITUTIONS IN THE REFORM ERA

In the early 1980s, the Chinese state and Party changed fundamentally. The reforms that had started with Deng Xiaoping's *de facto* rise to power, in December 1978, entailed radical changes in the political constitution of the nation. The core leadership demanded that the structures of the state and the Party should be separated fully, and the Party and state structures were reformed in order to accommodate the politics of the new era. The Party structures were simplified in the 1982 Party Constitution, and the state structures in principle reverted to those of the 1954 Constitution.

The Chinese People's Political Consultative Conference

In 1978, the CPPCC was reinstituted after having been defunct for about 15 years. Its new structure resembled its structure in the 1950s, but its scope of tasks were watered down to even less than the original CPPCC. It had been degraded from a deliberative assembly with a poorly fitting denture to a toothless discussion club which provided its members with yearly free excursions to Beijing, special shopping opportunities (high-grade goods and/or foreign goods at bargain prices) and free gifts. But this is not the whole story. The meeting of the CPPCC on 4 February to 28 March 1978 was an important, symbolic step back to power for Deng Xiaoping, who chaired the meeting. While Hua Guofeng held the apparently most powerful positions in the country, as the chairman of the Central Committee of the Chinese Communist Party and as the premier of the State Council, Deng Xiaoping became the chairman of the CPPCC, a post which Mao Zedong held in 1949, and which Zhou Enlai took over in 1954 (while Mao was announced 'Honorary Chairman of the CPPCC') and held until the CPPCC became defunct after 1964. Deng was thus able to claim to represent the legacy of the two great leaders at a symbolic level. After the CPPCC had served as a stepping-stone it was neutered. In August–September 1980, all those in the CPPCC leadership who held or were appointed to other senior political posts under Deng Xiaoping's leadership reorganization retired from the CPPCC. In 1983, the CPPCC was chaired by Zhou Enlai's widow Deng Yingchao.

The National People's Congress

In contrast, the National People's Congress was reinstituted as a potentially stronger organization than before, in order to create a framework for the dispersal of power at top levels that were part of the reforms under Deng Xiaoping. The NPC had convened in 1975 to pass the 1975 Constitution and to elect a new state leadership. However, the NPC in 1975 did not represent more than a poorly veiled compromise between conflicting groups in the leadership. It was an attempt at balancing the factions by manipulating the state leadership posts.

In 1978, the NPC convened to pass a new constitution and to elect a new leadership, confirming Hua Guofeng as the premier of the State Council, following Zhou Enlai's death in 1976, and electing, among others, Deng Xiaoping as a vice-premier of the State Council.

The NPC meeting in August–September 1980 saw perhaps the most important historic compromise in the politics of the People's Republic: Hua Guofeng stepped down as as premier, while Deng Xiaoping and the other vice-premiers also stepped down. The new premier was Zhao Ziyang. This step was of immense importance because it introduced a rejuvenated state leadership which symbolized a division of powers – senior leaders refrained from holding both top Party posts and top state posts. However, it also, ironically, instituted Deng Xiaoping's position as 'peremptory arbiter', as the senior, retired leader who would still have decisive control, based on patronage and personal standing.

Incipient reform of the political system

The formal structures governing the Chinese political system had barely gained legitimacy with the 1978 Constitution, and the leadership shuffle in 1980 did not in itself imply a genuine reform of the political system. This only started after 1983.

In 1979, an electoral law was passed for the local-level People's Congress elections. Unlike the previous practice, it assured that there were more candidates allowed than places to fill, and it also made possible the nomination of candidates who were not selected by the authorities in charge of the election. Although a few non-official candidates stood for election, and in rare cases won a seat, the general attitude of the established power structures was so negative that such candidates were harassed in all the elections that followed.

The 1982 Constitution

The reform leadership was intent on creating regularized frameworks for political life, and revised the written Constitution thoroughly, inspired by Deng Xiaoping's call for a 'political restructuring' to accompany the economic reform. Only minor amendments were made to the formal structures of the state: most notably the presidency of the state (i.e. the head of state) was reintroduced, and People's Congresses were explicitly established at all levels, and urban administrative structures. This new structure meant that the people's communes were formally abolished and replaced by jurisdictions (Figure 5.3) which without any doubt belonged to the structure of the state (rather than the original ambiguous position as units of collective ownership).

1962–1983			1983–present	
State	County		State	
Collective	People's commune	Townships and towns		
	Production brigade	Administrative villages	Collective	
	Production team			

Figure 5.3   *Rural jurisdictions before and after the reform*

Pre-reform basic-level organization

The basic-level administrative structures in the rural areas changed radically throughout the post-1949 period. The counties were the lowest level of state structure, with people's congresses and people's governments. Below that level, the administration was in the hands of the collectives, i.e. the people's communes, following the collectivization in the mid-1950s. In 1962, the administrative structures of the rural people's communes were settled in a policy document from the Central Committee of the CCP in a form which was to remain virtually unchanged for between 16 and 20 years. The administration of the people's communes would be directed by a committee, which combined Party and economic-administrative functions. During the Cultural Revolution this would become the 'Revolutionary Committee'. A small number of offices would be in charge of practical administration. The people's communes were subdivided into production brigades, each of which had a small committee, normally consisting of five Party members in charge of day-to-day administration. Below the level of production brigades, the production teams were in charge of practical coordination of production activities, each having a head, an accountant and a bursar. The management under this system integrated production, civil administration, social welfare provisions, public utilities and policing into one unitary structure.

Expansion of local administration

The restructuring of rural administration was thorough. The Constitution was accompanied by a policy of separating economic and political management of the rural collectives, a policy which meant that the new township people's governments and the township people's congresses were not in the long term in charge of the day-to-day management of collective assets. They were to retreat to a position as political entities, regulating an independent economic sphere. The lower levels of rural organization were also affected. The administrative village replaced the production brigades. The village was outside the realm of the formal organizations of the state, being an institution of the people's self-organization; the villages were led by villagers' committees. Teams which had been important units of economic organization and production in the communes were disbanded or retained depending on local circumstances.

This means that formal state administration was extended far deeper into the rural society than ever before.

Post-reform basic-level organization

The people's commune system was eroded in the years between 1978–1983. The political administration and economic management were separated, and the Party functions were in theory disconnected from the administrative organs of the collective. The new administrative units were townships (*xiang*) and administrative villages (*xingzhengcun* or *cun*), roughly replacing the communes and brigades. In some places the teams continued to exist, but with limited functions.

The rural reforms in 1978–1983 privatized production activities and divided the use-right of the land among the peasants. This meant that the collective ceased to act as a production unit, and took upon itself the role of public authority.

The new structure meant a loss of direct influence in rural areas, a phenomenon the Chinese Communist Party countered by expanding the primary Party organizations down to village level where they had not been strongly represented before. According to the 1982 Constitution the township governments became the lowest level of state administration in the rural areas, indicating that the formal state control was expanding downwards. The villagers' committees were described as the organs of the people's self-organization, indicating that they were outside state administration. However, during the latter part of the 1980s the state issued detailed legislation on their organization and administration, and also from the beginning of the 1990s started to introduce more rigid and more uniform practices for villagers' committee elections.

The Party's and state's presence in the countryside has thus been increased by:

- regularizing and strengthening the township;
- opening representative offices of county-level authorities in the townships;
- seeking to regularize and standardize the villagers' committees; and
- intensifying Party grass-roots control.

The ownership issue

The provisions of the 1982 Constitution on ownership rights were very cautious, very reluctant steps away from the strict forms of public ownership. However, the judicious move away from exclusive socialist ownership in the 1982 Constitution was supported by policies that were not published at the time, but which implied that private ownership of means of production at any scale was allowed (Box 5.5). Amendments to the 1982 Constitution in 1987 expanded the scope of private ownership.

Regularizing the political process

The coming to power of Deng Xiaoping in 1978 meant that great political changes took place. The main task that Deng Xiaoping faced was to regularize administration and political decision making after the 'chaos of the Cultural Revolution'. The reinstitution of Party authority in 1969–1970 had been based on a system where Mao as the supreme leader had been able to dominate decision making, but where formal structures of institutional responsibility

---

Box 5.5   *Socialist ownership*
The ownership structures in China include three types of public ownership of the means of production:

1. the ownership by the whole people, i.e. state ownership, where the state represents the people's ownership and administrates this ownership;
2. the collective ownership by the labouring masses, i.e. urban collective ownership, where the ownership belongs to all the members of the workforce in a factory or a shop – this form of ownership came about as a merger of small private enterprises in the mid-1950s;
3. the rural variety of the collective ownership by the labouring masses, i.e. rural collective ownership, where all inhabitants of a rural jurisdiction (normally a production team), irrespective of age or labour participation, were joint owners of the totality of local means of production, the ownership relation being formally expressed in their local household registration status – this type of ownership came about in the rural collectivization drive in the mid-1950s and was codified in a policy document from 1962 which governed the operation of the people's communes until the early 1980s.

---

were gradually restored. The erosion of political institutions during the 1960s and the unification of state and Party functions at most levels of authority impeded effective governance. While day-to-day administration regained a formal shape, policy issues were dealt with in campaigns and wasteful political mobilization, which not only disrupted production, but also confused lower echelons in the Party hierarchy. There was a general lack of laws, regulations and rules which could help shape the functioning of the nation, and instead a profusion of broad policy decisions, often sparked off by specific incidents, were used as policy guidelines. Interventions on specific issues from the leadership took the form of instructions and commands to be complied with. China was not under-regulated in the 1970s, but it was poorly regulated by an abundance of irrational policy instruments.

Separation of Party and state

The main aim of the 1982 Constitution, and more importantly the administrative reform with which it was combined, was to bring administrative regularity to China. Implicit in the Constitution was the formal separation of state administration and Party activity. The full-scale reinstatement of the National People's Congress and of the Chinese People's Political Consultative Conference was an important step towards regularization. The legal system was rapidly improved, so that laws passed by the NPC and various types of regulations passed by the people's governments grew in numbers and reflected a more comprehensive system of administrative law and practice.

At the same time the economy was gradually to be wrenched away from the grip of the state, so that production and economic exchange were no longer governed by the state plan in any detail. Incidentally, the state plan, which originally was a plan setting specific production targets and was called the 'Economic Plan', was rebaptized to become the 'Plan for Social and Economic Development', setting out broader targets of development. The 5-year plan for the period 1991–1995 even included general living standard indicators to be attained.

The 1982 Constitution, therefore, cannot be seen in isolation from the political project of Deng Xiaoping: the creation of a political and economic system which followed general, formal rules to replace the idiosyncratic rule by individuals that had come about during the Cultural Revolution. The retreat of the Party to general policy formulation and political supervision; the practical formulation of policies, laws and regulative frameworks within a state system which encapsulates differing views and preferences; the implementation of policies and law by a professional administrative system; and the execution of decisions on production and trade, based on individualized economic interest: all these aspects reflected the overall ambition of formalized governance.

Characteristics of Deng's reforms

Deng Xiaoping's reform project aimed at power dispersal, regularization of political life, and professionalization of administration. The development of the National People's Congress since the mid-1980s can be seen as a reflection of the relative success of these policy ideals. By around 1985 the National People's Congress had already asserted itself by its weeding out in the bills put forward by the State Council for approval; and debates in the National People's Congress attracted public attention to specific provisions of laws and possible alternatives to them. The scrutiny in parliamentary committees meant that legislative bills had to be withdrawn and worked over again, and that some aspects of the reform policies were rejected because they were not sufficiently clear or thought through.

A new trend has been emerging, which cannot yet be fully confirmed, but which may emerge as a pattern. Senior politicians in the State Council (state councillors and ministers) are now asked to retire in their early 60s, in order to allow for rejuvenation of the political system. They are then subsequently elected for the National People's Congress and are made members of parliamentary committees within or close to their original field of work. As a consequence, the National People's Congress may become a very interesting and powerful player in the political system, where venerable elder colleagues check the power of the State Council and its subordinated commissions and ministries.

An example of this is the Committee for Environmental Protection under the National People's Congress, which was established in the early 1990s, headed by the pensioned head of the government's Environmental Protection Agency (an office under the State Council). This has important implications for environmental legislation, upgrading the importance of the field.

The National People's Congress, thus, reflects a trend to regularize the operation of the state by increasing power dispersal.

Vertical power dispersal: Branches and areas

There exists a fundamental, systemic conflict between the administrative bodies of the central state and the local governments at various levels.

Seen from the centre (except in the cases of the People's Liberation Army and the Chinese Railways), the policy-implementing bodies are offices under local governments. The line of command is clear: local offices of a ministry or commission must follow the instructions of the central ministry or commission. However, the appointment of cadres and the budget for these local offices are mainly a matter for the local government, which represents a comprehensive view of the needs of its jurisdiction, and so may be in conflict with certain central policies.

The Chinese leadership has, during the 1950s to the 1990s, revised the central–local relationships, mainly in favour of local management of local affairs. This has led to a situation where the centre controls only a small proportion of all financial incomes, and where wide powers are deregulated down to provinces, cities and counties. On several occasions, however, the centre has experienced the difficulty of this power dispersal, and has therefore instigated the 'reining in' of local authorities.

During the 1950s till the early 1980s the planned economy meant that it was in the interest of the central government to devolve much decision-making power to the provinces, in order to be able to concentrate central state planning on the core elements of the economy, while planning in the localities would complement central planning. By maintaining strong central control of fossil energy (oil and coal), heavy industry, railway transport and shipping, international trade and the financial system, as well as core agricultural products, the state was better off, leaving detailed decisions on other aspects to the local governments. In the 1980s the reforms shifted the focus away from central planning, and the new field of conflict became the fiscal revenue, the financial expenditure and the banking system. The central state did not have sufficient leverage to control the flows and size of investments, and therefore China experienced serious inflation in consumer prices.

The state tried to curb these trends by 'reining in' some of the powers given to local authorities, but it was not until a banking and financial reform in 1994 and 1995 that the structural problems started to subside.

THE DISTRIBUTION OF POWER

The middle echelons: Local and sectoral leaders

The rule by individuals who set up their own power centres became a problem in the 1950s, and the tendency for certain provincial and local leaders to become excessively powerful due to patronage increased with the years. The local or provincial Party secretary was in most cases able to amass a very strong power base. The status of the CCP and the adherence to the principles of democratic centralism enhanced this trend. The fact that the nomenclatura was *de facto* in the hands of the Party secretary gave him a natural role as a patron. The Party had in the 1950s adopted an anti-factionalist principle, which forbade members of the Chinese Communist Party to coordinate voting or to form groups within the Party. This prohibition left few opportunities for Party members to confront individual leaders to achieve change.

The strong Party secretaries, of course, derived their power from above, and their status in the final analysis always depended on their loyalty to leaders in higher echelons. However, their loyalty could shift from one group of leaders to another, and so their bargaining position was often very strong.

It is always expected that sectoral or local leaders' policy preferences represent their office in the first instance. There is a very liberal attitude to dissenting views on policies which originate in regional or sectoral interest. Local and sectoral leaders are expected to fight to maximize the benefits for their county, province, ministry, university or army unit. Leaders transferred from one post to another accordingly speak out in favour of their present post and are not expected to express specific loyalties towards their former position. Leaders in the middle echelons, hence, are not partisan beyond the level of their present official post.

The strong sectoral leader type was further affirmed in his power by the work-unit system. All Chinese either belonged to an urban work unit or to a rural production brigade. All their activities were confined to the work unit, so that the enterprise has been described as 'small society', comprising all aspects of life for life, often even catering for the education, employment and social framework of the children's generation. The sectoral identification, therefore, was based on strong ties within the work unit and few ties outside it.

Power dispersal after the reforms

The reforms during the 1980s sought to cope with these problems in various ways. The arrest of the so-called 'Gang of Four' in late 1976 started a process of cleansing the ranks of the Party and state organs of their followers, which lasted until the early 1980s. In itself this toppled many almost autocratic local and sectoral leaders, bringing a breeze of fresh air into the Chinese administration. The policies pursued by the new leadership under Deng Xiaoping after December 1978 aimed at avoiding double posting. A provincial governor would normally not at the same time be the provincial first secretary (of the Party), the headmaster of a school would not be the chairman of the Party branch, etc. The holder of the non-Party top post, however, would be vice-chairman of the Party branch. The structural dispersal of local power on the local people's congresses, local governments, local Party branches, etc., has markedly reduced the incidence of excessive power concentration on individuals. However, it has not done away with it and up to the mid-1990s quite a proportion of local leaders enjoyed almost unchecked power within their jurisdictions.

These intermediate levels of politics (the ministries and the local governments at county to provincial levels) indicate the nature of the political system. They not only determine the degree to which central policies are carried out, but they also form the basic structures on which the edifice of the top leadership rests.

Alliances and cleavages

An ideal-type Marxist collective leadership is likely to base its decision making on shifting alliances of big political players (top leaders, powerful ministries and large state-owned companies), forming flexible coalitions on a broad spectrum of issues. Each individual player in such a system would join the winning coalition and seek to influence to its own purpose the issues agreed on; at the same time each player would seek to avoid too strong commitments to any other player, in order not to suffer from sudden shifts in coalition composition. Individual leaders would gain and lose in importance depending on their position in the coalitions. The Maoist system of the Cultural Revolution, and after, implied that players would seek to influence the top leader, Mao Zedong, and were caught up into complex, sycophantic relationships of dependency in order to further their interests.

The disruptive nature of concomitant leadership cleavages and the paralysis of the system due to stalemates in the policy process, combined with the general lack of skills, knowledge and professionalism which characterized decision making, caused Deng Xiaoping to strive towards a more predictable and professional governance form. Harking back to the formal divisions of power in the 1950s Constitution, introducing an increasingly meritocratic system for cadres (with an ultimate vision of a professional civil service), and rejuvenating the leadership, the foundations for a new type of leadership were laid in the early 1980s. The local authorities and the ministries gained an immense independence from central authorities.

Reciprocal accountability

If we look to where power originates and how it is distributed in China, we must consider the main players: the top leaders, the Central Committee, the People's Liberation Army, the ministries, the provinces and the National

People's Congress. The top leaders in the Political Bureau are elected by the Central Committee of the Chinese Communist Party, and top leaders in other (e.g. state) functions are appointed or vetted for election by the Political Bureau, which holds the nomenclatura power for top posts.

Top leaders, accordingly, tend to represent (the interests of) major constituencies which are represented in the Central Committee. On the other hand, given the principles of the nomenclatura, the top leaders vet the appointment and/or election of senior officials in the state structure, the military, and major companies. Furthermore, with the mechanisms of democratic centralism and the mechanics of electing and convening the Central Committee they have a strong hand in determining their own electorate.

There is a similar relationship between the top leadership and the State Council, where the central administration of the state, i.e. the large commissions (e.g. the State Planning Commission), the ministries, the Bank of China, etc., set the stage for policy making. Ministers and commission heads are appointed by the National People's Congress, but the appointments are invariably vetted beforehand by the top leadership in the Political Bureau.

This structure has been termed 'reciprocal accountability' by Susan L. Shirk (1993). The consequences of this for political decision making and power relationships are huge. With increasing autonomy and assertion of sectoral and local interest following the reforms in the 1980s, the large heavy industrial ministries, the People's Liberation Army, and the provinces constitute important and powerful constituencies to whose interests the top leaders in the Political Bureau are accountable.

The strength of top leaders

The top leaders do have a number of ways of manipulating their constituencies. They set the agenda and are able to convene meetings where decisions are made. A method which has been used quite often to put a matter on the agenda and to force through a decision is to convene a meeting of provincial Party first secretaries instead of the Central Committee. The decisions in 1980/1981 giving detailed shape to the rural reforms were made at such a meeting. This means that the People's Liberation Army and the main ministries were not able to have any profound influence over this policy.

It is important to note that the Chinese Communist Party – as implicit in the practice of democratic centralism – makes its decisions by vote rather than by consensus. No minority has any right to veto any decision. This ensures that the structure is not excessively conservative, and that decisions on new developments can be made rather swiftly. The top leadership can, of course, use this principle to force through decision making. If, for example, the members of the Standing Committee of the Political Bureau fear that there might be opposition in the Political Bureau, they are likely to convene an enlarged meeting with representatives of particular interests. This may shift the voting patterns radically in favour of the Standing Committee of the Political Bureau.

The Standing Committee of the Political Bureau, apart from anything else, sets the agenda for meetings and is likely to have greater overall political knowledge of the issues involved. The relative flexibility and superior overview at the top levels, i.e. in the Standing Committee of the Political Bureau and in the Political Bureau, have been confronted with institutional conservatism in parts of their constituencies. Policies that are unpopular in important constituencies cannot be implemented due to lack of consent.

Reorganization

The central leadership has various methods of circumventing such situations of political stalemates. They can reorganize the ministries and commissions, upgrade or downgrade them, divide them or amalgamate them, dissolve them or establish new ones. The administrative reorganization of Chinese central administration in 1982 was radical, reflecting a veritable system change; the full scope and effects of this change have not been examined in the literature. An example of this change was the amalgamation of two ministries and a bureau to form the Ministry of Agriculture, Animal Husbandry and Fisheries, which changed its name to Ministry of Agriculture in 1988. This meant that the semi-military administration of state-farms merged with general, civil administration of agriculture and aquatic production. Pulling the military out of the small, but not insignificant, state-farm sector was not only a step to secure a sound development of the rural reforms, but also to professionalize the army.

Another important change in 1982 was the establishment of the very influential State Commission for the Reform of the Economic System. This top-level organization was aimed at instigating cumulative change in the political structures, breaking down barriers to development and creating proper administrative frameworks for the reforms, quite often based on large-scale trial implementation. During the 1980s this System Reform Commission (the abbreviation in Chinese is *Tigaiwei*) took care of the establishment of many new institutions, initiated non-plan market structures for core commodities (the last restricted product to be released was cotton in the early 1990s), and in the mid-1990s was fully occupied with negotiations on a social insurance system.

In 1988 the formerly powerful State Economic Commission was dissolved and parts of its functions and staff went to the State Planning Commission, whose tasks also altered radically during the 1980s. Also in 1988, the Ministry of Power and Water Conservancy was split into two separate ministries.

These changes to a certain extent all reflect changes in administrative tasks, and a more rational division of administrative labour. The changes, however, also reflect the intention of the leadership to control the unruly parts of its constituency.

The State Economic Commission, for example, functioned as a very strong calming element in the Chinese administration and had great authority in bringing together various parts of the administration in compromises. Its task was to formulate and effectuate policy coordination. Disbanding it created a new balance of powers, and broke a conservational element in the central administration. Breaking up the Ministry of Power and Water Conservancy has been understood by some to solve the problem of a strong opposition to the Three Gorges Project within the original single ministry.

A different method of controlling the constituencies in the ministries and commissions has been to introduce various think-tanks and *ad hoc* leadership bodies.

Fragmented power and institutional frictions

As already discussed the ministries, commissions and other authorities tend to nurture their own interests in the execution of power. Their leaders are generally supposed to represent institutional and sectoral interest, and their employees are normally disposed towards a very high degree of loyalty to their employer. Ministries and commissions are generally organized vertically into structures of command, with the head ministry/commission at central government level, and offices belonging to provincial, city/district, and county governments, which are at the same time subjected hierarchically to the head ministry/commission. This type of structure is called a *xitong* by the Chinese. *Xitongs* are typically much broader than just administrative bodies, they encompass a wide range of functions.

For example, most *xitongs* have established a multitude of universities and colleges to provide graduates for their own staff replenishment, and many have fully fledged research academies under their control. In this sense they do not rely on general universities and colleges under the State Education Commission to provide candidates, but generally prefer to train their own people. Some even sustain theatres and orchestras in addition to the cultural establishments provided by the Ministry of Culture. *Xitongs* have affiliated companies and other types of structures which supply needed semi-commercial services.

Institutional balancing

A severe problem for the Chinese leadership has always been the lack of collaboration between the *xitongs*, and their unbridled quest for more power, more funds and more influence. Good leadership in China, therefore, aims at avoiding steps that can upset a balance of inter-*xitong* interests, which is finely tuned and agreed in uncountable bilateral and multilateral negotiations.

Divide and rule governance, of course, brings some advantages to the top leadership. It prevents collusion between departments, and is therefore seen as advantageous for policy implementation. It may, for example, be noticed as very peculiarly Chinese that at central levels financial policy is vested in three main *xitongs*, the Bank of China, the Ministry of Finance and the Tax Bureau, while the State Planning Commission must vet large state expenditure programmes. The dispersal of power in several *xitongs* over a single policy area gives rise to continuous conflicts of interest, into which the top leadership can intervene in order to create balance between the *xitongs*, but also to ensure that no policies and interests of any one of these *xitongs* prevails at the cost of central policy.

Conflicts between *xitongs*, even over small issues, can take grotesque dimensions and are occasionally detrimental to the good and smooth functioning of the state. Conflicts over authority boundaries are frequent and cause paralysis in parts of the administration, and compromises involving higher-level authorities and protracted negotiations are required to solve what Chinese bureaucrats euphemistically refer to as 'frictions'.

Institutional protectionism

Institutional power maximization implies that *xitongs* do not normally share resources, and if they do, they do it based on scrupuously worked-out contracts which ensure that every party obtains an equal benefit. There is a general lack of information between *xitongs*, and concomitant squandering of resources. The Ministry of Transportation or the Academy of Sciences will make their own land surveys and have their own cartographic staff, not because relevant maps do not exist, but because they are kept by the cartographic authorities. Information on similar initiatives under different ministries is normally not exchanged, due to institutional secrecy. Detailed tabulations from the State Statistical Bureau are not available to other parts of the Chinese administration unless they are paid for (at prohibitive rates) or are part of a collaborative project in which the State Statistical Bureau participates. Other commissions and ministries, therefore, have their own statistical collection mechanisms.

Policy coordination

The paralyzing and wasteful perversion of the *xitong* system causes the top leadership to respond with various measures.

One very common measure is to convene working parties between stake-holding *xitongs* to reach overall agreement on policies. Semi-permanent arrangements are found in committees (also termed leadership small groups) headed by vice-premiers of the State Council and in which vice-ministers or ministers from relevant commissions and ministries take part. An example of such a committee is the Committee for the Economic Development of Poor Areas. Recurrent policy coordination can be carried out in such fora with a rather high degree of efficiency. Conflicts over funding and authority related to specific policy areas can thus be solved in businesslike and regular negotiations. Permanent policy coordination takes place in certain State Council Commissions which are established as permanent bodies, with permanent secretariats, and with broader, but distinct, policy areas as their brief. Such State Council Commissions also often comprise specially appointed scientific advisers. Examples of such commissions are the Environmental Protection Commission, the Commission for the Preparation of the Establishment of Hong Kong Special Zone, and the Commission for Place Names. Typical for these commissions is that they govern an area of policy which transcends the borderlines of ministries. The authority of these working parties, committees and commissions is that they do not have authority in themselves and are not part of the official administrative structures of the state. Their membership is mainly ex officio, meaning that the vice-minister in charge of a policy area will be a member. The only exceptions to this are the scientific consultants of the State Council Commissions who are appointed due to their expertise. The practice of using these *ad hoc*, semi-permanent and permanent types of policy-coordinating bodies was introduced in the early 1980s and increased rapidly towards the end of the 1980s.

The associations

A more indirect way of dealing with the strong boundaries between *xitongs* is to promote horizontal, cross-departmental links. These are mainly furthered in the wide range of professional associations which sprang up during the 1980s. This type of organization is characterized in the official jargon as a 'societal entity'.

They are officially registered and based on charters which are officially recognized, formally by the Ministry of Civil Affairs, but in reality by the responsible Party branch. They are normally composed of members from many different work units and *xitongs* who share a profession or certain types of interest, and they are often headed by Party notabilities, retired leaders, etc.

Their function throughout the 1980s and 1990s has been to open up cross-departmental debate and broaden out the background of policy coordination. In this sense they have been extremely successful in moderating *xitong* loyalty and simplistic policy interpretations. The importance of various professional associations in shaping the intellectual background of professional debate for environmental policy and rural development policy is well known, and they have also created a broad professional ethos in favour of the economic and administrative reforms.

Associations exist at all levels of government. While they are formally not linked to any specific authority, it is possible for them to share offices and support staff with government bodies. Some are very independent and others are closely knit together with government bodies, to the extent that some can almost be regarded as informal extensions of a government agency.

The mass organizations

The Chinese mass organizations are central to the structure of the state. The main organizations are the All-China Women's Federation and the All-China Federation of Trade Unions. The Communist Youth League is also considered to belong to this category.

These organizations have similar history and similar purpose. The Federation of Trade Unions claims heritage to the first National Labour Conference in China in 1922, which was held in Guangzhou, and which represented 230,000 members of trade unions. The Chinese labour movement was, from the very beginning, strongly influenced by the Chinese Communist Party, although in its infancy it also included nationalists, anarchists and non-aligned members. The Chinese Communist Party, by controlling and coordinating trade union policy, gained a strong presence among a broader proletarian constituency and was able to rally non-communist progressive forces.

The Communist Youth League was also established in 1922, and was from the very beginning seen as an organization for recruiting socialist youths into the Party; its elected leaders have always been influential leaders of the Chinese Communist Party.

The Women's Federation was formally established in early 1949, when it gathered together 'democratic women' in a national organization. In this way large numbers of women who had been associated with various women's organizations (some of which had been existing since the early 1920s) were given the opportunity to join a federation under the leadership of the Chinese Communist Party.

The distinct role of these organizations, historically, was to be the CCP's face towards society, and they are therefore still called 'mass organizations'.

WOMEN'S POLITICAL PARTICIPATION IN CHINA

The question of women's participation in Chinese politics is complex. China, like other socialist states, ideologically commits itself to gender equality, and through strong policies has promoted high female participation in the workforce; mobilizes and organizes women in the All-China Women's Federation; ensures a high rate of female representation in political bodies; and actively protects women from violence and hardship. Chinese women, however, do not have real political equality with men. While some women do have significant and important posts in the leadership, they form a small minority, and they normally do not have positions of significant power. Of almost 30 people who have sat on the Standing Committee of the Political Bureau of the Central Committee of the Chinese Communist Party between 1969 and the early 1990s, not one was a woman. Of approximately 70 members of the Political Bureau in the same period, only three were women, namely Deng

Yingchao (the widow of Zhou Enlai), Jiang Qing (the wife of Mao Zedong), and Ye Qun (the wife of Lin Biao); and among about 15 persons serving as alternate members of the Political Bureau, only two were women (Chen Muhua and Wu Guixian).

Among the 15 people who served as chairmen and vice-chairmen of the Central Committee between the late 1960s and the early 1990s, not one was a woman; among almost 725 people who served as members of the Central Committee in that period only 35 were women; and among almost 600 people who served as alternate members of the Central Committee in the period, about 10 per cent were women. No women served on the Secretariat or Central Military Commission of the Central Committee, but Deng Yingchao (Zhou Enlai's wife) served for a short period as a second secretary on the Central Discipline and Inspection Commission.

In the organs of the state, the highest post ever held by a woman was that held by Song Qingling (the widow of Sun Yat-sen). She was vice-chairman of the state before the Cultural Revolution and was made Honorary Chairman of the People's Republic after the 1978 Reforms had started. Among approximately 60 vice-chairmen of the Standing Committee of the National People's Congress, only 8 were women, while no woman was ever president of the Standing Committee. Among almost 600 members who served on the Standing Committee between the late 1960s and the mid-1990s about 13 per cent were women.

Male equivalence

Of the women who have belonged to the top leadership over the last two decades, four stand out as being either the wife or the widow of a party elder. This 'male equivalence' is probably best demonstrated by Song Qingling's high status in the Chinese political system. Her role as the widow of a revolutionary leader meant that she gave a specific legitimacy to the United Front policy of the Chinese Communist Party. As the widow of the revolutionary leader Sun Yat-sen, she represented a link back to the 1911 Revolution and the United Front with the Guomindang. After the Shanghai Massacre in 1927, Song Qingling formed an opposition to Chiang Kai-shek, and created the Revolutionary Committee of the Guomindang, which took side with the communists in the subsequent battles. Hence, Song Qingling became a symbol of national unity and of reverence for Sun Yat-sen's contribution to the revolution.

The fact that Zhou Enlai's, Mao Zedong's and Lin Biao's wives became direct members of the leadership can essentially be ascribed to their husband's position. It should be noted that Deng Yingchao did not gain a top leadership position until Zhou Enlai had died; she, in a sense, was chosen to symbolize continuity after his death.

Apart from Jiang Qing (Mao Zedong's wife) no woman in a top leadership position has had a strong political position. Jiang Qing's position as the most ambitious leader of the Cultural Revolutionary Group is unique and has gained her a less than pleasant position in Chinese history books. Ye Qun stood fully in the shadow of Lin Biao, her husband, and did not have any independent political power. Kang Keqing (Zhu De's wife) had a multi-faceted political carreer with many different responsibilities, but she never participated in real political power in the top leadership. Jiang Qing's case shows that once a woman has gained an organizationally important position, she is able to negotiate a power base independent of her husband.

Women who reach the pinnacle of power in China are not viewed kindly by their male colleagues. The campaign after the arrest of the 'Gang of Four' in late 1976 was particularly vicious and carried gender-specific overtones directed against Jiang Qing, for example, comparing her to the Empress Dowager (Ci Xi) of the Qing empire, who is depicted in Chinese historiography as cruel, whimsical and deeply reactionary. The campaign was, in other words, carried by sexist prejudices and stereotypes about strong women.

Female political career patterns

Other women in the Chinese leadership reach their position in a more regular career pattern. For women, the main pathways to political recognition and political posts are within the sphere specifically earmarked for women within the system, e.g. the All-China Women's Federation. A small minority of women are able to climb to important posts based on a combination of political and administrative skills, specialist knowledge and patronage. Such women are rare in the top leadership, but do exist in greater numbers in medium-level management. Chen Muhua is perhaps the best example of a woman whose career was mainly meritocratic and, who carried out functions in relatively high positions, her career taking her from the State Family Planning Commission to become Minister of Foreign Trade and Economic Relations and eventually Director of the People's Bank of China. In spite of her high ranking in the state system, she only made it to alternate member of the Political Bureau.

Women in intermediate leadership roles

Chinese political life is predictably male dominated, but individual cases of women within leading positions indicate a certain tolerance towards women in politics, and also provide some scattered role models for younger women. The relative absence of women in the top leadership is very conspicuous given the fact that women in China are much more active in the labour market than in most other countries, and do have the opportunity to acquire leadership skills. The reforms have not changed this situation much. If one looks at the female ministers (vice and full) in the 1980s and 1990s, they constitute between 6 and 7 per cent of all ministers, more than the approximately 4 per cent in the 1960s and 1970s. The proportion of female delegates to the National People's

Congress is about 21 per cent, a number which has remained stable since 1975. Since the reforms, however, the proportion of women in the more powerful Standing Committee of the National People's Congress has fallen drastically, from 25 and 19 per cent in 1975 and 1978 to 9, 12 and 13 per cent in 1983, 1988 and 1993, respectively. As already noted, the most powerful organs of the party (the Political Bureau and its Standing Committee) do not include women. About 6 per cent of the Central Committee of the CCP are women, a number which has basically not changed over the years (except in 1973 when it was about 10 per cent). The proportion of female alternate members of the Central Committee, however, was 17 and 18 per cent in 1973 and 1977, and has fallen to between 9 and 10 per cent in the 1980s and 1990s, indicating that less women are in the process of being groomed for full membership.

In state-owned and urban collective industry there do exist women directors and top managers, but they form a tiny minority. Women who have a politically powerful family background may gain significant posts in politics or industry, but examples of such women who have both the required skills and the family links indicate that they mainly provide a springboard for their husbands to attain even higher positions. Marriage to a high-level cadre's daughter is a well-known and often-used career pattern for ambitious men.

Rural women

For rural women the situation is different. Rural marriage patterns are predominantly patri-local so that the woman will live together with her husband in his village; most marriages are traditionally between partners from different villages, although some Chinese anthropologists and sociologists in recent years have noted a trend towards marriages between people from the same village. This pattern of marriage has been reinforced by the household registration system and the rural collective ownership. The household registration system was introduced in the late 1950s in order to prevent migration from the countryside to the cities, and so every Chinese had to obtain special permission to move to another place to live. This permission was virtually given only to female peasants in conjunction with marriage, while it was very unlikely for men to move to another place (except if they got a higher education or had served in the People's Liberation Army). The household registration system was relaxed gradually during the 1980s, but the collective ownership structures in the countryside mean that men from outside the village are seen as intruders who are claiming a share of the communal property, so villagers' committees normally do not give permission for a man to move into the village. The consequence for women is that they are in strange territory with long communication lines back to their kinsfolk, friends and social networks, and exposed to the united will of a well-organized male-dominated community, whose norms are traditionally imposed by a relentless mother-in-law, herself originally also a stranger to the community. Within this context, a woman's role is all too often designed by social norms which are hard to break, even for the most enterprising, and women do not tend to reach real decision-making positions in rural areas, although they generally participate actively in labour outside the home.

Women in rural leadership

Some rural women are active in local government due to their gender, being in charge of health, family planning and women's work, thus ensuring a certain level of social organization of women, and career opportunities in politics for some few.

In more recent years training of junior officials in public administration involves placement in the countryside for a 2–4 year period in order to gain work experience. Young graduates (including women) from vocational schools and universities thus may find themselves in a situation where they gain very powerful local positions due to sheer superiority in administrative skills. These people are normally not of peasant origin, and they are not locals. However, the example of young women in such positions may have a function as role models for young rural women.

Rural women and economic power

Some have suggested that the power of women in the family context has increased during the last two decades, due to the increased focus on entrepreneurship. Marriage, according to such an interpretation, has become an important aspect of generating and cementing business links, and this is thought to have enhanced the influence of women directly and indirectly: they are supposedly the carriers of investment capital and market information. Such explanations can also be turned around: Women are instruments for male entrepreneurial endeavours, and they only perform a function as a moral bond of obligation between business partners; they must give birth to the next generation and be a mortgage in a business transaction between men; this is more humble than powerful (see Chapter 12).

Equal representation

It is an important aspect of the Chinese political system that there is a degree of equal representation of the sexes in China. However, this is based on quotas demanding a certain proportion of women delegates to the NPC and of members in the CCP. This has secured a representation which, when compared in numbers only, is quite impressive for a Third World country. Posts and offices have been given to women who have proven able through their work in the NPC or the local branches of the CCP. With the introduction of multi-candidate lists in 1979, there has been a marked tendency to elect men instead of women in local elections. However, this does not severely affect the delegation of women to posts in higher-level people's congresses. A general impression is that these formally advantageous opportunities for women have not been borne out in real participation in decision making.

To sum up, women in China were given an official status of strength in Chinese society, but they still do not have access to the fora where real decisions are made on the future of Chinese society.

CONCLUSIONS

The problem of the socialist state was to establish power structures which reflected the ideals of the revolution, and at the same time were able to provide a sufficiently sophisticated governmental and administrative structure to ensure the development of the country.

The Chinese political constitution has been torn between, on the one hand, balancing of interests and power dispersal (in order to maintain the CCP in the leading role) and, on the other hand, continued revolution to break down centres of power within the system.

The reform policies introduced by Deng Xiaoping at the end of the 1970s and the beginning of the 1980s have created room for broad power dispersal and a professionalization of the administration, and have brought more stability to the political system.

FURTHER READING

Analytical works: an historical outline of Chinese politics, which is easily read and which covers the whole period up to the mid-1980s, is found in Meisner (1986). The core issues of political governance are described best and most comprehensively in the 'old classic' *Ideology and Organization in Communist China* (Schurmann, 1966–1968), and more recently by Shirk (1993) and Lieberthal and Oksenberg (1988).

6 Political processes: mobilization and participation

This chapter examines the changing character of the Chinese political system, processes of participation and forms of protest. The chapter will chart the processes by which the political mobilization of the Maoist period has given way to management of protest in the post-Mao phase of Chinese politics. We suggest that this management, while innovative in the Chinese context, is not very effective because the political institutions are unable to respond flexibly to the growing demands generated by the privatizing economy and the regenerating civil society. This could, in the long run, pose a threat to the legitimacy of the Chinese state.

WHAT DO WE MEAN BY POLITICAL PARTICIPATION?

The Chinese political system has been routinely described in a language of totalitarianism, with Mao Zedong cast as the Red Emperor and the Chinese people as 'blue ants' tugged and pushed by a corps of cadres and completely powerless to resist the demands of the Party/state (see Chapter 1). This chapter will examine the evidence for such claims in the light of the history of Chinese political practice under the communists from the immediate post-1949 period, through the Hundred Flowers Campaign, the Cultural Revolution and the post-Mao protest movements from 1976 to the present, including the Tiananmen Movement of 1989. We will argue that the totalitarian discourse does not take into account the limitations on state power which arise as a result of the vastness of the country, poor communications, local interests and a system of *guanxi* which at times works against the grand projects of a centralized state. It also does not acknowledge the importance of the many forms of resistance that the Chinese people have employed in their interaction with the Party/state.

Political participation: The case against

Political participation is a contentious concept. It has been seen as unrealistic in the setting of the modern nation state – most people do not *want* to participate in political life, they do not understand the full implication of the various choices that political elites have to make, they do not have the time, and if they did participate they would probably get things wrong, and be manipulated by charismatic, populist leaders which might lead to a non-democratic society (Dahl, 1961; Almond and Verba, 1963; Huntington and Nelson, 1976; Schumpeter, 1947). The people, or the 'masses' (a word often used in the Chinese context), are thus characterized as ignorant, intolerant and irrational in comparison with the political elite which is educated, reasonable and trained to make difficult decisions judiciously (Lipset, 1960). A further criticism of the idea comes from Huntington (1968), who makes a point that is of particular relevance to our study of the Chinese political system. He argues that institutionalization of democratic processes is a prerequisite for inclusion of 'new social forces' into politics if participation is not to lead to 'political decay' and destabilization, and therefore prove a danger to the very system of democracy it seeks to promote and strengthen. This argument has been explicitly used by the present-day economic reformers in China who argue for a political space to implement economic policies unhindered by democratic critique.

Political participation: The case in favour

Arguably, the most potent defence of the concept of political participation is its resilience – despite the barrage of criticism, it continues to hold the imagination of the people. It would be difficult to argue against it with the students in Tiananmen Square in June 1989, or with the people on the streets of Berlin, Prague and Bucharest in the same year. Participation has also been defended as a normative value. From ancient Greeks to Rousseau, and Marx to Cole, social and political theorists have argued that individuals need to participate in civic life in order to distinguish between private and public interest. Further, it provides a yardstick by which to judge existing public political practices – transparency and efficacy of decision making and implementation of policies by public institutions. Political participation concerns itself with the right and ability of citizens to influence the direction of local and/or national policy and control policy-making bodies through various political processes and institutions – elections, recall, demonstrations, and activities of political parties.

Three levels of participation

We can identify three levels of participation (Pateman, 1970). People can be mobilized to participate in the public sphere by institutions that remain largely outside the effective control of those mobilized. Mobilization suggests *active* partipation – demonstrations, 'struggle meetings', rallies, sit-ins, mass meetings, etc. The Cultural Revolution was an example of mobilized participation. The second level of participation can be called licensed participation which 'allows a degree of open or thinly veiled negotiation or bargaining to take place between the regime and the group, and shifts the sole burden for success or failure of particular policies away from [the authority structures]' (Strand, 1989: 54–5) Such a process allows for only a critical elite to bargain with the incumbent leadership for particular demands. This is what we witness in the Hundred Flowers Campaign, and this is what perhaps Deng Xiaoping had in mind when he spoke in 1983 of 'political restructuring' of Chinese political institutions. The third level of participation is autonomous participation. It emphasizes the importance of individual opportunity to participate but also insists upon a civil space for groups of individuals that come together in interest-representing organizations. This is what most, though by no means all, of the post-Mao protest movements have demanded.

STRUCTURAL CONSTRAINTS ON POLITICAL PARTICIPATION IN CHINA

As we have seen in Chapter 1, demands for democratic participation were an important part of the political revolution that engaged Chinese elites. 'Mr. Science and Mr. Democracy' were political characters created in 1916, and came centre stage during the May Fourth Movement. They have been embedded in the imagination of the Chinese political elites. The call for their revival was made again and again by students and intellectuals, and yet the two never again came centre stage due to political structural constraints. Mobilization not participation was the dominant political *modus operandi* in Mao's China; the lack of institutional reform has frustrated the extension of a limited, licensed participation in Deng's China.

The individual, the *danwei* and the state

One of the most important organizing mechanisms of the Chinese communist political system in urban areas has been the tying of the individual to his or her work unit (*danwei*). The work unit caters for the social needs of its members, quite apart from the professional aspect of the production the unit might be engaged in (teaching in a school, making shoes in a shoe factory, etc.) (see Christiansen, 1994: 154). A network of *danwei*s constitute a *xitong* which is normally overseen by a ministry at the provincial and national level. The flow of resources network is organized vertically, and horizontal mobility levels are low. The dependence of individuals on the work unit is enhanced by this social welfare aspect, what Andrew Walder has called 'organised dependence' (Walder, 1986), together with the control of the local Party leadership over the *danwei*. The local leadership is able to use social benefits as incentives and disincentives that encourage 'clientelist' relations (Walder, 1986) on the one hand, and constrain individual political participation on the other. While the above discussion focuses on state power and its use of work units to organize mobilization of individuals, we must also examine the opportunities that this system provides for protection against, and subversion of, state power in China.

The loyalty and dependence that the *danwei* system creates is also a resource that is used by individuals against the local leadership, the local leadership against provincial leadership, and provincial leadership against national leadership. Writing on the rural *danwei* system (the commune administration), Vivienne Shue has called this network of subversion and protection the 'honeycomb polity' in which community solidarity insulates and protects the collective member from the state (Womack, 1991: 317). However, while the *danwei* provides the individual with a protective community, and opportunities for subversion of official policies, it also encloses the individual in a fragmented political system which is not conducive to participatory politics (Christiansen, 1994: 155). The slow dilution of this network of work units, as the economic reforms progress, will necessarily have an impact on the terms of organizational control available to the state, as will have the increased mobility of populations. However, despite policies of breaking lifelong job security associated with the *danwei* system, it is proving a resilient organizational pattern, hard to break. This fragmentation also hinders the growth of a civil society, which has been long associated with participatory politics.

Civil society and political reform

Civil society has been described as the sphere of voluntary, autonomous activity which takes place in the public sphere situated between the state and family. Associational activity is at the heart of the idea of civil society. As we shall see, starting in 1978, Chinese cities saw the mushrooming of various types of societies, associations and salons. Unofficial journals also began circulating, and private bookshops proliferated. Roadside cafes provided meeting points for the local population, as well as for the increasing migrant population crowding the cities. The introduction of economic reforms also introduced a new socio-economic actor on the Chinese political stage – the individual entrepreneur (*getihu*) who runs small businesses. The *getihu*, as a social stratum, are of increasing numerical significance. However, due to a political culture linked to the *danwei* system they are often forced to operate in a grey zone which is not fully regulated by legal provisions. They are therefore vulnerable to accusations of being 'illegal' and looked down upon by other groups in society. The growth of associational activity, and a market economy, led to expectations of the growth of civil society in China, facilitating the expansion of public space for political participation. However, is the language of civil society an appropriate language to assess the current Chinese political situation?

It has been pointed out that the term 'civil society' fails to capture the diversity of associations that have emerged in post-Mao China. These can be classified as official, semi-official, popular, and illegal, and at times straddle more than one category (Howell, 1995: 81). While official associations are obviously not autonomous of state controls, other legal associations, in most cases, are not also not independent of state control – they are officially registered, and their leaders are recruited from local elites embedded in the Party/state system. The resources at their disposal are small, which does not allow for efficient functioning (Christiansen, 1994: 157). We have commented on the dominance of the work units in the organization of public life in China. It has also been argued that the concept of civil society has a 'particular history in Western political thought, but this creates its own set of specific problems for studying China' (Howell, 1995: 81). These problems arise from the oppositional role that the civil society occupies in relation to the state in Western political theory, and from attributing the rise of civil society to the introduction of the market system. It is argued that neither attributions are relevant in the Chinese case, which cannot mirror the particular history of the rise of capitalism and the conflicts between social classes in Western Europe (Howell, 1995: 81–2). Finally, we can witness the growth of associational activity mainly in the cities; rural areas, while experiencing market reforms and the breaking up of the commune system, have not witnessed the growth of associations. Can we speak of civil society in China, when most of the country remains removed from associational politics?

Civil society is often regarded as oppositional to state power. Such placing situates the sphere of individual freedom in civil society, and characterizes the state as hostile to a public sphere. However, as we have argued elsewhere, such a positioning is indicative of a patriarchal liberalism which fails to take into account the fact that for many sections of society – women, and ethnic minorities for example – the social sphere is not a site of freedom, but a fraught space where freedom is not nurtured but attacked (Rai, 1994; Rai and Zhang 1994). In China, the reconstitution of social space was justified, among other reasons, by pointing to the way in which traditional society perpetuated women's exclusion and oppression. The state's attack upon that traditional social sphere, while by no means entirely liberating for women, did open up a significant new public space that was not available to them before. This is not to imply that the state is the creator of autonomous spaces for women (far from it), but to problematize the characterizing of civil society as a sphere of freedom.

Given the scepticism about the concept, is it useful to employ the term 'civil society' in the context of China? This is a difficult question to answer. If we accept that both the state and civil society are constantly negotiating (from different positions of power) their place in the polity with the various groups constituting society, then a sociological description of civil society allows us to chart the changes that might be taking place in the relations between the state and society in China. This is important because, while not mirroring the growth path of Western capitalism, China is witnessing largely state-initiated changes in its economic and social arrangements which are affecting the balance of power between the state and the rest of society. These changes, of necessity, create their own dynamics – some that are predictable, others that are not.

In order to deal with the new demands that arise within a changed economic and social climate, the state needs to respond institutionally as well as politically. The Chinese state has done this in particular, limited ways which have led to further responses and demands. The state has not been able to contain these demands within the institutionalized system of the Party/state, and so a limited sphere of autonomous social space has been created. In order that we can examine this newly created, gradually widening social space, 'civil society' can be a useful term to use.

In the next sections, we will examine the history of political participation in China and see how the theoretical issues discussed above translated into the Chinese political system and discourse.

POLITICAL PARTICIPATION AND MOBILIZATION IN THE MAOIST PERIOD

Mao's analysis of participation was formulated in terms of 'mass line' which we have discussed in Chapter 3. We saw that the two competing and unreconciled elements of Mao's analysis of participation remained the creativity of the masses on the one hand, and the importance of leaders on the other. While remaining consistently suspicious of the 'leaders', Mao could also never completely trust the 'masses'. This contradiction became evident during the two major political campaigns that Mao was associated with: the Hundred Flowers Campaign of 1956/1957, and the Great Proletarian Cultural Revolution of 1966–1969, both resulting in much confusion, and even tragedy.

Chinese politics under the CCP has been dominated by campaigns of one sort or another. The status and nature of the campaign is critically important to its resources. A campaign can be either a *yundong* or a *huodong*. A *yundong* has a special flavour in Chinese politics. It is a national-level campaign that has been officially endorsed by the dominant faction of the party. It is well resourced, and mass mobilization has been an important feature of all such campaigns. *Huodongs* are generally smaller campaigns and mainly concentrated in specific geographical areas (Rai and Zhang, 1994: 52). The two, however, share the characteristics of administrative practice: specialized work groups are given the task of going through a number of formalized steps eliciting participation from the target group though party-organized meetings.

The Hundred Flowers Campaign

'Let a hundred flowers bloom, let a hundred schools of thought contend' was the slogan that launched the *yundong* in 1956 that took its name from it. Mao and the Chinese Communist Party invited the intellectuals, artists, and managers of its economic enterprises to review the work of the communists in rebuilding China after the success of the revolution. It was an invitation that seemingly was accepting of a pluralist approach to China's development. It was an opportunity for China's intelligentsia to evaluate, criticize and make suggestions to those in power about the balance sheet of the communist programme between 1949 and 1956. But why did the CCP allow Mao to open this Pandora's Box? And why did Mao want such an open discussion of his and the Party's work? It does not make sense if we accept the totalitarian model of politics for China. Unless, like some, we construct an explanation for this movement solely in terms of a sinister plot laid by Mao to flush out the critics by inviting them to criticize the Party and then arresting them in the most cynical of ways. A loss of control at that scale, however temporary and devious, does not fit in with the paramount concern for control of a totalitarian state. Another explanation, perhaps more likely, lies in the tension between Mao's views as we have outlined above. Mao wanted the validation of the masses for what the Party was doing. The masses, as we saw in Chapter 3, were characterized, in the language of the United Front, as not only those belonging to the proletariat and the poor peasant class, but also to those of the petty and national bourgeoisie, and the middle peasants. The rationale behind the theory of the United Front also presupposed a unity of purpose – to make China great again – which was embedded in nationalism.

The background

As the response of the intelligentsia was to show during the campaign, this turned out to be a false presumption. The broad mass of the Chinese people might have supported the CCP during the war against Japan, but policies of the communists after the success of the revolution had gradually alienated the middle classes both in the countryside (with the increasing pace of collectivization) and in the urban areas, as pressures to conform ('re-education' campaigns) to communist agendas increased. We can witness these growing pressures in the campaigns to discredit various philosophers, artists and writers that were launched during the 1950s (Gray, 1990: 293–5). However, Mao's hope was for criticism to flow like 'a breeze or mild rain' rather than the storm that was unleashed during the campaign. This hope was tied to Mao's conviction that the leadership of the CCP was essential to the success of the nationalist and socialist project on which China was embarked. This was, however, not an unproblematic issue for Mao as his concern for the relationship between the masses and the leadership meant that the evaluation of the style of leadership was a constant theme in his political discourse.

It was not only his own convictions, however, that led him to seek better relations with the masses. International events too persuaded him to address this issue. In particular, the secret speech of Khrushchev and the support it got from a wide range of people within and outside the Soviet Union, and the revolt in Hungary against communist rule, convinced Mao that bridge building with the intelligentsia was essential for political stability and for economic development, especially with the launching of the First Five Year Plan in 1953. As usual, it was a complex set of reasons that prompted the launching of the Hundred Flowers Campaign – ideological, political and pragmatic.

On handling contradictions

Mao's speech 'On the Correct Handling of Contradictions Among the People' in 1957 (Mao [1957]) set out the theoretical ground for the campaign. Its core message was a clear and public departure from Stalinist dogma, perhaps made possible by the death of the Soviet leader and Khrushchev's stinging critique of the Stalinist period. In his speech Mao emphasized that even in a communist country, in its socialist stage, conflict of interests must arise, especially between the government and the people. Conflict was inevitable; the issue at stake was how to resolve it.

In his speech (Box 6.1) Mao made a distinction between two different types of contradictions that arose in society – antagonistic and non-antagonistic. The former embodied class conflict and could not be resolved in any way other than by the elimination of the 'enemy' – the comprador bourgeoisie or the landlord for example. Non-antagonistic contradictions, however, were contradictions among the people and must therefore be resolved through negotiation. While radical in formulation, Mao did not wish to challenge the authority of the Party. There was also a general suspicion among other leaders of the Party about opening up the political space to critics of the Party. Liu Shaoqi and Deng Xiaoping were among those leaders who wanted Mao to let well alone, and keep Party rectification an internal matter. As a result of all these political issues, negotiation as a process was not institutionalized within the political system but remained contingent upon the initiatives of the leadership to involve the masses. The same was true for negotiations between factions within the CCP. The recognition of fundamental disagreements that surfaced, during both the Hundred Flowers Campaign and the Cultural Revolution, did not lead to a discussion about the processes by which they might be articulated in the political sphere. The insistence upon the primacy of the political sphere on the one hand, and the unchallenged primacy of the Party in the political sphere, led to a strengthening of the position of the Party after both these movements (see Rai, 1991: Chapter 1).

The campaign

The campaign itself was brief, lasting from 1 May 1957 to 7 June 1957. The intellectuals were initially wary of this invitation to participate in a critique of the regime but soon joined in with enthusiasm and frankness that the Party had not expected. What persuaded them to participate was the fact that the Rectification Campaign launched in 1957 entitled the movement to 'rectify the style of work' within the Party. The idea of the *zheng-feng* Campaign, as it was

---

Box 6.1 *Extracts from Mao Zedong's speech 'On the Correct Handling of Contradictions Among the People',*
27 February 1957

The unification of our country, the unity of our people and the unity of various nationalities — these are the basic guarantees of the sure triumph of our cause. However this does not mean that contradictions no longer exist in our society. To imagine that none exist is a naive idea which is at variance with objective reality. We are confronted by two types of social contradictions — those between ourselves and the enemy, and those among the people themselves. The two are totally different in their nature ... The concept of 'the people' varies in content in different countries and in different periods of history in the same country ... The contradictions between ourselves and the enemy are antagonistic contradictions. Within the ranks of our people, the contradictions among the working people are non-antagonistic, while those between the exploited and the exploiting classes have a non-antagonistic aspect in addition to an antagonistic aspect ... there are still certain contradictions between the government and the people ... [and] are also contradictions among the people ... This democratic method of resolving contradictions among the people was epitomized in 1942 in the formula 'unity, criticism, unity' ... it means, starting from the desire for unity, resolving contradictions through criticism or struggle and arriving at a new basis. ... Today ... [the] large-scale and turbulent class struggles of the masses of the previous revolutionary periods have in the main ended, but class struggle is by no means entirely over ... the class struggle in the ideological field between the proletariat and the bourgeoisie will continue to be long and tortuous and at times will even become very acute. In this respect, the question of which will win out, socialism or capitalism, is still not really settled.

(Source: Mao [1957])

---

called, was to find out how the Party had misused its powers, through criticism by 'outsiders', after which the Party would reform its functioning. There was a second reason for the intellectuals participating in the campaign: the Confucian tradition whereby scholars were obliged to speak out, even against the emperor, whenever they saw misgovernment. This obligation, however, was limited, in that protest 'amounted to the creative reworking of the dominant moral order' (Pieke, 1995: 295) rather than its overthrow, and did not lead to the development of institutional pluralism.

Once the intellectuals and non-Party people decided to take up the gauntlet, criticism of the CCP's post-revolutionary record became severe. Speaking for the intellectuals, Lo Longqi pointed out, for example, that 'There are students of philosophy who work on the compilation of catalogues in libraries, students of law who take up book-keeping work in offices, students of dye chemistry who teach languages in middle schools and students of mechanical engineering who teach history in middle schools' (MacFarquhar, 1974a: 20). For the democratic parties that were tolerated constitutionally but made ineffective by the monopoly of power of the CCP, Zhang Boqun said, 'Inasmuch as democracy is to be developed, why stress the leadership of the Communist Party, why stress democratic centralism?' (MacFarquhar, 1974a: 21). While cautious, such criticisms of the CCP provoked a robust response from the Party fairly quickly, especially from the wing of the Party that had been initially sceptical of the entire project of 'blooming and contending'. First, this response was in the form of limiting the licence to participate. Deng Zhumin drew 'Four Circles' around the 'Contending Schools' as early as April 1957. These were that the contending schools must have: (1) leadership of Marxism–Leninism; (2) direction of socialism; (3) a boundary that allows only 'people' and not 'enemies' to take part; and (4) a criterion of practice (MacFarquar 1974a: 29).

As the sense of unease with the movement grew at pace with the strengthening of the criticisms of the CCP, Liu Shaoqi evoked a scenario of chaos and loss of leadership by the Party: 'The universities . . . are already on the move. If the worker masses, the teachers from . . . schools, and other mass organizations also start mobilizing then we won't be able to stand our ground . . . If we don't control things, then in a jiffy millions of people will be on the move and then we won't be able to do anything . . .' (MacFarquhar, 1974b: 221). While we might think that conservative elements in the Party sought to cajole its members into withdrawing the licence of participation from the masses, Liu's predictions did seem to come true during the Cultural Revolution. At the heart of the dilemma before the Party was the question of institutionalization of political participation – and this remained unresolved as the Party swung behind the conservatives to launch an Anti-Rightist Campaign to curb further criticism of the CCP. By not addressing this dilemma Mao was unable to give a lead in developing a 'third way' socialism that he might otherwise have been able to; it also weakened his position within the Party, leading to his acquiescence to the savage counter-attack of the Anti-Rightist Campaign upon the critical intelligentsia. The 'fragrant flowers' of the campaign turned into 'poisonous weeds' by the end of July 1957. Problems of agricultural production, and a concerted attempt by the moderates within the Party, produced a compromise between the warring factions of Mao and Liu, papering over the divisions within the Party which were to emerge yet again in the 1958–1960 Great Leap Forward initiative, and, of course, during the Cultural Revolution. The intellectuals felt betrayed and let down, though this did not stop them from making another attempt at reforming from within in the period after Mao's death in 1976. But before that period they had to live through arguably the bleakest period of their lives in communist China – the Cultural Revolution.

THE GREAT PROLETARIAN CULTURAL REVOLUTION

'More than the sum of its parts' would perhaps be an accurate description of any revolution, and so it is of the Cultural Revolution which Mao launched and directed (insofar as he could) between the years 1966 and 1969. It is, however, a whole decade that is labelled under this term in the official CCP historiography – 1966 until 1976, when Mao died. The Cultural Revolution has come to symbolize many different (even opposing) political values and processes during and after this decade. It has marked China, its people, its leadership, its images, and its policies profoundly. This movement tells a continuing story of a tension within Maoist political discourse about participation. The Cultural Revolution was perhaps the biggest mobilizational movement that the world has witnessed. It was a movement in the name of the 'masses' – a movement to empower them; it did not achieve this. It was a movement that set out to 'purify' China of 'revisionism' by debureaucratizing its revolutionary system; this failed because the first was definitionally impossible, the second not feasible in the context of a one-party rule and a command economy. In essense it was an 'idealistic' movement – as such, scripted for failure. Its strength lay in the questions it raised about political practice in socialist states; its fundamental weakness was its inability to resolve the issue of political participation.

The context

The Tenth Plenum of the CCP's Eighth Central Committee, held in September 1962, signalled the start of the Cultural Revolution.

It has been suggested that the elements that Mao put together to make up the heady cocktail of the Cultural Revolution were the following: nationalism that took the form of a belief in the unique contribution that the Chinese people and revolution could make to world (revolutionary) history; a struggle for power to consolidate his position within the Party after the bruising it had got by the withdrawal of the Hundred Flowers Campaign in 1957 and the failure of the Great Leap Forward in 1959; and finally, a need to implement policies that Mao thought were best suited to Chinese conditions and goals (Schram, 1973: Chapter 1). China's uniqueness took the form, during this period, of a critique of the Soviet Union (discussed at length in Chapter 9). Mao insisted that the Soviet leadership had betrayed the goals of the Russian Revolution by not challenging the growing power of the elites and the institutionalization of privilege leading to the development of a new class of bureaucrats who were not in touch with the masses. This, of course, was not a new criticism – the Yugoslav dissident Milovan Djilas had already written about the 'New Class' that had emerged in the Soviet bloc countries. The startling difference in Mao's call to the Chinese youth to 'Bombard the Headquarters' of the CCP was that he was the head of the Party he was attacking. Mao's presumption was that the CCP could be reformed from within through a 'continuous revolution' in the ideological sphere carried out by the masses, especially the working classes and the poor peasants. This was a time of ideological class conflict where non-antagonistic contradictions became antagonistic in order to stop China sliding down the 'revisionist' road along which the Soviet Union was progressing. The Cultural Revolution finally destroyed any sense of unity in China and divided the society into 'masses' and 'enemies', completely reversing the political compromise framed by New Democracy.

Why and how this happened, and what role political mobilization played in this reversal of political policies is the substance of the next section.

Campaigns and mobilizations

The first educational initiative of the Cultural Revolution came soon after Mao's speech to the Tenth Plenum, in the form of the Socialist Education Movement (Box 6.2). Corrupt rural cadres were criticized or dismissed, 'spontaneous capitalist tendencies' in agriculture came under attack and a new institution was established called the Poor and Lower Middle Peasants Association. In the cities, a campaign for the 'class education of youth' was launched and the role of the PLA as an ideological model made prominent through the 'Learn from Comrade Lei Feng' campaign in 1963, and the 'Learn from the PLA' campaign in 1964 (for more on this see Chapter 10). In the same year Mao made an attack upon the cultural establishment, accusing them of 'revisionism' and pointing to the need for a 'rectification campaign on the front of art and literature'.

The launching of the Cultural Revolution in May 1966 faced opposition from within the Party itself. The Central Committee was wary of Mao's radicalism disturbing the fragile economic and political stability achieved after the upheavals of the Hundred Flowers Campaign and the Great Leap Forward. Knowing this, Mao decided to force the issue on the Party leadership instead of trying to build a consensus around the need to change China's direction. He left Beijing and went to Shanghai, where a younger and more radical provincial leadership was eager to do his bidding. Yao Wenyuan, one of the Shanghai radicals, then wrote an article criticizing the play *Hai Rui Dismissed From Office* written by Wu Han (Deputy Mayor of Beijing and one of the 'moderates'). The play was said to attack Mao; Yao's article was a warning to 'revisionists' within the Party that they could not afford to oppose Mao. Mao also mobilized support within the PLA through Lin Biao (who was at first to be officially named as Mao's heir at the end of the Cultural Revolution, but was later found guilty of plotting to assassinate Mao). In July 1966 Mao swam the Yangtze River to indicate that he was 'fighting fit' and not a political pushover, and gave his blessing to the formation of youth groups who called themselves the Red Guards. This reaching over the head of the Central Committee to mobilize support among the 'masses' and the army was unprecedented in Chinese communist history and violated all political norms associated with 'democratic centralism' (see Chapter 5).

Box 6.2 *Chronology of events: the Cultural Revolution*

24–27 September 1962	The Tenth Plenum of the Eighth Party Congress at which Mao makes a speech 'Never Forget Class Struggle'
2 May 1963	'Learn from Comrade Lei Feng' campaign is launched with Mao's instructions published in *Chinese Youth*
20 May 1963	The Socialist Educational Campaign in the countryside
14 July 1964	Mao's 'On Khrushchev's Phoney Communism and its Historical Lessons for the World' is published
10 November 1965	Yao Wenyuan (one of the 'Gang of Four') publishes an article attacking a play by Wu Han (Deputy Mayor of Beijing) called *Hai Rui Dismissed from Office*
18 April 1966	*Liberation Army Daily* calls for the launch of the 'great socialist cultural revolution'
16 May 1966	The Politburo sets up Cultural Revolution Group under its Standing Committee
16 July 1966	Mao swims the Yangtze River
1–12 August 1966	Eleventh Plenum of the Eighth Central Committee issues the Sixteen Points Decision
5 August 1966	Mao's poster 'Bombard the Headquarters' is published
6 August 1966	Central Committee issues a 16 point directive to guide the Cultural Revolution
18 August 1966	Mass Cultural Revolution rally at Tiananmen, at which the Red Guards appears for the first time
September 1966	Publication of the *Little Red Book*, the Thoughts of Mao Zedong (Mao, 1972)
23 October 1966	Liu Shaoqi and Deng Xiaoping produce self-criticisms
January 1967	The 'January Revolution', when radicals organize the seizure of power in Shanghai
5 February 1967	Shanghai People's Commune is created briefly
April 1967	Serious violence mounts
1 September 1967	Zhou Enlai orders all Red Guards to return home, abjure violence and cease attacks on foreign embassies
27 July 1968	Worker–Peasant–Mao-Zedong-Thought Teams sent into Qinghua University

Continued over

Box 6.2   *Continued*

14 October 1968	Central Committee orders resumption of classes at all levels of education
13–31 October 1968	Enlarged Twelfth Plenum of the Eighth Central Committee adopts a new Party Constitution (see Chapter 5)
31 October 1968	Liu Shaoqi is expelled from the Party and dismissed from all posts
1–4 April 1969	Ninth National Congress of the Communist Party produces a new Party Constitution with Mao-Zedong-Thought as the theoretical basis

---

We have seen that the dominant faction within the CCP, led by Liu Shaoqi, was reluctant to allow the Party to be criticized by non-Party members during the Hundred Flowers Campaign. This faction wanted to keep a tight organizational control over policy making and implementation, with Party cadres as the main instrument of persuasion and control of local populations. Mao on the other hand felt that the two organizational elements of Leninist party functioning – democracy and centralism – could go hand in hand, as is evident from his conceptualization of 'mass line' politics. It was this difference in approach to resolving political differences in China which was at the heart of the Cultural Revolution.

The Sixteen Points Decision, reached by the Central Committee during the Eleventh Plenum of the Eighth Central Committee in August 1966, emphasized that the Cultural Revolution was a movement to 'mobilize the masses without restraint' in order that the masses get the opportunity to 'educate themselves'. They would do this by attacking the 'Four Olds': old ideas, old culture, old customs and old habits. Included in 'old ideas and culture' were the ideas of feudalism and capitalism that were undermining the purity of socialism by taking the form of 'revisionism'. Revisionism became a catch-all phrase indicating a tendency within the CCP itself whereby the cadres, under the influence of the Soviet Union and the Communist Party of the Soviet Union (CPSU), were becoming alienated from the masses, selfish, privileged and corrupt. Their education by the masses was a second theme of the Cultural Revolution. The revisionist cadres within the CCP were supported by a growing intellectual elite outside the Party which gave a privileged position to 'expertise' in comparison with the 'revolutionary enthusiasm' of the masses. 'Red versus Expert' thus became a third strand of ideological difference exposed during the Cultural Revolution.

The issues

The major issues that gained prominence during the Cultural Revolution were the following:

- the importance of the political organization, especially of class, in social organization;
- the accountability of Party cadres to the masses through the implementation of mass-line politics;
- decentralization of management in both economic and political organization; and
- the politicization of education and cultural production as a means of 'thought reform' essential to counter 'revisionist' tendencies in social and political life.

These broad directional issues translated very unevenly into policies. The centring of class in political life not only broke with the politics of the United Front, it also created a culture of 'labelling' which tore the social and political fabric of China apart. It also created a contradiction within the logic of the Cultural Revolution. On the one hand, the emphasis placed on class meant that the economic position of people, and even their families (sometimes going back three generations), came to determine their politics; an assumption was made that linked people's ideology with their actual economic position. On the other hand, education and culture were mobilized in the interest of 'thought reform', suggesting that through this process anyone could acquire 'correct ideas' and then presumably rise above the political constraints imposed upon them by their class.

A second theme linked to underscoring the importance of the political organization was the strength of mass mobilization as a strategy of organization. This echoed the guerrilla tactics pursued by the CCP during the revolutionary war. It was political will not better equipment and arms that would win the war for the communists. Similarly, it was mass action/education that would make China a world economic and military power, not elitist-led scientific production. Industrial and agricultural organizations were both affected by this understanding of the value of people's participation. Mechanization of agriculture and the whole labour-incentive system were reorganized in line with this political position. Individual incentives were to be replaced by collective incentives; both agricultural and industrial management were reorganized by introducing 'three-in-one (peasant/worker–PLA–party cadre) revolutionary committees' that would replace the one-person management system currently in place. Decentralization thus became another issue for debate during the Cultural Revolution (Box 6.3).

Box 6.3 *The main political characters of the Cultural Revolution*

Mao Zedong   Chairman of the CCP, the 'Great Helmsman' and the initiator of the Cultural Revolution.

Liu Shaoqi   President of the People's Republic of China, 'China's Khrushchev', and the main target of the Red Guards, and of Mao's attempt to dislodge the 'organizational wing' of the Party under Liu's leadership.

Zhou Enlai   Premier and close confidant of Mao; a moderate by instinct who tried to curb the worst excesses, not always successfully.

Lin Biao   A veteran of the revolutionary period and the Long March, Lin became the exponent of the concept of 'People's War' during the Cultural Revolution years; he was mandated constitutionally to succeed Mao in 1969, but fell from grace in 1971 and died fleeing to the Soviet Union in that year.

Cultural Revolution Small Group (or 'The Gang of Four' as they were called in 1978)   This sobriquet became prominent after Mao's death. The group was composed of the four most prominent radicals of the Cultural Revolution, with their power base in Shanghai. Headed by Jiang Qing, Mao's wife, it included the former Shanghai cultural affairs official Zhang Chunqiao, former editor Yao Wenyuan, and former labour organizer Wang Hongwen.

Deng Xiaoping   Long March veteran, he came to be called the 'number two person (after Liu Shaoqi) in authority taking the capitalist road' during the Cultural Revolution. Dismissed from his office three times, Deng returned in 1977 to take the leading position in the CCP and take China down the road to the 'Four Modernizations'.

The ninth stinking category: Intellectuals in trouble

Intellectuals were particularly affected by the emphasis on class and the importance of the political organization. 'Cultural intellectuals' were not engaged in direct production like the scientists and engineers, and were therefore vulnerable to political pressure by the Party, which was conscious of their crucial role in transmitting ideas and attitudes to the younger generation. Further, as experts they were in a position of privilege within the Chinese society which, together with the elitist nature of 'cultural production' in which they were engaged, made them very vulnerable indeed to initiatives of 'thought reform' during the Cultural Revolution. As schools and colleges closed, and the Cultural Revolution gathered momentum, the intellectuals suffered greatly. Thousands were the targets of 'mass criticism' by their students, colleagues and the 'people'; thousands were labelled as 'revisionists', 'capitalist roaders', and 'the ninth stinking category' of the Chinese society; thousands were sent down to the countryside under the *xiafang* policy to 'learn from the peasants'. They were harassed and harried and many committed suicide. (For a vivid account of the life of an 'intellectual family' during the Cultural Revolution, see Dai, 1987.)

A whole generation of intellectuals was lost – either by an interrupted education, or by the alienation fostered by such treatment between the intellectuals and the Party. However, very often the results of these extreme policies pursued against the intellectuals obscure the fact that several thousands of young people who would never have had a chance to get higher education were drawn into the system of education during this period. This was done through a policy of recommendation whereby revolutionary committees would put forward to universities names of young people selected on the basis of their 'correct political attitude' and their working class/poor peasant background. While, inevitably, such a system soon spawned corruption, the issue of decentralization of educational privilege was an important one.

The form that the Cultural Revolution took, however, with its mass mobilizations, its dogmatism and its increasingly internecine power struggles, overshadowed all issues of substance. The growing splits within the ranks of the Red Guards into Centre, Left and Ultra-Left led to growing violence that, in 1967, threatened to bring down the whole edifice of the state (for an account of the progression of the Cultural Revolution on the Qinghua University campus in Beijing, read Hinton, 1972b). The Red Guards also displayed a 'self-centredness' which allowed no compromise among the various groups on the Left, and Mao increasingly felt that they were getting out of control. Therefore, in the summer of 1968 the PLA was asked to restore order in the country. Millions of Red Guards were sent to the countryside, university campuses were 'retaken' from the control of the Red Guards, schools were reopened and a semblance of order soon restored. The Red Guard phase of the Cultural Revolution was at an end by 1969 with the Ninth Party Congress of the CCP in April that year enthroning Lin Biao as Mao's successor, and Mao-Zedong-Thought as the basis of party ideology, together with Marxism–Leninism (see Chapter 5).

The Cultural Revolution had been launched with the hope that a new China would be born out of the destruction of the revisionist China that the Red Guards had attacked. This hope was belied. The reasons were many, but perhaps the foremost of them was that the Cultural Revolution broke the consensus within the country that had been built with such painstaking care by the Chinese leadership, Mao included. Contradictions that were non-antagonistic, even according to Mao's own definitions, were turned into antagonistic contradiction, the resolution of which could only be through the destruction of opposition. Opposition itself was identified and demonized everywhere, at every level. No institution – social, economic or political – remained safe from attack. Millions of people suffered, especially in the cities. A whole generation lost out on education, and, worse, on legitimacy, leading to tensions between the Cultural Revolution generations and those who saw themselves as the children of reform (see Rai, 1991: 140–8).

The Cultural Revolution did not result in much that was positive. Challenging privilege, authority and hierarchy had been one of the key themes of the Cultural Revolution. However, in the end it was the army that restored order; the Party, position, structure and functioning remained unchanged; the personality cult of Mao defied belief and created an unchallenged source of authority, and spawned a dogmatism that was a far cry from Mao's encouragement to the Red Guards (Box 6.4) to 'doubt everything' at the start of the Cultural Revolution.

Box 6.4   *Some slogans from the Cultural Revolution*

Sailing the seas depends on the helmsman, the growth of everything depends on the sun, and making revolution depends on Mao Zedong's Thought.

We face a mountain of swords and a sea of flames, but we also have a bright beacon light – Mao Zedong's Thought which will surely guide us to victory.

Revolutionary spirit of Peking's Red Guards, the spirit of daring to think, to speak out, to act, to break through and to make revolution so that all of China will be set ablaze by the revolutionary flame of Mao Zedong's Thought.

Chairman Mao has said: 'In the last analysis, all the truths of Marxism can be summed up in one sentence: "To rebel is justified"'.

The Golden Monkey wrathfully swung his massive cudgel,
And the jade-like firmament was cleared of dust.

(Source: Anon, 1966)

Indeed, Mao said at the end of the Cultural Revolution:

> The slogan of 'doubt everything and overthrow everything' is reactionary. The Shanghai People's Council demanded that the Premier of the State Council should do away with all heads. This is extreme anarchism, it is most reactionary . . . In reality there will still always be 'heads'. (Schram, 1973: 95)

The tension within the Maoist approach to political participation – between the creative energies of the masses and the need to hold cadres accountable, and an acceptance of the Leninist position on the structure and functioning of a revolutionary organization – meant that when the dust settled on the mobilizational politics of the Cultural Revolution, the CCP and the army emerged strengthened in their positions. This strengthening of the traditional institutions of power was rendered more potent because of the attack upon organizations which represented non-class-based interests during the Cultural Revolution. The All-China Women's Federation, for example, was not allowed to function during this period. Even allowing for the fact that this organization was functioning within the limits imposed on it by the CCP, it was deemed as distracting from the resolution of the 'main contradiction' – the class contradiction in Chinese society.

POST-MAO POLITICS: FROM MOBILIZATION TO MANAGEMENT?

With Mao's death on 6 September 1976, the question of succession became important. The Radicals, united under the leadership of Mao's wife Jiang Qing, were pitted against the Moderates, led by a group that Zhou Enlai had helped put together in 1974/1975 before he died in January 1976. The Radicals lost and for a short time it seemed that China would return to traditional socialist politics under the leadership of Mao's successor, Hua Guofeng. However, Hua soon gave over to the emerging strength of the 'modernizers' within the Party, and by 1980 the balance of power had shifted fundamentally away from old-style socialist cadres to this group under the protection of Deng Xiaoping.

'Political restructuring' and licensed participation

The new leadership rejected the mobilizational and personalized politics of the Maoist period in favour of one more geared towards institutionalized control to promote a new consensus that would support the grand project of the Four Modernizations which included the modernization of agriculture, industry, science and technology, and defence (see Chapter 10). Deng's starting point was a redefinition of key concepts which had been in circulation in the Chinese public sphere for a long time – politics, ideology, class, class struggle, egalitarianism, mass line and Mao-Zedong-Thought. This was essential for constructing a new basis of legitimacy for the CCP after the internecine warfare between factions during the Cultural Revolution. Deng identified the problems facing the post-Mao Chinese political system in terms of 'bureaucracy, over-concentration of power, patriarchal methods, life tenure in leading posts and privileges of various kinds' (Deng, 1984b: 309). To tackle these problems Deng proposed a programme of 'political restructuring' which included an attempt to disentangle the Party from the state institutions. This was to be tried at the grassroots level first, leaving the central Party leadership unchallenged while the local-level Party committees were to be opened up to criticism by the people. The people themselves were no longer targets of mobilization but were to be 'persuaded' and 'educated' in the new agendas and policies of the Party. This process was to be carried out by, first, acknowledging the existence of differentiated, generally professional interests that were not simply based on class, and, second, by regulating the various organizations that represented these. It is interesting to note here that though some professional groups were allowed to form associations, these were built around the area of expertise shared by the members and not their positions in the processes of production. At the same time the Party leadership set out the 'Four Cardinal Principles' (Box 6.5) with the leadership of the CCP as the fundamental political tenet (Rai, 1991: 16–29).

Box 6.5   *The Four Cardinal Principles*

The Central Committee maintains that to carry out China's four modernizations, we must uphold the four cardinal principles ideologically and politically. The four principles are:

1. We must keep to the socialist road.
2. We must uphold the dictatorship of the proletariat.
3. We must uphold the leadership of the Communist Party.
4. We must uphold Marxism, Leninism, and Mao Zedong Thought.

(Source: Deng, 1984c: 172)

The concept of New Authoritarianism emerged in the Chinese political discourse, formulated by state-sponsored political 'think tanks'.

New Authoritarianism

New Authoritarianism drew its theoretical inspiration from the work of Samuel Huntington, and empirical evidence from the experience of the newly industrialized economies of Singapore, Hong Kong, Taiwan and South Korea. The intellectuals promoting this concept – Zhang Bingjiu, Xiao Gongqing and Wang Juntao – pointed out that China 'does not have a tradition in the rule of law, is economically backward, has an undereducated populace, and lacks the prerequisites for entry into the developmental stage where economic freedom and political autocracy achieve a balance'. What was needed for China was to use authority to 'smash obstacles that block the development of individual freedom in order to protect individual freedom'. Two distinctions were thus made – between economic and political freedom, and between individual freedom and democracy. Like the Deng leadership, this group of intellectuals gave primacy to economic modernization, and also to individual freedom which was equated with the freedom of economic entrepreneurship. A case was made therefore for a strong state that would work with an intellectual elite to chart the course of China's economic modernization. The 'New Authoritarian' stage would be transitional, and lead slowly but surely to the next stage of full representative democracy. There was in this analysis an implicit rejection of class politics in regarding economic modernization as an 'objective' goal to be achieved through the merging of a strong state/Party and the technological intelligentsia. Thus, the pattern of political practice espoused by the post-Mao leadership tried to combine organizational, licensed participation with an unchallenged position of primacy in the political sphere for the Party.

The response to 'political restructuring'

After the betrayals of the Hundred Flowers Campaign, and the traumas of the Cultural Revolution, the intellectuals were again asked to engage in political debate with the Party leadership. The licence to participate, which had been taken away during the Cultural Revolution, had been renewed.

The intellectuals responded in three different ways. The first, the 'New Authoritarian' response has been discussed above. The second response, which became influential in the late 1970s and early 1980s, but has been increasingly marginalized in Chinese political debate, maintained its link with socialist ideology. Su Shaozhi, Wang Ruoshui and Su Ming were representatives of this response and called themselves socialist humanists. This group was influenced by the Frankfurt School of Marxism, and took issue with the Chinese regime on two counts. First, they insisted that modernization is a broader concept than the Four Modernizations; it must include social and cultural modernization. Second, they claimed that China needed a socialist system, but one that was 'humanistic' and whose starting point was the freedom of the individual. However, while these critics urged a re-evaluation of Marxism, they were unable to bring together the socialist concern with equality and the political impulse towards greater participation.

The third response, that was most dramatically translated into the events that led to the Tiananmen Square Incident in 1989, was from a group of radical liberal democrats who presented themselves as the real 'political modernizers' of China. Yan Jiaqi, Fang Lizhi, Wang Ruowang and Sun Liping were the foremost members of this group. Influenced by Western liberalism attracted to representative democracy, this group demanded that the leadership, and indeed the country, learn the lessons of modern Chinese history. Leaders were fallible, 'good cadres' turned bad all too often, and therefore structures and conventions, rules and regulations were needed to keep their power in check and ensure that a change in leadership could be brought about if and when needed. Rule of law was needed to protect individuals against a malfunctioning authority which could be either individual like Mao, or it could be organizational like the CCP. A 'political responsibility system' must complement the economic reforms; accountability must be placed at the heart of the political system. Mobilized and licensed participation were both under attack; the alternative suggested was 'constitution writing' and 'direct and free elections'. However, these intellectuals seemed unable to get away from an inherently instrumentalist approach to democracy. Increased participation was a corrective for existing ills, not a value in itself. They were also elitist, giving to the technical and cultural intelligentsia a position of authority which stemmed from a constructed notion of 'truth' that could be reached through a 'scientific method' and not majority opinion (Nathan, 1990). It was this strand of democratic thinking that became immensely influential in the 1980s, especially among young people. It inspired a whole generation of students and young people to become politically active. This political activism revealed the limitations of licensed participation as a strategy of political management.

THE LIMITS OF LICENSED PARTICIPATION: THE DEMOCRACY MOVEMENT

The winter of 1978 witnessed a spontaneous emergence of what is loosely called the Democracy Movement in several of China's major cities. Beijing was at the centre of this Movement that tried to articulate the many different responses to the politics of the Cultural Revolution. These responses came in the form of literary contributions, political comment and associational activity. All these three forms have now become part of the Chinese political culture on the margins and provide us with important indicators of the terms on which the Chinese state is licensing participation in China.

The Democracy Wall Movement

The Democracy Wall Movement followed on from the Qingming or April Fifth Movement of 1976, which saw hundreds of people take advantage of the Chinese festival of honouring the dead to pay their respects to Zhou Enlai. This was seen by the radical wing of the Party as a critique of the Cultural Revolution, as Zhou was a well-known moderate and had opposed the later excesses of that movement. The Deng leadership, on the other hand, recognized the Qingming Movement as a 'revolutionary' movement. The Democracy Wall Movement had its origins, in part, in the political space provided by the struggle for power between Hua Guofeng and Deng Xiaoping in November 1978. While Hua tried to build on the mandate of Mao, Deng sought to move the political agenda away from the ideological dogmatism of the Cultural Revolution years. 'Practice' and not ideology was emphasized by Deng, and, in a context where ideology had wreaked such havoc in society, the Chinese people welcomed this change of emphasis. The Party machinery was demoralized at this time, with few clear guidelines to work to, the policy units were in flux and there was a sense of a momentary political vacuum with relaxed controls over grassroots organizations. There is also the view that the 'practice faction' of Deng encouraged the critique provided by the 'democrats' of the Mao years to put the 'bureaucratic

Left' headed by Hua under added pressure. Whatever the conjunction of events, the Democracy Wall in Beijing became the focus of attention for people from all walks of life who wanted to express an opinion about the state of the Chinese political system.

On 19 November a political stir was caused when a wall-poster (*dazibao*) claiming that Mao had made mistakes in his later years was posted on a wall (soon to be called the Democracy Wall) near the official residences of the Chinese leadership, a whole series of posters followed expressing criticism either of individual Party leaders, or of particular aspects of the Cultural Revolution. Citizens of Beijing soon began to gather around the wall to discuss the posters, and to listen to an increasing number of speeches by poster-writers and others. The wall also became the venue of distribution of new journals that emerged during this period, the most prominent being *Enlightenment*, *April 5th Forum*, *Beijing Spring* and *Exploration*. In the course of the next few years several hundred journals emerged, creating a focus for associational activity of a new kind. Most of the writing of this time (see Chen, 1984, for example) remained within the broad Marxist framework. There were, however, prominent exceptions like the writing of Wei Jingsheng which was strongly pro-Western liberalism. While not fundamentally rejecting the socialist system, such journals soon became irritants for the new CCP leadership that emerged strengthened from the Third Plenum of the Eleventh Party Congress in December 1978.

This was because these journals were going beyond the officially sanctioned and tolerated criticism of the Party and its officials, and were airing the concerns of not simply a few intellectuals but a range of oppositional groups. These included the large number of peasants who began arriving in Beijing to petition the authorities about the conduct of rural Party cadres during the Cultural Revolution, and the large numbers of *xiafang* (sent down) school leavers. They protested that the local bureaucrats were not letting them return to their home towns and cities, despite an official policy which was passed in December 1978 at the Third Plenum and allowed the *xiafang qingnian* to return. The 1979 war with Vietnam, in which the PLA forces did much worse than anticipated, also produced a pressure within the Party to restore 'unity and stability'. By April 1979 a number of writers and activists were arrested, the most prominent being Wei Jingsheng, who was sentenced to 15 years' imprisonment in October 1979; the Democracy Wall was closed down later in the same month. The activists, however, persisted in their attempts at keeping the movement alive until 1981 through participation in the National People's Congress elections, which the Electoral Law of 1980 had thrown open to individuals and China's eight 'democratic parties' (see Chapter 5). By early 1980 most unofficial journals had been forced to close down, though some continued to publish. In 1981 an official campaign was launched against 'ultra-democracy' and 'anti-party and anti-socialist activities', which then broadened into the 'anti-bourgeois liberalization campaign' of 1981. In the 1983 Constitution, wall-posters were no longer an accepted form of public expression of individual opinion.

The Democracy Wall Movement is important for several reasons. It was the first of a succession of attempts by the Party and the 'masses' to renegotiate the licence for public participation. It set the pattern for expression of views by citizens in the public sphere which was very much part of the communist tradition – after all the Cultural Revolution started with the putting up of posters. It also introduced new elements into Chinese public life with the proliferation of journals, and, throughout the 1980s, many informal associations. But perhaps most importantly, its significance remains symbolic – after the oppressiveness of the Cultural Revolution years, it pointed to a thaw in political dogma, and indicated to the Chinese people, and the world at large, that change was afoot in post-Mao China.

The 1980s: A march to Tiananmen Square?

When the Democracy Movement re-emerged, first in 1985 and more openly in 1986/1987, it took on a different character to that of the Democracy Wall Movement. This was primarily due to two reasons. First, during this period the economic reforms introduced by Deng Xiaoping had taken off. The early to mid-1980s were a time of economic growth, and optimism about the new leadership. Second, the agenda of economic modernization had led to strenuous attempts by the leadership to woo the Chinese intellectuals. However, this wooing yielded only partial results for the CCP. With the economic reforms came the pressures of competition in the market, a squeezing of student grants, rising prices, for the first time a fear of unemployment for China's young people, and the 'open door policy' which allowed an exchange of ideas and heightened expectations that could not realistically be met. The context in which the Democracy Movement of the 1980s matured was thus completely different from that of which the Democracy Wall Movement was a product. Thus, while the disadvantaged, and the exiled youth of the Cultural Revolution had formed the vanguard of the 1979 movement, by 1989 it was university students, one of the most privileged sections of the the Chinese population, who carried the banners.

During the 1980s the intellectuals gradually became disenchanted with the Deng leadership. One of the articles in the Hong Kong journal *Chengming* pointed out 'five insufficiencies' in the reform programme: a lack of theoretical preparation, the lag between economic and political reform, a rigid policy-making pattern, an inability to keep up popular support for the reform, and a lack of honest self-appraisal (April 1989). As the self-confidence of the intellectuals grew, the Party became alarmed. By 1989 cracks began to appear in the alliance that had been made between the intellectuals and the Party in the early 1980s. There were several factors that contributed to this break – the reforms in the higher education system resulted in unforeseen contradictions emerging between various groups of intellectuals based on generational differences, competition for promotions, etc., and between the intellectuals and the local Party bosses on questions regarding the proposed withdrawal of the Party from the academic decision making in the university. The rhetoric of 'political restructuring' generated exaggerated expectations which, when not entirely met, resulted in friction. The acknowledgement by Deng and other Party leaders of the importance of the intellectuals to economic modernization gave this group tremendous bargaining power which it used to press its case for greater independence; and the self-perception of the intellectuals as the rational voice in a Chinese political system which needed extensive reworking.

This period of growing disaffection led to student demonstrations. In the spring of 1985 the first round of student demonstrations was organized leading to the Party's call to fight 'bourgeois liberalism'. In December 1986, students of the Science and Technology University in Hefei, where Professor Fang Lizhi – one of the most prominent oppositional voices in the growing democracy movement – was based, demonstrated. Soon, over 150 campuses in at least 17 cities saw students organizing demonstrations. Beijing emerged as the centre of student protest. While the official students' organizations – the Students' Unions and the Communist Youth Leagues – did not participate in these demonstrations, it was obvious during 1986/1987 that various autonomous student groups were involved and were 'linking up' with each other and forming an efficient network for the dissemination of information. Technology helped the students too – faxes and inter-city telephone facilities were used to relay information to dispersed groups.

The demands put forward by students in their demonstrations were minimal, and within the boundaries that the Deng leadership had drawn. The demands were related to both the immediate concerns of the students – the quality of food served in university canteens, the time at which lights were put out in dormitories, etc. – and concerns about the reforms in the country. The students urged the reformers within the Party to accelerate the pace of reforms, to extend and strengthen representative institutions, particularly the National People's Congress, and to allow a greater freedom of expression and press. The rhetoric of the students was liberal – the emphasis was on individual identity and freedom, on legal rights of individuals against the state, and for a non-Marxist usage of the concepts of democracy and freedom. The response of the Party reflected the strains under which it was functioning. On the one hand, Hu Yaobang, one of the prominent reformers of the CCP was sacrificed to appease the more hardline group in the Party. On the other, it was also made clear that the partnership between the intellectuals and the state would continue. This was also a period when the Democracy Movement remained largely a campus movement; the demonstrators neither wished nor attempted to 'link up' with other social groups. In such circumstances it was easy for the Party not to revoke the licence to participate, while at the same time sounding warnings that it might.

The Tiananmen Square Movement

The foreign and dissident critique of the events of 4 June 1989 has focused on the violation of human rights by the Chinese regime, and suggested that the CCP cannot reform itself while it retains the monopoly of power. Images of a totalitarian regime suppressing the Chinese people have been employed to make fresh attacks upon the political system still officially tied to the ideology of Marxism–Leninism. While the violation of human rights witnessed on June Fourth was clearly evident, we need to explain the reasons why the Deng leadership seemingly jeopardized the reforms it had itself initiated. Our study of political participation may give us some clues.

We have examined the various responses to the Party/state's offer of a renewal of political licence to the intellectuals. Those who engaged in the debates about democratization of the Chinese political system, however, were a minority even among the intellectuals. The majority of intellectuals were concerned with more immediate problems – price rises and deteriorating conditions of living as fixed incomes were eroded by inflation. The same could be said of the students who worried about making ends meet and securing good jobs. However, the conjunction of a limited political reform with concerns about the material impact of reform on the living conditions of intellectuals produced a powerful boost to the growing disaffection of the intellectuals. It led to more generalized claims against the Party/state. The anger of this section of the population was fuelled by the raised expectations resulting from Deng's assertion that the Party ought to leave the administration of universities, and indeed production, to the experts. When this withdrawal did not occur apace, opposition to growing corruption within the Party spilled out on to the streets. Starting at the local, parochial level, demands for reform soon took the form of a general rhetoric of democracy which the Party could not accept. This was largely because the Party did not have the institutional mechanisms to respond to demands made against it, even though it could deal with most demands made upon it.

Hu Yaobang, who had been dismissed from office after the 1986 demonstration, died on 15 April 1989 and his death proved a flash point for the Beijing demonstrations. What followed has a curious echo of the Tiananmen Incident of 1976 when students had used the Festival of the Dead to commemorate Zhou Enlai's moderate leadership, and thereby indirectly criticize the radicalism of Mao and the Gang of Four. In 1989 students went to Tiananmen Square to pay their respects to Hu, the premier reformer who the Party had rejected, and by implication to criticize its decision, and they stayed on. Many autonomous student and citizen groups were formed during this period including the Federation of Autonomous Students' Unions and the Beijing Autonomous Workers' Union. Though these represented various social groups, they were held together primarily by the momentum of the movement. The student and intellectuals groups did not seek to build alliances with the workers or the peasants, but to lead them.

The response of the Party was at first muted; it did not want the protests to escalate due to heavy-handed policing. Ironically, however, this measured response might have been seen as a sign of weakness, or even an invitation by the reform faction of the Party to continue protesting. In late April, Deng Xiaoping intervened in the growing dispute between the students and the Party, on the side of the Party. He denounced the student movement as anti-Party, and his article in the *People's Daily* and all major newspapers laid the basis of the eventual dismissal of the reformist Premier Zhao Ziyang who had criticized the personalization of power in China during a conversation with President Gorbachev of Soviet Union. However, it became clear that personalization of Deng's power within the CCP contributed to the limited options that the Party was left with in responding to the students (Benewick, 1995). Deng lost face as the students remained defiant and continued to occupy the square, and compromise became more difficult to secure. The presence of the international media, due to Gorbachev's visit, reporting all the details of the approaching confrontation between the Party and the students also limited the Party's options for action. The Party's position was again undermined when, on 12 May, students went on hunger strike to press for their demands. Popular sympathy for the students increased many-fold during this period. The Party was getting boxed in by events that were outside its control, and by the very limited constitutional and institutional levers that it could effectively use. As negotiation would have meant providing legitimacy to the students' associations, a dialogue was attempted between the hunger strikers and Premier Li Peng who had replaced Zhao Ziyang. The televised meeting was acrimonious and unproductive, and only produced further sympathy for the students as one of them – Wang Dan – fainted after haranguing the premier. A State of Emergency was declared in parts of Beijing on 2 June, and the army marched into the square to clear it on 4 June.

CONCLUSIONS

The suppression of the student movement by the Party leadership can be read as a comment on the limitations of the reforms introduced by the Deng leadership. It was also symptomatic of the problems of reforming a centralized state and economic system from above. In the course of the reforms many new interests and contradictions have emerged that are not always compatible with the broader goals of the Party and state. The need for and process of articulation of these interests has become a critical factor in the Chinese political system. The demand for autonomous interest-representing organizations is becoming more pressing as economic reforms progress. This is important for the efficiency of the reforms themselves. The 'new authoritarian' option, employed by many East Asian states, would be for the state to work with the peak interest groups in society in order to keep the political demands made upon it confined within economic boundaries. This is not a realistic option in China, as the new emerging social groups do not as yet command enough economic clout to force the state to negotiate with them. On the other hand, state power has become dispersed with some devolution of power to local and provincial governments which pursue their own particular interests. Indeed, as we have pointed out above, the *getihu* remain socially marginalized. Bargaining through networks of *guanxi* remains the only option available to these new social groups. The Party's determination not to share power, while at the same time experiencing a devolution of its powers, allows it very little political room for manoeuvre. The only realistic option that it has, and that it has employed effectively, is that of 'licensing' participation. The problem with this strategy, as we have seen, is that the licensee need not always function within the bounds set by the licence. At such times the licensor is left with little option but to use force. The question of institutionalization of power that might lead Chinese political practice beyond licensed participation remains as yet unanswered.

FURTHER READING

For an understanding of the debate on political participation see Dahl (1961), Huntington (1968), Schumpeter, (1947) and Pateman (1970).

For a discussion of participation in the context of China see Rai (1991), Schram (1973) and Strand (1989).

For a survey of the Hundred Flowers Campaign see MacFarquhar (1974a, b).

The Cultural Revolution and its critique is well covered by Dai (1987), Deng (1984b), Gray (1990) and Hinton (1972b).

Post-Mao political practice is analyzed in Christiansen (1994), Nathan (1990), Pieke (1995) and White (1994).

7 The People's Liberation Army

In Chapter 3, the discussion of the revolutionary movement in the 1930s and 1940s made clear how integral the growth of the Chinese military was to the emergence of the Chinese state. The networks of leadership of the CCP and the army overlapped, which strengthened the ties between the political and military wings of the post-revolutionary state. In this chapter we will examine how this complex relationship was managed in the post-revolutionary period, and to what effect. We will examine the role that the military has played in Chinese politics, and the changes that have occurred in the military, and its relations with the Party in the post-Mao period.

RED ARMY TO PLA: THE FORMATION OF THE MILITARY

The formation and the role of the People's Liberation Army (PLA) has been of particular significance in Chinese political history. The army in China developed out of the revolutionary process and therefore its relationship with the political wing of the movement was a very close one. It is 'a measure of party dominance of the system that the PLA is sworn to defend the Communist party rather than the state' (Lieberthal, 1995: 205). This closeness affected the post-revolutionary power arrangements, and also the ways in which the military was included into the political structures of the People's Republic. The Chinese defence minister, for example, has always been included in the Politburo of the CCP, unlike in the former Soviet Union where the military elite was assiduously kept away from the structures of political power. In 1969, at the height of the PLA's influence in the political sphere, 47.5 per cent of the elected Central Committee members were soldiers, and in 1971 half of the State Council members were soldiers. In 1973, 37 per cent of the Central Committee members were from the armed forces, and 33 per cent in 1977. The position has changed radically in the post-Mao period, indicating a shift in the relationship between the military and the Party; only 12 per cent of the Central Committee members were from the military in 1987. These last figures do not necessarily indicate the lessening of importance of the military establishment in China, only a changing relationship between the Party and the army, and the role that the army is expected to play in the country.

Dual role of the army

The period of the first civil war, from 1921 to 1927, which resulted in the Shanghai Massacre, demonstrated to the CCP the vulnerability of a revolutionary party which lacked strong military backing. The Nanchang Uprising on 1 August 1927 marked the beginning of the Red Army – to this day, 1 August is celebrated annually as 'Army Day'. In April 1928 several armed units were amalgamated into the 'Fourth Red Army'. From then on, problems of political and military power were regarded as inextricable. Mao's theory of 'people's war' was a theory of the relationship between political and military power, and a view of the social and political role of a revolutionary army which distinguishes it in many basic ways from the usual model of military practice in the West.

Perhaps the key elements of Mao's thinking on military matters during this period can be summarized in terms of two famous slogans: 'Political power grows out of the barrel of a gun' and 'Our principle is that the Party commands the gun and the gun must never be allowed to command the Party'. Maoist strategy was to develop a politicized military in at least two senses: first, the military was to be subordinated to the political leadership by organizational means – simultaneous membership of soldiers in the Party, and the system of political commissars in the army; second, officers and soldiers were encouraged to take a political and not simply a 'purely military viewpoint' through: political study . . . participation in a range of non-military activities . . . and both propaganda work and economic activities; and to develop a 'military democracy' that involved the abolition of ranks and egalitarianism between officers and men (Box 7.1).

Box 7.1   *The Maoist view of the military*

The Chinese Red Army is an armed body for carrying out the political tasks of the revolution . . . the Red Army should certainly not confine itself to fighting; besides fighting to destroy the enemy's military strength, it should shoulder such important tasks as doing propaganda among the masses, organising the masses, arming them, helping them to establish revolutionary political power and setting up Party organisations.

(Source: Mao [1929]: 106)

We have an army for fighting as well as an army for labour. For fighting we have the Eighth Route and New Fourth Armies; but even they do a dual job, warfare and production. With these two kinds of armies, and with a fighting army skilled in these two tasks and in mass work, we can overcome our difficulties . . .

(Source: Mao [1943b]: 153)

This intermeshing of the political and the military roles also had an important impact on the leadership networks of the Party and the military. Most of Chinese political leaders – Mao Zedong, Deng Xiaoping, Zhu De, Ye Jianying and Lin Biao – had military careers during the revolutionary war and they were all Long March veterans. In the Soviet Union the Red Army was created after the revolution, and had necessarily included elements of the old tsarist regime as the people's militia proved inadequate to stop the counter-revolutionary offensive. The Soviet Communist Party, always suspicious of the loyalty of these tsarist generals therefore attempted to keep them under tight surveillance, and set up an elaborate network of political commissars to do so. In China, the close and overlapping relationship between the military and the political leadership led to a blurring of the boundaries between the two elites; they were all revolutionaries and responsible for the fate of the revolution. Peng Dehuai, defence minister in the People's Republic of China, spoke out against the Great Leap Forward in 1959 at the Lushan Conference. Lin Biao actively participated in the Cultural Revolution, and even after Mao's death, Ye Jianying was for a time the focal point of opposition to Deng's economic reforms.

The participation of the political elite in military operations also meant that there was little emphasis on formal training of officers. Together with the politicization of the objectives of the military, this lack of professional training meant that the question of professionalization of the Chinese army was not addressed with any seriousness, either before or after the revolution. 'Red' was always considered better than 'expert' even in the army. After Mao's death and the launch of the programme of four modernizations this became an issue in the military.

The politicization of the army also led to the developing of the 'mystique' of the PLA as a disciplined, politically aware force engaged closely with the task of rebuilding the nation. Soldiers were required to memorize the Maoist creed called 'the Three Main Rules and Eight Points for Attention' which emphasized the importance of treating the masses with respect (Box 7.2). This was important to distinguish the PLA from the armies of the KMT, as well us to secure the help of the local populations in the guerrilla war that the communists were waging.

Finally, the army was used as an economic resource as well as a political one. Soldiers participated in food production, wherever the Red Army set up base, to supplement the reserves of the area and lighten the burden on the local population on whose support the communists depended. After the setting up of the PRC, the PLA played an even more important domestic economic role. The huge armies of the civil war were demobilized to a large extent by setting them to civilian production, though they retained a military organization. Soldiers participated in agricultural and industrial production, and they also assisted in the land reform process, in setting up state farms, and collectivization (the state farms were fully turned civilian in 1983/1984).

Box 7.2   *The Three Main Rules and Eight Points for Attention*

The three main rules were:

1. Obey orders at all times;
2. Do not take a single needle or piece of thread from the masses; and
3. Turn in everything that has been captured.

The eight points for attention were:

1. Speak politely;
2. Pay a fair price for what you buy;
3. Return everything you borrow;
4. Pay for everything you damage;
5. Do not hit people or swear at them;
6. Do not damage crops;
7. Do not take liberties with women;
8. Do not ill-treat captives.

This dual role of the army was reiterated by the General Political Department of the PLA as late as 1985 when it enumerated the functions of the PLA as: (1) economic construction; (2) coping with emergencies; (3) establishing public welfare undertakings; (4) lessening the people's burden; and (5) building spiritual civilization.

The structure of the army

As described in Chapter 5, a *xitong* is a grouping of bureaus that together deal with broad tasks of governance. The military forms one such *xitong*, but is distinct from the others. Party control is exercised via the Military Affairs Commission, below which there is a General Political Department which oversees Party activity in the PLA, including security and counter-espionage together with military personnel recruitment and discipline (Lieberthal, 1995: 205). The PLA also has a General Logistics Department that runs a vast industrial and transport network over which the economic *xitong* does not have any control. The General Staff of the PLA, while including all divisions of a military regime – army, air force and navy – is dominated by the concerns of the army (Figure 7.1). The army had, until the reforms instituted by the Deng leadership, 4 million soldiers under its command, making it the largest such force in the world.

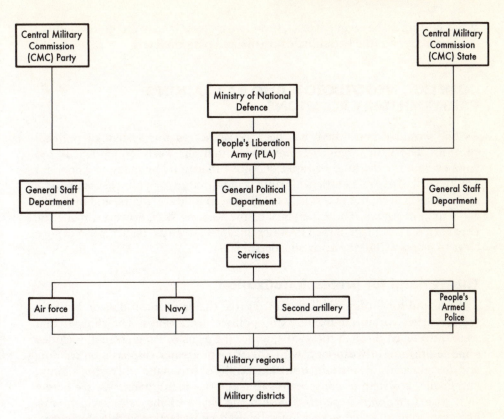

Figure 7.1   *The military structure of China*

The system of political control

While the military *xitong* gives the impression of being a 'state within a state', this has not prevented the Party from building a system of political control in the army. This was based on the principles applied by Trotsky to the Soviet Army, and had two elements:

1. A Party committee hierarchy from the 'centre' (the Military Affairs Committee of the Central Committee) to the regiment level – the Party committee of a given unit was to consist of its military commander, its political commissar and one or more of its main staff members.
2. A hierarchy of 'political departments' staffed by political officers and commissars stretching from the General Political Department of the PLA headquarters down to the Political Office of the regiment. Unlike the former, this is part of the army structure and not an 'external' organism like the Party committee system. Similarly, elections of PLA delegates to the NPC are carried out separately from all other delegates.

While distinct at the regiment level, these two systems tend to merge lower down the hierarchy, viz. the battalion, company and platoon levels.

CONFLICT, NEGOTIATION AND BARGAINING: PARTY–MILITARY RELATIONS

As one would expect, there has been resistance to this system of political controls. The main arguments have been that the Party committee is too cumbersome for the kind of rapid decisions that must be made in a modern army, particularly in a battlefield context; and that many political commissars are non-specialists, not necessarily competent in military affairs, and may take the wrong decisions. The experience of the Korean War, however, made the need for a reassessment of the PLA's organization, strategy, tactics and weapons clear to many within the army's leadership.

The demand for professionalization

The demand for professionalization triggered the first serious divison between two branches within the military and political leaderships. The changes that were introduced through the 1950s, under the aegis of Peng Dehuai, included a modernization of weaponry, with Soviet help; greater emphasis on training and discipline and the introduction of hierarchy of command and responsibility; and finally, a system of conscription to regularize recruitment. We see here a shift to a *functional imperative* within the ranks of the army, which was, however, soon attacked as revisionist by the Maoist faction within the Party.

It is important to note here that the divisions were not simply between professionals and the political leaders, but between two different sorts of revolutionaries – a group that looked to the Soviet Army for inspiration ('red professionals') and the Maoists who emphasized the uniqueness of the Chinese experience (the 'revolutionary reds'). There have been 'revolutionary reds' (such as Lin Biao) among the top army leadership as well as 'red professionals' (such as Peng Dehuai). Further, it would also be wrong to assume that there was a growing rift between the army and the civilian leadership. While the Party and the PLA are two separate units, we have seen that they are intertwined and interpenetrating organizations. Relations between them, therefore, have two aspects: first, between two separate institutions, with personnel specializing in different areas; and second, between two wings of the same institution.

The debate between the pro-Soviet and Maoist factions within the army leadership centred around several key issues:

1. The importance of weapons – the Maoists believed that a correct ideology and political education were the most important resources of a revolutionary army, while the pro-Soviet group put more emphasis on technology and training.

2. Relations between officers and soldiers – what was the impact of hierarchy on political morale on the one hand, and decision making on the other? Issues of elitism, and revolutionary commitment were debated.
3. Military involvement in non-military areas – to what extent should the army involve itself in activities such as running farms and doing political propaganda?
4. The Soviet Union's example – to what extent was the military model provided by the Soviet Union relevant to the Chinese conditions, and to what extent should Chinese military policies be based on the assumption of continued Soviet assistance and nuclear protection?

While the pro-Soviet faction came under attack in 1957/1958, the Maoist faction was put on the defensive in the aftermath of the dislocation caused by the Great Leap Forward. However, the pro-Soviet faction led by Peng Dehuai was defeated, and Lin Biao (whose military policies expressed the position of Mao Zedong at the time) was made minister of defence. This was encapsulated in a slogan coined by Lin extolling the 'Four Firsts' : man over weapons; political over other work; ideological over routine work; 'practical thought' over book-learning. This position dovetailed with the general political position towards which Mao was to take China during the Cultural Revolution.

In the early 1960s there was a series of campaigns in the PLA to carry out the reforms – party membership was expanded; party organization at the basic level was reorganized and new branches built; there was a stress on the ideological training of the officers and greater emphasis on the class background of military personnel; and the influence of the Soviet Union was combed out of military textbooks. In short, the PLA increasingly became the organization that epitomized Mao's ideas in action. As a result, the political profile of the PLA, and of Lin Biao personally, began to increase: military personnel such as Lei Feng were made heroes during the Cultural Revolution; a campaign was launched to 'Learn from the PLA' in 1964; and a new apparatus of political control in government and economic units, modelled on the PLA's political control system, was introduced. The army emerged from the chaos of the Cultural Revolution with greatly increased position and powers.

Deterioration in Sino-Soviet relations through the 1960s, and serious armed clashes in 1969, meant that technological advancement again became an issue towards the end of the Cultural Revolution. Greater emphasis was placed on training, and military budgets were increased. China's nuclear programme was boosted. The 'revolutionary professional' wing within the army was given a further fillip when Lin Biao fell from grace in 1971. Lin's fall had many causes – one of the most radical policies of the Cultural Revolution; factionalism within the ranks of the Maoists (especially conflicts between the Cultural Revolution Small Group and Lin Biao) and Chinese negotiations with the USA at this time. His mysterious death while he was ostensibly on his way to Moscow was followed by a purge of officers loyal to him. In December 1973 Mao rotated eight out of the eleven leading military positions in different regions, reasserting the Party's control over the army. There was also a reorganization of the militia to make it more urban based, and to include public security among its functions. It was given the same status as the PLA in the 1975 Constitution. In January 1975 Deng Xiaoping took over as PLA chief of staff and was appointed to the Central Military Commission (CMC) as well. Purged yet again after the Tiananmen Incident, he was rehabilitated in 1976 and appointed as the vice-chair of the CMC, and he took on the job of professionalizing the army in the new political context in China.

During the revolutionary and Maoist years, there was a major change in the social image of the military. Traditionally, the military in China had very low status, even though there was a folklore built around romantic soldiers and virtuous military heroes. However, the depradations of the military in the Qing period as well as the warlord period meant that soldiers were regarded with justifiable suspicion by the people: 'good iron is not made into nails, a good man does not become a soldier' the saying went. This image changed dramatically during the revolutionary war, and because of the societal imperative that created it. As a result, joining the PLA became an aspiration for young people, particularly for those of worker or peasant background. Acceptance by the PLA almost automatically led to acceptance by the CCP, whose membership was most important to furthering one's career prospects. The PLA gave opportunities to young people to acquire skills that were useful in civilian life; demobilized soldiers were honoured in their villages and had good access to the local bureaucracy. Many became local cadres themselves, providing status to their families. The PLA, therefore, had a support base that was wide and strong in the countryside and the cities among people of the 'working classes'. This base has been eroded in the years since the introduction of economic reforms, and has important implications for the future development of the PLA, and its relationship with the CCP.

REORGANIZING THE MILITARY: THE POST-MAO YEARS

The overriding change of policy *vis-à-vis* the PLA has been a reversal to professionalism. The central tenet of Mao's military policies, however, remains the same: the Party must command the gun.

Post-Mao changes in the PLA's organization

The Maoist doctrine of a 'People's War' has been reworked in the military rhetoric as a 'People's War under Modern Conditions', with greater emphasis on modern weaponry and technology, and positional instead of guerrilla warfare. The 'original name is retained most to emphasize continuity with the past, when in fact the doctrine represents a sharp break with past practice'

(Dreyer, 1993: 252). Professionalization has also meant a reduced emphasis on the political study that formed such an important part of a soldier's training during the Maoist period. The emphasis now is on the study of strategy and tactics, and training in particular geographical areas and conditions. Emphasis on advanced defence systems has led the Chinese state to look to both indigenous as well as foreign sources to augment existing resources. There is also a renewed interest in nuclear technology. Perhaps one of the most dramatic changes has been the streamlining of the organization of the PLA. A million people, 25 per cent of the army personnel, were to be demobilized, and the number of military regions reduced from eleven to seven. The rank system has been reinstated, and older personnel encouraged to retire. The army wants to present a younger, more professional image to the country and the world. The vast majority of the new recruits are between the ages of 18 and 39; only 2.5 per cent are 50 and over (Wang, 1989: 199). There is also an emphasis, in parallel with the Party, to pay greater attention to the education of military personnel. 'About 25 percent of the officers on the active list had a college education in 1986' (Wang, 1989: 198) Recruitment and promotion procedures now favour youth and formal educational qualifications, and provide disincentives for those without. A National Defence University was founded in 1985 by merging three PLA academies – military, political and logistical (Dreyer, 1993: 254).

As far as the relationship between the military and the Party is concerned, the Deng leadership has carried out major reorganization primarily to try and separate the PLA organization from that of the Party. The political importance of this is significant. 'By 1990, there were no individuals with a primarily military background in the Standing Committee of the Politburo', and a change in the Party constitution dropped the requirement that the chair of the CMC must be a member of the Standing Committee (Dreyer, 1993: 254). The People's Armed Police was created from the PLA to oversee internal security functions which were supervised by the army. While there has been an effort at a functional separation within the PLA, it has been only partially successful.

The PLA continues to provide for its own food and other needs, and in the late 1980s the army went into business on the strength of its industrial base over which it retains control. This became important as, between 1979 and 1990, the military saw a relative decline in its official budget and needed to supplement its income to meet its needs. Its enterprises cater for both military and civilian sectors, and are also involved in exporting goods to other countries. The PLA employs about 700,000 employees in its 10,000 enterprises, and by the late 1980s it had set up its first transnational corporation, the Sanjiu Enterprise Group. It also runs collective enterprises and joint ventures with both domestic and foreign partners. The businesses include non-military ventures like property development and the hotel industry. However, arms sales provide the largest profits to the military. The CMC changes the tax laws in order to get most of the profits for the PLA (Bickford, 1994: 460–9).

The politics of resistance

The reforms met with strong resistance by the PLA establishment. There were different sources of resentment that provoked this negative response. One cluster of issues concerned the refurbishment of the PLA. The commanders wanted more money; the Party leadership refused to accede to this demand. Economic modernization was the priority for Deng, not the modernization of the military. China's expenditure on the military fell from 14 per cent of the budgetary allocation in 1983 to 10.5 per cent in 1985, where it has stabilized. There were also differences about who should supply China's needs for modern weaponry – indigenous or foreign sources – and over which kinds of weapons ought to receive priority.

A second issue was a loss of privilege. People joined the PLA as a job for life. Streamlining the PLA involved shedding a million jobs. The decisions about who would go and who would stay were difficult, especially as most soldiers stayed in the same units for the entire time they spent in the PLA. The unit (*danwei*), as noted in Chapter 6, is a close-knit community, and any divisions within it led to much bitterness. When decisions were made on the basis of *guanxi* – personal contacts and nepotism – resentments grew further. Added pressures on those already in the PLA, such as improving their formal educational qualifications, were added irritants. The 'Red' versus 'expert' controversy raised its head again, as an emphasis on expertise was seen as an attack upon the Maoist principles of 'politics in command' that had served as the PLA's creed for decades.

If it was difficult to retire people from the PLA, the economic reforms introduced by the Deng leadership also created problems for recruiting new soldiers. This has been for both economic and non-economic reasons. The recruiting base of the PLA has always been the countryside. Young men who wanted to escape the rigours of poorly paid agricultural labour were attracted to the PLA as a high-status alternative. With the introduction of the family and individual responsibility system in agricultural production, it became much more lucrative for young men (90 per cent of the PLA is male) to remain in their villages. Further, the losses in the Vietnam War, and the de-emphasis on politics meant that the PLA's status in the eyes of the people was reduced. The dual role of political education and military defence that the PLA had performed was undermined by the reduction of political rhetoric. If politics was no longer to be in command, the political role of the PLA was not viable and there was no non-economic incentive to join it. The reluctance of country youth to join began to change recruitment patterns of the PLA, as it looked to the cities to fill the empty places. A complex process of bargaining ensued as potential recruits sought to improve their living standards through the military. In some cases, military units have resorted to illegal means to meet these demands.

The consumer boom in China, and the erosion of security that the old state system provided, the rising inequalities in income, together with the opportunities provided by PLA's incursions into the sphere of business, have all contributed to an alarming rise in corruption in the PLA. Bribery, embezzlement and smuggling are the three main areas of corruption within the PLA. These corrupt practices occur for collective as well as private gain. With demobilization came the threat of unemployment or reduced incomes. To avoid this, officers and soldiers often find it necessary to either offer bribes, or involve themselves in private business, and at times even both. Corruption is difficult to monitor in most situations. However, as information about corruption in the PLA is treated as a military secret it becomes even more difficult to regulate. An internal regulatory system has been instituted to combat corruption. PLA business units cannot create holding companies; equipment still in service cannot be used for business activities; and there are no profit targets for these business units. These regulations, however, are routinely subverted (Goodman, 1994: 4). The image of the PLA has suffered enormously as a result of corruption scandals, and has caused concern to the 'political' wing within the military elite.

While resentments grew within the PLA, this did not necessarily mean that they were expressed by its leadership through political intervention. Most regional commanders are part of the Party/military establishment, and would not want to be accused of anti-Party activities. However, some more politically oriented officers did coalesce, in the early 1980s, around one of the most respected military/Party men – Marshall Ye Jianying. A major issue of difference between Deng and this group was the evaluation of Mao Zedong's role in China's revolutionary history. Related to this is the importance placed on ideology by the Deng leadership and by this military grouping. Veteran army writer Bai Hua's screenplay 'Bitter Love', which told the story of an artist hounded by Red Guards during the Cultural Revolution became a target for this group of officers. They felt that in the old Chinese tradition, Bai was reflecting the views of Deng on Mao's legacy. Feelings ran strong enough for Hu Yaobang to initiate a compromise whereby Bai made a self-criticism in order that an attack on the playwright by sections of the military may not be read as an attack upon Deng. This group of officers also attacked 'liberal' tendencies in the Chinese political culture. As much of the mystique of the PLA during the Maoist years was built around a 'correct' ideological position, it is easy to say why the erosion of ideological rhetoric in public life would matter to this section of the military. They denounced 'bourgeois liberalization', being encouraged by the new economic and political policies of the Deng leadership. Deng's economic policies, especially the decollectivization of agriculture, were also targeted by this group. We have already noted the problems arising for military recruitment and corruption within the PLA ranks because of this change in policy. The Deng leadership, however, has not brooked any opposition for long. This group of military officers came under attack in 1982, and Wei Guoqing, the director of the PLA's General Political Department, who was one of the members of this group, was removed from office (Joffe, 1984: 30). The death of Ye, soon after, removed the lynchpin of this coalition of opposition. This did not, however, remove all friction between a section of the military officers and the Deng leadership, as was evidenced during the events leading up to and during the PLA's operation on 4 June 1989. However, such friction should not lead us to think that the cleavage between the military and the political leadership is very deep or wide, or that the military is an alternative to the current reformist leadership. This will become clearer as we take an overview of the events around the June Fourth Incident.

THE JUNE FOURTH INCIDENT AND THE PLA

Much was written about the role of the PLA during the Tiananmen Square Movement. There were reports of military commanders' unhappiness at being involved in political skirmishes, and of the refusal of some commanders to march into the square. It had been clear that the military was divided in its response to the reformists' agenda – the promise of modernization of the PLA's aging technological base lured the military leadership to support Deng's reforms. However, concerns about the political fallout from these reforms led to opposition to the more enthusiastic members of the reform circle in the Party. On both counts – professionalism and political purity – the involvement of the PLA in the events of the June Fourth Incident were difficult to accept by the two wings within the military. A compromise was reached with the PLA after the incident and this seems to be holding.

The June Fourth Incident

Martial Law was declared in parts of Beijing as empowered by Clause 16 of Article 89 of the Constitution. The mayor of Beijing reported that the measures to 'stop the turmoil' were taken at a meeting attended by 'cadres from the Party, government and military institutions' in Beijing on 19 May 1989. Zhao Ziyang, the prime minister and the leading reformist after the fall of Hu Yaobang, refused to attend this meeting. What developed during the next week was, therefore, not simply a matter of law and order for the authorities, but a leadership struggle in which the PLA was asked to intercede by becoming the main law-enforcing body. This ran counter the assurances of professionalization of the PLA as promised by Deng.

The opposition to this demand upon the PLA came from those who thought that, as a professional institution, the PLA should be protected from the internecine battles of the Party, and that the separation of the military and political functions should be established as a principle. Those who were against professionalism and thought it an attack upon PLA's traditions of 'serve the people' and 'politics in command' were also opposed to its involvement in clearing the square. They did not want PLA soldiers to be seen to be attacking the people they were meant to serve. The protesters made use of this known concern by publically claiming that the PLA would never attack the people. Deng was the only leader that both the reformists and the traditionalists within the military trusted, and he was able to use his considerable persuasive skills to get the army into line behind him, and to clear the square.

Compromises and continuities

As the PLA involvement in the events of 4 June was a compromise brokered by Deng, there was a political bill that had to be met by the Party authorities. This was done in different ways that spelled a compromise not only between the military and the political leaderships, but also between the professional and the amateur wing of the military. After the suppression of the student movement in 1989, there was an attempt to renew the mystique of the PLA (that was so damaged in the eyes of ordinary Chinese) by emphasizing the importance of politics to the military. The separation of a professionalized military from the party was underplayed. Further, old heroes were resurrected to emphasize the PLA's history of serving the people – Lei Feng was, for example, relaunched as a PLA soldier to emulate and revere. Hagiographic histories of the PLA's role in Chinese revolutionary struggle were sponsored and published in 1989/1990.

While these attempts were made to conciliate the amateur wing of the military, the professionals were offered more money for modernization of the army: an increase of 15 per cent in its budget in 1990, 12 per cent the following year and 13.5 per cent in 1992 (Dreyer, 1993: 261, 265). While being an important gesture in the context of inflating budget deficits of the government, these increases did not make up for the erosion of monetary value due to the high inflation that China has been experiencing through the 1990s. While there were mass transfers made after the June Fourth Incident, these were not made in a punitive spirit. Most personnel were transferred from one area to another, rather than being demoted, dismissed or promoted for the roles they played and positions they took during the incident. An influential personality in the military leadership, for example, was General Yang Shangkun, the Chinese president and the general secretary of the CMC. He was the focus of opposition to increasing the pace of reforms without taking into account their political implications. Yang's younger brother, Baibing, was also influential in the military establishment, which gave rise to speculation about the Yang family faction dominating the military. Both brothers were promoted after June 1989 – Yang Baibing was made general secretary of the CMC when Yang Shangkun became vice-chair of the CMC. At the same time, however, Jiang Zemin was made chair of the CMC when Deng resigned from the post. However, the modernizers regrouped their influence and resources and by 1994 the amateurs in the army were on the retreat. Yang Baibing was persuaded by Deng to resign from his post at the CMC with a promise of membership of the Politburo. Baibing resigned, but was not included in the Politburo, signalling to the amateurs in the military that the reformists still had the upper hand in the Party.

The hand of the professionals was strengthened further after the Gulf War, when the technological superiority of the United States became painfully evident to the PLA leadership. The military establishment was concerned on two counts – the ease with which the US military overwhelmed a supposedly highly politically motivated army put paid to the rhetoric of 'people's war' as a strategy of modern warfare. Second, the swiftness with which the United States was able to put together a UN-backed Western military coalition against Iraq underlined for the Chinese leaders the impact of the collapse of the Soviet Union; there seemed no check on the United States in the global political arena. China needed to modernize to counter both aspects of the equation – the technological gap and the power vacuum (Dreyer, 1993: 264–6).

CONCLUSIONS

The amateur wing of the military, however, continues to have a presence in the PLA. As we have noted above, the PLA is involved in not only military but also economic activities, and the principle of Party control over the army continues to be asserted. This tension between the professionals and the amateurs is set to continue. The dice seems loaded in favour of the professionals, however, as China's economic and political climate continues to change in favour of liberalization.

FURTHER READING

For a review of the relations between the Party and the PLA see Joffe (1967, 1984), Dreyer (1993: Chapter 9), Whitson and Huang (1973) and Jencks (1982).

For post-Mao reforms in the military and their impact on the PLA see Bickford (1994), Joffe (1987), Goodman (1994) and Lovejoy and Watson (1986: Chapter 8).

8   China and the world

This chapter examines the bases upon which the Chinese Communist Party has conducted its foreign relations. It reviews the claims that Chinese foreign policy has been driven by two irreconcilable claims – the claim to territory that was part of the greater Chinese empire, and the claim to ideological leadership in the Third World. It will do this by setting out the historical and contemporary trajectories of Chinese foreign policy in relation to three groups of countries and territories: (1) the United States and the former Soviet Union; (2) China's Asian neighbours; and (3) the 'near abroad' of China that might also be called Greater China – Hong Kong and Taiwan.

THE BASES OF CHINESE FOREIGN POLICY

It is widely assumed that historical tradition has conditioned the foreign policy of the People's Republic of China. The history of the Middle Kingdom (see Chapter 2) is often seen as relevant to modern China's perception of the rest of the world. Mao, in such writing, takes the place of the emperor, and is seen to take China down a road of self-important delusion. For example, C. P. Fitzgerald wrote:

> These arguments [about Marxism with the Soviets] amounted to a restatement in modern terms of two of the fundamental postulates of the old Chinese view of the world: that China was the centre of civilization, the model which less advanced states and peoples should copy if they were to be accepted within the pale, and that the ruler of China was the expounder of orthodox doctrine; that after all and always, Chinese interpretations were the right one; truth and right thinking must come from China and conform with Chinese teaching. (Fitzgerald, 1964: 49)

'Face' as a concept in Chinese cultural tradition is presented as a central concern in foreign relations (Shih, 1990). While there is a considerable impact of tradition on any aspect of Chinese state functioning, it is problematic to transpose imperial patterns of governance on a thoroughly modern Chinese nation-state in a new world order. Further, truth claims are made by all ideologies and ideologues, as the claim to universal validity of an ideology rests upon these. All ideologies draw their legitimacy from the claims to universal viability of their paradigms.

The People's Republic came into being, as we have seen in Chapter 3, as a result of the harnessing of two different forces in Chinese society and polity – nationalism and Marxism. National interest and ideology, therefore, have both been important to the construction of legitimacy of the state and hence are necessary components of all policy making in China. Most times these two impulses have worked together, though at others they have seemingly conflicted. The Chinese leadership has used the rhetoric of both nationalism and socialism effectively, though, increasingly, ideology is becoming less apparent in the conduct of China's foreign relations. China emerged as a nation-state when the world system was polarized because of the Cold War; today, globalization seems to be the dominant trend in world politics. The space that China occupied in the world system has been affected by these changing trends, while at the same time China has also been an active and autonomous agent in its relationship with the world beyond its boundaries.

Chinese nationalism and national interest

The two immediate issues exercising the Chinese leadership in 1949 were nationalist issues – national security and economic reconstruction. Chinese nationalism fuelled the victory of the communists, and socialist ideology became part of the new nationalism that the CCP constructed – the language of equality was used effectively as anti-imperialist rhetoric while China sought its place in the world after the humiliations of the eighteenth and ninteenth centuries. Nationalism also strengthened the CCP's attachment with the socialist movement. China emerged in the post-war world to be faced by the polarization of nations behind the two superpowers. The choices open to the new China were limited. There was the US-inspired economic blockade of China, and the declared threat to the existence of the PRC by its KMT/Taiwanese allies. The Soviet Union seemed to be the only bulwark against this threat to the new nation-state, and the affinity provided by the ideology and the organizational links between the CCP and the CPSU was there to build on. Nationalism and ideology seemed in harmony at this stage; at least there seemed little choice in making friends that would defend the interests of the new state. If the interests of national security were served by allying China with the Soviet Union, so were China's economic interests. The economic blockade imposed by Western powers meant that the Soviet bloc was the only major economic partner of China, and China was in no position to decline the help offered. China and the Soviet Union signed a Treaty of Mutual Alliance in 1950.

Through the late 1950s, however, we see China's relations with the Soviet Union deteriorating sharply. There were several reasons why this happened – the death of Stalin, and Khrushchev's 'secret speech', the Hungarian revolt in 1956 and its handling by Khrushchev, and his call for *détente*, among others. However, what is of interest to us here is that national interest was interpreted very differently by the various factions within the CCP. This was a time of re-evaluation of strategies within the Party with Mao preparing the way for the Great Leap Forward. Ideological divisions within the Party affected China's foreign relations greatly. If the logic of a self-reliant Maoist model of development was carried through then there was a limited need for high-level technological inputs into the Chinese economy which the Soviets were providing.

In terms of national security, however, the break with the Soviet Union is more difficult to explain, unless Khrushchev's attempt to build working relations with the United States were seen by China as an abandoning of the Soviet commitment to the protection of China. Given his preoccupation with ideological issues, one might argue that Mao saw the erosion of socialist values that he was witnessing in the Soviet Union as a threat to the 'purity' of China's socialism, and therefore detrimental to its national interests. During this period which lasted between 1960 and 1971, China stood alone against the two superpowers, and between 1969 and 1970 engaged militarily with the Soviet Union. China's stance against both the superpowers is therefore difficult to explain simply in terms of national interest.

Is it possible to identify national interest? The idea of national interest presupposes a singularity of purpose that seems to underplay the importance of the tensions of domestic politics, and to situate the nation-state in a singular space that is unfractured by considerations of time-bound relations at the regional and domestic level. Chinese foreign policy has reflected the leadership's changing and at times divided understanding of national interest. Its nationalist goals have varied in different periods – securing its borders, economic reconstruction, ideological 'correctness', expanding its sphere of influence regionally and globally, economic modernization, and the continuation of the rule of the CCP have all been woven into China's foreign policy considerations.

Ideology and international relations

Ideology has been the other pillar of China's foreign policy. The formulation of principles upon which China would base its diplomatic relations was always in terms of China's independence – in terms of sovereignty as well as ideology. In China, as in other state socialist countries, Marxism–Leninism was the official ideology. However, ideology also suffers from similar problems as the concept of national interest. It is variously interpreted by different factions within the ruling elite, and by different national parties adhering to it. China's dispute with the Soviet Union has its origins in many issues, but also in fundamental disagreements about interpreting Marxism–Leninism (Box 8.1). The definitions of class and class struggle, the nature of imperialism, the relations between capitalism and socialist states were all disputed issues between the two countries.

To say that Marxism–Leninism was the official Chinese ideology, is clearly not enough, as we have seen in our study of domestic Chinese politics. China

Box 8.1   Ideology and Sino-Soviet split

The facts of the past seven years have amply proved that the differences between the Chinese and Soviet Parties and within the international communist movement have arisen solely because the leadership of the CPSU has departed from Marxism–Leninism and the road of revisionism … [The] present differences within the international communist movement are differences between the line of adhering to Marxism–Leninism and the line of clinging to revisionism between the revolutionary line and the non-revolutionary and anti-revolutionary line, between the anti-imperialist line and the line of capitulation to imperialism. They are differences between proletarian internationalism and great-power chauvinism, sectarianism and splittism.

(Source: Editorial Departments of Hongqi and Renmin Ribao, 1963: 99–100)

was increasingly isolated during the 1960s and played virtually no part in the global institutional politics. This self-inflicted isolation was explained by the Chinese leadership in largely ideological terms – it was China's 'correct' stand against Soviet 'social imperialism' that had resulted in the concerted efforts of the two superpowers to isolate China. However, China would not submit to such pressure.

During the Maoist period, especially between 1966 and 1976, ideological and doctrinal debates weighed heavily on all aspects of policy making; the role of ideology now is less important in itself, though not entirely absent as legitimizing the monopoly of power of the CCP. The Deng leadership has kept the ideological framework, as we have seen in Chapter 6, by emphasizing the Four Cardinal Principles which set out a political, as opposed to an economic, interpretation of Marxism–Leninism. The problem with different interpretations and reinterpretations of ideology by various factions within a national party, and within the international movement, is that the process delegitimizes ideology itself; which interpretation is considered valid is largely reliant upon which faction is dominant. Ideology becomes a rhetorical devise. However, rhetoric also imposes certain constraints upon its users; even in a one-party state, legitimacy is a key element in governance.

If ideological rhetoric is deemed important as a basis for policy formulation, it is difficult then to turn around and say that it isn't. However, stretching ideological boundaries too much in order to justify current policies further erodes ideological credibility. In post-Mao China an entirely different set of priorities and policies to those pursued by the Maoist leadership have been framed within the ideological paradigm of Marxism–Leninism–Mao-Zedong-Thought. Such a reinterpretation is not convincing, especially as the Party in all phases of Chinese politics has given hegemonic place to the dominant faction's interpretation of ideological principles. This makes reconciling the Maoist and post-Maoist interpretations of the same ideology a difficult task. National interest and ideology, therefore, give us only partial clues to foreign policy making in China. We need to examine foreign policy agendas in the context of competing domestic interests, political and ideological constraints, and current security needs. In its 1982 Constitution the Chinese leadership declared: 'The future of China is closely linked with that of the whole world. China adheres to an independent foreign policy as well as to the five principles of mutual respect for sovereignty and territorial integrity, mutual non-aggression, non-interference in each other's internal affairs, equality and mutual benefit, and peaceful coexistence . . .' After the Maoist emphasis on ideological rhetoric, and international class struggle, this signalled a more pragmatic period in Chinese foreign policy.

While seeking to undermine a simplistic understanding of national interest and ideology, we want to convey a complex relation between the two that has been and is affected by domestic factionalism, external pressures, and issues of legitimacy and political stability. It would be difficult to isolate one particular element of the above as dominant in foreign policy considerations.

CHINA IN A BIPOLAR WORLD

As already noted above, China emerged out of an anti-imperialist and a civil war into a bipolar world. The two superpowers dominated the world system, and this was reflected in the international institutional arrangements, as well as diplomatic relations between their allies and 'enemies'. The two blocs were sustained by hostile political ideologies, competing economic systems, and antagonistic military networks. It was an 'us' and 'them' world, and new China had to make its choice.

China's early overtures to the United States got no answer. Though the Truman administration toyed with the idea of recognizing the People's Republic, the logic of the 'Domino theory' and its sense of loyalty to the KMT regime in Taiwan overruled this option. By 1950 China had signed the Treaty of Friendship with the Soviet Union, and the Korean War had started; the divisions and hostilities between China and the United States that were to last for more than 20 years had begun. The relationship between the Soviet Union and China, however, did not turn out to be smooth either. The bipolar world was not able to contain China within its narrow boundaries.

Sino-Soviet relations in the 1950s

Even though the Friendship Treaty ensured China's inclusion into the Soviet bloc, it did not provide a blanket commitment from the Soviet Union to come to China's aid. China made several territorial concessions to the Soviet Union, which became irritants as relations between the two socialist states deteriorated. The treaty committed the Soviet Union to engage militarily in China's defence only if China was attacked. A conflict initiated by China would not be supported in the same way by the Soviet Union. This caveat proved important – though the United States was dissuaded from attacking Chinese military targets because of the provisions of this treaty, in the case of the Sino-Indian conflict in 1962 the Soviet Union decided to treat the dispute as a bilateral affair. Stalin showed a distrust of the Chinese leadership that was interpreted by the Chinese as reflecting the historical suspicions and racist attitudes of the Russians towards the Chinese.

However, the treaty provided China with desparately needed financial and technical resources from the Soviet Union, even at the cost of increasing Chinese dependence on the Soviets. Fifty per cent of China's foreign trade in the 1950s was with the Soviet Union. Between 7,000 and 10,000 Soviet experts – engineers in particular – were sent to China to help in the construction of 211 major industrial enterprises. It is noticeable, however, that no large grants were provided to China by the Soviet Union, whose aid to India and Egypt was more generous. However, the impact of Soviet technology, management and education was considerable in China's early attempts at economic development.

China in regional politics

During the mid-1950s China tried to forge relations with countries of South and East Asia, and become involved in political initiatives to strengthen ties between Third World nations. Several factors contributed to this moderating of its policy of 'lean to one (Soviet) side'. The death of Stalin in 1953 removed many constraints from the Chinese leadership. Stalin's successors were not as dogmatic about other countries being completely loyal to the Soviet bloc; certain flexibility at the regional level was accepted. This became politically possible for China as decolonization got underway in large areas of old colonies, making imperialism less of a threat. The Soviet leadership after Stalin also did not command the stature in the international communist movement that Stalin had, which resulted in the movement fracturing soon after. Finally, the truce signed in Korea in 1953 provided some stability on the eastern border of China, which allowed it to look to its other borders.

Between 1954 and 1957 China began a charm offensive on its neighbours in order to reduce tensions on its borders, and gain a prominent place in regional politics. It played an important role in formulating the treaty that led to the partition of Vietnam at the 1954 Geneva Conference. In June 1954, Zhou Enlai met the Indian prime minister, Nehru, to work out a basis for good neighbourly relations between the two countries. India had been the first country to recognize the People's Republic, and to recognize that Tibet was part of China. The two countries shared a disputed border, but decided to tone down the differences on the border issues in an attempt to make the region more stable.

> **Box 8.2 Panchsheela *or the Five Principles***
> 1. Mutual respect for each other's territorial integrity
> 2. Non-aggression
> 3. Non-interference in each other's internal affairs
> 4. Equality and mutual benefit
> 5. Peaceful coexistence

This meeting led to the formulation of the Five Principles or *Panchsheela* which framed Chinese foreign policy during this period (Box 8.2).

India was a founder member of the Non-Aligned Movement, and played an important role in bringing together diplomats from Asian and African countries at Bandung in Indonesia in April 1955. The Chinese attended this meeting and contributed to discussions on cooperation among the newly independent countries on the basis of *Panchsheela*. China thus situated itself very much in the Third World, and presented itself not simply as a communist state that was part of the international communist movement. The peaceful coexistence that the Five Principles included was understood by the Chinese leadership to apply to the countries of the Third World, and did not undermine its hostility towards the United States. The Bandung period was an important period for China – it established the country's credentials as an independent nation among the Asian and African countries, and gained much goodwill. It is to this period that the Chinese leadership has looked to formulate new foreign policy initiatives in the post-Mao period.

The Sino-Soviet split

The tensions between the Chinese and the Soviet leaderships had historical roots. The triumph of the Maoist strategy of guerrilla warfare had been in the face of stiff opposition from Moscow (see Chapter 3). Stalin therefore was not favourably inclined towards Mao, whose independence from the Stalinist orthodoxy was clear in practice if not in his rhetoric. Further, even as late as 1945, Stalin had signed a treaty with the KMT to protect Soviet interests in Manchuria. However, while Stalin lived, even Mao could not challenge his leadership of the international communist movement. Further, China's economic dependence on the Soviet Union confirmed this subordinate position. We have already referred to Chinese resentment about the provisions of the Friendship Treaty, though they were in no position to press their case given their dependence on the Soviet Union. The Chinese leadership also felt that the Soviet Union did not give enough material and military help to China during the Korean War. However, until Stalin's death in 1953, the relations between the two socialist countries remained stable, with China dependent on the Soviet Union economically as well as politically.

After Stalin's death however, Sino-Soviet relations deteriorated sharply. At a personal level, Khrushchev and Mao did not get on. At the political level, they did not share views on scarcely any issue. A bitter dispute ensued, especially after Khrushchev criticized the Great Leap Forward in 1957, refused to back China when the Americans moved their fleet into the Taiwan Straits in 1958 after the bombing of Quemoy Island, and reneged on a promise to share their growing nuclear technology with China. Mao, for his part, decided to challenge the Americans when speaking at the Moscow Meeting of Communists and Workers' Parties in 1957 by declaring that 'the East Wind is prevailing over the West Wind. That is to say the forces of socialism have become overwhelmingly superior to the forces of imperialism'. Such talk was not welcome in Moscow at a time when Khrushchev's policy on *détente* was being put together. Several other irritants emerged at this point that increased tensions between the two countries (Box 8.3). In 1969 there were armed border clashes when Chinese soldiers opened fire on a Soviet patrol on a small island in the Ussuri River. China's isolation from the international community was nearly complete and its borders seemed vulnerable to attack.

Box 8.3 *The politics of the Sino-Soviet split: the Chinese view*

The following are the main facts about how the leaders of the CPSU have sabotaged Sino-Soviet unity:

1. ... any fraternal Party which rejects the erroneous line and programme of the CPSU ... is looked upon as an enemy by the leaders of the CPSU, who ... try and subvert its leadership by every possible means.
2. ... The leadership of the CPSU broke off diplomatic relations with socialist Albania, an unprecedented step in the history of relations between fraternal Parties ...
3. The leadership of the CPSU has continued to ... make outrageous attacks on the Chinese Communist Party ...
5. In April and May 1962 the leaders of the CPSU used their organs and personnel in Sinkiang, China to carry out large-scale subversive activities in the Ili region and enticed and coerced several tens of thousands of Chinese citizens into going to the Soviet Union.
6. In August 1962 the Soviet Government formally notified China that the Soviet Union would conclude an agreement with the United States on the prevention of nuclear proliferation. This [would] deprive China of the right to possess nuclear weapons ...
8. The leadership of the CPSU has become increasingly anxious to collude with the Indian reactionaries and is bent on forming a reactionary alliance with Nehru against socialist China.

(Source: Editorial Department of Hongqi and Renmin Ribao, 1963: 93–7)

With Chinese economic and political policies becoming more radical through the Hundred Flowers Campaign of 1957, and the Great Leap Forward in 1958, a clash of the giants became inevitable. The CCP emphasized its commitment to socialism, an international socialist movement and to anti-imperialism. It was the latter that was to become an important element in China's bid during the 1960s to claim for itself the role of the leader of socialist movements and parties in the Third World. During the 1960s we also see China actively supporting communist movements in other East and South Asian states – the Indonesian Communist Party and the Communist Party of India (Marxist–Leninist), for example, both received political and some material aid from Beijing during this period. The Soviets were at this time talking the language of *détente* and did not want instability in East Asia. Their relations with not only the Communist Party of India, but also with the ruling Congress Party, were very good, and to have another communist country destabilizing regional political balance was not in Soviet interests.

Another issue that divided the two leaderships was regarding the unity of the international communist movement against 'American imperialism'. Khrushchev's talk of *détente* alarmed China as it suggested a *rapprochement* with the enemy, who China saw as fundamental to the continued oppression of many Third World countries by its dominance of the world capitalist system. America was also of course the primary supporter of the KMT leadership in Taiwan, and routinely used its influence and its veto to keep China out of international organizations such as the UNO (United Nations Organization). Khrushchev's weakening of the international communist movement was unacceptable to China; however, by not accepting the decision of the Soviet Union to formulate a policy of *détente*, China also signalled an open break with its former ally.

The Sino-Soviet dispute became increasingly bitter following Khrushchev's fall in 1964. The Chinese press published many critical and alarmist stories – that the Soviet Union was planning a pre-emptive strike against the Chinese only nuclear installation in Xinjiang Province. It also published the Chinese leadership's denunciation of the crushing of the Prague Spring in 1968, and, by implication, the Brezhnev Doctrine – that other socialist countries had the right to interfere when events within a socialist country were endangering the whole socialist bloc. This doctrine seemed to be a direct threat to China, especially as the Soviet press was calling the Cultural Revolution the product of the insane imagination of Mao.

Ideological differences thus played an important part in China's relations with the Soviet Union and the Eastern bloc nations. China's 'correct' ideological position became an important issue in its diplomatic relations. One could interpret the break with the Soviet Union as one motivated by growing Chinese expansionism in East Asia, but it would be difficult to overlook the role played by ideology and disagreements over its various interpretations.

Sino-American relations in the 1950s to the 1960s

The account of Sino-American relations could be one of missed opportunities by the United States. As Fairbank points out, 'we are left to contemplate how the United States could so signally have failed to see the possibility' in 1950 (1986: 311). Having missed the opportunity, the logic of the Cold War took over. The Korean War crystallized for the Americans and the Chinese their suspicions of each other; the direct involvement of both added bitterness to their relations that was to keep them at loggerheads until 1971. As the Korean War progressed, the Americans hardened their opposition to any claims by the Chinese on Taiwan, and moved their Seventh Fleet to the Taiwan Strait. This was perceived as a direct threat to China's security by its leadership, which then tried to force the issue by bombing the offshore Taiwanese island of Quemoy in 1954. The US response was to sign a mutual defence treaty with Chiang Kaishek's government.

It became impossible to establish diplomatic relations in this situation, further preventing dialogue between the two countries. China also supported the Vietnamese struggle against the French in Indochina, and sent arms and supplies to Ho Chi-minh. When the American government became involved in the conflict the relations between China and the United States worsened further. The US administration under President Eisenhower and Secretary of State Dulles were concerned with controlling the 'spread of communism' and increasing the American sphere of influence in East Asia. The Chinese leadership wanted to remove the US presence from the area as it posed a threat to its security.

Throughout the 1960s China faced complete isolation on the international stage. It was not only shunned by the two superpowers and their allies, but also by many regional states where Maoist revolutionaries had received Chinese support, such as Indonesia and India. During the Cultural Revolution the Red Guards attacked the embassies of various governments in Beijing. The Chinese leadership was so self-absorbed in its internal squabbles that foreign policy got very low priority.

THE THAW: CHINA REJOINS THE WORLD COMMUNITY

The 1970s saw dramatic changes in the world balance of power, and China was centrally involved in these changes. This period also reflects the growing importance of national security concerns in the Chinese leadership circles. The role of ideology is less clear here, though it was not entirely absent. The major development during this period was that of Sino-American *rapprochement* which led to realignment of world forces. While the Cold War was no longer virulent in the 1970s, the divisions between the superpowers were still deep. The Brezhnev Doctrine further exacerbated these hostilities; both the United

States and China felt threatened by this attack upon the policy of maintaining 'spheres of influence' that had been crafted during the Khrushchev years. The change in Sino-American relations should be read in the light of this new aggressive stance by the Soviet Union.

Paper tiger plays ping-pong

The American people's opposition to the Vietnam War had prompted presidential candidate Richard Nixon to suggest a reduction of American forces in East Asia during his campaign. However, while the American administration wanted to pull out it did not want to lose face in doing so; its status as a superpower meant that its withdrawal had to be presented as a considered decision rather than a defeat. The Chinese links with the Vietnamese communists were strong, and could be used to encourage accommodation at the Paris Peace Talks on Vietnam. This was of direct relevance to the Chinese who were feeling extremely threatened by the Soviets. While the erstwhile American imperialist 'paper tiger' was in withdrawal, the newly aggressive 'social imperialist' Soviet Union was engaged in extending its sphere of influence, and, as the Czechoslovak case had demonstrated, directly interfering in the internal affairs of sovereign nations. Having stood against both superpowers during the 1960s China had experienced isolation from the international community, and realized that its interests were not being well served. Economically and politically it needed to be part of the world system and this could not be achieved from behind the 'bamboo curtain'. The question before the Chinese leadership was which superpower to approach in order to regain access to international diplomatic channels.

The answer was not simple, and both national interest and ideology were important in the ensuing discussions within the Party leadership. The radicals, at this time led by Lin Biao, were opposed to approaching the United States because it was a capitalist and imperialist country. Instead they wanted to approach the Soviet Union, arguing that despite all the ideological differences between the two socialist states, both were still socialist. They shared the language of Marxism–Leninism, and an opposition to imperialism. It has been suggested that the Sino-Soviet military clashes were engineered by the Zhou Enlai faction, supported by Mao, that wanted to lean towards the United States, in order to discredit the radicals within the leadership (see Dreyer, 1993: 412–13). Whatever the situation, with the death of Lin Biao in 1971 in an air crash, as he allegedly fled to the Soviet Union, the starting of the Paris Peace Talks, and the Ussuri Island Incident, all became factors in the construction of a new Chinese policy of seeking *rapprochement* with the United States. There was caution on both sides, especially as Taiwan still presented a problem, though, as the coming months and years would show, not an insurmountable one.

The first indication of changing relations between the United States and China came when President Nixon relaxed travel and trade restrictions with China.

The Chinese leadership responded by inviting the US table tennis team to visit China, an invitation that was accepted with alacrity. 'Ping-pong diplomacy' was on.

Nixon's visit to Beijing in 1972 made the relationship public, and resulted in the Shanghai Communiqué which affirmed the desire of both countries to build a good relationship. The Taiwanese question was skirted around, though the United States did accept that 'All Chinese on either side of the Taiwan Strait maintain that there is but one China and Taiwan is a part of China'. The United States did not, however, make clear whether it agreed with this position. To break relations with Taiwan was not in the United States' interest as it would give the wrong signal to other allies of the United States; loyalty needed to be seen to be rewarded. With this question on the backburner, the relations between China and the United States continued to grow, culminating in the establishment of full diplomatic relations on 1 January 1979. The United States decided to end its formal relations with Taiwan, with the proviso that the United States would continue to provide Taiwan with defensive weapons. With the United States on its side, China also secured its seat in the UN Security Council in October 1971.

China and the Third World

With China back in the international arena, it began to tackle its relations with its neighbours, and with other Third World countries. In 1974 Mao posited 'a theory of Three Worlds' in which the First World comprised the two super-powers; the Second World comprised the satellite states of the superpowers – east and west European states, respectively; and a Third World which was struggling to overthrow the rule of 'superior nations'; Mao placed China in this last category. We have seen that Mao had placed China in the Third World in his original formulation of the theory of the Three Worlds. In 1974 he reaffirmed that world view, while pointing out that the Second World was economically and politically more independent than before. By placing itself in the Third World the Chinese leadership was not only accepting its economic position, but also staking a claim for the leadership of this world as its biggest and most powerful member.

Its stature enhanced by the permanent membership of the Security Council, the Chinese leadership set out to mend fences with its neighbours, in particular with India. It made clear to the radical political groups in India that they could no longer depend upon China's support. These groups had been splintered by sectarian doctrinal feuds, and had also been suppressed by the power of the Indian state during the internal emergency in 1975 making it easier for China to withdraw its support. China also withdrew support from the separatist movement in the Indian province of Nagaland on the north-east border of India. While its relations with Pakistan remained strong, it refrained from supporting Pakistan's claims against India. On the boundary dispute which was at the root of the problems between the two countries, both decided not to raise the issue, though neither withdrew its claim on it. Diplomatic relations were established between the two countries in July 1976.

While China improved relations with many non-socialist countries, ironically, its relations with socialist Vietnam reached an all-time low in 1978/1979. After its reunification, Vietnam had leaned towards the Soviet Union rather than China, which led to vicious political attacks by China on the new Vietnamese leadership. There was also the problem of overseas Chinese in Vietnam. When the Vietnamese communists 'expropriated' the assets of the 'capitalists' after the reunification, the Chinese protested at the treatment of the Chinese, eliciting a predictably dismissive response from the Vietnamese. Things came to a head when Vietnam invaded Kampuchea in December 1978. China saw this as a direct challenge since Kampuchea was one of its strongest allies in the region. The Sino-Vietnamese war ensued in February 1979 with Deng declaring that Vietnam must be 'taught a lesson'. The defeat of the PLA in this war had an important effect on the internal political dynamics in China (see Chapter 10), and also emphasized the security needs of the Chinese military.

China had learnt an important lesson in its conflict with Vietnam, and did not repeat the mistake of becoming directly involved when the Soviet Union invaded Afghanistan in December 1979. It did, however, break off negotiations with the Soviet Union on a new treaty to replace the Treaty of Friendship of 1950 which it had abrogated in 1979.

While China wanted to be the leader of the Third World, its economic interests increasingly undermined its political ambitions in that area. For example, China chose to join the World Bank and the IMF (International Monetary Fund) and is pressing for the membership of GATT (General Agreement on Tariffs and Trade), rather than becoming involved with the Non-Aligned Movement, or even OPEC (Organization of Petroleum Exporting Countries). In Asia, China began to turn more to Japan for economic investment, and in 1978 the two countries signed a Sino-Japanese Treaty of Peace and Friendship. Overseas Chinese were encouraged to invest in China, and even the Muslim minorities were used to persuade Arab countries to develop relations with China.

By the time that Mao died and the succession battles within the Party were over, China had come of age on the international stage. For the first time since the late nineteenth century, 'China is seen as a powerful and legitimate force in international affairs' and not as either dependent or deviant (Harding, 1987: 241).

CHINA IN A NEW WORLD ORDER

The 1980s saw China emerging as a major economic power in Asia, and the world. The economic reforms initiated by the Deng leadership led to immense opportunities for multi-national corporations from the West to invest in and trade with China. The result was a growing need to tie China further into the international economic system through membership of various international organizations. China, too, wanted to use this new mood of the Western powers to its advantage. As the 1980s wore on, it became clear that the Soviet Union and the East European countries were going through major crises, and 1989 saw the dissolution of the Eastern bloc with the success of the 'Velvet Revolution' in East Germany, Czechoslovakia, Hungary, and later, even Romania. The old polarities, which had already been undermined by Gorbachev's *glasnost*, became irrelevant during this period. It was clear by the end of the 1980s that state socialism had lost out to the economic power of international capitalism; the Western alliance was triumphant. China's situation was a unique one during this period. It was a socialist state, but not on the losing side; on the contrary, it was being wooed by all Western powers. However, the ideological fallout of the collapse of the Cold War system generated a tremendous rhetoric about the validity of liberal democracy as inextricably linked to capitalism; China's political model did not fit. This tension between the success of China's economic reforms, and its political system, has led to some difficulties in its relations with major Western powers. The major issues that China has faced and is facing in the last and the coming decade are the following: (a) security and sovereignty – resolution of border disputes, absorption of the treaty territories of Hong Kong and Macao, and the issue of Taiwan; (b) regional ethnic conflicts – Tibet, and growing Islamic influence in the north-west (see Chapter 13); and (c) pressure to improve human rights within China. However, on balance, it is the economic logic that has prevailed in the West, leaving China in a very strong position in its quest to enhance its international stature in the 1990s.

China, the Soviet Union and Russia

Sino-Soviet relations improved after the death of Brezhnev, and the eventual rise of Mikhail Gorbachev. As part of a process of reducing Soviet military expenditure and political liabilities, the Soviet army was recalled from Afghanistan. Troops concentration on the Chinese borders was greatly reduced on both sides. At the level of informal relations, border trade was encouraged, and many delegations exchanged at the middle level of state bureaucracies. Gorbachev's visit to Beijing in May 1989 was of great symbolic significance as marking the end of the two-decades-long schism between the two countries. However, the Soviet Union continued to pose problems for the Chinese leadership. The Chinese found the internal situation in the Soviet Union was a cause of concern. The disintegration of the Eastern bloc signified to them the collapse of state socialism, a system they supported in China. Politburo member Yao Yilin's advice to Honecker to crush the democracy movement in Germany, though embarrassing later, was given in all seriousness. At the international level, the praise that Gorbachev got from Western governments for his policy of *glasnost* – a political 'opening up' – seemed an implicit criticism of China's refusal to follow suit. The Chinese leadership found this criticism unacceptable, and felt justifed in maintaining a centralized authority of the state in light of the collapse of the Soviet Union; the collapse of which also marked the end of the familiar triangular relations among world powers. China would have to find a new framework within which to place its foreign policies.

While the border tensions between the Soviet Union and China had receded under Gorbachev, there is a growing sense of alarm among the Chinese leadership about the expanding influence of Islamic states in the neighbouring Muslim states of Azerbaijan and Tadjikistan, and the impact of religious affiliations on Muslim minorities in China's Xinjiang Autonomous Region (see Chapter 13). Without a centralized power in Moscow to keep the minorities in check, the Chinese fear that its minorities will find succour in these newly formed Islamic states, leading to internal tensions in China. There is little that it has been able to do, as yet, to stem this growing influence of religion in the area.

China and the United States

The Tiananmen Incident adversely affected China's relations with the United States and the West. There was a considerable slowing down of investment in China between 1989 and 1991. The US administration suspended all official exchanges with China at or above the level of assistant secretary, and imposed a ban on military sales to China and high-level military exchanges. The European Community followed suit, as did Japan. The World Bank and the IMF halted new lending and GATT negotiations on China's membership were also suspended. The Gulf War and the Nato bombings in the Yugoslav–Bosnian conflict have underlined the unchecked dominance of the United States on the world stage. The conjunction of internal and external pressures, for a time, undermined the Chinese leadership's confidence. Its response was two-fold: first, to emphasize China's sovereignty and independence, and its resistance to foreign pressures to modify its internal policies; and, second, to clarify that the Chinese leadership would not reverse its economic reforms. There has also been an increase spending on defence (see Chapter 10). China has used a combination of threats, incentives and concessions to regain ground it had lost after 4 June 1989.

Taiwan and Chinese foreign policy

An important irritant for Chinese relations with the United States has been the US position on Taiwan. Under the provisions of the 1979 Taiwan Relations Act, the United States continued to sell arms to Taiwan. This was unacceptable to the Chinese leadership as a long-term situation, and its pressure on the United States resulted in a communiqué in 1982 wherein the United States agreed to reduce and eventually cease arms sales to Taiwan, but no timetable was laid down. The arms sales, however, continued at a high level until 1992 when President Bush announced the sale of 150 f-16 fighter jets to Taiwan. While this was intended as a boost to the arms industry in the United States, its political fallout was negative. More recently, a row broke over the granting of a US visa to the president of Taiwan; China protested furiously, and the United States, while standing by its decision, has indicated that another such visa would be unlikely in the near future.

While these irritations wax and wane, the Chinese leadership has continued to provide incentives for Taiwanese economic investment in China. Since 1987, Taiwan's economic investment in China has increased sharply, especially in the Xiamen region and Fujian Province (Lieberthal, 1995: 325). As one of the areas that constitutes China's 'near abroad' (Lieberthal, 1995: 323), and because of the history of the conflict with KMT, the resolution of the sovereignty issue has been given high priority by the Chinese regime. Rhetorically, it has called for the unification of China on the basis of a policy of 'one nation, two systems' indicating acceptance of the Taiwanese economic system. It has also also encouraged 'people to people' exchanges. Under a policy of 'flexible diplomacy' it no longer requires the countries it deals with to cut their relations with Taiwan. However, the situation has become more complicated because of a growing indigenous Taiwanese movement that wants independence from China, under whoever's leadership it is constituted. If a formal declaration of independence is declared by the Democratic Progressive Party, it will provoke a crisis for China. It is difficult to anticipate how this might be resolved.

Hong Kong – the extension of sovereignty

The 'one nation, two systems' slogan is also important in the process of China's reabsorption of Hong Kong in 1997, which is the other territory constituting China's 'near abroad'. The United Kingdom and China signed a Joint Declaration on the transfer Hong Kong on 19 December 1984. China agreed that Hong Kong would be granted the status of a special administrative region (SAR) and will keep some powers of self-government, while Beijing would take over the making of its foreign and defence policy. The attempts of the last British governor of Hong Kong – Chris Patten – to increase the political ambit of the Legislative Council of Hong Kong have not been acceptable to the Chinese leadership, leading to confrontation between the United Kingdom and China on the one hand, and between the Democratic Party in Hong Kong and the Governor (who is seen by many as unable to deliver on his promises) on the other. There has also been controversy over the plans for the building of a new international airport in Hong Kong. China was not consulted and demanded a freeze on the project. After a lot of posturing on both sides, the Chinese won, and the British assured them that they will be consulted in the running of the territory in the period leading up to 1997.

Human rights and international diplomacy

China has come under some pressure on the issue of human rights at international fora like the World Conference on Women in Beijing in September 1995. Both non-governmental organizations (NGOs) like Amnesty International and professional organizations like the Pen Club, and the governments of Western powers – in particular the US administration, have pressed for the need to take issue with the Chinese state on the issue of human rights. China's political prestige, and even its economic position in the world economic system, have at times been threatened by this issue. It has been pointed out that while the Chinese Constitution guarantees individual freedoms, it also includes the Four Cardinal Principles which undermine those freedoms by asking for unquestioning loyalty to the CCP. Once the basis of 'counter-revolutionary' practice is laid in the constitution, those dissenting from the Party become easy targets.

A number of rights such as the privacy of correspondence, of political association, etc., are not sufficiently respected by the Chinese authorities, and a general culture of intolerance and high-handed treatment of individuals which emerged in the 1950s is still very much in evidence.

Offences of espionage, betrayal of state secrets, and subversion of the state, have been used to attack individual freedom to dissent. The Chinese courts, in dealing with political offences, mete out very harsh prison sentences, often up to 15 years, followed by an additional number of years deprivation of political rights. Lenient sentences are used if the prisoner cooperates with the authorities. The lack of strong legal guarantees for the defence, and justified doubts about the professional and political independence of the Chinese judiciary, have given rise to a questioning of convictions and the due process of law in China. Rules of detention and arrest strongly favour the public security organizations against the individual, whose rights are very limited. The Chinese penal system includes the death penalty for a number of offences, like economic crimes, which in most Western countries would be treated more leniently. The announcement of death penalties at large rallies and the public parading of convicts before execution are seen by many as incompatible with a sound judicial system.

The extensive use of the death penalty has caused concern at a time when China is witnessing a general rise in levels of crime due to migration and increased social difference in the country. The Chinese law enforcement agencies, which originally based themselves on internal, community-based control and surveillance techniques, have found it difficult to police a population on the move. The difficulty of law enforcement has been in the combination of poor training of the public security organs to deal with new types of crimes, and also the fact that local powerholders have been entangled in alliances with criminals, holding back the police and judicial system from taking action against some sections of organized crime syndicates.

In a unipolar world, the liberal democratic rhetoric is dominant, and China is criticized in the international fora and media for not meeting what are considered to be international standards of human rights. Liberal democratic theory makes two suppositions about the state–individual relations: first, that the individual has rights *against* the state, and second, that the individual needs a civil space uncoerced by the state to exercise these rights. Both these suppositions lead to an anti-state stance. Given the predominance of the state in the socialist societies, it was easy to target the political system in these countries. Human rights and the dominant state thus became important instruments to attack the socialist system – first, during the Cold War, and then again after the fall of the Soviet Union and the communist bloc. In the post-communist world system, there has developed the concept of 'political conditionality' which is explicitly linked to the spread of liberal political systems in the aid-seeking countries. This conditionality was also applied to China, especially after the Tiananmen Incident, through constant threats by the United States to withdraw the Most Favoured Nation status from China if it does not improve its human rights record. The Western governments have also given support to particular dissident groups in China. While there has been some dissident activity in China, unlike such activity in the Soviet Union, it is largely limited to a small section of intellectuals who are being supported by groups of Chinese political exiles. The issue of censorship and media monopoly has also been taken up by international organizations. Without independent media, the Chinese rely on informal networks of information about China. However, the widespread generalizations and inaccuracies of reporting on the Chinese political situation undermine the confidence among ordinary Chinese in the international media, and so have an adverse effect in the forming of a critical opposition in China.

China has responded to this pressure with characteristic robustness, maintaining that any interference in its internal affairs is an unacceptable infringement of its sovereignty. It has also referred to the principle of non-interference to resist any pressures on the human rights issue. China seeks to dissociate the issue of human rights from economic relations with the West. It points out that Chinese developmental imperatives, its political system and philosophy, and its political culture do not view the relations between the individual and the state in the way that the liberal political theorists do. The discussion on New Authoritarianism (see Chapter 6, pp. 140–1) is relevant here.

However, when there has been the threat that verbal battles over human rights might damage the growing economic relations between China and the Western countries, especially the United States, both parties have thus far opted for compromise and negotiation. While an irritant, the human rights issue is not one that seems an insurmountable obstacle to the growing importance of China in world affairs.

China and nuclear weapons

Another issue that is of significance concerning China's relations with the West, in particular the United States, is that of nuclear weapons. China did not agree with the Partial Nuclear Test Ban Treaty of 1963; it wanted a total ban on nuclear weapons. However, in October 1964, China carried out its own first nuclear test. Given its isolated international position during the 1960s, it justified its nuclear programme as a part of its defence against superpower (especially Soviet) attack. It did not change its stance on the destruction of all nuclear weapons, pointing out that the two superpowers between them possessed 95 per cent of the world nuclear arsenal. During the 1970s, China's criticism of the Soviet nuclear programme was much more stringent than that of the American one. In the 1980s, China resisted US demands to curtail its nuclear programme on the grounds that the nuclear weapons of the superpowers and the Western powers constituted a potential threat to its national security. With the reduced military budgets of the late 1980s, China was able to claim that it was reducing the size and scope of its nuclear programme. It has, however, been cautious about the prospects of a nuclear-free world, and has continued to develop its nuclear programme; for example it carried out nuclear tests in 1995, despite supporting the Nuclear Non-Proliferation Treaty.

CONCLUSIONS

China has emerged as a significant international player during the 1980s and 1990s. Its size, the phenomenal growth in its economy, the opening up of China, and its military capacity have all contributed to China's important position on the international stage. This growth in China's stature is set to continue, especially if China's economic success continues. In the context of China's growing economic strength, there has been a increasing discussion of a concept of a Greater China. While being without a precise meaning, broadly speaking it emphasizes the increasing interaction among the economies of China, Hong Kong and Taiwan. It is argued that cultural bonds and convergence of economic interests will combine to bring about a political union encompassing these distinct areas. The union with Hong Kong is already assured; Taiwan will present a greater problem, especially as there is a growing movement of indigenous Taiwanese who would like to be independent of Chinese domination, whether it be of the KMT or the CCP. China's policy of 'one nation, two systems' is regarded as an attempt to facilitate the transition of Greater China from concept to reality. Whether this dream is realized or not will depend largely on the way succession to Deng is managed; and the way the process of transfer of power in Hong Kong from the United Kingdom to China is carried out.

China is well placed to benefit from the success of its economic reforms in its relations with other world powers. There are some imponderables – the question of Taiwan, the process of reabsorption of Hong Kong, for example – that continue to exercise the Chinese leadership and Western governments. However, for the most part, its ongoing progress in establishing itself in the international community seems set to continue.

FURTHER READING

See Fairbank (1968) for China's perceptions of the world, and especially see Schwartz (1968) and Fitzgerald (1964). For more recent psychological profiling of China, see Shih (1990).

For an overview of the Maoist foreign policy, see Yahuda (1978). For Sino-Soviet relations, a Beijing-biased book would be Mehnert's *Peking and Moscow* (1963); also see Zagoria (1962) and Medvedev (1986). For Sino-Indian relations, see Maxwell (1971).

For overviews of China's post-Mao foreign policy, see Harding (1984), Kim (1984), Yahuda (1983) and Lieberthal (1995: especially Chapter 12). For Sino-Taiwan relations, see Long (1991); also, see Deng (1984a).

PART III
The economy

The Chinese economy is in all respects an important political factor. The Chinese path of development has been based on the planned economy. The political structures for managing the economy have, throughout the period, been of prime importance in the Chinese state and have determined the availability of policy options. The two chapters in this part focus on the political–economic apparatus and its dynamics, which are very different from those in capitalist countries. Chapter 9 describes the economic system of the 1950s to the 1970s, outlining the justifications and inherent problems of the planned economy. Chapter 10 examines the Chinese economic system since 1976, indicating two strategies for growth: Hua Guofeng's unsuccessful attempt, and the reform policy initiated by Deng Xiaoping. The legacy of the planned economy and the continued state intervention in the economy proved to constitute a dynamic stimulus for economic growth.

9 The Chinese economy I (1949–1976)

China's economy in the 1950s until the early 1980s was a fully fledged socialist economy, and thereafter it has increasingly turned into a mixed economy, which officially is called a 'socialist market economy'. Here we explore China's unique path to economic development in two chapters. In this chapter we present the formation of the socialist economy in the early and mid-1950s, discuss the shock of the Great Leap Forward, the stabilization of growth in the early 1960s, the stagnation of the Cultural Revolution and the suppressed development of the early 1970s.

THE FOUNDATIONS OF THE SOCIALIST ECONOMY

The socialist economy, as it was introduced in China in the early 1950s and continued to exist for over 30 years, differs radically from liberal market economies. The state controlled the economy by enforcing a state plan. It also monopolized the distribution of all goods and commodities. Instead of attempting a formalistic definition of a socialist economy here, we want to outline the moral justifications and ideological origins of the economic formation in China, and describe how it was brought into reality by the Chinese Communist Party.

The Chinese Communist Party's political mission is to establish a communist society in China, a society which does not allow exploitation of people by other people – a genuinely classless society characterized by an equal distribution of wealth and opportunities. This ideal reflects the last stage on the development ladder as prescribed in Marxist–Leninist ideology, where societal formations (or, in Marxist terminology, modes of production) must pass from primeval or primitive communism through slavery, feudalism, capitalism and socialism, in order to reach the utopian goal of communism. In the Chinese case, the development of capitalism was stymied. This was because the forces of imperialism and feudalism joined together to suppress the bourgeois revolution and quell the rise of domestic capitalism. As a consequence, the Chinese Communist Party must first make a bourgeois revolution, creating the conditions of capitalism. After this, the revolution of the proletariat must lead the country into the socialist phase. Socialism, and accordingly socialist economy, are not the ultimate goal, and thus do not reflect the ideal state of development, but constitute a transitional phase leading up to communism. The socialist economy must hence be understood both as a moral mission and as an imperfect structure.

The socialist economy seeks to achieve justice and social equality by:

- enabling the dictatorship of the proletariat, i.e. political control, which minimizes the risk of exploitation;
- allowing socialist public ownership of the means of production – in China this takes three basic forms: ownership by the whole people (state ownership), and ownership by the labouring masses (manifested in urban collective ownership and rural collective ownership);
- planning of the economy at central levels of government; and
- distribution of wealth according to labour.

These fall short of the communist utopia, which would know only common ownership, which would ensure all humanity a distribution of wealth according to need, and where the edifice of the state would have disintegrated. Socialism by its very nature only imperfectly approximates the benign aspects of the communist ideal.

The socialist economy is considered to be morally superior. It defines itself as different from other modes of production, which all represent exploitative relations between people. Equal economic rights and moral justice are dispensed by the leadership of the Chinese Communist Party. According to the theory, the party exercises dictatorship over those who intend to subject others to exploitation. The socialist mode of production is the only mode of production which is considered able to promote the development of the forces of production in synergy; all other modes of production must fail and end in revolutions because they become incapable of giving direction to the development of the forces of production; they become constraints to progress of social production and must subside. The socialist mode of production, however, is based on the correct understanding of the objective laws that govern progress, and so the progressive class, the proletariat, is enabled to consciously realize communism by perfecting the socialist mode of production and adapting it to the evolution of the productive forces. Accordingly, the transition to communism from socialism will not take the form of a revolution, but will be a gradual process.

This socialist economic dogma is an essential underpinning of the socialist system and forms an important barrier to the acceptance of different economic systems; and it has had an important influence over the choice of options during the reform period in the 1980s and 1990s.

MODES OF PRODUCTION

The Marxist theory regards the advance of history as determined by the way in which social production (i.e. the production which is necessary to uphold human society) is organized. According to this theory, the fundamental determinant is the level of the productive forces, i.e. the tools, skills and technologies available to society. The relative complexity of the productive forces requires different types of relations of production (i.e. forms of social organization) in order to be utilized in the most rational way. Together, the productive forces and the existing relations of production form a mode of production. The most simple mode of production is primitive communism, a sort of primordial society in which there is no scope for anybody to exploit fellow humans. In primitive communism, tools of production and technical skills are simple. In human history the next mode of production is slavery, in which production has reached a certain scale of operation and needs a large input of organized human labour. The exploitation takes place as the slaveowner's confiscation of the total product of his slaves' work; at the same time the slaveowner must ensure his slaves' lives and reproduction. The forces of production underlying slavery generally represent a low level of technology. Feudalism is the third mode of production in Marxist theory; it is based on the physical extraction of a part of the tenant farmers' product by the landlord. Production under feudalism is technically more varied and advanced, requiring a level of skill and a scale of operation which exceeds the capacity of slavery, i.e. the forces of production are more advanced. Capitalism represents the large-scale production for a market, where the owners of the means of production (the capitalists) hire in workers (the proletariat) to work for them; the capitalists exploit the workers by only paying them a fraction of the value of the work which is embedded in their product. The forces of production of capitalism are highly advanced. The last mode of production is communism, a system where nobody exploits anybody else, and reflecting the highest possible level of technological development, i.e. further-advanced forces of production. Socialism is only a transient phase between capitalism and communism, and does not constitute a proper mode of production in itself.

According to this theory, at certain incisive points in history, the development of the forces of production is constrained by the social relations of production, and so the objective basis for a change in the mode of production has appeared. This occurs in the form of social revolutions, by which old ownership structures are replaced by new ownership structures.

REVISIONISM AND RADICALISM IN THE CHINESE POLITICAL ECONOMY

The 1950s and 1960s were dominated by the disagreement over how to interpret the socialist economic dogma. The struggle between political lines (or, in a different formulation, between factions within the leadership) was determined by the exegesis of Marxism–Leninism–Mao-Zedong-thought within a radical or a revisionist framework. Throughout the period between

1949 and 1978 the radical interpretation prevailed, but was strongly contested, especially in the mid-1950s, the early 1960s and the early 1970s.

What do the terms mean? How could they be of such dominating influence over the political system? The first point to make is that neither 'revisionism' nor 'radicalism' are terms that their proponents would use to classify themselves with. We use these terms because they give a clear indication of the meaning. Those in the Chinese leadership who associated themselves with Mao Zedong were 'radicals', while those associated with Liu Shaoqi and Deng Xiaoping were 'revisionists'.

Revisionism

The main argument carried forward by the revisionists was that the socialist mode of production was advanced, while the stage of development of the productive forces was backward – that there was a mismatch between the structures organizing production and the technological level of production. Progress, in the revisionists' opinion, could only be achieved if all political and economic activity was aimed at promoting the development of the productive forces, while gradually adapting the socialist mode of production.

Revisionists emphasized private, individual interest as a way to improve production and economic efficiency, so they favoured the use of economic incentives, small-scale private production, bonus payments to effective workers and the contracting out of production tasks to individuals. They also favoured a prolonged policy of nationalizing the national capitalist assets. They regarded the socialist period as protracted and focused on economic growth. Revisionism, in this sense, could also be termed 'economism'. The incentive to produce was located in the individual's personal gain.

Radicalism

The radicals, however, emphasized that the change of the ownership structures to public ownership and the introduction of a fully fledged socialist planned economy, as well as the abolition of differential treatment between labourers, would enable the development of the productive forces. The moral superiority of the socialist system would instil the right spirit in the working masses, and those who had not fully understood that their interests and those of society coincided, could be educated and mobilized for the development of the economy. The incentive to produce was located in moral pressure and the ability of the party to instil political motivation and social responsibility in the workforce.

Allowing personal interest and individualist incentives would, in their opinion, breed capitalist or feudalist exploitation, and therefore revisionism was considered to be retrograde or restorationist, wanting to re-establish past modes of production. The emphasis on the will of the leadership could lead us to term radicalism as 'voluntarism'.

The conflict between these two approaches was very intense and fundamentally irreconcilable. It is the key to understanding some of the most prominent problems during the Great Leap Forward, the Great Proletarian Cultural Revolution and the struggles in the 1970s. However, we must keep in mind that both are understandings of socialist economy, interpretations which have a place within the framework of Marxism–Leninism and the moral mission of socialism. It is wrong to characterize revisionism as capitalist.

THE ECONOMY AND CLASS ANALYSIS

The transition of China towards socialism in the early 1950s took place in two stages. The first stage represented the New Democratic Revolution, which established the people's dictatorship, aiming at abolishing imperialism and feudalism. The second stage was the socialist transition, which aimed at doing away with the national capitalist element in the economy, and at socializing production activity. The second stage reflected the beginnings of the 'dictatorship of the proletariat'.

In both stages the main task for the Chinese leadership was to establish which types of persons could be included in the economy. Those who represented feudal exploitation (landlords) and imperialism (foreign capitalists and their Chinese aides) would have to be deprived of their power in the first stage; those who represented the (more benign) national capitalist class, and thus capitalist exploitation, would have to be suppressed in the second phase. Following this logic, rights must be distributed according to class status in a Marxist sense, i.e. defined by the ownership of the means of production and thus the nature of the relationship with the labourers.

The Chinese Communist Party had from its inception in 1921 sought to capture the structures of social and political reality in China by conducting class analysis, dividing the Chinese population into various economic categories to gauge their potential strategic and political support for the revolution. While the origin of the class analysis was based on economic status, i.e. ownership, it soon became an exclusively strategic notion, which enabled the Chinese Communist Party to designate the friends and foes of the revolution. The act of allocating class status moved from objective description to subjective prescription, and it hence became an arbitrary allocation of rights.

Institutionalized class status

Class status was institutionalized as a political and institutional ranking of Chinese citizens between 1949 until early 1979, when 'bad' class status was abolished ('good' class status was never abolished). It took two basic forms: that of class status and that of family background. Those who had positively belonged to, say, the landlord class, before 1949, had landlord class status, while children of landlords, born after 1949, had landlord family background.

Class status and family background fixed the economic and social rights of their bearers, and so played an immensely critical role in the economy – for 30 years determining the social mobility of people, both occupationally and in marriage patterns.

The majority, those who were lucky enough to be classified within the range of classes which were considered to belong to the 'people' rather than the 'enemies of the people', enjoyed rights as co-owners of public assets under the public-ownership systems.

THE ROLE OF THE STATE

The economic plan

The economy was modelled on the Soviet Union's planned economy. The idea was that the state by centrally governing the flow of resources could achieve an optimal distribution of production factors (labour, investment capital, raw materials, energy, equipment, land, etc.) and thereby the most rational production.

The structure of state planning takes several forms, manifested in the long-term strategic 10-year plans, the medium-term 5-year plans, and the plans for the current year. Five-year plans and current-year plans were the most important policy documents in China since the first 5-year plan period which started in 1953. They were from the very beginning written into the constitutions, and the government must each year give a report on plan fulfilment.

The state plan was based on balancing industrial input and output targets for specific regions, sectors and enterprises. By creating a table of all supply demands and production targets, as well as their projected growth rate, it was possible to project production. The central plan stated the national framework, which was then filled in by the ministries and by the provincial government, deriving the relevant targets from the central plan. The planning procedure was replicated down to the individual factory or village. The 'material balances', were very large calculations, which involved substantial adjustments and negotiations each year. Chinese industrial management during more than 30 years was focused on achieving advantages under the plan, which would allow for upholding the material standard of each *danwei*.

Each plan included the production targets to be achieved, and also the allocations of production factors (including capital investment) which could be expected. The central plan normally listed all large investment projects.

The planned economy required a large political and administrative apparatus, and planning was in reality spread between a number of discrete institutions at the centre, as well as becoming increasingly decentralized after 1957 (Figure 9.1).

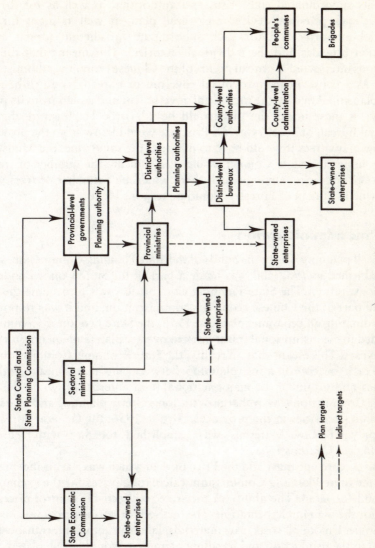

Figure 9.1 *Planning system in the 1950s to the 1980s in China*

The state plans have a dual dimension: they are sectoral and regional alike. Below the level of the central state plan, there are plans for: (a) each ministry and all its subordinated enterprises and authorities, as well as for (b) each province; each province devised an overall plan, as well as plans for each provincial authority and for each subordinate jurisdiction (down to the production brigades and the individual factories). This means that the plan tabulations intersected at crucial points of the Chinese economic administrative system. As a consequence, provincial government bureaux were to be under both a plan stipulated by the provincial government and a plan from its parent ministry; at these nodes the plan could be adjusted. To illustrate this: the Provincial Bureau of Forestry in XX Province would know from the provincial plan how many trees it would have to plant; at the same time, the Ministry of Forestry under the State Council would also indicate the number of trees to plant in XX Province, among which there would be a number of trees which the Provincial Bureau of Forestry would be responsible for.

Economic administration

The overall planning was in the hands of the State Planning Commission, which was established in 1952 and was made a part of the State Council under the 1954 Constitution. The State Planning Commission was to become the most powerful part of the Chinese economic administration, and it was responsible for coordinating all economic plans. In 1956, the State Economic Commission was added to the institutional framework to oversee plan implementation in the current years. This means that, in reality, the State Economic Commission took up the task of coordinating planning between the many heavy industry ministries and a number of major national-level enterprises, while the State Planning Commission was in charge of the longer-term planning and overseeing the planning activities in the provinces. Also in 1956, the General Bureau for the Supply of Raw Materials was established together with the State Technological Commission.

To this picture one must add the Price Bureau which was a semi-independent part of the State Planning Commission, calculating prices for the exchange of goods and for retail. The ability of the state to effectively control prices was crucial for the plan implementation. The method for setting prices was inspired by the Soviet Union: all costs (raw materials, labour, equipment, transport etc.) involved in the production and handling of an item would be calculated, using standard cost tables which would be revised every year. The Marxist theoretical foundation for the price-setting exercise was to let the price reflect the socialized labour embodied in the commodity. Once the prices had been determined by the Price Bureau, they would be officially passed by the State Council in order to ensure that all departments were bound by them.

Production was organized in large industry-specific ministries, which had large subordinated companies. They were directly in charge of the large state-owned companies, and at the same time responsible for the supervision of provincial and lower-level administrative bodies.

Chinese state ownership of the means of production has two dimensions: type and level – state ownership is defined as different from collective ownership, and is organized by level of ownership. State-owned enterprises can be owned by the national government, by provincial governments, by city governments or by county-level governments. Each level of government has an appropriate authority which controls the subordinated enterprises.

The local government bureaux are hence subjected to two types of authority: the local government and the line ministry under the State Council. Enterprises are administrated in an ambiguous structure where local and central interests intersect. The Chinese term for this is '*tiaotiao, kuaikuai*', meaning 'branches and areas' (Figure 9.2).

The administrative level of ownership has a number of consequences for understanding the structure of the Chinese economy. An obvious point is that

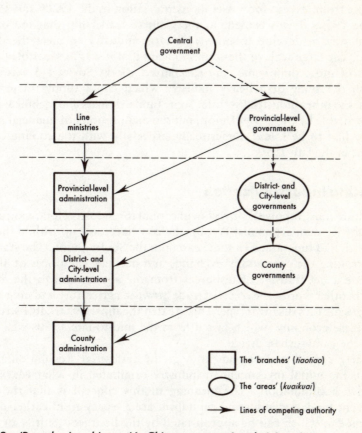

Figure 9.2   '*Branches' and 'areas' in Chinese economic administration*

the situations of two neighbouring enterprises can differ radically due to the level of ownership. Centrally funded enterprises normally had priority, more power and influence, better provisions and better funding than local ones. Large, centrally owned enterprises do not contribute to the local economy; their profit remittances (until 1982) went directly to the centre, and, being self-contained units, they encompassed all provisions and were only marginally integrated with local economy.

DEVELOPMENT AND INDUSTRIALIZATION STRATEGY

One of the most difficult tasks for a country which has a low degree of industrialization is to achieve rapid growth rates in industrial production. Capital accumulation for industrialization in early capitalism followed many different patterns, which could not easily be emulated in a poor country in the twentieth century. The Chinese communists did not have many models of development to choose from, except for Soviet industrialization in the 1920s and 1930s.

In the 1950s it was evident to the Chinese leadership that the only way forward was to develop a sufficiently large industry to meet the domestic demand. The large scale of the country meant that it was not feasible to rely on imports of more than some very specialized goods. Soviet aid was spent to establish the spine of a heavy industry which could supply materials and machines to other industrial sectors. Some funds, designs and technical aid were made available by the Soviet Union, but the main sources of financial inputs to industry had to be found domestically, especially with the cooling of Soviet relations in the late 1950s.

Financing industrialization

Agriculture must supply the investment capital for industry, following a scheme which the Russian economist Preobrazhensky had come up with in the 1930s, and which had functioned to some extent in the Soviet Union. The state could, by controlling the commodity exchange and deciding the prices of all goods, effectuate a net transfer of resources from the agricultural to the industrial sector. In other words, the terms of trade between agriculture and industry must be in agriculture's disadvantage. This created the most remarkable structure of the Chinese economy, which lasted from the mid-to-late 1950s well into the 1980s: the rural–urban divide.

In early capitalist development (e.g. the Industrial Revolution in Great Britain), the initial investment in industry originated in what Marx termed 'primitive accumulation'. The meaning of this concept is that the original investment funds for industrial capitalism are a legacy from earlier phases of development, which can be appropriated by the bourgeoisie: it is an external resource, freely available for industrialization.

By analogy, the Chinese state would have to regard Chinese agriculture as an external resource, which could be freely exploited for the sake of industrialization. But for ideological reasons (exploitation being considered immoral), the socialist state could not accept exploitation and had an obligation to prevent dire poverty from emerging.

Also, the blind development of a heavy industry in China, which was pursued in imitation of the Soviet model, gave rise to political concern in China. Mao Zedong, making a speech in 1956 on the 'Ten Great Relationships' argued for the prudent coordination of industrial and rural development. In order to be able to profit from the products of heavy industry, agriculture must be modernized, and excessive focus on industry would have a negative effect on agriculture.

For these reasons the Chinese embarked on a unique development strategy which in theory allowed accumulation to originate in agriculture, and at the same time ensured modernization of agriculture and a levelling of social differences in the countryside. A main difference between the Chinese model and the feudalist/capitalist extraction of surpluses for industrialization was that the other systems rely on exploitation of one class by another class as a pivot between agriculture and industry, while the extraction in China took place through administrative structures. An egalitarian distribution prevented the emergence of relative deprivation and of excessive poverty. This is not to say that there was no poverty in rural China, but this poverty did not reflect different classes in the countryside. We will in the following sections explain the structures adopted in China in more detail.

Also, if we make comparisons with other developing countries, the Chinese industrialization model was unique, because industrialization was relatively more capital intensive and less labour intensive than one would normally expect in a developing country.

The rural–urban divide

The Chinese development model was based on the strict division of the economy into the agricultural and the industrial sectors. The Chinese state authorities gained control over the flow of resources between the two sectors, in order to pursue the development of heavy industry as a strategy (Box 9.1).

The flow of resources, most importantly, included control over migration and labour allocation. In the following we shall discuss the terms of resource flows between the two sectors by looking at the five major elements: labour, raw materials, markets, investment capital and food.

The major flaw in this sectoral division was that it was impossible to limit the division functionally to two sectors of the economy. The division was in reality between two parts of society, and covered a much larger field than only economic exchange.

Box 9.1   *The Three Big Differences*
In Chinese political discourse, the rural–urban divide is phrased in the language of the 'Three Big Differences'. The three big differences are:

1. the difference between industry and agriculture;
2. the difference between cities and the countryside; and
3. the difference between intellectual and manual work.

These differences continued to exist after the introduction of socialism, but they must be eliminated before China can proceed to become a communist country.

As is obvious from the analysis in this book, the division lines between industry and agriculture, and between cities and countryside, were pretty much reinforced by the socialist state. The way in which the state controlled the flow of resources between them meant that the differences widened rather than narrowed during the socialist period.

Labour

In order to control the allocation of labour to all aspects of production it was necessary to define the need for labour. This was done positively for the industrial and service sectors, but negatively for agriculture. Ideally, those people who were needed in industry and service were recruited, while the rest, by default, were labourers in agriculture.

The administrative system set up to control the labour force was effective from around 1957: it was the household registration system. Each inhabitant in China was registered in a place of residence – by default, the father's place of origin. Changes in residence could only occur with the permission of the authorities both in the original place of residence and in the receiving place (the only really common way of relocation was marriage: a woman would leave the paternal village for the groom's village). In addition to this, the household registration system indicated whether a person had an 'agricultural household status' or an 'urban resident household status'. Only people with an 'urban resident' status were entitled to employment through the labour administration of the state, those with 'agricultural' status by definition belonged to the collective economy of the people's commune system, and their employment was a matter for the production brigades and production teams.

While the place of registration followed the paternal line, the registration status (agricultural or urban resident) followed the maternal line; any children under the age of 16 would be registered in accordance with their mother's status and their father's place of registration. Some residents in rural areas had urban resident status, including leading cadres of the people's commune (who were considered to be a type of state employee), workers in state-owned factories and mines in rural surroundings, some senior teachers in rural schools, etc. While their residence was rural, their status was urban. It was very difficult to change household registration status; the main avenues to change it from agricultural to urban status were to serve as a soldier or to take a higher education.

The rationale of the system was to bureaucratically distinguish between those eligible for work in state enterprises and those who were not – only people with urban residence were qualified. The labour administration bureau was, in theory, in charge of distributing the labour force rationally between the state-owned enterprises; recruitment of new labourers was a state monopoly. It was the task of the Labour Administration Bureau to match the supply of new entrants (school leavers, university graduates, returned soldiers, etc.) with the demands of state-owned enterprises.

The labour allocation system, however, became quite farcical in the late 1950s, when the supply of new entrants far exceeded the demand for labourers because the state pursued a policy of capital-intensive industrialization. Because the system was based on entitlement to employment for all urban residents who reached the working age, the labour administration bureaux in reality became responsible for overstaffing the state-owned enterprises, rather than ensuring a rational allocation of labour.

As a consequence of the strain on resources this caused, the state, in 1962, started the policy of sending urban school leavers ('rusticated youths' or 'young intellectuals') to the countryside to work. These young people lost their urban resident status and thereby their entitlement to job allocation in state enterprises. This policy was pursued for 16–17 years, and was abolished in 1979. In that period in excess of 17 million school leavers were sent to the countryside. The whole policy was couched in Maoist rhetoric about the young having to learn to lead a frugal life, learning from the peasants, and experiencing the 'taste of bitterness' (*chiku*), and it was coordinated intimately with Red Guard mobilization during the Great Proletarian Cultural Revolution, exploiting group pressure among the youngsters. Stripped down to its economic rationale, however, this mass movement can be understood as an attempt to make both ends meet in the balance sheet of the state under conditions where there was no market mechanism that could equilibrate supply and demand in the labour allocation.

Between the 1950s and the end of the 1970s the state took in considerable numbers of rural labourers to work in state-owned industry, mainly to take charge of menial tasks considered to be too dirty or dangerous for urban residents; this was of a relatively short duration which did not merit a recruitment for life. The majority of these rural labourers were employed as temporary workers or 'peasant workers'. Most never received urban household status or rights equivalent to those of their colleagues. However, on several occasions, there was a policy to accommodate longer-term rural contract workers, and some were accordingly awarded urban resident status and officially joined the ranks of workers. For peasants, temporary work in state enterprises did not constitute a regular way out of agriculture to an urban career.

How could the migration control of the household registration system be upheld so effectively? The system was supported by a host of other measures, most notably the total state domination of trade, especially in food products. All core products were rationed, and could only be purchased with the right coupons. If one had no grain and other foodstuff coupons from the relevant city authorities, one could not even buy a meal in a restaurant.

The state control of labour allocation was inherently flawed because it divided China into peasants and urbanites and allocated structurally different rights to the two groups. It was incapable of fulfilling its task of limiting staffing in state enterprises at rational levels because the natural increase in the urban population at working age was greater than the demand for labour.

The system was truly an instrument for industrialization rather than for rational allocation of labour in all sectors. This is because it did not consider the development of agriculture, and assumed that agriculture could accommodate any number of labourers who were not used in industry.

Raw materials

Agriculture supplied important raw materials for industry. These include cotton, hemp, silk and other fibres for the textile industry, raw materials for food and feed processing industries, leather and hide industries, etc.

The supply of raw materials was monopolized by the state. The Ministry of Trade (internal trade, that is) was responsible for coordinating the procurement of non-grain agricultural products. The local rural processing of cotton and silk was prohibited in the mid-1950s, and all plant-fibre crops and silk had to be sold to state-owned enterprises. The agricultural sector supplied the agricultural products to industries at prices set by the authorities and did not have other outlets. Production was enforced within the current yearly plan.

Markets

Agriculture also constituted one of the most important markets for industrial products. Prices for goods sold to the rural sector were fixed by the Price Bureau. The crucial question was to what extent the rural sector had the means to buy industrial goods. The main constraint on the rural sector's function as a market lay in its ambiguity: it was supply-led and had prices which were low in the sense that they did not reflect the scarcity in the market. For this reason, the rural sector never functioned as a dynamic market for industrial goods. There were several reasons for this. The relatively high density of rural labour to land meant that farm mechanization proceeded more slowly than it would have if labour had been transferred away from agriculture. The market for farm machinery, therefore, was probably lower than it could have been; despite this, the supply from state-owned enterprises never exceeded demand. The Chinese industrial-ization relied on developing heavy industry rather than light industry, and for this reason the state did not at all explore the full potential of the rural consumer market. The market was huge, and it was not until the early or mid-1980s that the demand for bicycles, wristwatches, sewing machines, radios, alarm clocks and petty electrical goods was saturated, or rather that these goods were universally taken off the coupon. The state was incapable of expanding industry to a degree which reflected the real potential of the rural markets for industrial products and so had to concede to the rural areas the right to engage in manufacturing themselves to satisfy the basic needs.

As a result, the rural areas constituted a large, unsaturated market which was able to absorb whatever the state-owned enterprises sold (provided it was not too expensive). The existence of such a stable, unsaturated market, in other words, gave the state-owned industries little encouragement to innovate, but rather to stick to old products and designs.

Investment capital

The state set artificial terms of trade between the agricultural and industrial sectors, which are often termed the 'price scissors' or the 'scissor's gap', in order to transfer capital from the countryside to finance urban industrialization. This meant that the cost calculus of commodities for agriculture fixed the price higher than it should have been. Agricultural products for the urban market were set at a lower price. This meant that farm incomes were kept low in real terms.

How did this generate investment capital for state-owned industry? It didn't directly. The income from the scissor's gap did not take the form of a revenue which could be seen in the state budget and directed towards an investment project by the state. The scissor's gap meant that urban expenditure levels were very low (salaries, raw materials, etc.), so that budgeted investments could have greater effect for the same money.

The transfer of funds, accordingly, created a soft economic environment for all urban enterprises, and did not provide for targeted investments in production. The main flaw of this system was that what was in theory a temporary, initial transfusion of funds, which would be reversed once the industrial sector made higher profits than agriculture due to superior productivity, in reality became a permanent support for urban consumption and a discouragement to increased productivity in the urban industry.

Apart from the capital transfer based on the price scissors, agriculture also contributed funds through the agricultural tax. This was a levy for the state, based on the production of core crops. The tax was relatively light, and did not constitute a large source of income for the state. Its proportion of the state budget fell between the 1950s to the 1970s. This tax was levied in kind by the grain procurement stations.

Food

During the first 5 years of the People's Republic the authorities severely limited private trade in agricultural products, and finally monopolized it in 1955/1956. The main concern was grain. A special administration under the Ministry of Trade was in charge of grain procurement, and its branch offices, the grain procurement stations, were present in all townships/people's communes. Other trade of agricultural products was monopolized by the trade and marketing cooperatives, which were in name cooperatives, but in reality functioned as local branches of the Ministry of Trade (between the mid-1950s and the 1980s their formal status oscillated between decentralized cooperatives and more-centrally controlled state offices).

The Grain Bureau received both quota and above-quota grain; the above-quota grain was normally paid for at higher prices. Peasants' own consumption of grain was handled through the production teams, so the grain retained for their own use was distributed equally among the members of the production team.

Grain thus purchased in the countryside was then sold to urban residents through special grain stores, selling different types of rice, flour, edible oils and noodle products. Consumer prices for grain were set very low, and urban customers were required to pay both with money and rationing coupons, which were issued in the same jurisdiction. Special, bureaucratically complicated provisions existed for those who travelled with permission; they could use a special type of coupon. Some peasants who specialized in non-grain production, and those who for some other reason did not have sufficient land to produce grain for their own consumption, or who had been struck by natural disasters, were given coupons to purchase reverse trading grain (*fanxiaoliang*). They were under no circumstances authorized to trade directly between themselves or even between neighbouring villages.

Trade in other agricultural products was, as mentioned, also strictly controlled by the state, and here also quotas would apply. However, in practical administration there was a high degree of laxity, and for long periods between the 1950s and the late 1970s there existed a semi-'private' market, which was condoned as long as it did not involve large-scale private operators. This semi-'private' market was reserved for agricultural products grown on the peasants 'private plots', small pieces of land reserved for individual households to grow vegetables (officially for their own consumption, but in reality for the market). The bulk of agricultural products for the cities were marketed through the official channels, and sold in various ways. In most cities and towns large marketplaces were divided into sections for state-shops, collective marketing cooperatives and private traders. Some major bulk products would be sold through the work units, while other products were sold through specialized shops. The semi-'private' or 'free' markets were constantly under great pressure, and especially in the early and mid-1970s they were seen as inappropriate under socialism, and closed down in many places; private production and sale were regarded as 'capitalist tails', which were likely to generate a capitalist restoration. Due to the importance of free markets in most rural areas, they were normally reopened once an 'anti-capitalist policy wind' had subsided. It was not until 1977 that they were given a strong, central regulation which protected them from arbitrary interference. Throughout the period major food items (like meat, eggs, milk, etc.) were rationed on and off, depending on relative availability.

Agriculture was basically able to provide the required food for the cities, even at low prices. Serious shortages occurred during the great famine in 1960/1961 (Box 9.2), and occasionally as a result of hoarding around traditional festivals. Local and temporary shortages occurred due to natural disasters, poor management, or political campaigns, but agriculture's supply of food for urban China was in general terms sufficient and well organized, and the retail prices remained low.

As a proportion of the Chinese population the urban areas were small, only about one-fifth of the population having non-agricultural household registration status. The greatest population growth took place in the countryside rather than in the urban areas. Provision of food for the nation, therefore, throughout the first 30 years of the People's Republic, remained predominantly a question of rural self-sufficiency with a relatively small marketed surplus.

In conclusion, the system instituted for the rural–urban exchange of production factors had a strong urban bias. The general criticism that can be directed at such structures is that they cannot ensure rational distribution of production factors in the way that the planned economy aspires to. In particular, the irrationalities of labour recruitment and investment transfers demonstrate the weaknesses of the planned economy. The fact that a planned economy could be sustained for such a long time was due to continuous political intervention and revisions of the rules.

Box 9.2 *The great famine in 1960/1961*

Following the Great Leap Forward (1958/1959), the situation in Chinese agriculture turned bad. A combination of disintegration of rural work, adverse weather conditions and the depletion of reserve stocks during the Great Leap Forward caused widespread famine in virtually all parts of China, the worst famines to occur in China since the 1920s.

The famine continued during two to three harvests and took a toll of between 30 and 50 million lives, mainly among the peasants. However, the famine was also strongly felt in the cities, where supplies were low or cut off for long periods. The famine is still a psychologically painful issue which most Chinese feel uneasy about.

EVOLUTION AND ORGANIZATION OF THE URBAN ECONOMY

The urban economy emerged from a *mélange* of traditional, modern and international forms of enterprises and trades existing at the eve of Liberation in 1949. The Chinese communists took a gradual approach to regularizing urban economy according to their own blueprint. The seediest businesses went first, with the Chinese Communist Party offering re-education and training to prostitutes and petty criminals, while clamping down on the secret societies and criminal gangs which controlled both illegal trades and parts of the more respectable economy. Bordellos, casinos, 'dance halls', and opium dens were closed, and property was seized from the gangs. The KMT had left the Chinese mainland, bringing along with them parts of the bourgeoisie and many officials in the former KMT regime. Capital belonging to the nationalists was confiscated at the time of liberation. In particular, property of the 'four big families' was taken over by the new government. In many cases the transfer was uncomplicated, with the staff and directors of the companies, already being infiltrated by the Communist Party, declaring their allegiance to the new government.

Foreign companies were nominally allowed to continue functioning, but they were being increasingly cut off from resources and markets and eventually most foreign companies left, *de facto* being dispossessed.

Companies run by Chinese capitalists were allowed to continue for 5–6 years, albeit under close supervision by the new government. Eventually directors were bought out of their enterprises by the government, some of them remaining in the leadership of the companies as salaried directors.

Petty trades and the urban lumpen-proletariat were encouraged to pool their assets in larger, collective firms.

New Democracy in the economy

The policies followed corresponded narrowly to the ideas of New Democracy and the class analysis. Imperialist, feudal, and bureaucratic capitalist forces were dealt with by confiscation of their assets. In the case of the secret societies and gangs, these were considered to be feudalist; their 'victims' (prostitutes, drug addicts, petty criminals, etc.) were carefully separated out from their leaders, who were tried and executed or jailed, and they were given a chance to 'turn a leaf'. Foreign firms were seen as imperialist; the Chinese leadership took a firm line, eventually confiscating most foreign assets without compensation, but adopting a slow, seemingly ambiguous strategy in order not to provoke direct retaliation from foreign powers (especially during the Korean War). The KMT had represented bureaucratic capitalism in the sense that powerholders in the KMT had monopolized public assets and had used their position to enrich themselves. Chinese capitalists belonged to the 'good' classes and so were encouraged to operate privately. The Chinese state gradually started taking over such enterprises under the Socialist Movement of the mid-1950s.

Ownership

The state thus became an important owner of confiscated and nationalized assets. These assets were considered to belong to the whole people, but they were administrated on behalf of the people by the state.

The urban collective ownership of the means of production arose out of the petty traders and the small independent urban labourers and artisans; a policy was drawn up to lead them onto socialist forms of organization. The state did not confiscate their assets, but encouraged them to work together in cooperative forms, while the ownership of these assets was declared the 'collective ownership by the labouring masses'.

The main source of state ownership, however, was the continuous investment by the state in large industrial complexes after the model provided by the Soviet Union.

The state-owned enterprises

The state-owned enterprises were owned by the whole people, but the administrative power was vested within a *xitong* and a level of government. A *xitong* is a ministerial line of command, so an enterprise could be part of the Ministry of Textile Industry, the Ministry of Transport, or the Ministry of Chemical Industry, or any other ministry-level authority. As already discussed, it could be owned by the state at national, provincial, district, city or county level, and be included in the relevant state plan for that level of authority.

Being part of the administrative system, enterprise managers were appointed as cadres, vaguely similar to civil servants in other countries, while workers were on a worker payroll, but also enjoyed guaranteed permanent employment (the 'iron rice bowl').

Enterprise management in the early 1950s was relatively straightforward, based on what one could term the 'director-in-command': the appointed enterprise director was in charge of overall decisions on production, appointments, contracts, external negotiations, etc. He normally supervised the work of the subordinate functional directors, and transferred limited decision-making powers to them. They were in charge of day-to-day management of their respective divisions or functional departments. The enterprise director was normally a person who combined technical knowledge with managerial skills, and he was generally expected to be an administrator. Of course, some large and influential enterprises were given a political leadership of revolutionary veterans who acted as nominal directors; in those cases, the vice-director was the real decision-making person, and the nominal director was more a patron and spokesperson.

Workers' congresses

The socialist transition policy in the mid-1950s meant that the Chinese Communist Party extended its control from external, indirect structures of influence and established Party committees in virtually all enterprises. The Party committees were the highest decision-making bodies in Chinese state-owned enterprises between 1957 and the heyday of the Cultural Revolution in 1966/ 1967. The promise to the working class of making the proletariat 'masters in their own house', the idealism of New Democracy and the ideals of the written Constitution, also meant that the newly established workers' congresses were given strong, subsidiary powers within the enterprises. As a result, the function of enterprise directors was reduced to the third rank after the Party committees and the workers' congresses were given strong powers. The director made decisions in constant consultation with the functional directors on the enterprise board. The enterprise director, therefore, not only was subjected to a supreme enterprise management by non-professional, political leaders and a strong worker participation in management, she or he also shared more responsibility with the functional directors (Box 9.3).

This new type of management system had both political and economic significance. It was geared to a situation where plan fulfilment was of supreme importance, and where production was coordinated under the plan rather than competitively in the market. Ideally, the co-optation of worker interest in strong

---

Box 9.3 *The enterprise management system*

The enterprise leadership has oscillated between 'professional' and 'political' during the history of the People's Republic. The original system of the 'director in charge' meant that control could only be external and *ex post facto*, to the great annoyance of the leadership. The imposition of Party committees in 1957, seconded by workers' councils, gave the leadership more direct influence over the management.

The chaos of the Cultural Revolution meant that spontaneous 'communes' and 'workers' committees' broke up the regular structures and disbanded the Party committees, which were often accused of harbouring 'capitalist roaders' and other 'counter-revolutionary scum'. In 1968 and 1969, a new system was instituted, aimed at breaking the new local powerholders of the Cultural Revolution who 'stopped production in order to make revolution' (*tinggong nao geming*). These were the three-in-one committees, which (in the absence of the experienced Party cadres) consisted of officers from the People's Liberation Army, the workers' councils and the directors. This system was changed into revolutionary committees in the early 1970s, when the military was withdrawn and the Party moved back in. It was not until into the 1980s that this system was finally given up.

workers' congresses was important in order to make sure that the workers could accept the more unpleasant sides of the plans. Workers' congresses should in no way be considered instruments for 'economic democracy' and the like; they were an import tool for controlling the workforce and for creating a counterweight to technical/administrative management.

The environment of a planned economy meant that the interests of the enterprise were best served with political influence which could effectively sway the allocation of resources (machines, raw materials, funds, etc.), the formulation of production targets and the long-term investment patters in direction of the enterprise. A Party committee and a more politicized leadership of the enterprise was much more useful than a single director with a mixture of entrepreneurial, administrative and technical skills.

However, this 'division of labour' in the mid-1950s caused a schism to appear in the urban enterprises, the likes of which had never existed before; the schism, between the 'professionals' (*neihang*) and the 'politicians' (*waihang*), was to cause constant problems for enterprises during the next 40–50 years. Management decisions were often constricted by the Party committee, and competition over authority gave rise to severe frictions and conflicts.

Danwei: *The work units*

The nature of urban enterprise organization in China was probably unique in the world. As we have seen in Chapter 6, the *danwei* system fundamentally affected the relationship of individuals and the state, mediated by the *danwei*. The enterprises were 'work units' (*danwei*), whose workers were bound to them for life. Work units normally created their own all-inclusive facilities for the workers, including housing, child care, schools, clinics, shops, services, post offices, etc. Workers' access to social resources outside actual labour functions was, accordingly, controlled by exactly the same persons who directed production activities. The most critical problem in all respects was related to the allocation of living space. Unmarried or single employees would normally have only a bed in a dormitory, while married people had small flats of between one and three rooms. The work unit had a crucial role in social administration (marriage registration, child-birth, family planning, care for the elderly), and so could manipulate by not allowing marriages to go through in order to avoid problems in providing housing, or, conversely, allow marriages to take place on the condition that no claim for better housing was submitted. From the mid-1950s it became increasingly common that married couples lived in different work units, often in different parts of the country, because transfers of one spouse could not be matched with the transfer of the other spouse. Only the reforms of 1978 began to address these problems.

The lifelong dependency of employees on their work units thus gave rise to patronage relationships between workers and their managers; these, however, never crystallized into a employee–management dichotomy. Employees were too heterogeneous and had too many mutually conflicting interests to develop a class/interest (they were competing for the same limited favours and privileges – housing, employment for their offspring, leave of absence and travel permits to visit a spouse, or even transferral of a spouse – from the managers), and they chose to further their individual interests by courting those managers who had the power of allocation.

Managers, including the Party committee, had one need: the workers must help them fulfil the state plan. This gave the workers room for potential collective pressure. If they chose to strike or work below standard, the management was in trouble, since they could not normally dismiss workers and did not have very wide disciplinary powers. The structure favoured ostensive egalitarianism and private favouritism, as well as official co-optation of worker interest, discipline of troublesome workers and promotion of vociferous and popular workers into workers' committees or other trusted functions.

The trade unions (*gonghui*) were official parts of the All-China Federation of Trade Unions, a mass organization centrally led by the communist authorities. The main functions of the trade unions were not to represent worker interests in labour disputes or wage negotiations, but to perform practical tasks in the distribution of certain social goods, making sure, for example, that enterprises had functioning pension schemes, etc.

To sum up, the work units through the iron rice bowl had a problematic internal power structure, which was partly conditioned by the need for optimal performance in the planned economy, and partly reflected the need to control the employees.

Spatial distribution

From the mid-1950s until the early 1970s, investments in new industries reflected the determination to shift industry from the coast into the central and western parts of China. Two factors played a role. The industrial development had taken place mainly along the coast in the treaty ports and their immediate hinterlands, in a way similar to colonial development in other parts of the world, and the CCP had a spatially more balanced development as a strategic priority, perhaps most clearly expressed in Mao Zedong's famous speech in 1956 on the 'Ten Great Relationships' (Box 9.4).

However, after the break with the Soviet Union in the early 1960s, and especially after the start of the Vietnam War in the mid-1960s, the Chinese leadership developed a siege mentality, which caused them to relocate large industrial complexes deep into the western parts of the country. In particular, military hardware factories and heavy industries were located in places distant from their natural markets, in order to make it difficult for an enemy to strike at China's core industries.

This development was wasteful, using up resources which could have realized more rapid development of the economy. However, it meant that poorly

---

Box 9.4 *The Ten Great Relationships*

The major problem of development as it emerged in the mid-1950s was that the economy became difficult to manage from a central point of view. Mao Zedong, in April 1956, expressed this concern in a speech on the 'Ten Great Relationships', i.e.

  (i)   between heavy industry, and light industry and agriculture;
 (ii)   between industry in the coastal regions and industry in the interior;
(iii)   between economic construction and defence construction;
 (iv)   between the state, the production units and the producers (in Marxist terminology 'producer' means 'worker');
  (v)   between central and local authorities;
 (vi)   between the Han and the minority nationalities;
(vii)   between party and non-party;
(viii)   between revolution and counter-revolution;
 (ix)   between right and wrong; and
  (x)   between China and other countries (see Mao [1956]).

In this speech Mao outlined the dangers of one-sided and unbalanced development. The points raised by Mao on industrialization argued that heavy industrial development should be in harmony with agricultural development and light industrial development. Light industry and agriculture must be given sufficient attention and investment in the state plan, because they are the main consumers of heavy industry's goods, and because agriculture supplies goods needed by industrial production. He also addressed the skewed regional development and the opportunity cost of large-scale military industry. Mao's speech did not have much influence in its time, and it was never published during his lifetime. It was not until Hua Guofeng found that he could use it to justify his new policies in the late 1970s that it was published (Hua, 1977).

---

developed places received technologically more-advanced inputs and some economic spin-offs from the greater contact with the national economy. However, such work units were closed communities in themselves, catering for their own workers (only few were hired locally), and fenced off from the local economy (no profit transfers accrued to the local authorities). The advantages for the local economy were thus indirect, by improvements of the infrastructure, creating a market for local goods, offering some job opportunities for local people, etc. Some large complexes simply became industrial zones outside the jurisdiction of the counties.

The urban collective enterprises

The urban collective enterprises were different from the state-owned enterprises in terms of origin and status within the economy. Such enterprises were labour intensive and often poorly equipped, and were more geared towards producing for local consumption.

In principle, they did not have fixed salary scales for employees, but practised profit sharing. However, larger urban collective enterprises were linked up with the state plan and were given production quotas. These 'large collectives' became increasingly similar to state-owned enterprises in their structure, and often introduced salary schemes similar to those in state-owned industry.

At the lower end of the scale, during the 1960s and 1970s, small collective enterprises started flourishing in the cities, operating outside the state plan, and under the control of neighbourhood committees. Such enterprises had the purpose of creating employment opportunities and at the same time locally needed goods and services.

Urban social welfare

Social welfare in the cities was provided through the work units. They paid pensions, allowed pensioned employees to continue to live in living quarters, ran clinics, etc. Urban residents were normally provided with employment through the Labour Bureau. On paper, there was no unemployment.

The agencies of the Ministry for Civil Affairs were in charge of overseeing the situation for the disabled and the poor in the cities.

The main social problems which existed throughout the period in the cities were related to poor and crowded housing, while the lack of unemployment and the low consumer prices, combined with the egalitarian wage structures, precluded the emergence of large-scale destitution and poverty.

THE RURAL ECONOMY

Agriculture: from land reform to the people's communes

The land reform of 1949–1953 brought about huge numbers of small-scale individual farm households. Land was taken from landowners who had more land than they could till using only the labour of the able-bodied persons in their household, and landlords were evicted from the land. Land belonging to temples and clans was divided up for use by the individual farm households. Each head of household received a title to his land. The land distribution was, in order to be fair, often carried out by giving each household a lot of small parcels scattered around in the village. Individual management also meant that some peasants did not possess sufficient draught animals or farm implements.

The Chinese Communist Party did not intend to let the peasants become small capitalist farmers, and sought to lead them into forms of 'socialist' cooperation. This built on a number of discrete approaches. One was the gradual monopolization of rural credits by the establishment of government-controlled rural credit cooperatives; another was the control of the market by the establishment of supply and marketing cooperatives. The most important was gradually inducing the peasants to cooperate on production.

The assumption was that most peasants would share implements and swap labour in peak periods in order to gain mutual advantages, and so the CCP mobilized peasants into such forms of cooperation. The party promoted the establishment of so-called mutual aid teams which would share implements and swap labour, but were based on the individual ownership of land and the individual rights to the crop. The systems which became broadly used were very different from traditional forms of swapping and neighbour help. Traditional arrangements had been bilateral between specific types of partners for specific functions, and each household would have many different labour swapping arrangements with other households. The 'book-keeping' practice was settled directly between partner households. The practice promoted by the Party was centralized, needing an accountant to supervise the labour contribution of individual households, and it was indiscriminate in terms of the use of labour. While the traditional practice had given priority to efficiency based on selective use of partners, the more centralized and mechanistic approach adopted by the Party was slightly inefficient. However, it had the advantage of being easy to monitor, and easier to control externally.

The socialist transition was gradually stepped up, so that the peasants were urged to till the land collectively, and take shares of the total crop, rather than harvesting their individual crop. The so-called 'higher agricultural producers' cooperatives' fell short of abandoning the land titles of the individual households.

Towards the people's communes

Mao Zedong is considered to have promoted rapid social transition of agricultural production against the collective will of the Party leadership, who had decided on a slow progression of the transition process. Mao took the initiative to press for a rapid transition by starting a campaign in 1956/1957 which aimed at doing away with the land deeds, so that all peasants pooled their land and draught animals.

The formation of production brigades and production teams as permanent institutions for labour utilization and for the allocation of incomes in kind and cash was the foundation on which the people's communes were built. Mao's political opponents, mainly Liu Shaoqi and Deng Xiaoping, found that the development to a fully fledged collective economy should be protracted to allow agriculture time to stabilize and to gain new impetus. Allowing farmers to pursue their own interests was considered by them to generate growth in the rural economy. However, the permanent productive cooperation and surplus sharing in the production teams (which consisted of anywhere between 10 and 50 households), and the overall management in the production brigades (normally consisting of several hundred households), which took over the peasants' individual titles to the land, as well as other large assets and infrastructure, were introduced swiftly between 1956 and early 1958. The socialist nature of the transformation was signified by the fact that the local governments were renamed 'communes' (*gongshe*).

The Great Leap Forward

The Great Leap Forward pressed the socialist ideas even further: not only agricultural production, trade and credit management should be socialized; the functions of the family were to be included too. Women were to participate in production equally with men, and so large refectories and crèches, kindergartens and homes for the elderly were promoted. The general displeasure with such steps caused this policy to be stopped abruptly after a couple of months.

In accordance with Mao Zedong's policy of linking agricultural and industrial production (as put forward in 'Ten Great Relationships'), the Great Leap Forward also promoted the establishment of local industry. The policy was both misconceived and carried out in such a rigorous manner that it caused huge losses. The idea to develop rural industry was, in itself, laudable and could have achieved important growth, but it was carried out as a political campaign to achieve targets for which there was no basis in the affected localities. Lack of machines, capital and raw materials, and seasonal differences in the availability of the workforce were not taken into consideration in the implementation of the policy. The most commonly cited example of this is the 'backyard furnaces' which were used to produce iron for the new rural industry. The lack of iron ore meant that scrap iron and all sorts of perfectly good iron utensils were commandeered to provide raw materials for the furnaces, which produced unusable third-rate iron. Labour was commandeered away from agriculture, even in peak periods, to participate in the industrialization. The peasants, no longer personally responsible for agricultural production under the collective management, joined in the new trend, neglecting the harvest, sowing and planting seasons.

Following the Great Leap Forward, there was a 2-year severe famine which affected all of China – a disaster, which caused the deaths of about 30 million people.

Stabilization of the people's communes in the 1960s

Although Mao Zedong was challenged as a leader at the Lushan Conference in 1959, he remained in power, albeit in a much weaker position. In the emergency years 1960–1962, Liu Shaoqi and Deng Xiaoping pressed for a reorganization of agriculture, and in 1962 the Central Committee passed a policy document which was to become the legal framework for the structure of the people's communes until the reform which took place between 1978 and 1983.

The document was a compromise between the Liuist and Maoist views of agriculture. Production was collectivized and land ownership was collective. Trade and credits were also collective. The organization of the people's communes was in production brigades and production teams. The outlines of an internal financial structure in the people's commune were drawn up, and guarantees were given to orphans, and elderly and disabled people.

The people's communes which had been established in 1957 had been very large, and in 1961–1963 they were split into several smaller people's communes, and at the same time land under urban jurisdiction, which was not yet built up, was separated out as people's communes or attached to people's communes. Small rural towns which had been included in the large people's communes in 1957 were separated out. These general trends were realized with some differences in different parts of the country.

Peasants were guaranteed the right to produce for their own consumption on so-called 'private plots' (the ownership belonged to the brigade, but the production on these plots was outside the collective), and they were allowed to raise small animals for their own consumption also.

The few viable rural industrial enterprises which emerged during the Great Leap Forward were taken over by the county governments and their workers were transferred to become urban residents under the household registration system. The rest were closed down.

The Maoist ideas of 'walking on two legs' in the countryside (having both agriculture and industry), and the opposition against private production even for own use, had to subside. The Liuist ideals of private incentives and private organization of production were not realized, but the result was an effective structure for transferring surpluses to the urban centres and for generating growth in production, and so fulfilled the most important of Liu Shaoqi's and Deng Xiaoping's demands.

Structure and functions of the people's communes

The unique organization of the people's communes was able to generate growth in a structured way, because the large scale of operation meant that labour and the means of production could be utilized very effectively.

From the early 1960s until well into the 1970s, rural labourers were mobilized for large infrastructural projects, most notably irrigation and terracing, which provided an important basis for increasing productivity and efficiency. The concerted use of labour also meant that the green revolution, which gradually replaced low-yield species with new crops, could be pursued with great efficiency. Productivity increased at an astonishing rate, which fully covered the increasing demands from the growing population.

Ideally speaking, collective management should also give better opportunities for farm mechanization. However, the high prices demanded for mechanical and chemical inputs, as well as the insufficient capacity of urban industry to supply these, made the continued use of physical labour more rational. The relative surplus of agricultural labourers meant that productivity per labourer rose only a fraction of the rise in productivity per unit of land.

The distribution of surplus was based on the following principles:

- Each member of the team received an equitable share in the food grain, measured on the basis of average consumption (slight differences were made between male and female members and adults and children).
- The brigade received a share of each team's marketed surplus for communal purposes (for accumulation, administration, production, social welfare, culture, etc.). It also transferred the agricultural tax and contributions to the people's commune.
- Those in a team who had participated in the actual labour received a share of the income from the marketed surplus (after deduction of the contributions to the brigade, agricultural tax and the people's commune). This was calculated by the accountant and cashier of the team as work points. Young, able-bodied men were normally given higher points than older men, and women were given less than men, based on assumption of their labour's overall value for production.

Radical attacks in the 1970s

In the early 1970s, the radical wing of the Party started to attack this distribution, arguing that not the team, but the brigade should be the accounting unit, thereby increasing the scale of management. At the same time they sought to do away with the 'private plots', which they saw as 'capitalist tails', which drew labour away from the collective production. In order to increase efficiency and to further revolutionize the peasants, they must learn from the production brigade in Dazhai, which had accounting at brigade level, and which had allegedly been successful in large-scale terracing and mechanization.

The hope was for the rural mechanization to gain impetus by large-scale operation. The brigade leader from Dazhai, Chen Yonggui, rose to leading positions in the Party as the only peasant ever to become member of the Political Bureau. Dazhai's success was in reality based on its function as propaganda showcase, heavily funded by the central authorities.

The conflict over this in the 1970s reflected not only ideological disagreements, but more a general concern that the Chinese agriculture might not be able to provide sufficient food for the nation without changes in the system of production and extraction. Lowering marketed surpluses and severe crises in parts of the countryside had caused this concern to arise.

Rural industry and trade

The Chinese Communist Party had effectively disrupted the functioning of private trade in the Chinese countryside by 1955. Small towns had lost their functions as marketplaces, small-scale artisan production was gagged, and cotton and silk trades were monopolized fully by the state, doing away with traditional rural textile handicrafts. The peasants were drawn out of the rich and varied peasant economy and reduced to becoming collective farmworkers. Except for the hectic spate of activity during the Great Leap Forward, where everybody was mobilized to become industrial workers, the period until the beginning of the 1970s was marked by almost exclusive agricultural production.

Some peasants, of course, worked in the collective administrations in charge of procurement, and some worked as technicians or in public facilities. But, besides those few who dared to continue petty artisan trades, all private rural trade and industry was closed down.

In 1970, however, the incapacity of the urban industry to supply the needed production factors to agriculture meant that the state allowed the people's commune to set up small factories to produce cement, machinery, fertilizer, etc. These enterprises were to complement the small state-owned enterprises at county level which produced similar products. The main difference was that the workers were to remain registered as members of agricultural households, and that the investment should be found within the people's communes. These enterprises were to be outside all state plans, but were given some preference in state allocation of energy, machines and raw materials.

This new sector grew fast, and was nurtured by the people's communes because they generated not only employment, but also cash surpluses for the local finances. Also, materials produced locally saved the cost of buying them from state-owned enterprises. The workers in these enterprises were given a share in the surplus like those working in the fields, based on work points. The enterprises were flexible, and could be stopped during agricultural peak periods.

The enterprises therefore became crucial elements in rural accumulation, and they could be used for chain investments in other production lines.

CONCLUSIONS

To sum up this chapter, it describes the structures underlying the Chinese economy until the mid-1970s. The intimate links between the political system and the economic structures are evident. It is difficult to say what is in command: ideology, politics, economy or something else. Which dynamic spurs China's economy on? What causes the reform of the economic system?

It is impossible to answer this last question. The lack of market information in the planned economy, and the absence of real market exchange makes it difficult to assert that the economy is in command. However, there is a limit to politics in command. If the economy does not deliver food and other consumer goods, the political system enters a crisis, and economic and administrative institutions are changed.

If we recall the results of the Great Leap Forward in 1957, we see that the structures of the people's communes and jurisdictional divisions were changed as an outcome of the great famine in 1960/1961, which was caused by the Great Leap Forward.

The right for urban residents to be allocated employment after graduating from school became untenable and from 1962, and with greater intensity since 1965, millions of young school leavers were sent to the countryside, and deprived of their urban resident household registration.

The lack of rural mechanization caused the government to allow the establishment of supply industries under the people's communes from 1970.

The overall crisis in agricultural production in the 1970s caused the radical policy of 'Learn from Dazhai in Agriculture' to emerge. In spite of colossal propaganda efforts, this policy was never accepted by the peasants, and was hardly implemented anywhere.

So, are politics in command? Or ideology? Ideology helped shape the structures of the economy, gave rise to the distinctions between different types of ownership and the planned economy. But ideology cannot determine the performance of the economy, it can only interpret conflicting trends. The schism between the radical and revisionist schools shows two fundamentally different stances within the same set of ideological dogmas. And the two schools have resulted in different institutional solutions to the same types of problems.

FURTHER READING

There is a vast literature on China's economy, and it can be difficult to select appropriate works for further reading. Early works (written between 1950 and 1979) often lack the knowledge of hindsight, and more importantly have been unable to profit from the publication of data on the period which followed the open-door policy of the 1980s. On the other hand, publications after 1980 tend to be preoccupied with the reforms, and only hark back to the earlier period in a superficial manner. For the most comprehensive description of the Chinese economy, see Riskin (1987). A number of 'classic studies' of China's economy are worth consulting: Donnithorne (1969), Eckstein *et al.* (1968), Chen and Galenson (1969), Howe and Walker (1989) and Howe (1978). A rather kaleidoscopic outline of the economy in the 1960s is found in Joint Economic

Committee of the US Congress (1968). Maxwell (1979) gives topical introductions to China's development.

On rural development, the classic *Socialist Upsurge in the Chinese Countryside* (Anon., 1957) makes excellent reading. On this topic also, read Crook and Crook (1979) and Hinton (1972a).

On labour issues, see Howe (1971).

On the household registration system, see Christiansen (1990).

10   The Chinese economy II (1976–1995)

The leadership under Hua Guofeng which took over after the death of Mao Zedong in September 1976 and the arrest of the 'Gang of Four', set high targets for the economic achievements to be made. However, the ambitious plans were moderated by the Deng Xiaoping leadership in 1978/1979, and a process of total reform of the economy was set in motion, a reform which continued in the 1990s.

FOUR MODERNIZATIONS: HIGH ASPIRATIONS

When Mao Zedong died in 1976, Hua Guofeng took over the leadership. Having come to power by a coup, he sought his legitimacy in presenting himself as the ideological 'heir' to Mao, pledging to continue Mao's line, based on the idea that 'whatever Mao had said and whatever Mao had done was correct'. This necrosanct sycophantism led him into an ambitious interpretation of the 'Four Modernizations' which Zhou Enlai had proposed, declaring very ambitious targets for production, and stating that China could take in the developed world at a fast rate. The hollow rhetoric was followed up by more substantive policy initiatives.

Hua Guofeng's version of a socialist economy was based on large-scale operations that were based on state ownership. The new leadership designed several large-scale projects which were to be built with the use of advanced foreign technology. The idea was to use large, modern industrial enterprises as a locomotive for the economy. Provincial governments were given almost carte blanche to enter into contracts with foreign enterprises, and the projects resulting from the subsequent gold rush by the provinces were far too burdensome for China's currency reserves, and had to be curbed in 1979/1980.

The vision of rural development was also to achieve large-scale management. Rapid agricultural mechanization in large production units was seen as the solution. The accounting unit of the production team was seen as too small for rational accumulation of investment funds, so, first the production brigade, and later the whole people's commune, were to become socialist agricultural 'factories'. The peasants must be torn out of their semi-socialist collective-cum-small-producer relations and be thoroughly proletarianized, to become salaried workers in ever-growing agricultural 'industries'. Collective ownership was to be sublated into the state ownership. The leadership (influenced by Deng Xiaoping who was on his way back to power after he had been demoted in 1976) was unable to agree on such visions, and the Second Dazhai Conference in 1978 sent out rather vapid signals. Consequently, the Hua Guofeng leadership's ideas were never presented in a consistent form. They only exist in scattered formulations and in some specific policy measures; an example of the latter is that the supply and marketing cooperatives in 1978 were administratively reorganized to become branches of the Ministry of Trade, showing the statist determination to restructure the rural communities into state-owned enterprises.

Except for Hua Guofeng's embarrassing retreat, the hastily and pompously pronounced modernizations failed to convince the Chinese bureaucracy, the ambitious plans had no effect, and were followed by an austerity period instigated by the new *de facto* leadership of Deng Xiaoping.

TOWARDS NEW STRUCTURES FOR THE ECONOMY

Deng Xiaoping's new leadership after December 1978 set out to change the structures of the economy profoundly, following concepts that totally negated Hua Guofeng's visions of China as a gigantic socialist work unit rapidly leaping towards the communist stage of societal development, and taking in the advanced industrial countries in a couple of decades.

Pragmatism

The type of revisionist or *pragmatic reform* which the new leadership embarked on excludes the utopian vision and teleology of the radical school promoted by Mao Zedong, the 'Gang of Four' and Hua Guofeng. The pragmatist reform does share the utopia of communism with the radical school, and builds its ideological legitimation on the argument that only pragmatism can eventually attain communism. However, it pushes the perspective of this attainment into the far future (rhetorically 50–100 years from now), and discards socialist norms of, for example, egalitarian distribution, for the present. Pragmatic reform as introduced in China in 1978/1979 was aimed at gradual change of the economy and improvement of the economic performance of society; the means for this were not to be dogmatic, the only criterion being that they produced results. Deng Xiaoping's commitment to results rather than ideological cleanliness has been expressed in his own terse fashion. He thought that the 'colour of the cat was irrelevant, if only it caught mice', and he protested vehemently against the dogmatists who 'occupy the loo without shitting'.

The ideological underpinnings of the reforms were not formulated at the outset. They were assumed in the negative, as the opposite of the poor state of the economy. The Party was exposed to a number of internal campaigns instigated on the behest of Deng Xiaoping during 1977 and 1978, during which tragic examples of sustained rural poverty during the previous 30 years were reported in great detail, and during which examples of bottlenecks and irrationalities in the planned economy were disclosed. Examples of this kind cannot have come as a surprise for most party cadres, many of whom welcomed the fact that such issues were addressed structurally rather than swept under the carpet or attributed to some poor scapegoats. The inadequacy of the existing system was sufficient justification for seeking new ways.

Hu Qiaomu's speech

The new economic structures were introduced gradually and selectively. There existed some blueprints for economic reform, which outlined a number of preliminary principles that could be pursued. The most important of these blueprints is a speech given by Hu Qiaomu (1978) in front of leaders during the campaign to get Deng Xiaoping back in power, and it was conveniently published in October–November 1978, immediately before the Third Plenary Session of the Eleventh Central Committee of the Chinese Communist Party which marked the transfer of *de facto* power to Deng Xiaoping.

The fundamental principle was that all economic activities in the socialist economy should be quantified in contractual relationships, so that their relative value could be visible. Under the overall regulation of state planning, the allocation of resources should take place to those parts of the economy where they could have the greatest impact for society. If a resource was scarce, the best way to ensure its maximal social utility was to direct it to the highest bidder, instead of allocating it according to fixed quotas at artificially low prices.

The contractual relationships were seen as universal, penetrating all levels and entering into even trivial economic exchange relationships. The government and enterprises; enterprises and enterprises; corporations and factories; factories and their subordinated workshops; workshops and individual workers; individual persons and individual persons – all were to engage in contract relationships in order to enhance productivity, rationalize the allocation of resources, and do away with bottlenecks in the economy.

Precursors for contract relationships

One would think that the main problem in such an endeavour was that the economy did not have sufficiently clear structures for introducing the concept of contracts. The absence of agreed forms of contract, the absence of established price relationships, and uncertainty about who is entitled to sign a contract and how it is enforced, must frustrate any attempt to introduce contracts into a socialist planned economy. There did exist, however, procedures for negotiating plan quotas, and work units, and the persons legally representing them were known. On the basis of such rudimentary structures it was possible to let a new system of contract relationships emerge, allowing horizontal links between partners which had previously been officially barred from direct interaction (both having to report upwards until they reached parental authorities which were entitled to negotiate, or referring the matter to the State Planning Commission). As it happened, the horizontal links *did* exist under the planned economy – illegally. The bottlenecks in the allocation of raw materials and other supplies had taken such grotesque dimensions that illegal swap arrangements had emerged, based on personal relationships. Such arrangements, therefore, became legalized with the reforms.

Economic legislation

Early in the reform period, the leadership established the 'Principles of Civil Law' which with the status of a law indicated the economic rights of natural and legal persons. Laws and regulations on contractual relationships followed. Most importantly, the 'Economic Contract Law' in 1981, and detailed regulations on financial, insurance, trade, livestock procurement, lending and credit, and other types of contracts, followed during the next few years. In 1982 a Law on Court Procedures in Civil Cases was issued, and in 1985 a Law on Inheritance was passed. The gradual evolution of economic legislation and the expansion of a regulatory infrastructure for dealing with a private economy was essential for the economic development. However, the economy developed faster than the legal frameworks, following dynamics that were unpredictable. These issues will be discussed in detail in the following sections.

Not all economic relationships were turned into contracts with one stroke, but the leadership let the contract relationships spread gradually, and also directly intervened in their development.

AGRICULTURE: THE HOUSEHOLD RESPONSIBILITY SYSTEM

The first and most important sector to be affected by the reforms under the Deng Xiaoping leadership was agriculture. The leadership was concerned that agriculture could not produce sufficient grain, and so sent out four signals to agriculture:

1. Grain procurement prices were to be raised by 20 per cent for the summer harvest in 1979, and in subsequent seasons, and the price for industrial inputs to agriculture was to be lowered similarly.
2. Political guarantees were given that the rural collective ownership was intact and could not be infringed upon by anybody.
3. Wrong done to anyone by local leaders would be redressed and the perpetrators would be punished; the bad class labels (landowner, rich peasant, etc.) were lifted.

4. The central leadership tacitly agreed to the division of land to the peasant households in some of the poorest areas, which was actively promoted by provincial leaders as a way out of poverty.

These measures, however small they may seem, set in motion a gigantic shift in the relationship between the government and the rural areas, and there was an immediate increase in the grain sold to the state. Each of the measures had a decisive effect. Increasing the procurement prices meant that the depressed rural economy could be invigorated, and that greater rural purchasing power came about, while agricultural output rose. The political guarantees sent a signal that former radical policies were to be abandoned, and immediately took away the peasants' hostility to central policies. Redressing wrongs and removing class labels was probably the most momentous move; within days of the decision in December 1978, Beijing was swamped by peasants who had been exposed to wrongdoings, and who now went on *shangfang* (i.e. contacted special centres for lodging complaints) to get their cases heard. While special authorities investigated the cases, peasants were sent home, and many received justice in due course. A purge of the ranks of the local cadres ensued, so that most places had new faces in the leadership of production brigades and people's communes. The local promotion of the division of land to individual peasant households in poor areas was based on well-known measures which had been taken during the great famine in 1960/1961 and during natural disasters; in order to restart production fast, land was handed back to the peasants to till.

Dividing the land

In 1978/1979, the new leadership under Deng Xiaoping was unable to reach agreement on allowing a permanent division of land in poor areas, in spite of the fact that very detailed descriptions of the devastating state of affairs in the countryside were circulated in the Party. Not having reached agreement, some provincial leaders, including Wan Li in Anhui Province, actively promoted the policy of dividing land in poor communes and thus created several models of the success of this policy (for example Fenghuang County). Later the policy was presented as a bottom-up initiative taken by the peasants since it was believed that it acquired better recognition in this way. The impact of this was enormous: Local rural leaders were encouraged to experiment with different new ways of organizing agricultural production, and they broadly received positive responses from the peasants. Meetings of the first secretaries of the CCP branches in the provinces in 1979 and 1980 (convened to circumvent the opposition in the Central Committee of the Party) called for consultation and experimentation with new types of rural organization.

There were uncountable ways of organizing agricultural production tried out 1979–1983. Some split the land to households, but retained a full-scale centralized redistribution of grain and cash income; some involved only the division of work tasks into groups, and let the groups share their incomes; some divided land to individual persons and required procurement of a fixed amount, etc. The leadership's initiative had brought forward many examples of management, which it summarized in large surveys, from which it crystallized what it considered to be the most suitable system – the 'Household Responsibility System for Agricultural Production', in Chinese termed '*bao gan dao hu*', literally 'contracting the work to the individual household'.

According to this system, which was made official policy in 1983, the land of production brigades was divided to the households. The method used often but not always divided the land for food grain into equal sizes for each member of the brigade, while the land for state grain quotas, agricultural tax, and for other crops sold to the state was divided in equal sizes for each able-bodied adult agricultural labourer. Each household would thereafter have a number of plots reflecting its size and number of labourers, and would of course also have the original 'private plots'. The households were contractually obliged to sell a specific quota of grain and other products to the relevant procurement station, and could keep the rest for their own use. They also had the option of selling products at a higher price to the procurement station, or, in the case of most products (initially not grain, oilseeds and cotton), on the free market. The land was not given in ownership to the peasants, but was on a 3–5 year land use contract. In 1984, the duration of the contract was prolonged to 15 years, and forestry plots and wasteland reclaimed by peasants was generally offered to them on 50-year inheritable contracts.

Budding rural enterprises

Non-land assets, like large pig-farms, poultry-farms, farm machinery, etc., were auctioned off or given in contract to a manager. Under the circumstances in 1983, tractors, lorries, threshing machines, and other machinery were thus sold (at prices that reflected their limited use in a stagnant economy) to the highest bidder within a brigade, so the prices paid were quite small when compared with the incomes that could be generated with the help of this equipment in an expanding rural economy. In the beginning, management contracts only reflected limited incomes, and, since they were on fixed terms for a certain period, the contractors could often spin a large profit.

The immediate result was that small groups of very entrepreneurial peasants were able to generate high incomes, using non-land assets they bought or contracted at the outset of the reform.

In tandem with the household responsibility system, rural China also experienced an exponential growth in small businesses. Originally, they had been explicitly prohibited in central policy documents, but they were officially allowed according to a policy document from 1983. In the official version of the policy they were allowed to consist of eight employees, i.e. five workers and three apprentices. But in a secret version of the policy document, which was actively transmitted to rural cadres, it was indicated that larger private enterprises were to be tolerated.

The emergence of small private enterprises, run by the most successful local peasants, meant that a new entrepreneurial class started to emerge in the countryside.

Adverse effects of decollectivization

Many observers of Chinese agriculture were strongly concerned that, with declining redistributive roles of the collectives, the communal facilities would fall in disrepair. Irrigation systems, for example, are very sensitive to lack of maintenance. It was also claimed that short-term land use contracts would lead to predatory management, and thereby to a decline in the fertility of the soil.

Even more importantly, the rapidly increasing rural wealth and the expansion of rural private enterprises took their toll of the land. House building became a major area for investment in China's rural areas. New, large, modern houses were constructed in such great numbers that the leadership grew concerned about all the good farmland that was sacrificed to living space. From 1982 when the problem became a concern, several measures were taken to limit the building of new homes. The most radical measure was to introduce a separate Land Administration Bureau that was to give out licences for non-agricultural use of land. Such use was subject to a special tax, the revenues of which were earmarked for the development of new land. A Land Administration Law was also introduced by the National People's Congress after a long and heated debate.

The grain policy

The overall rise in productivity meant that the state was confronted with a much too large commitment to buy grain from the peasants in 1984. While 1984 was a triumph for those who sought rapid growth of agricultural output, the bumper harvest was a catastrophe for the state's coffers. The conditions on which the peasants sold grain to the state had become very favourable: they received a low price for the first 30 per cent of the quota grain, a higher price for the next 70 per cent of the quota grain, and an even higher price for above-quota grain, which the state was obliged to purchase. This system caught the state with insufficient financial means to purchase the agricultural products, and a lack of storage and transport facilities. During the following decade, the state sought to get to grips with a situation where regulation of prices, private trade and procurement conditions must be harmonized with the state's procurement plan for agricultural products.

Agricultural policy in the period 1985–1993 was focused on getting the procurement right – a task which was very difficult. Peasants' cropping decisions and the decisions of whether or not to supply the agricultural products to the state were determined by other variables than just the price of the agricultural products, namely the incomes to be generated outside agriculture, the increasing costs of fertilizers, pesticides, diesel oil and plastic foil (used for simple 'hothouses'), the changes in pork prices, etc. The situation was not helped by the fact that the state's system for procurement of grain and other agricultural products broke down in large parts of China during the late 1980s. The allocation of grain procurement funds to the grain procurement stations was handled by the Agricultural Bank of China, which was often unable to make the cash available due to internal administrative constraints and local cash flow problems. As a result peasants were given IOUs instead of cash payments. At the same time the state started operating a policy of preferential prices on fertilizer and diesel oil, and of cash advances on crops if peasants signed special procurement contracts. The administrative systems around this also broke down, and gave rise to grave corruption by which local cadres and work units pocketed the difference between the strongly subsidized price and the free market price for products. The outcome of this was great dissatisfaction among peasants, distrust of local cadres, and occasional riots and unrest in parts of the countryside.

The gradual withdrawal of the grain quotas

The immaturity of the administrative systems, and the lack of experience in coordinating planning and price-sensitive behaviour, therefore turned rural policy into a highly politicized and controversial topic in the late 1980s. The fact that peasants do not have officially recognized interest organizations aggravated the situation, causing the peasants to resort to spontaneous violent action against local officials, rather than being able to negotiate solutions to the problems.

A further complication was the fact that some provinces, like Guangdong, effectively gave up enforcement of grain contracts, and also dissolved the subsidy on urban grain retail; as a consequence, private markets in Guangdong (and other similar places) diverted grain away from state procurement in neighbouring provinces, which then imposed rigid bans on cross-border trade. An illegal private wholesale market in grain evolved during the latter part of the 1980s, which made it additionally difficult for the authorities to make production, state procurement, planning targets and actual retail match. In 1993, the urban retail of grain was taken off the coupon in all of China, and the procurement of grain was, during 1994 and 1995, gradually liberalized so that licensed private and semi-private grain traders could operate legally. The state, however, is still supposed to occupy a dominant position in the grain, oil seed and cotton trade, and grain will continue to be a major field of economic policy making in the future.

State investment in agriculture

The decline in farmland, the drying up of investments in farm production, and the declining quality of agricultural resources in general, gave the state an impetus to seek new avenues for securing sufficient agricultural investment to improve the productive base of agriculture.

The household responsibility system, as we have already indicated, gave the peasants a structural disincentive to invest, due to: (a) the low competitive prices of agricultural products when compared with the better earning opportunities in non-agriculture; (b) the small scale of operation and the fear of free-riders in local cooperation; and (c) the fact that communal mechanized services (no matter how primitive they were in the first place) in many places disintegrated. In the 1980s, the state, therefore, set up or expanded county-level centres for agricultural extension with well-trained agricultural technicians in order to disseminate new agricultural techniques. It also made targeted investments available for areas which agreed to develop specific agricultural commodities according to state-imposed norms. The most famous (apart from numerous 'grain base areas') are for the production of lean pork and for vegetables.

In the latter part of the 1980s, the state initiated a large-scale investment programme for agriculture, which aimed at raising the per-hectare productivity of farmland by irrigation, draining, soil improvement, planting of hedgerows (against wind damage), change in farming structures, introduction of new techniques, etc. The programme also foresaw the reclamation of large tracts of wasteland. This Comprehensive Agricultural Development Programme began in 1987/1988 as a joint effort between many different ministries under the supervision of a State Council Committee, and relying strongly on the coordination by an office under the Ministry of Finance. The Ministries of Agriculture, Water Conservancy, Forestry, Finance, etc., carried out projects in conjunction with lower-level authorities. The demand that those who profited should themselves raise a significant amount of money and supply labour for the projects in order to obtain aid was very important for the success of the programme, and the demand that large areas should be handled for a time under external supervision largely solved the problem of free-riders. The system was based on a combination of grants, rotating grants and bank credits, which were matched by the peasants' own contribution and labour. The central government would contribute one-third of the grants, the provincial governments another one-third, and city, district and county governments roughly the remaining one-third. This system linked local governments into a management structure which ensured that grants from above were actually used for the purposes intended, and which also forced them to make their own financial contributions to the scheme.

THE DEVELOPMENT OF A MARKET ECONOMY

How does a market economy sprout on barren ground? The institution of contractual relationships, principles of civil law, etc., are an important starting point, but they are neither imperative nor sufficient for a market economy to emerge. What really matters is that the actors of the economy enter into open exchange relationships which reflect the scarcity of goods and services; closed, exclusive types of exchanges are not really a market economy.

Privatization of ownership was never considered seriously by the Chinese leadership, and the political influence of the huge industrial ministries and large heavy industry corporations prevented privatization of state-owned industry. This 'conservatism', ironically, was a dynamo for the development of the market economy. The planned economy failed to supply sufficient services and consumer goods to the Chinese population, so there was a large market for everything from hairdressers, bus and taxi transport, hotels and catering, and retail shops, to manufacture of furniture and building materials. State-owned enterprises also needed many services, which could not be sustained in-house and which were in short supply in the state sector: mainly transport, but also supplies of goods outside the allocated quota. These huge neglected areas were an open area for private investment, and accumulation for further growth was held in private hands, so that the private sector grew in a parasitic coexistence with the state sector.

Preferential policies

The state adopted active policies to support the emerging private economy (officially termed the 'individual economy', *geti jingji*). Regulations were issued, ordering the planning authorities to set aside a proportion of goods to be sold to the private sector, e.g. goods for retail like cigarettes and clothes, and also production factors. Work units were encouraged to rent out unused space to private enterprises, banks were ordered to give a portion of their credits to sound private projects, and local governments were asked to adopt policies to further the development of these 'individual households' (*getihu*).

The state set up administrative frameworks for licensing private ('individual') enterprises – a complex procedure, where the local Industrial and Commercial Administration issued a permit based on statements from the family planning authorities (the applicant must sign a document acknowledging the one-child policy); the relevant local trade association; the tax office (documenting proper tax registration; the local labour administration (that proper registration as an 'independent labourer' had taken place); the health authorities (documenting that relevant arrangements on refuse collection, etc., had been made); the bank (on accounts and availability of operational funds); and many other authorities, depending on the type of enterprise. Many did not bother to register officially.

Without the encouragement, active support and formal structures introduced by the state, the growth of the private sector would probably have been very difficult.

EMPLOYMENT

The rationale of developing a private economy outside the narrow scope of the planned economy emerged as a combination of factors, of which the most important was the political will to promote market exchange in order to achieve growth in the economy. Another prominent reason was the difficult labour situation, which had become an administrative headache.

The relatively slow growth of the urban industry, and the capital intensive industrialization strategy that followed, meant that the real need for labourers in industry was much smaller than the supply of people with entitlement to job allocation. The household registration system (which divided people into agricultural and urban residents) was devised in such a way that all children of women with urban residence status were ensured allocation to a job in the state-owned sector. In the period 1962–1978 the system of job allocation had lost its original purpose of ensuring rational distribution of the labour force to state enterprises, and state enterprises had been forced to accept the numbers of new employees allocated to them, irrespective of whether they were needed or whether their qualifications were acceptable. In the same period, the state had forced about 15–17 million school leavers to go to the countryside, removing their urban residence registration, and nullifying their right to employment in the state sector.

This policy had been unpopular *both* in the countryside where the peasants saw the 'rusticated youths' or 'young intellectuals' as intruders on collective property; *and* in the cities where the division of families and deprivation of perceived rights aroused strong sentiments. In 1978, between 5 and 6 million young intellectuals were still in the countryside. The new leadership under Deng Xiaoping decided to allow them back to the cities, and issued policy documents to this effect immediately following the Third Plenary Session of the Eleventh Central Committee in December 1978.

Employment policy of 1979

To accommodate the young intellectuals returning from the countryside, several avenues were opened. A large number of university places were made available to mature students in two academic years through very competitive entrance examinations, and the army was asked to recruit large numbers too; in these ways the burden on the Labour Administration Bureau was reduced somewhat, but from early 1979 and for several years onwards, the registered urban unemployment (i.e. entitled people awaiting job allocation, *daiye renshi*) was very high. Urban enterprises were asked to take a higher number of workers, in spite of the fact that most of them were structurally redundant within the enterprises and depressed their overall profitability. Furthermore, the fact that the 'sending down' of school leavers was abandoned meant that the Labour Administration in one stroke lost its main administrative lever.

From the early 1970s, a sub-stratum of collective enterprises at neighbour-hood committee level had been introduced with the view to absorb excess labourers. These enterprises were often in charge of menial tasks or primitive handicraft production, and were outside the state plan. They were administra-tively called 'small collectives' (*xiao jiti qiye*). By the end of the 1970s, these enterprises were saturated by labourers, and they were loathed by the urban population because working for them was seen as demeaning.

A Labour Conference at the outset of the reform introduced a set of policies to cope with the pressure of unemployment. In addition to allocating more people to urban enterprises, three genuinely new approaches were identified, which were immediately carried out with great success:

1. The introduction of job inheritance. Any worker who decided to retire before retirement age could nominate his or her offspring as a substitution. This *dingti* system offered a number of advantages to induce early retirement, and was widely used between 1979 and 1984, when it was abandoned.
2. The introduction of labour service enterprises (*laodong fuwu gongsi*), which were established either as subsidiaries of the city government or large state enterprises. These enterprises were outside the state plan; state-owned enterprises could invest retained profits in such enterprises with the aim of employing the offspring of their employees. They rapidly became popular money-spinners for their parent enterprises and could often offer their employees attractive wages to compensate for the loss of some other entitlements.
3. The introduction of registration of individual enterprises (*geti qiye*), meaning that the state no longer had to employ a person with such a registration. The number of registered individual enterprises rose drastically during the following years.

But labour was not a commodity on a free labour market. The reforms at the end of the 1970s and beginning of the 1980s added complexity and further fragmentation to the originally irrational labour allocation system. The structures which emerged can in no way be described as a labour market, and they did not ensure rational matching of skills and jobs. What they did do was set in motion strong and irreversible dynamics towards market behaviour in the socialized exchange of goods, production materials, capital and services.

Smashing the iron rice bowl

In the latter part of the 1980s and the beginning of the 1990s pressures mounted on enterprises to clear their ranks of redundant workers. The pressures were:

● administrative: enterprises were asked to make individual assessments of labourers' productivity in a labour optimalization (*laodong youhua*) drive;

- relative deprivation: average state wages fell drastically compared with incomes in the private sector (to keep effective and essential employees, enterprises would need to offer them competitive conditions); and
- market competition: a gradual hardening of the economic environment forced enterprise managers to take direct action against idle workers and absentees.

In the early 1990s many people started to leave state-owned enterprises on a large scale, afterwards entering the private sector. Leaving secure employment was soon dubbed 'to dive into the sea' (*xiahai*). New job opportunities were opened by allowing state enterprises to invest in taxi leasing companies, which signed leasing contracts with individual drivers, and also by approving of private ownership of taxis. New spending powers and refined tastes lured many state employees into the catering industry, either as owners or employees of private establishments. Former in-house services were often dissolved, and the employees allowed to bid for leasing contracts.

THE STATE SECTOR: INCENTIVES AND ENTERPRISE BEHAVIOUR

The market dynamics unleashed in the early 1980s did not leave the state-owned sector untouched. To the contrary, while at the central political level the large corporations and heavy industry ministries were conservative and sought to minimize the steps towards a market economy, they soon changed their actual behavioural patterns to gain as much as they could from the reforms.

The first main step was the government decision to replace profit transfer with taxation. A batch of experimental decisions was issued in July 1979, and a system was in place roughly by 1982, when all state-owned enterprises were allowed to retain their profits, but instead had to pay various taxes. Under the pure planned economy, all profits made must be turned over to the Ministry of Finance. Under the new scheme there was an incentive for enterprises to make a profit, ideally by efficiency savings. The scope within which companies *de facto* could utilize the profits was very wide: improving conditions for employees, and allowing bonuses, investment in new production and techno-logical innovation. The state early on introduced a prohibitive tax on bonuses, penalizing enterprises which allowed large salary increases, in order to reduce the price inflation.

Enterprise leaderships soon recognized that the future was in profitable investments which could generate high income outside the state plan requirements. Well-managed and profitable enterprises, while still being under the planned economy and state ownership, started to behave as independent, profit-oriented agents in the marketplace. This was the greatest impetus of all to the market evolution. Production outside the plan yielded products which could not be sold profitably through the state trade agencies, and enterprises relied on private traders to retail the goods, an activity which also increased the need for private transport services, etc. Unused workshops, land around campus walls, equipment, and vehicles could be leased to private entrepreneurs and could so generate an additional income for state-owned enterprises.

The labour service enterprises were in most cases very successful investments which generated high turnover and high profits.

Although a bankruptcy law was introduced in 1986 it was hardly ever used during the following 7 or 8 years. In 1992 and 1993, however, the autonomization of state-owned enterprises was effectuated, and the 'soft' economic environment started to 'harden' for the less successful urban units. Enterprises which had been structurally underfunded, had poor and backward technology, had poorly educated workers who were difficult to train, had produced commodities that were not in demand any more, and which had suffered from mismanagement, had not been able to profit from the emerging market economy, but were subsidized by the state through credits and soft money allocations. It has been claimed that about one-third of all state-owned enterprises belonged to this category. The response of the state has been not to close them down, unless in very special circumstances, in order to avoid the misery and unrest that invariable follows from large-scale unemployment. The strategy has been to link them up with profitable enterprises, which are given a strong hand in reforming them. With the policy in the 1990s of enterprise autonomy, enterprises now to a greater extent seek to force unsuitable and indolent workers into early retirement: they give them symbolic 'golden handshakes', they fire them on disciplinary grounds, etc.

Successful companies, conversely, often suffer from structural underemployment. They have been able to expand their activities successfully deploying all workers on the payroll, and are now unable to attract suitably skilled persons, or their skilled personnel leave them because they can get better wages in the private sector. The most valuable skills throughout the 1980s and 1990s were those of drivers and cooks. A measure to deal with shortage of skilled workers was to initiate in-house training on contracts which bound the trainees to the company for a 3- to 5-year period; if they left early, they would have to pay for their training.

The state-owned enterprises in all respects contributed to the evolution of the market economy, exactly because the industrial ministries prevented them from reforming thoroughly until the early 1990s, and altogether avoided their privatization. The mixture of inefficient plan fulfilment, and shrewd and scheming manoeuvring in the marketplace revealed state-owned enterprises as ambiguous and dynamic agents of change.

RURAL INDUSTRIES

Rural enterprises as a category developed rapidly between 1970 and 1978. Their significance in the Chinese economy increased drastically throughout the 1980s and 1990s. By 1990 the number of employees in rural enterprises exceeded the numbers of employees in state-owned enterprises, and their generation of foreign currency was about one-third of the national foreign currency earning in 1991 (Figure 10.1).

The impressive growth in this sector reflects a number of dynamics set in motion by the rural reforms, within a strongly fragmented economic environment. The rural enterprises basically started as rural collective enterprises which handed over their profits to the people's communes or production brigades. In 1983, following the policy of the leadership, most rural enterprises were made more or less independent of the collective authorities. Some were based on contracts with the director, who leased the enterprise, paying a fixed lease to the collective; others were based on appointment of directors, who had to transfer part of the profit to the collective; others were based on joint management between a number of persons; and yet other (mainly small) units were auctioned off or sold directly. A broad array of ownership forms emerged, which were regulated uniformly by the state in a single regime: they were termed 'township and town enterprises' (*xiangzhen qiye*), encompassing individual, joint, cooperative, private (after 1988), village-owned collective, township-owned collective, neighbourhood-committee-run, and town-owned collective enterprises. Township and town governments established branches of the industrial and commercial administrations, and the enterprises were registered at county level.[1] The question of ownership is important. It is obvious that the lowest jurisdiction of the Chinese state is the township and the town; these levels of authority, however, are rooted in the history of the people's

Figure 10.1   *Employees in rural enterprises in China, 1978–1992*

---

[1] It is worth noticing that much Western literature misleadingly refers to the township and town enterprises as township and village enterprises (TVEs). This term is misleading, since it can be confused with the narrower definition of enterprises owned by the villages and townships (i.e. collective enterprises). The best usage is 'township and town enterprises' or 'rural enterprises'.

communes, in the rural collective economy. This means that the ownership of collective enterprises directly owned by and subordinate to the towns and townships is in theory hybrid; in reality, these enterprises are outside the state plan, their workers are (in most cases) not urban residents, and they are subjected to policies and regulations which are entirely different from those regulating state-owned and urban collective enterprises.

The large number of different enterprise types and ownership forms initially caused problems in the overall policy making. A major problem was the fact that many enterprises were private in nature, but officially registered as collective in order to avoid restrictions imposed on non-collective enterprises. It was a major bone of contention whether large private enterprises, i.e. enterprises employing more than five apprentices and two workers in addition to the owner, were to be allowed. In 1983, the Central Committee had *in reality*, in one unpublished paragraph of a policy paper, endorsed their existence *secretly*, while the matter was debated and researched by the Party. In 1988, they were finally officially permitted and given legal recognition.

Reasons for rural industrial growth

What is the background of the enormous success of the rural enterprises? The first main reason was their special status in the rural economy. The privatization of rural production in 1979–1983 gave the peasants the right to dispose of their time in the ways they thought fit, and instilled strong profit motives in the behaviour of the individual peasants. The commercialization of services opened new markets for non-agricultural and agriculture-related activities. Those who bought their means of production early got a headstart and were in most cases able to accumulate further investment funds. The new entrepreneurs were very sensitive to new niches in the market, where transport, furnishing, house building and sub-contracted production were the most popular sectors. The collective enterprises, once they were freed from direct management of the brigades and communes, could take bolder management decisions, and they could often retain a part of the profits for reinvestment. These enterprises were all very competitive with the urban enterprises because: (a) they did not have any expenses for social overheads, i.e. no pension schemes, no free or cheap housing for employees and no service institutions; (b) they had an ample supply of relatively cheap labour, due to the low income levels in agriculture compared with the much higher gross salaries (including salaries, bonuses and subsidies); (c) they were more flexible than state-owned enterprises, being able to change production lines very fast; and (d) they had a low capital investment level and were in most cases labour intensive.

The second reason was the linkages with the state-owned industry. Especially in places like southern Jiangsu and Shanghai's rural areas, urban enterprises regarded it as profitable to invest in rural subsidiaries. A village or township would supply land and manpower, while the urban enterprise would supply machinery, blueprints, technological supervision and market outlets for the products. This was possible because urban enterprises had free money to invest (due to the new policy of replacing profit transfers with taxation); investing in urban expansion was quite expensive and had to pass through many planning authorities. The allocation of urban land for industrial expansion was almost impossible, and expansion in the suburbs would involve requisitioning of farmland by the state, a procedure which was both cumbersome and expensive. Decisions were easier and the investments more effective if a direct deal was struck by an urban enterprise and a rural enterprise. Many such enterprises then produced parts and spares for the parent enterprise, or new products which had a good market outside the plan.

The third reason is that rural enterprises enjoyed an active preferential policy from the state authorities. Initial 3-year tax holidays, the availability of bank credits and other measures were employed to give the enterprises very good conditions to work under. At the end of the 1980s, the state also arranged for an association of township and town enterprises to be set up, and the top leadership made strongly reassuring signs to the sector (with the exception of about 6 months, from July 1989 to early 1990).

The fourth reason is the impact of communal economy. Township and town governments became known for levying large contributions from enterprises for a wide range of purposes. The local government saw itself not as a parasite of the enterprises, but as an overall manager, able to transfer funds into new initiatives and investments. Similarly, the enterprises were often required to take on redundant peasants as workers in order to solve local unemployment problems, so that while the profit motive may have eroded somewhat, the enterprises helped local government alleviate distribution problems. The symbiosis of rural collective enterprises and town or township government was often extended to local private enterprises, which frequently contributed to the local finances in return for protection and support from the local government. The ability of town and township government to shift resources between enterprises and also to extract funds from them for local government finance has accounted for the vitality of the sector. New initiatives could be started, based on local financial inputs. In some cases, it may have reduced the speed of development, mainly where local government 'killed the chicken to get the egg' (i.e. imposed such high taxes and burdens on rural enterprise that they went bankrupt).

A fifth reason applies in some parts of China, namely the links between rural communities and the rusticated youths. The rusticated youths, after returning to the cities, were in a precarious situation. Some got further education, some gained access to state employment, and yet others became private entrepreneurs in the budding market economy. However, they formed relationships of shared experience, facilitating contact and enhancing mutual trust. Thousands and thousands of the former rusticated youths in major cities have finemeshed networks of contacts, and have informal meeting places (in Beijing alone about

10 different restaurants and clubs). They formed economic bridgeheads between rural enterprises and the urban economy, securing market knowledge, technological information and finance. Many of the early enterprises in the 1970s were established mainly by and for the rusticated youths (who were seen to be a burden on agriculture) in the first place.

Political profile of rural industry sector

The range of rural enterprises is very wide, and it is difficult to summarize this whole sector in a simple way. They include small restaurants; bicycle repair shops; local cement factories with dozens of employees; large soft-drinks companies with several thousand employees and nationwide distribution of their products; specialized mining equipment, boiler and engine manufacturers supplying goods to their markets through specialized brokers; textile and clothing factories supplying directly to the world market, receiving their designs from foreign chainstores; and household appliance firms supplying mainly to the domestic market, but using Japanese designs, Hong Kong electronics, German steel, American microprocessors manufactured in the Philippines, etc., in their manufacture. They also include travel agencies, theme parks, and whatnot. These enterprises have little in common, except the official classification and the policies of the 1980s which helped the sector grow very fast.

Rural enterprises caused strong political and ideological unease. In spite of the fact that Deng Xiaoping had called for some regions and some individuals to become rich first, the sudden affluence and the emergence of a rather exploitative rural middle class was seen by some to be a surrender to hedonist values and a rise of capitalism. The rapid dynamics of their development precluded a sufficiently stringent regulation of the enterprises, but they were, from the very beginning, monitored closely by research teams from the state and the CCP. State regulation in the beginning was very open-ended and permissive, and accorded many advantages to their development. Local governments colluded with their enterprise leaders to even further facilitate their advance, shifting taxable incomes around, allowing false registrations of private enterprises as collective enterprises in order to gain access to bank credits and preferential policies, encouraging restructuring of enterprises to obtain tax vacations, etc. The dual price systems during the 1980s encouraged corruption among officials, and the lack of clear regulation caused immoral and dysfunctional trades to emerge (like pirating of video tapes, printing of pornographic materials, etc.). The perceived economic disorder and the shock of seeing what some thought were plump and uncultivated peasants emerge as rich and influential people gave impetus to a significant undercurrent of displeasure within parts of the leadership, thus dragging out the decisions on how to regulate rural enterprises.

In 1987, the leadership under Zhao Ziyang finally gained support for full legitimization of the sector. Symbolically, 10 rural entrepreneurs were received by Zhao and given official reassurances. Within a year, new legislation was enforced, and soon an Association of Rural Enterprises was established which could be seen as a political framework for political participation of the sector. But it was not plain sailing for rural entrepreneurs. The consumer price inflation and the general state of illegality within which large parts of the sector existed caused an austerity campaign to be directed at the sector. Enterprise registers were cleaned up, tax registers were brought up to date, etc. At the same time bank credits to the sector were reduced and new rules introduced to canalize them into such sectors that the state wanted to give priority to (especially processing of agricultural products, farm machinery and agricultural inputs). Empty and loss-making enterprises were forced to close. The austerity preceded the economic austerity policies which were introduced in 1989, following the Tiananmen Incident, and so continued until early 1992 when the national austerity measures were lifted.

As a result, the rural enterprise sector became stronger and more competitive, and plays an important role in China's modern economy.

AUTONOMIZATION OF STATE ENTERPRISES

State-owned enterprises were, from the early 1980s onwards, given an increasing authority to make their own decisions. The enterprise tax reform, which meant that they could retain profits, but had to pay taxes, was perhaps the greatest step forward. Also, the institution of a new enterprise management system in 1984/1985, substituting for the revolutionary committees, was an important step (Box 10.1).

The large heavy industry ministries and large corporations, however, delayed a genuine enterprise reform for many years. The Commission for the Reform of the Economic System proposed several forms of enterprise legislation, labour regulation, etc., but these were rejected until after 1992. A bankruptcy law from 1986 was, for example, only used in very rare cases, while it was obvious that there were many enterprises with such an unhealthy economy that they ought to be closed down. The reason was that the Chinese state had not yet developed a system for coping with urban unemployment on a large scale. Redundancies due to closing of work units would add to urban discontent with the reforms and could lead to unrest. At the same time, ministries sought to protect their subordinate work units in spite of their poor performance.

During the early years of the 1980s the enterprises were asked to improve productivity by monitoring workers' performances, and by placing workers with little or no productivity outside the work groups. This 'labour optimalization' was the first attempt during the People's Republic of China to measure individual productivity of workers as a matter of policy. The large 'unemployment within the factories' (*changnei shiye*), thus revealed for the first

> **Box 10.1   *New enterprise management in the 1980s***
>
> The 'revolutionary committees' had been set up during the Cultural Revolution in 1965/1966, and formed collective leaderships of each work unit. Basically, the decisions of the revolutionary committee were transmitted directly to the functional departments. Under this system there were no enterprise directors solely in charge. Such an organization was impractical under a system where contracts were to be signed and where responsibility for individual economic activities was crucial.
>
> In 1984/1985 the management of Chinese work units was put under the effective leadership of a director, appointed by the parent ministry or corporation, vetted by the Party committee, and elected by the workers' committee. The director was the legal representative of the work unit, and signed contracts on its behalf. The workers' committee and the Party committee would both have representatives in the enterprise management board, which was mainly composed of the director and the functional directors. Decisions were carried out by the functional departments, in accordance with instructions from the functional directors who were responsible to the board.

time, swayed the urban state-owned enterprises towards a thorough enterprise reform.

From the outset of the reforms in 1978/1979, many urban state-owned enterprises had been able to profit from the expansion of the non-plan economy and had adapted their behaviour in the direction of the market and competition. But internally, their administration of the planned production targets was conservative, and uneconomic practices were buttressed by the security provided by the state. There was little incentive to tighten up productivity. However, as soon as the scope of the internal unemployment had become obvious, and enterprises were given the right to decide over the recruitment of labourers, they started to become very cost sensitive.

Perhaps the gradual transition towards a more market-oriented behaviour with a long learning period gave urban state-owned enterprises the needed scope to adapt, and equipped them with the skills that eventually would see them through the transition. The shock therapy which was suggested by the Chicago School of Liberal Economists, and which was adopted in Eastern Europe and the Soviet Union, would probably have had very bad consequences in China, and would have led to political destabilization.

THE SPECIAL ECONOMIC ZONES AND THE OPEN DOOR POLICY

China in the 1960s and 1970s was virtually out of bounds for foreigners. A handful of foreign enterprises maintained permanent representative offices in

China throughout the period, but with little or no business, since they were restricted in all respects. Foreign experts, students and tourists could travel in China between a small number of cities open to foreigners, and only with prior permission (in the form of 'green travel cards'); contacts were strongly controlled, and only a few authorized hotels and other establishments were open to foreigners. Except during the 1966–1970 period, overseas Chinese and compatriots from Hong Kong were allowed to visit relatives, but contacts were uneasy and made difficult by the authorities; contact with Taiwan was almost impossible, although a number of people from Taiwan arrived in the mainland with the intention to live there.

External contacts were thus highly regulated and controlled, and limited the scope for economic exchange. In 1979, twenty or so cities were opened to foreign travel, and the 'green travel cards' were abandoned. Foreign businesses started moving in, strongly reassured by the resumption of full diplomatic links between the United States and China. Representative offices of multi-nationals and other foreign firms were established in many Chinese cities.

The Chinese leadership adopted the so-called 'open door policy' in order to attract foreign technology and foreign investment, and to open foreign markets to Chinese goods.

The general policy was followed by a number of concrete steps. In 1979, the establishment of 'special economic zones' (*jingji tequ*) in Guangdong and Fujian was prepared, and ratified by legislation in 1980. In 1981, detailed rules followed and administrative procedures were formalized. The purpose of these special economic zones (SEZs) was to create an advantageous environment for foreign investment. The method was to introduce a special set of economic regulations, institutional frameworks and infrastructure planning within enclaves on Chinese territory. In this way the land lease, labour relations and wages, taxation, planning, and other problems related to foreign investment could be swept aside, easing the way for investors. The main points included that the zones were allowed to sign very long land lease contracts; that taxes were lower than elsewhere in China; and that labour costs were higher than in other parts of China, but competitive in comparison with foreign labour markets. The original hopes were to gain high-tech production lines, ample foreign investments and total export of the products. In reality, these objectives were not attained. Investments were moderate, albeit significant; the imported technology was mainly intermediate levels of assembly or production, typically using unskilled, young female labour; and two-thirds of the products were sold within China.

The aspirations of foreign firms were not totally in line with the stated purpose of the SEZs. While the zones were immensely easier to handle for foreign firms than other places in China, the purpose of producing containers, soft-drinks and electronic gadgets in south Chinese SEZs was to have a foot in the Chinese market. The idea of attracting high technology to areas with no local tradition of engineering, and at best a university in its early state of development, is not convincing; foreigners did not see any purpose of investing in very advanced technology-intensive projects in such an area. Cheap labour was one attraction, but if the aim was to export 100 per cent of the products, other export-producing zones in East Asia were more attractive for investment, both in terms of wage levels and infrastructure.

THE SUCCESS OF THE SEZs

This apparent failure of the zones to meet the stated aims does not mean that they were unsuccessful. They were exceptionally successful. The three zones in Guangdong were strategically situated, so that they could profit from Hong Kong and Macau. The biggest SEZ, Shenzhen, was a large strip of land across the peninsula on which Kowloon is situated. Once the border was opened for trading with Hong Kong, the investment from Hong Kong grew rapidly. The zone began to serve as a tourist resort for Hong Kong residents, and provided cheaper conditions for production than Hong Kong.

Since 1980, Hong Kong underwent a revolution of its production structure, from manufacture to trade and services, banking and finance, and high technology. The relocation of Hong Kong manufacture onto the mainland to a large extent bypassed Shenzhen, and took place in other parts of Guangdong, so that the companies could profit from even cheaper labour. But the SEZs served as an important catalyst for this development also.

From being a desolate, underdeveloped border town (and the last stop on the railway from Guangzhou, where passengers for Kowloon Station had to disembark before walking over a narrow bridge into the British Crown Colony to continue by trains belonging to the ambitiously named Kowloon–Guangzhou Railway), Shenzhen suddenly grew to become a city of great importance, having affluence without parallel in the Chinese mainland. It was not simply the foreign investment, but the infrastructure, facilities and opportunities offered by the special policies, the easy access to Hong Kong, and the status associated with the place which caused it to grow. Major Chinese enterprises, research institutions and several ministries opened commercial or industrial branches in Shenzhen. Chinese scholars returning from study abroad settled in Shenzhen in significant numbers, and highly educated people from the mainland were directly employed there. The high-tech profile that Shenzhen eventually acquired was mainly based on brain-drain from other parts of the mainland and the fact that returned graduates found Shenzhen more attractive. Overseas Chinese and Hong Kong tycoons were particularly helpful in donating immense sums to the development of the local educational infrastructure – Schools, colleges, Shenzhen University, and libraries – thereby creating one of China's best areas for education, also strongly enhanced by advisory boards composed of prominent scholars from the best mainland educational establishments.

In the mid-1980s, the first Chinese stock market exchange was opened in

Shenzhen, listing Chinese mainland businesses. Part of the trade was kept in Chinese hands, but certain categories of shares were tradeable to foreigners. The stock market developed fast, but even though it was soon matched by the establishment of the Shanghai stock market, it could not cope with the investors' demand. From the outset, the trade was highly speculative and insufficiently regulated; after a number of unfortunate incidents, including a shareholders' riot in 1993, the stock market has become better organized and is technically very advanced. Regionally, it remains insignificant compared to the Hong Kong Stock Exchange, but it has generated a hitherto unseen dynamism in Chinese business financing.

While the original purpose was to attract foreign capital and create an export processing zone, the result is much richer and more complex: a mixture of foreign, domestic, Hong Kong and Taiwanese investment; a high-status city for an emerging bourgeoisie of technocrats and merchants; a city with a high-tech profile, assembly industry, vacation resorts for Hong Kong people, and also sweatshop-like manufacturing with poor and dangerous work conditions. Shenzhen, as a zone, is also carefully cordoned off from the rest of the mainland in order to prevent it from being swamped by migrants.

The other zone in the Pearl River Delta, Zhuhai, just north of Macau, is also relatively successful, but suffers from poorer communication lines. Unlike Shenzhen, however, Zhuhai has the advantage of natural conditions for a deep-water harbour which is gradually being built, serving a different type of industrial development. The development of Macau (the enclave under Portuguese rule which started its decline long before 1900, due to its inability to accommodate deep-going vessels) depends much on the new harbour and airport provided by Zhuhai, and also the construction of a motorway connecting Zhuhai with Shunde, Guangzhou and Shenzhen.

Other zones, Shantou in northern Guangdong and Xiamen in Fujian have had a less pronounced development than Shenzhen, but play important roles as regional development boosters.

Other regional preferential policies

After the special economic zones were established in 1980/1981, some preferential tax legislation was extended to 14 coastal cities in 1984 in addition to the SEZs. These cities were Dalian, Qinhuangdao, Tianjin, Yantai, Qingdao, Lianyungang, Nantong, Shanghai, Ningbo, Wenzhou, Fuzhou, Guangzhou, Zhanjiang and Beihai.

It was decided in 1987/1988 to establish an independent Hainan Province. Hainan Island, distinct by its tropical climate, had belonged to Guangdong Province. To ensure rapid development of Hainan, preferential policies were also implemented here, so that the province *de facto* became a large special economic zone.

At the end of the 1980s the Shanghai Municipality began developing a business and industry zone aimed at foreign investors, the Pudong Area (literally the 'Area East of the Huangpu River'). Some preferential regulations were also implemented here, and the large-scale infrastructural improvements of Shanghai (motorways, bridges and a metro system) have been crucial for Shanghai's revival as the most dynamic economic centre in China. The development of Pudong, however, has been retarded due to the uncertainty among Western investors about where the core services in Shanghai were planned. One core question was whether the waterfront of the Huangpu, along Zhongshan Road (among Western expatriates, called 'The Bund') was to be made available to the Western firms that were accommodated there before 1949, while the city government and Party branch now housed there would move to other parts of the city. The lack of decision on these issues meant that few Western firms initially invested in Pudong. Another issue which set the development back was that an internal dispute broke out between the Shanghai City Government and the central government, over whether the zone fell under city or central authority.

In 1995, the area of the projected Three Gorges Dam was given special preferential policies, which in some respects even exceeded the conditions in the special economic zones. The new economic area aims to bring rapid development to one of the poorest regions of Sichuan Province. Once the dam is finished (realistically around 2010), it will provide large amounts of electrical energy and will enable transport by deep-going vessels as far as Chongqing, thus giving access to a market of approximately 130–140 million people by 2010. The special reservoir zone comprises a number of counties which are directly affected by the huge dam project.

The open door policy also included the opening of border trade, which has since developed rapidly between Russia, Central Asian states, Laos, Vietnam, etc., and China.

Investment from Hong Kong and Taiwan

The impact of the open door policy and the establishment of the special economic zones was to create enclaves of fast development. However, their effect has been to generate economic development in other areas as well. Overseas Chinese, Taiwanese and Hong Kong business people have gone much beyond the special economic zones, investing directly and indirectly in highly profitable ventures. The strategy has been to minimize political risk by investing limited amounts in high turnover, rapid-return projects, and by basing themselves on personal contacts rather than juridical and contractual safeguards, which foreign business people in general regard as a *sine qua non*. Taiwanese investment in the mainland began gradually in the 1980s. Until 1987, travel by Taiwanese citizens to the mainland was virtually impossible, so much investment was canalized through the United States and Canada, from where overseas Chinese business people, with for example US citizenship, undertook the investment in the mainland. After the gradual opening of the contacts (mainly tourism) between Taiwan and the mainland in 1987/1988, and eventually the lifting of the official Taiwanese ban on investment in the mainland, such business increased rapidly to become one of the most important sources of external investment in the mainland economy.

REFORM OF THE STATE FINANCES

The main problem for Chinese development during the reforms has proven to be financial policy. The evolution of the financial institutions has been very fast, and they have developed into very strong and independent players.

The main agents are: (a) the state bank, the People's Bank of China, which has an overall regulatory role in the banking system; (b) the foreign currency bank, the Bank of China, which regulates Chinese exchange rates; (c) state-owned commercial banks (e.g. the Bank of Industry and Commerce, the Construction Bank of China, and the Agricultural Bank of China); and (d) the 'policy banks' (e.g. the Agricultural Development Bank). Apart from these institutions there are also local banks, the People's Insurance Company of China, the rural credit cooperatives, urban credit cooperatives, various trust and investment corporations (e.g. Chinese International Trust and Investment Company, CITIC), financial companies, leasing companies and securities companies. This set of institutions, in general terms, form the *xitong* of the People's Bank of China, and are officially referred to as such. However, the banks have very wide independent powers and in all respects, except the appointments of their top officials (which are vetted by the top leadership), their relationship to the People's Bank of China is merely overall regulation.

The Ministry of Finance is the major administrative and regulatory body for state finances, but it also regulates economic policy. It is, strictly speaking, also in charge of tax policy and administration of tax laws because the State Tax Office is subordinate to the Ministry of Finance. In reality, however, the State Tax Office is a State Council Office at vice-minister level, directly subordinate to the State Council in policy matters, and with direct access to present proposals and reports to the State Council. It is subordinate to the Ministry of Finance only in matters relating to internal administration. A further authority is involved in financial policy, namely the State Planning Commission, which, among its many tasks, is also responsible for ratifying large-scale investment projects.

Before the reforms started, the central financial system, i.e. the ways in which the state canalized incomes and expenditure, had been very unstable, reflecting the shifts in the political situation, for example between 1968 and 1971 where all incomes and expenditures went through the central financial authorities in order to assure that at least the core functions of society remained intact. So incisive had the Cultural Revolution been that local financial authorities were largely unable to function due to local political strifes and stalemates. A similarly crude system was introduced in the mid-1970s whereby local (roughly meaning 'provincial') and central shares in the revenue were fixed proportions of a target (with separate proportions for above-target revenues) and local expenditures were set according to a fixed target (meaning that localities must cover overshooting of expenditure themselves).

The many unstable systems for sharing the revenue from the early 1950s until 1980 had one lasting effect on the financial reform: financial matters were an issue between the central government and the provincial governments. The reforms invariably meant that the localities gained power *vis-à-vis* the central government. By relocating the responsibility for incomes and expenditures to local decision making, the centre relieved itself of an administrative burden, and allowed better local control with development. The original lack of refined central control mechanisms for governing local finance meant that the state finances increasingly became a negotiation game between the centre and the localities, where officials were bogged down in detailed *ad hoc* rules in a process which was very sensitive to other centre–province relations. While negotiations were mainly bilateral between the centre and the individual localities, the relative balance between localities impinged on all negotiations. Supreme leadership intervention was often a prerequisite for reaching agreements.

The financial policy system

In the following we will sketch out some features of this policy field. We will not discuss all major aspects of it, but will give an impression of the most important dynamics and principles.

The first point to be made is that 'locality' (*difang* in the slang of Chinese financial policy makers) points at the level of provincial administration. However, in addition to the provinces, the three cities Shanghai, Beijing and Tianjin, and the autonomous regions, a number of cities have been declared 'direct planning cities' (*jihua danlie shi*). These in financial administration, negotiate directly with the centre like the provincial-level 'localities'. They include Harbin, Shenyang, Dalian, Chongqing, Wuhan, Ningbo, Qingdao, and effectively also Shenzhen; they have, in relation to higher levels of government and in relation to foreign countries and regions, the same powers of decision making as provinces, and they have the same authority as provincial governments to approve decisions from their subordinate counties. This further complicates the negotiation structure between the centre and the localities, since they also must recognize various transfers between the direct planning cities and the provinces in which they are located. There are special historical reasons for the awarding of this type of structure, the most important being that all these cities are major centres of large state owned industry, but in the cases of Ningbo, Qingdao and Shenzhen, the special status in rapid development of foreign investment has been the major factor. In order to facilitate smooth administration of the (largely centrally owned) industries without the interference of 'irrelevant' provincial-level interests, and in order for the centre to have a more direct grip on the profit transfers and taxes from the industrial sector, the institution of direct planning cities has been an effective tool. A number of direct planning cities are excluded from direct relationship with the central financial authorities and have to pass through their respective provincial authorities in these (but not in certain other) matters; these include Changchun, Chengdu, Xiamen, Guangzhou, Nanjing and Xi'an.[2]

Financial reforms

In the financial reform of 1980, strongly differential approaches were adopted to share the revenue between the centre and the localities. Roughly four different systems were applied, all of which were at the time characterized as 'moving from the system of "eating at the same stove" to "eating at separate stoves"'. The result was that the localities were given strong economic independence, and that they were able to pursue their own investment programmes. Additionally, the principles for the financial agreement in 1980 were fixed for a 5-year period in order to avoid annual arguments and conflicts over central–local financial sharing. Special rules applied for Guangdong and Fujian provinces. As a matter of principle they were to cover all their financial expenses from their own financial incomes (except for the financial incomes and expenditures relating to central-state-level institutions and enterprises). Guangdong was, in addition to this, obliged to pay the centre 1 billion yuan annually, while Fujian received 150 million yuan annually in subsidy from the centre.

The financial reform of 1985 aimed at a more shared responsibility between the centre and the localities. Different types of taxes and financial incomes were levied exclusively for the centre, while other taxes and financial incomes were levied by the localities. Some taxes were shared between the centre and the localities, and some local contributions were to be made to central regulation funds. In principle, the structure for financial expenses remained, which was that the centre paid for those activities which were owned by the centre, including large construction projects, central-level administration, centrally owned schools and universities, central funds for agriculture, water conservancy, etc., and the rest were paid for by the localities. Additional rules were introduced to regulate fluctuations in incomes and expenditures between provinces, and annual increments were introduced for the subsidies to localities with the status of autonomous regions. A precedence for earmarked taxes was also set with the introduction of the Urban Construction Tax in 1985, a practice which was expanded in the following years, and which fell outside the

[2] Note that the reference to direct planning cities reflects the situation around 1992–1994, and that there is a considerable fluctuation in this category over time.

above-described-tax-sharing arrangements. Guangdong and Fujian continued the special arrangements which had been laid down in 1980.

The 1985 finance reform was revised in 1988. The state had radically lost its share in the revenue due to inefficient tax collection and the eroding effects of inflation. Annual increments in financial incomes were budgeted, based on 1987 as a base year, and the localities were forced to make up for a difference between the budgeted central income and the central incomes actually levied by the localities. Increases in the local financial incomes exceeding the budgeted increments were to be retained by the localities.

In 1993/1994, a minor tax reform took place, relocating some local incomes between levels of authority, and instituting a formal township and town level financial administration. Some (but not all) earmarked taxes linked to particular types of expenditure and various types of *ad hoc* regulation funds have disappeared in order to straighten out the state budget.

Within the structure of these general rules, which are the results of endless negotiations, a whole culture of centre–local bargaining has emerged, which dominates other economic decisions, and which has consequences for many aspects of society. This is not the place to explore this in full, but it is worth noticing that the central government's relations with the provinces are constrained by the financial system.

The new role of the banks in the 1990s

Similar, but not identical, problems surrounded the banks as they emerged in the 1980s. The major commercial banks played a new and dual role in the economic system. Apart from their function as institutions for extending credit and receiving savings deposits, they also functioned as the channels by which the government transferred funds to local governments for various purposes. Serious conflicts arose in the mid-1980s, where bad debts (especially to rural industries) caused the commercial banks to reach their credit ceiling. If they transferred government funds (which were technically credits), the banks would break their credit ceiling. Due to very strong government regulation of the banking sector, aimed at suppressing the money circulation and consumer price inflation, the banks were liable to pay heavy fines if they violated the government imposed ceiling. Consequently, the banks had great difficulty in paying out the government funds. Government credits, also, were not given in the full amount, but in a proportion of the amount, urging the banks to earmark a portion of their deposits to supplement the government credits up to the target. Local governments, especially township, town and county governments, often waited for months for funds due to them, and were often unable to pay peasants for their products or initiate development projects. This miserable situation is obviously to be blamed on the lack of coordination of policy objectives and the poor overall organization of the banking system.

A banking reform in 1994, initiated by Zhu Rongji, set out to divide the banking system into three types: commercial banks, policy banks and cooperative banks. Existing banks were split into commercial and policy institutions and strictly separated from each other. The cooperative banking system was based on the rural credit cooperatives, whose savings deposits had partly (about 25 per cent) been claimed as savings deposits for the Agricultural Bank of China, and on the urban credit cooperatives.

Creating a rural finance system

One of the fundamental problems of economic development in China has been the lack of formalized and administratively strong financial structures in the villages and townships. The ambiguous economic structure, somewhere between a collective and state administration, has made local public finance a great problem.

The villages, and especially the townships, are responsible for a vast amount of public amenities, including schools, social care, health provisions, drinking water, infrastructure, electricity, family planning, extension of farming techniques, irrigation services, public administration, etc. They are also strongly involved in the investment in productive activities. They have mainly been able to cover expenses through contributions from farm households, profit transfers from rural collective enterprises, fees for using amenities (like forbiddingly high school fees), and various forms of levies.

The debate in the 1980s, especially after the crisis in 1984/1985 when the amount of grain sold to the state declined due to the new procurement structures and prices, has centred on the 'burden on the peasants'. This 'burden', it was thought, decreased the peasants' inclination to produce grain, cotton and oil seeds, and pushed them into more lucrative occupations. Also, it was considered to milk otherwise profitable rural collective and private enterprises to the extent that they went bankrupt. In the mid-1980s, the debate started to shift in the direction of regularizing and systematizing the sources of local government funding in order to distinguish between legitimate and rational levies and excessive or damaging ones. A rural finance system was partly introduced in 1993/1994, but has not had time to mature yet.

THE SOCIAL SECURITY SYSTEM

A major feature of the economic reforms has been to autonomize enterprises. This can only be achieved by relieving them of the heavy social overheads they are burdened with. While housing, as an asset, can be sold off to the occupants or be transformed to become independent enterprises, the social security system is a major problem. Until now, expenses for pensions, health care, child care provisions (if any), etc., have been shouldered by the urban work units. Unemployment benefits have, until the early 1990s, been non-existent.

The huge expenses involved will have to be taken over by the state or a social insurance system. China seems to opt for a social insurance system, to which the employing enterprises would contribute. During the 1980s, enterprises have already begun contracting out medical provisions for employees, signing contracts with hospitals and clinics. The state has already imposed a type of unemployment insurance by legislation, which is aimed at taking the brunt of destitution, but is totally insufficient to ensure a reasonable life for the growing number of unemployed. Pensioning schemes with the present age profile of the labour force are likely to be easy to introduce (the premiums can be kept relatively low).

The structures for urban social security have not been finalized, and rural social security has hardly been discussed; the rural system is based on a meagre aid to orphans, elderly without relatives and the handicapped. Additionally, hardship relief is often given to family members of 'revolutionary martyrs', i.e. soldiers or policemen who have died in service.

The immense difference between the urban and rural economic structures is gradually changing as a result of the reforms. Sub-urban rural areas and rural areas in Guangdong, Fujian, southern Jiangsu, etc., are prosperous to a degree which exceeds the major cities in living standards and incomes. Rural enterprise workers often earn salaries higher than workers in urban enterprises, and increasing numbers of people, both rural and urban, are employed in non-state enterprises. However, state enterprises are becoming more autonomous, and will probably increasingly look like non-state enterprises.

The main test point for a converging of these sectors will be the extent to which the Chinese state can regulate a universal set of social insurance systems independently of the ownership structures and the official household registration of the members of society.

GUANXI IN THE ECONOMY

Discussing recent developments of the Chinese economy, one is often tempted to take the market exchange mechanisms for granted. We will here introduce a term which brings the actual operation of the market system into a more realistic perspective. This term is *guanxi*. Literally it means 'relationship' or 'connection', and it is used in formulations like *la guanxi*, which means to 'use personal contacts' and *guanxixue*, which means the 'art of using personal contacts'.

The term has won broad popularity among foreign businessmen trading in China as a sort of managerial rule of thumb for how to deal with Chinese counterparts, winning them by trust and personal engagement. For other observers, the term almost signifies corruption and unfair dealing. The concept is very fluid and is perceived in many different ways, and one should be very careful not to pin it down on a simple definition. Then, why bother? Because *guanxi* reflects a broadly perceived reality of interhuman exchanges which follow a different logic than expected in a market exchange. The way in which foreign merchants perceive the term – as a gimmick to overcome some inhibitions in the market exchange – reflects a too narrow and insensitive understanding of how people interact. The idea that *guanxi* verges on corruption does not reflect its nature either.

Some observers, as already mentioned in Chapter 1 understand *guanxi* as clientelism, or patron–client relationships, where one (weaker) person gives support and personal attention to another (stronger) person in exchange for protection and favours. This is indeed an aspect of *guanxi*, which is important. The way we understand *guanxi* is as a strategy for managing functional inter-personal relationships in order to survive in an environment of scarcity of information, goods and services. The nature of *guanxi*, therefore, changes under different environments. In the 'classical' planned economy, the power of allocation of goods and services was: (a) constrained by scarcity, and (b) egalitarian. While the principle was egalitarian, the individual attribution of an opportunity, a product or a service was linked to the unique decision of an individual or a group of individuals who had the power to decide over allocation. With the information and power of allocation being structurally concentrated in some persons, other persons would seek to please them or support them in order to be given an opportunity, a product or a service. This explanation corresponds to the client–patron relationship. If we extend this principle to cover a wide range of opportunities, products and services, not all decision-making powers were concentrated in one person or one type of persons, but innumerable decisions on allocation were scattered on a large number of people; this means that the distribution of opportunities, products and services becomes tradeable between decision makers. The exchange, furthermore, was not monetarized, and nobody knew the exact market value of the traded items. The lack of a market and the lack of information make it difficult to estimate the price. Hence, transactions in this system were based on a loose, implicit agreement of mutual exchange, which originated in some sort of affinity (kinship, common place of birth, shared university education, friendship, or collegiality), or even specially constructed, artificial links. A reward (beyond customary symbolic presents) for rendering a service was not expected until the need arose. Often the service was rendered through several links, so that a chain of obligations arose. For example, if we needed to purchase a bicycle, we had to obtain a letter of introduction from our work unit to the shop (because bicycles were in short supply, and certain quantities were set aside for each *danwei*); our good friend, who managed the campus book-store, was a personal friend of the director in charge of the introduction letters, and it so happened that he had recently been able to sell him a copy of the new English dictionary, which had been sold out almost before it appeared; so the book-store manager would get us an introduction letter. We also knew somebody (an old school friend) in the textile department of the department store, who would help us convince the clerk in the bicycle department that our letter of introduction was all right. All we would do was to buy some fresh fruit for her. Later in the month the book-store manager would need us to ride a refrigerator home for a relative in the small three-wheeled vehicle that we were employed to drive. Another example: a director of a rubber tyre factory had got an allocation of steel beams that could not be used in production, and a coal mine was in need of steel beams to reinforce a new mineshaft. The brother of the tyre factory director worked in the provincial administration, and had gone to school with the coal mine director. An (illegal) barter deal could be arranged, by which the tyre factory received coal for the steel beams. The transport over a long distance had to be carried out by small carts and vans, since it was impossible to get an allocation of railway freight.

Guanxi, in this sense, enabled transactions which would otherwise have been impossible or very difficult and cumbersome. Of course, under this system some very big decisions were in few hands, and some people had little to 'pay back' with. This means that within the wider framework of exchange through *guanxi*, various unequal relationships emerged, which formed the basis of institutionalized corruption.

Guanxi and the market

The coming of the 'market' economy and the new economic relationships between people in the early 1980s caused the function of *guanxi* to change. Existing structures disintegrated slowly. By the early 1980s buying bicycles in shops was no problem any longer, and plenty of *getihu* would, for a money reward, transport your new fridge home. You could, in the new economic environment, continue to live as before, with some added convenience. However, those who chose to do so gradually came to realize that they were losing out. Their relatives, neighbours and others were actively engaged in new economic activities and gained from them, in terms of incomes, social status and wellbeing.

The problem with the 'market' economy was that it lacked perspicacity. The rules governing it were unclear, the opportunities were confusing, and some people were ruthlessly exploiting their position. The market also meant that money became an increasingly important asset, where previously the power to allocate had been paramount. The amount of money circulating in the economy increased drastically. This led to large-scale corruption. The reason was that the official prices did not reflect the scarcity of certain popular items. The officials, and sometimes whole enterprises or government offices, started receiving bribes for delivering the goods. The case of telephone lines was a clear example. In the mid-1980s the price of a private telephone connection was low – in official prices – while the bribe to the official in charge was about five to ten times higher than the price itself. In order to jump the queue, one would have to pay about 4,000 yuan in bribes. By the early 1990s the state price went up to between 4,000 and 5,000 yuan, and the problem of bribes basically disappeared. In many sectors, the state operated a so-called 'dual track price system', meaning that raw materials, production inputs, energy, etc., were partly distributed on fixed quotas at subsidized prices, and partly at a higher price which reflected a theoretical 'market' price (the latter was in reality an officially imposed, artificial price, misleadingly called 'negotiated price' or *yijia*). As a consequence, an illegal market emerged, by which officials or work units in charge of distributing the quota goods sold these at the 'negotiated price', thus gaining an illegitimate profit. Because the scarcity of specific goods was much greater than was reflected in the 'negotiated price', the goods could be sold off at even higher prices.

These types of corruption, of course, were facilitated by the existence of *guanxi* networks, and the strategy of those involved is likely not to have been a straightforward sale to the 'highest bidder', but rather distribution mixing the objectives of particular favouritism and extortion of the scarcity price. The (albeit small) risk connected with corruption, of course, meant that *guanxi* relationships were necessary to generate mutual trust.

In the wider economic environment of deficient market information, poor state regulation, poorly developed civil law systems, absence of consumer organizations and pressure groups, and omnipresent corruption, it was essential for almost every Chinese to expand their *guanxi* networks in order to protect themselves from being cheated. *Guanxi*, therefore, became a very strong defensive mechanism and an important calibrator in the emerging market economy.

The effort, resources and time spent on maintaining *guanxi* networks in a neo-classical economy are understood as 'transaction costs'. In China in the 1990s, the transaction costs in economic interactions are still very high. Many economic functions are now gradually being changed. New payment methods (e.g. credit cards), better communication (broad availability of inter-city telephone lines, fax machines, mobile phones and pagers), increasing reliability of the transport system, decreasing bureaucracy in some sectors, and the emergence of independent, vociferous consumer organizations, all contribute to lowering the transaction costs, and thereby the need for this type of *guanxi* relationship.

This, however, does not mean that the urge to expand *guanxi* relationships will disappear as a strategy. The forms and content may change over time. However, the best proof that *guanxi* does not disappear easily is that overseas Chinese all over the world engage in *guanxi* relationships when they do business. Even in highly monetarized systems there is enormous scope for non-economic considerations.

A final word must address the idea that the asymmetric reciprocity of *some guanxi* relationships is in favour of the stronger person, and gives him/her the opportunity to exploit the *guanxi*. We will cite two possible scenarios to argue against a clear-cut definition of *guanxi* as patronage:

1. A rich and influential farmer, who was head of the township, wished to build

a house; he strongly refused his (less well-off and less powerful) neighbours' offer to contribute labour and cheap materials, and he hired in non-locals at high expense, using more expensive purchased building materials, in order to avoid return obligations to the neighbour which would eventually be very expensive and burdensome.

2. A private restaurant was opened just in front of the gates of the district tax office, and the owner started serving free lunches for the employees and their guests, who, in return, agreed to lenient treatment in tax matters; the concessions actually extorted from the fiscal authorities were exceedingly high, and the restaurant owner had a fair 'income' as a go-between for people who wanted to present their case favourably to the tax office. He got back manifold the loss of income from lavish dishes. In the latter case, the powerful tax officials were weak in the hands of the restaurant owner, but they did not lose personally as they transferred the cost to the public.

WOMEN AND ECONOMIC DEVELOPMENT

The situation of women in the reform era has changed drastically. Until the reforms started, women and men were distributed to work units, more or less according to the same principles, and enterprises and state organs would generally accept them equally. With the increasing focus on productivity in all sectors, enterprises began to become selective, preferring male employees, who were considered more reliable and more stable. The prejudices against women mainly focus on: (a) child-birth, maternity leave, menstrual instability and the effects of the menopause on productivity; (b) less physical strength than men; (c) less assertiveness in negotiations; and (d) the expectation that women will yield to popular views of the role of women, e.g. they will marry, will support the husband's career rather than their own, and will follow the husband wherever he may be relocated. Even before the state-owned enterprises were fully autonomous in choosing their employees, they began sending women's files back to the labour administration unopened. At present, tens of thousands of women with excellent higher education records are each year turned away by companies, which instead prefer to employ less-qualified men.

The Chinese business culture in the 'free market' setting has, furthermore, developed into a distinctively male culture where the presence of women could be embarrassing. 'Trust', based on male friendships, is cemented in business dinners demanding considerable drinking skills at hours when women are expected to be at home looking after their children and husbands. Major business deals cannot be completed without such extensive and expensive events.

Mobility opportunities have given more women a way out of their social background. Migrant female labour is considerable, constituting perhaps 20–30 per cent of all migrant labourers. Most migrant female labourers are from the countryside, taking up jobs as housemaids, sweatshop workers, waitresses in private catering establishments, etc. The plight of migrant women workers is difficult. They are subjected to prejudice in the receiving community, regarded as boorish and plump, and are generally exploited with low wages for hard work. However, the relative economic independence and distance from home may protect them from arranged marriages and total dependence.

While urban women are less likely to find formal employment than men, and while more women than men have been laid off, increasing numbers of women do engage as private operators (in catering, retail, transport, small-scale manufacturing, etc.). The family strategies that emerged in large cities in the early 1990s included 'one family, two systems'. This means that one person would retain permanent occupation in a state enterprise, while the other would 'jump into the sea', as a private entrepreneur. The advantage was to retain the social benefits and subsidized housing provided by the work unit, and to have the higher incomes of the private sector. Each family would have its own strategy, based on individual conditions, and no typical male–female pattern emerged. Some sectors (retail, and catering) are more female dominated, while others (transport, wholesale, repair and manufacturing) tend to be male.

CONCLUSIONS

This chapter has examined the evolution of the reforms. It has been our prime task to demonstrate the dynamics of economic development, and the political and organizational factors, which contributed to growth. We have demonstrated that the notion of a market economy must be understood with great caution. It is not the case that an expanding market economy has wrenched open an unwieldy planned economy by the force of 'natural development'. The introduction of 'exchange by market mechanisms' was through political intervention and protection of the market in the initial stages. The state played on the inequalities in the economy to further the development of the non-planned sector, and allowed it to grow very fast.

While parts of the state sector were reluctant or even hostile to the new sectors at times, in overall terms they profited, and soon learned to exploit the new opportunities.

It has also been demonstrated that market exchange in China is moderated by *guanxi* relationships which have played a significant role in shaping the dynamics of change.

FURTHER READING

There is a huge literature on China's economic development since 1976. Carl Riskin's *China's Political Economy. The Quest for Development Since 1949*

(1987) covers the beginning of the reforms, but has been overtaken by events at the end of the 1980s. For an excellent up-to-date presentation, see Wong (1994). See also current World Bank Reports. Broader descriptions of the early stages of reform can be found in Harding (1987). The political environment around the economic reforms is well described by Baum (1994), and Shirk (1993) provides a profound analysis of economic reforms. For one of the most comprehensive descriptions of the objectives of China's reform, see Yu (1984).

PART IV
Society

In this part of the book, we address those areas of human life which are not politics or political economy in a narrow sense, but which directly affect the life quality of large groups of the population, and which, in probably the clearest way possible, characterize the political system and its capacity to regulate a complex society. In Chapter 11, we explore how China deals with the environmental crisis, how the Chinese state seeks to overcome the predicament of between 70 and 80 million poor people in China, and how China seeks to curb the growth of the population. In Chapter 12, we examine the situation of women in China; In Chapter 13, we examine the ethnic foundations of the Chinese state, and how China deals with ethnic diversity within its borders.

Although these topics may seem to go beyond politics, meandering into anthropological, feminist, geographical or environmental and sociological science territory, they form an important touchstone for a political system, and they provide the understanding that a narrow political perspective cannot. They indicate the cleavages upon which the political edifice has been built, and they lay bare the faultlines which may shake up the political system when otherwise-invisible tensions have grown.

11 The environment, poverty and population growth

The limited availability of resources and the growth of the population have become the major themes of the modern world, and since the 1970s they have set the agenda for debates on global development. In China, these two issues are also of acute significance. For one thing, China's economic development in the reform era is rapid and claims resources and causes pollution on a large scale. But China is also the largest nation in the world, and its ability to pursue sustainable development, find a balance between population growth and supply of grain and other foodstuffs, is essential for global development. In China there are 80 million poor (according to estimates from 1993). They are targeted for special development measures. This chapter describes China's environmental, population and poverty alleviation policies.

INTRODUCTION

There is a strong consensus that China faces a serious ecological crisis, and that China's crisis influences the global environment of food production and sustainable utilization of natural resources. Domestically, China's economic reforms, which have progressed since 1978, have been accompanied by an increased awareness of the ecological factors and by policies to solve imbalances in agricultural production and the depletion of the ecological environment. Internationally, the Brundtland Report of 1987 (WCED, 1987), as well as the papers from the Rio Summit in 1992, indicated China's importance for global development, being, as it is, the largest nation in the world, and having one of the world's highest growth rate economies. This means that China's environment cannot be seen as a domestic or isolated issue.

The problems of China's ecological environment have been described by many authors, perhaps most prominently and comprehensively by Smil (1984, 1993), Ross (1988) and Edmonds (1994a, b). In the following, we will outline some of the main problems in relation to major issues of development: population, poverty, agricultural production and urban environment.

POPULATION

The most common question is: how can China produce food for the growing population? However, the problem is broader and more complex. The main issues raised by the population growth are:

- the need for increased food production;
- the farmland area per capita;
- the development of non-agricultural employment;
- the energy consumption and concomitant pollution; and
- the consumption of non-renewable resources.

The issue of population growth is thus intimately linked with all other environmental issues. We will examine the main issues here, in order to see how they are dealt with in the context of Chinese politics.

Only about 10–15 per cent of the Chinese territory is suitable for agricultural and related use, and vast areas are in high altitudes, deserts and other conditions which make them uninhabitable. The population density in the fertile and more hospitable rural regions is more than 400 persons per km^2 and in some places even exceeds 2,000 persons per km^2. The average area of farmland per capita of the population is claimed to be less than 500 m^2, and is likely to be even smaller than this.

Continued growth of the population has strained the resources. There are several reasons for the growth in population. The most important is that Chinese development has led to a general improvement of the medical and nutritional situations. This, combined with the relative internal peace since the beginning of the 1950s, has drastically increased life expectancy so that it is now around 70 years as opposed to between 30 and 40 years during the first half of the century. In the 1950s to the 1970s, the collective structures in rural China *de facto* encouraged peasants to bear several children (to get a larger share of the collective distribution). For these reasons the *natural population growth* has increased, i.e. people die at a higher age, and until the early or mid-1970s they continued to bear many children (Box 11.1; Figure 11.1).

The Chinese government adopted a very rigorous policy on family planning in the 1980s, which in principle should reduce the rate of child-birth to one child per couple. However, in reality peasants are *de facto* allowed to bear two children per married couple. The high growth of the population in the 1950s through to the end of the 1970s means that the population at child-bearing age is expected to peak in the 1990s or later. Even with a very restrictive family planning policy, the population pressure on Chinese natural resources is likely to continue to grow until well after 2020, perhaps even to 2050.

The virtual ban on rural–urban migration between 1957 and 1984 means that the Chinese population is for the largest part settled in the countryside and is occupied in agriculture. The population growth in the urban population has

Box 11.1   *Basic data on China's population*
Population according to 1990 census: total: 1,130,510,638, of which
548,690,231 women and 581,820,407 men; the sex ratio was 106.04 men per
100 women; 1,097,776,366 persons lived in 276,911,767 family households
(average 3.96 persons per household).

Household registration status: agricultural 901,806,098 (or 79.72 per
cent of the total population), of which 456,673,886 men and 445,132,212
women; 884,726,134 persons with agricultural household registration were
permanent residents; non-agricultural 219,931,980, of which 120,821,432 men
and 99,110,548 women.

Illiteracy: 204,854,804 persons, of which 140,036,698 women and
64,818,106 men.

Other indicators

Life expectancy (in 1981): total population 69.3 years; female population
70.76 years; urban population 71.46 years; rural population 68.74 years.

Population density: 1950, 58 persons per km^2; 1982, 106 person per km^2;
1988, 114 persons per km^2; 1990, 119 persons per km^2; 1993, 124 persons per
km^2. Note: the regional differences are huge; in Shanghai, the density was 2,300
persons per km^2 in 1990; in Jiangsu, 670; in Gansu, 42; in Qinghai, 6.2; and in
Sichuan, 191. The population density is only slightly higher than Denmark's and
considerably lower than Italy's or the Netherlands'; however, only one-tenth of
the Chinese territory is arable, while between 60 and 100 per cent of the European
countries' land can be cultivated.

been relatively easy to regulate, while it has been more difficult to disseminate
the advantages of small family sizes to the rural areas.

Chinese leaders regard the rural bias of the population (which is somewhere
between 50 and 80 per cent of the total population, depending on the
definitions) as the most important development problem in China. The transfer
of the population to non-agricultural employment is considered to be a
precondition for the rational use of the farmland resources and thereby for the
potential for feeding the population.

POPULATION CONTROL

As mentioned above, China has a policy aimed at restricting child-birth. The
overall population pressure seen in relation to the scarcity of resources has been
the main reason for introducing this policy. The original ideas for the family

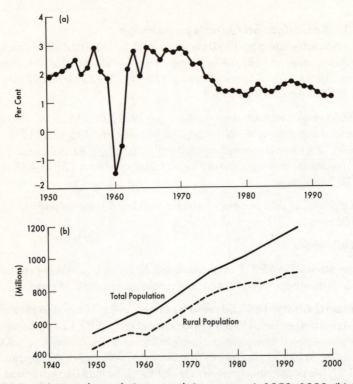

Figure 11.1 *(a) Annual population growth (percentage), 1950–1993; (b) China's population, 1949–1993 (Note: the proportion of the rural population fell due to rural–urban migration and reclassifications of the population; rural birthrates remained high)*

planning policy were put forward by the Chinese economist Ma Yinchu in the 1950s. His argument was that it was necessary to limit the growth of the population because otherwise the excessive supply of manual labour would retard China's technological transition, and thereby impair the economic development. His ideas were criticized after the Hundred Flowers Movement in 1957, and he was removed from all his posts. In the ensuing years, when the Maoist doctrine was in force, it was thought that a large population size was not a constraining factor, but rather an asset. Ma Yinchu's ideas were taken up again in 1979.

The Chinese fertility began to drop at the beginning of the 1970s, following the improved and more stable conditions in China since 1949, the only serious food crisis being the great famine in 1960/1961 (Figure 11.2). This stability induced a general trend of less births per woman, mainly in the cities, but also to a certain extent in the countryside. The people's commune system did very little to limit child-birth; some even argue that it promoted higher birthrates – that it was *pronatal*. The size of the family was the measure for distributing

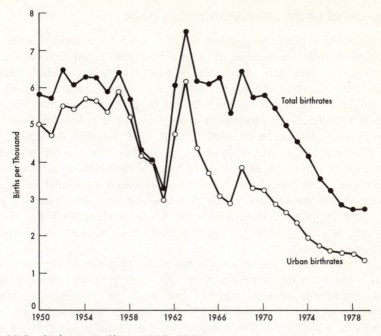

Figure 11.2   *Birthrates in China, 1950–1979*

food and allocating 'private plots'. At the same time the households did not have the limiting factor of farm size since production was collectivized; there was thus no individual incentive to restrict child-birth out of fear that the land could not feed the family. Finally, the care of the rural elderly was still a matter for the individual family, and so there was a strong incentive to want more children to give support in one's old age.

Conversely, urban residents had strong disincentives to bear children. Throughout the 1950s to the 1970s the available living space decreased rapidly, and urban occupations meant that both parents were normally employed full time, earning too little to support a large family. The uncertainties of the Cultural Revolution caused many families to be split up. While large families were not uncommon in urban China until the mid-1980s, the generation which came of age in the early 1970s was more likely to bear fewer children than their parents – for social reasons.

The reforms starting in 1978 did not basically change the incentives to bear more than one child per couple in the rural areas. The new direction of family-based production meant that more children meant more available labourers, and even 5-year-olds can be relied on to feed chickens or carry out other menial tasks. Greater affluence meant that there were less social constraints to child-birth, and housing space did not pose a problem in most of the countryside.

Background of the family planning policy

Family planning in China is a policy which is centrally directed. In the early 1960s there were some attempts at instituting family planning, and the State Council together with many provinces and cities established a Family Planning Office in 1964. However, due to the Cultural Revolution, it was only after 1970 that family planning came on the agenda. In 1969 and 1971, Zhou Enlai personally intervened to promote a family planning policy, and the State Council drafted a Report on Family Planning Work. In 1971, the state set up a Family Planning Committee with an administrative office in the Ministry of Health, and with an elaborate system of local administration down to county level. At the same time local offices or dedicated personnel in people's communes, street committees, production brigades, etc., were specially put in charge of family planning. From 1973 onwards, a rudimentary family planning practice was in place, concentrating on densely populated areas, information on contraceptives, etc.

After 1978, family planning was turned into a much more rigorous policy, which is based on central state planning: 'The state promotes family planning so that population growth may fit the plan for economic and social development' (Article 25 of the 1983 Constitution). Accordingly, the central authorities in a policy document demanded that 'state personnel and urban residents only bear one child per couple, unless they have received a permission based on special circumstances'. Originally it was the intention to extend this to all citizens in China, but it was not feasible. Rural residents are allowed to bear two children, provided they receive a permission to bear the second child. Detailed rules and conditions differ from place to place.

The family planning policy is led by the State Council Commission for Family Planning and commissions at each level of government.

Family planning policy during the reform era

The reforms coincided with the introduction of a serious one-child policy in both rural and urban China. While the compliance in the urban areas was high, there were serious problems in the rural areas. As a result the authorities sought to force through compliance by imposing Draconian punishment on those who did not comply. First, local officials were made personally responsible for meeting the targets of one child per couple, with a certain (large) proportion of women using contraceptives or being sterilized (after a certain number of births). Local officials – in order to protect their own personal interests – were often inclined to impose the policy in an even more heavy-handed way than they were meant to, abducting pregnant women to undergo forced abortions, destroying assets belonging to families having too many children, refusing to register (and report) the birth of excess children, etc. Accordingly, families expecting an excess child would seek refuge with relatives in other parts of the country, and would avoid registering excess children.

Due to the household registration system, only men are expected to stay in the parental village, so girls are no guarantee for their parents when they reach old age; also, more traditional concepts of continuing the male family line have played an important role. As many common Chinese say: 'You only raise girls for others to enjoy. They are no use'. For these reasons, families have avoided registering baby girls in order to have a chance of bearing a baby boy. Official statistics and school attendance indicate that there is a significant preponderance of boys in rural China. While there have been reported incidents of female infanticide, much of the explanation of the lower number of girls lies in non-registration and the fact that they are kept away from school to save tuition fees and to provide cheap domestic labour. Girls' education in many rural areas is taken lightly, since they are 'raised for other people' (i.e. their in-laws).

The improvement of conditions in the countryside, combined with a gradual urbanization, is likely to decrease rural fertility in the long run. Forced implementation has only led to a situation where many rural women do not have an official registration, are deprived of education and so are potential outcasts in society.

ENVIRONMENTAL PROBLEMS OF POPULATION GROWTH

Population growth seriously affects the ecological environment. It generates conflicts over resources and forces about changes in production which may reduce future availability of resources. It generates pollution which reduces the life quality and destroys resources which may be necessary for human survival. Here we shall discuss some examples of this in order to examine the extent to which Chinese environmental policy is adequate.

One important example of an environmental problem arising from population growth is the need for rapidly increasing food production. The technically fastest and most effective improvement in grain production is the use of chemical inputs (chemical fertilizer and pesticides) and of farm machinery. This is likely to disturb the ecological balance, for example by polluting ground and surface water, harming the soil composition (due to diminished use of organic fertilizer), and depleting scarce water resources. While higher yields are likely in the first few years, the long-term consequence is an overall decline in essential agricultural resources.

Another example is that the improving rural living standards are linked with employment in the growing rural industrial sector. The rational development of agriculture is to a large extent determined by moving labourers away from agriculture into local industry. However, the non-agricultural rural enterprises in China are very polluting, using labour-intensive processes and low-grade technology; most of them do not have sufficient economic strength to finance environmental protection measures. Local governments are too reliant on incomes from them to enforce such measures.

A further conflict over resources is related to the use of land. In economic terms, agricultural land use yields low incomes, while industries and service trades are more favourable to the local employment and economy. The development of such enterprises and the concomitant infrastructural improvement claims large amounts of land, often prime farmland like paddy fields.

The combined effects of pollution and the reduction in the farmland area mean that the basic resources for sustained food production are threatened.

The questions to be asked are whether China has an effective environmental policy, and whether the country is able to cope with these problems.

THE DEVELOPMENT OF ENVIRONMENTAL POLICY IN CHINA

An environmental policy came about in China in the early 1970s, and has since come of age. Participation in the Stockholm Conference on the Human Environment in 1972 caused the Chinese leadership to convene a National Environment Conference in 1973, at which it decided to establish an Environmental Protection Agency. Chinese environmental protection was, from this time, professionalized. The status of environmental policy making was ensured by placing it as a separate chapter in the Five Year Plans so that conflicts over targets and authority or problems of funding were mediated by the State Planning Commission.

The reforms of 1978 needed funding and financial flexibility, so in 1979/1980 China looked for the first time towards obtaining development aid and development loans through the international system, and sought accession to the World Bank and IMF. China agreed to adopt the procedures and practices attached to development loans, some of which were aimed at environmental protection projects.

In the early 1980s China, therefore, had ample contacts within the international development and environment regimes and became an independent and active participant in those regimes.

Initiatives in China included the compilation of the 'Programme for Environmental Protection in China' (1987), following the work of the Brundtland Commission, and of a Chinese 'Agenda 21' in 1993/1994 following the initiative of the Rio Conference.

China's domestic systems for dealing with the environment and development were created in the period since 1972. The Environmental Protection Agency began as an office under the Minsitry for Urban and Rural Construction, but was made increasingly independent. Since the mid-1980s it has been an independent office under the State Council, ranking as an office half a step down from a full ministry.

The Environmental Protection Commission under the State Council, which originated in the need to lead China's participation in the Brundtland Commission, was set up in 1984 and has gained increasing importance, headed by a vice-premier of the State Council and having a permanent participation not only by a wide range of ministries, but also by many scientific consultants. This commission puts strong weight behind the work of the Environmental Protection Agency. In 1993, environmental protection had been furthered even more by the establishment of a new permanent committee for environmental protection in the National People's Congress.

In the latter part of the 1980s and the first half of the 1990s China has adopted many laws and practices which are aimed at protecting the environment. These laws are still not fully implemented, due to a lack of properly trained manpower and funds. A major problem has been the conflicting local interests, which have made it very difficult to implement environmental laws in a serious and coherent way. In the most recent period, however, pressure from the central leadership and provincial authorities has led to concentrated efforts in special problem areas (like the Huai River, the Taihu Lake and Dianchi Lake). With strong political pressure and adequate funding (including loans from the World Bank) such specific projects stand a chance of being realized. However, it still remains to be seen how successful they are in the long term.

Issues and policies: Urban environment

China's urban development is typical of a modernizing state: rapid expansion of industry, construction of infrastructure, office space, housing and tourist facilities. The resulting situation has been a mixture of improvements and new problems for the urban population, as well as serious issues of the use of natural resources and of pollution. We will discuss the issues by examining the structural conditions of urban development.

Urban development in China can be divided into metropolitan and small town development, both of which have occurred at a fast pace in the post-1978 period. The development has, since the mid-1980s, been regulated by town planning, which is a legal requirement for all cities and towns.

The physical structure of Chinese cities is determined by: (a) the *danwei*-'syndrome', (b) public landownership and planning procedures, (c) population density and increasing demands for proper living space, (d) infrastructural and industrial demands, (e) needs for pollution control, and (f) demands for a pleasant urban living space.

Chinese urban areas in the 1970s were dominated by four main types of spaces: (1) the urban centre with shopping areas and public service agencies, laid out in the 1920s and 1930s, or in the 1950s (land in the centre was laid out in relatively large plots, built up to the street front, with each plot in principle belonging to a work unit); (2) old residential areas, with small, traditional one- or two-storey townhouses; (3) gigantic walled campuses for each large work unit, with main buildings, offices, workshops and service buildings, and residential areas; and (4) suburban villages and markets, often built around road crossings with poor buildings, surrounded by vegetable fields. This distribution of space from the 1950s onwards has set the agenda for urban planning in the 1980s and 1990s. Each work unit had very large land space for its use, and a wall around the campus took up much land; residential, administrative and industrial areas tended to be mixed, although it was normal that administrative work units, academies, colleges and universities were in one part of town, while industrial and transport units were in other parts of town. Both in the city centre and in the campus areas, work units dominated with their mixed functions and large scale.

Urban land was owned by the state, but in the 1950s the state had allocated the use right to the *danwei*s. When the reforms started, the land use right belonged to the *danwei*s, and they were encouraged to take advantage of this asset, e.g. by renting out space to individual and private enterprises. In some cities, the land use, especially in the central areas, was adjusted by the city government by relocating work units (in this context the level of jurisdiction was decisive, a city-level work unit was easier to evict than a provincial or central one), and investments in new construction projects were encouraged. The large size of the plots and the ability of the local government to clear large areas at one time meant that large-scale, modern hotels and shopping centres could be planned in central areas of the cities. In the campus areas, work units would rent out areas outside their walls to private enterprises who built 'lean-to' shops, restaurants and stalls which suddenly turned otherwise long, dull stretches between the kerb and the wall into busy areas. Some work units built their own high-rise hotels or shopping centres at the border of their campuses in order to derive an income from them. Residential areas and suburban villages were controlled by real estate corporations under the local government, and in many parts of China, old residential areas were bulldozed in the 1980s and 1990s to make way for new high-rise housing.

Urban development in the 1960s and 1970s had been stagnating, and had not been able to keep pace with the growth of the urban population. Living space tended to become more and more crowded, and many work units could not any longer allocate flats to married couples. Waiting lists for housing had become very long, and the allocation of living space had become a field for patronage and corruption. Housing provided by work units, conversely, was cheap or virtually free of charge, even considering the low income levels. At the beginning of the 1990s a gradual commercialization of housing started to take place. It is now possible to purchase owned flats from work units at subsidized prices. At the same time it became possible to buy living space in the free housing market. Since the mid-1980s, rich work units have been able to provide housing of increasing quality to their workers by taking shares in large real estate development projects. Poor work units continue to have abominable housing provision. In the 1990s there are still single workers and split families living in dormitories and store rooms, or sleeping on shopfloors after working hours, and there are plenty of people who cannot marry because they have not been able to solve the problem of housing. The regional differences are very large. A college teacher in Guangdong is likely to have a larger and better flat than a vice-minister in Beijing. The mismatch between living space and population size thus led to a priority for new housing construction, spearheaded by urban state-owned real estate corporations with the participation of rich work units. The result has been a rapid, large-scale development of huge residential areas with high-rise buildings.

The reorganization of the cities as a result of the town planning in the 1980s (by which work units in the city centres were rotated or moved so that new districts of certain industrial functions emerged) made the Chinese urbanites more mobile. Many had to leave the campus in order to go to work. The emergence of private and individual enterprises made new claims on public spaces. New shops, and new stalls and restaurants drew people into the streets. At the same time, the increasing needs for consumer goods increased the demand for transport. The city infrastructures were too limited, and priority was given to improving road networks to make space for more cars and lorries. Large cities built or expanded metro systems (Beijing, Shanghai, Guangzhou, Nanjing, etc.).

Infrastructure projects were in most large cities an outcome of long-term planning, and were as established in obligatory town planning procedures. However, the transport volume increased much more than ever predicted, and most large cities in China are characterized by traffic congestion in the 1990s. The town planning in the 1980s and after also reflects a reversal from the emphasis on production in the 1950s to the 1970s, and a new focus on services provided in the public space (rather than behind the walls of the *danweis*). Banking and other financial institutions, large joint-venture hotels, joint-venture restaurants, large shopping centres and supermarkets have been the strongest corporate players in shaping the city centres in the 1980s and 1990s. Heavy, and dirty, industrial production, as well as labour intensive industries are being moved further away, or renovated.

Industrial pollution is one of the worst problems of Chinese cities. The environmental protection authorities have been able to control much industrial pollution in the cities. Most large cities, however, still continue to have large polluting plants within their jurisdiction, which cause air pollution by emitting noxious gases and dust, and also pollute rivers and lakes by pumping wastewater into the river systems and by storing solid waste on river banks. Local environmental authorities are, in many cases, under great political pressure from local governments or powerful enterprises to turn a blind eye to pollution. The lack of coordination between levels of authority plays an important role here. Centrally-owned state enterprises can easily overrule local environmental authorities, and are able to calculate with the lack of manpower in the central environmental authorities to investigate pollution.

Popular protests and opinion forming on urban pollution are very limited. Individual citizens are not inclined to engage in protests, and there do not exist any genuinely popular environmental organizations. Public debate is toned down and conducted in an abstract way, not seeking to allocate blame for transgressions. However, internal investigations of such problems, accompanied by strong technical and scientific evidence, are made in many cases.

There is a risk that the reform policy in the long-term will threaten the Chinese system for collection of solid household waste. China has a very elaborate system for refuse collection, and treatment and recycling of solid waste; this so-far relatively efficient system is, ironically, an example of private initiative, combined with public regulation. Urban residents' committees and private refuse traders compete in the primary sorting of refuse, and useable items, like scrap metals, bottles, paper, textiles, plastic materials, etc., are collected and sold to special 'procurement centres' that resell the goods to factories which recycle them. Private traders make rounds to restaurants to procure cans, bottles, etc., and other waste. Because local government requires the restaurants to remove waste on their own, restaurant owners pay the private traders to carry off the waste; the traders can also have an additional income from reselling the waste to the procurement centres. The system is based on the fact that there is a large poor and unskilled workforce willing to do low-paid work. Waste food and vegetable waste is collected by suburban farmers to use as feed. As long as there is a poor, migrant population in the cities which is willing to eke out a small reward from this type of dirty and heavy work, the system will probably be maintained. However, large metropolitan centres like Beijing, Shanghai, Tianjin, Nanjing and Guangzhou produce increasing mountains of waste, which cannot realistically be handled by armies of waste collectors in rags, ploughing their way through the traffic jams on three-wheeled bikes.

Wastewater is becoming an increasing problem in many cities. Former systems by which suburban farmers collected latrine in carts or small boats are gradually being given up because of the dirty nature of the work, and the relative affluence of the suburban farmers who prefer to use chemical fertilizer rather than latrine which is more labour intensive. Water treatment plants are rare in China, and increasing surface water areas are being polluted by wastewater. Industrial wastewater is only partially treated, and many rivers and lakes in China are severely polluted by industrial waste.

Air pollution is the worst type of pollution in China, although many local governments have forbidden the use of small coal stoves and seek to regulate the use of fossil fuels in factories in urban centres. The increase in road traffic causes severe pollution from poor combustion of gasoline and diesel in technologically backward engines. The levels of air pollution in Chinese cities are very high, and they are almost impossible to control. It is particularly difficult to improve the emission from vehicles, since: (a) the demand for transportation is increasing more than the investment in transport facilities; and (b) new (less polluting) vehicles are so very expensive due to taxation, and the high demand means that older vehicles are not decommissioned even when their use is inappropriate for safety and environmental reasons.

An issue of enormous dimensions is the shortage of water. The new construction boom and the improving living standards have increased exponentially the need for urban water during the 1980s and 1990s. However, the groundwater reserves in North China have declined drastically in the last two decades. The groundwater level under Beijing and Tianjin has receded critically, and other cities in the north are likely to experience water shortages. The large Miyun Reservoir to the north of Beijing, which was originally built in order to supply irrigation water to agriculture, is now exclusively used for urban drinking water in Beijing. The local governments in large cities occasionally ration the use of water by cutting off supplies in parts of the cities. This policy does not apply to international hotels and similar establishments, thus causing resentment and public anger, albeit uncoordinated, directed against local government.

The Chinese have a tradition for well-developed urban spaces, based on a mixture of traditional concepts of geomancy and concepts of modern town planning imported in the 1920s. The model example of pleasant town planning was the way in which the nationalist government who set up Nanjing as the capital in 1927 renovated that city, creating broad, tree-lined boulevards and green open spaces, afforesting hilly areas outside the city. Ever since then the 'greening' (*lühua*) of Chinese cities has come to represent affluence. The Cultural Revolution did away with this, and the cities became drab, grey and dusty. The economic progress following the reforms and the greater emphasis on the environment have revived the notion of 'greening' – planting trees and sowing grass in public spaces and reserving land for parks, etc.

Developing the urban environment in the 1980s and 1990s was based on town planning, and reflects a legacy of the *danwei* structure of the earlier years, as well as the changing economic structures of the cities.

Small towns

Small town development, in principle, should also follow town planning rules, and town plans have been carefully drawn up, only to prove too difficult to follow. Due to the high costs of investment in regular development zones, much *real* urban development, especially of service industries, takes place along major roads. These long and ugly urban developments violate all town development plans, but provide a sufficiently cheap and effective basis for development of small private trade and industry. Due to the difficulty of controlling pollution in small places (where local government are close stake-holders in local industry), pollution levels can be excessively high in small towns.

Environmental issues and agricultural production

The linkage between the environment, economics and strategies for food production is at the core of development. In this section, we will explore the economic and social problems of agriculture to indicate how they impinge on the environment and the stability of food production.

Agricultural production in China has to develop further. The Chinese government's main problems with agriculture are within the framework of ensuring sufficient levels of grain, edible oil and cotton are supplied to the growing population, and to secure long-term stability of production. During the post-1978 reforms China has pursued a policy of giving peasants more direct choice in production, opening the markets, and allowing non-agricultural job opportunities in the countryside to expand. This has caused the incomes from grain production to decline radically in comparison with other rural income sources, and has encouraged a shift away from grain production to other products. Some large grain-price adjustments have taken place, as well as changes in the grain procurement mechanisms, but these have had limited effect.

The household responsibility system in agriculture means that each family in a village has received the land use right of a proportion of the land in the village. This often takes the form of small scattered plots with different obligations (taxes, local fees and quotas) attached to them. The result in large parts of Chinese agriculture is small-scale farming, which is regarded by many as irrational. In some parts of China, farming has become a week-end activity for farmers-turned-workers, and in other parts it has become impoverished due to lack of high-level investment.

One serious problem that was debated in the mid-1980s was that the household responsibility system would break down the collective structures of management, and especially that individual organization of agriculture would endanger the upkeep of irrigation and drainage systems, and that the lack of private land ownership would also lead peasants into short-term predatory management, neglecting investment in soil improvement. There is much evidence now that these concerns were justified.

It is essential for the Chinese leadership to devise policies which optimize the use of agricultural resources. As already metioned, the development options are complex and contradictory. The long-term protection of soil, forest and water resources to allow for future growth in agricultural production is one such aim. An aim for the short and medium term is to generate incomes for the peasants. Combining these aims can be difficult, especially if the short-term land use is harmful to the sustained fertility of the land. The state has therefore started investment schemes which aim to improve the agricultural resources, enabling long-term productivity while at the same time increasing peasant incomes.

The overall problems for agriculture, as mentioned, are: (a) the decline in farmland and the decline in fertility experienced as a result of soil erosion, salinization and alkalinization; (b) the lack of skill and ability among farmers, the skilled peasants being attracted by more lucrative work in other sectors; (c) the lack of investment in agricultural land, irrigation and roads; (d) changes of production methods, reflecting labour shortages (less use of organic fertilizer, switch to less-intensive cropping patterns, etc.); and (e) low prices for agricultural products. These problems cannot be solved by one simple measure, but must be addressed in many, complex ways.

The variables which determine outcomes for agriculture are: (a) ecological balance; (b) population and expected living standards; (c) agricultural prices and the supply of production factors, i.e. the economy; and (d) the political ability to balance these variables.

In 1987, the Chinese leadership started a large-scale investment scheme to solve some development problems for agriculture – the Comprehensive Agricultural Development Programme. This programme diverts a combination of central and local funds (credits and financial allocations) into specific land improvement, farmland irrigation, afforestation, and farm technology projects, aimed at increasing per-unit output from the fields and increasing peasant incomes. The townships and villages must contribute with a large part of the funding and the peasants must mobilize the labour themselves in order to receive central allocations and credits.

The Chinese government also has special investment programmes for promoting lean pork, vegetable production, farm technology extension, etc. These programmes aim at solving one of the most important problems of the Chinese development, the adaptation of agriculture to the new dietary demands of the population. The rapid urbanization of the population and the increasing living standard has shifted consumption away from a high starch (i.e. grain) content towards a larger protein (i.e. meat) content in the diet.

In addition to these measures, China has also begun to import grain on a certain scale, obviously to meet the food demand in a situation where it becomes increasingly difficult to squeeze extra grain from the available farmland resources.

The intense conflict between ecological balance and agriculture (both in terms of the economic organization and the external demands for increased food production) cannot be fundamentally solved by such policies, but can be temporarily alleviated to a certain extent.

POVERTY

Poverty in Chinese rural areas is a severe problem in spite of efforts to deal with it. The thrust of poverty alleviation policies is that the abolition of poverty is a matter for the poor segments of the population themselves, so that progress is earned, and that nobody in the end should depend entirely on the state. There are two government bodies for dealing with poverty:

1. the Ministry of Civil Affairs; and
2. the Poverty Alleviation and Development Committee under the State Council (formerly the Committee for Economic Development in Poor Areas under the State Council).

These two organizations deal with different aspects of poverty. Individual poverty and distress is a matter for the Ministry of Civil Affairs, which delivers various types of aid and enables the poor, the handicapped, elderly people without relatives, etc., to obtain various forms of direct and indirect aid. The Ministry of Civil Affairs is also in charge of relief in the case of natural calamities.

Poverty alleviation policy

The number of poor in China was estimated at 80 million in the early 1990s and the number was revised at 70 million in 1995.

What are the criteria for poverty? The norm used in China is based on household income. From the mid-1980s, China has taken a regional approach, and has based poverty alleviation work on designating poor counties, based on a calculation of the average rural household incomes. If the average household income was below (originally) 200 yuan a year (in 1992 the norm was updated up to 320 yuan a year, and in 1994 to 400 yuan a year), special aid was given to the county.

In 1994 there were 592 'poor' counties with a combined poor population of 58 million persons, the other 22 million poor being scattered in counties not designated as poor. Apart from poor counties designated by the state, each province can designate poor counties, townships and villages according to its own norms. For example there are 43 state-level poor counties in Sichuan, but at the same time Sichuan has designated an additional 40 provincial-level poor counties.

In 1994 China adopted a plan called the '8.7 Plan' which aimed at solving the poverty problems before the year 2000. The targets have been integrated into the Ninth Five Year Plan, which runs from 1996–2000.

The Poverty Alleviation Office under the State Council Committee is in charge of regional poverty. Since the mid-1980s, whole jurisdictions in China have been classified as poor, and have received development aid. The reform policies meant that the role of the central state changed. The central reallocation of funds to provinces was changed stepwise, so that provincial-level administration was made more directly responsible for their incomes and expenses. In order to ensure that the poorest areas did not lose out, the Chinese government instituted the poverty alleviation policy in the mid-1980s, earmarking central funds for poor areas and encouraging provinces to top up these funds. The policy originally started as a number of disparate financial transfer schemes at the beginning of the 1980s, directed at different types of areas which were all considered to be poor. These have been summarized as *lao-shao-bian-qiong*, i.e. 'old revolutionary bases', 'ethnic minority areas', 'distant border areas', and 'poor areas'. The old revolutionary bases were those areas where the Chinese Communist Party, in the late 1920s and 1930s, had strongholds from which they waged guerrilla warfare against the nationalist government troops. These areas, for example the Jinggang Shan Soviet, were situated in remote mountainous terrain with limited resources and poor infrastructure. The communist presence and warfare added to the poverty of the areas, and eventually the exodus of the young, able-bodied men (who joined the Long March) broke the local economy to the extent that it did not recover for more than 50 years. In the eyes of veteran cadres in the CCP these areas deserved special treatment in recognition of their role in the history of the Party. In the early 1980s special aid schemes were put together for them.

National minority areas and border areas were targeted, mainly due to the shifts in the financial structure at the beginning of the 1980s. It was recognized that central funding schemes were of particular importance for strategic reasons. Large-scale support for pastoral communities in the north-west is an example of such a programme. In the case of these areas, it was understood that they were relatively poor, but they did not belong among the poorest communities in rural China.

The poor areas as a category had not been recognized properly before the mid-1980s. It was known within the Party that parts of the countryside existed under intolerable conditions. Monthly cash incomes of 0.02 yuan, families with only one pair of trousers, families not having one decent meal every day, recurrent hunger-migrations from specific areas, people living in primitive huts and sheds, all these and other aspects of rural poverty were known through internal reporting. Aid to those struck by poverty had been given rather summarily, as emergency funds or loans (which were never returned). Once the household responsibility system had been introduced, poverty began to shift, and by 1983–1985 it was obvious where the real, structural poverty was. Many poor areas turned around between 1978 and 1985, due to the shift in leadership and the individual incentives for production, and such areas made a rapid recovery from the poor situation. Those areas which remained backward did so due to scarcity of resources. Accordingly, the poverty alleviation policy introduced in 1985/1986 avoided cash grants, and required local accumulation and self-reliance as part of the conditions for central aid.

The relative poverty in parts of the Chinese countryside causes further damage to the ecological environment, and also causes agricultural resources to be inappropriately utilized. Environmentally destructive behaviour includes over-grazing, harmful firewood collection and damage to the vegetation cover, and subsequent soil erosion.

Farewell to poverty?

In June 1995 State Councillor Chen Junsheng stated that '10 Million People Have Said Good-Bye to Absolute Poverty' (*Farmers' Daily*, 7 June 1995). This statement reported the results of the poverty alleviation plan, stating that the poverty-stricken population dropped from 80 million to 70 million between the end of 1992 and the end of 1994, so that the poor rural population fell from

8.8 per cent of the rural population to 7.8 per cent. It also stated that the poverty alleviation work in 1994 alone had created 664,000 ha of new farmland and 914,000 ha of new orchards and forests, solved drinking-water problems for 6.8 million pigs and cattle and for 7.2 million people, while 20,000 km of new roads had been constructed and 30,000 km of electric trunk lines had been installed. The plan is to reduce the poor population by 10 million each year until the year 2000.

The methods used to achieve these results, according to the *Farmers' Daily* (24 April 1995), include local mobilization, increased state investment, increased procurement prices of agricultural sideline products, various measures to alleviate the economic and financial burden on peasants, as well as the development of rural industries. All these measures had increased the average per capita income in rural areas to 1,220 yuan per year.

The news that '10 million people have said good-bye to poverty' has a hollow ring. It is not sustained by serious, detailed statistics and there is no indication of the geographical distribution of the success. Neither is there a reference to detailed surveys or any indication of the next stages of development for these 10 million previously poor. One may ask whether it only serves to indicate that China solves the poverty problem 'according to the plan'.

Poverty and the environment

Economic development of poor areas often entails the destruction of fragile ecosystems or further destabilization of areas already severely damaged ecologically. Extraction of water or increasing use of firewood in an attempt to generate local production may deplete local water and forest resources beyond repair, causing soil erosion and economic decline.

The typical problems of poverty include lack of safe drinking-water for people and livestock, absence of basic wherewithals, depleted firewood resources, etc. The problems are vastly different in the arid and semi-arid areas in the north-west, and in the mountainous areas in the south. The Chinese authorities seek to alleviate poverty through a multi-faceted approach which is sensitive to local conditions and based on a high degree of local government participation both in financing and execution.

Infrastructural projects (drinking-water, roads, irrigation systems, bridges, etc.) are mainly carried out as *yi-gong-dai-zhen* projects where the workers are locals paid in kind with grain and clothes. Projects aimed at establishing productive capacity are mainly in the form of credits which have to be returned after a number of years. According to official policy, the authorities must seek to restrict projects which are aimed at shortsighted profits, but may incur environmental damage; they must seek to further projects that use the specific advantages of the locality (medicinal herbs, minerals, local handicraft products, traditional skills, etc.), and they must also encourage labour export, because remittances from kinsfolk working in the richer coastal areas give an important contribution to the local economies. Such policies, of course, are difficult to carry out, and it is not likely that they will become reality.

Depletion of resources coinciding with poverty is often due to predatory exploitation of *common goods*. The legacy of the socialist ownership means that forestland and pastures were, and in many cases still are, owned by the state or the collectives, and people using the commons have no incentive to invest in their maintenance; the collapse of communal work patterns and collective control mechanisms means that the commons are free for everybody to use. Development projects in poor areas, therefore, are often linked with measures to allocate use rights to individuals for long periods, in most cases 50 years, or on unlimited contracts which may be inherited. Such measures are most common in afforestation programmes and pasture maintenance programmes. However, fencing and surveillance is difficult or uneconomical, and the new practices occasionally are in conflict with the traditional grazing patterns.

Special cases of poverty

To help solve the economic problems of disabled people, the Ministry of Civil Affairs gives support to enterprises which employ a certain proportion of disabled people in their workforce.

A final note on poverty must address the problem of reservoir refugees. Since the early 1950s, China has constructed immense reservoirs. Each time, large numbers of people have been removed from the flooded areas and resettled in other parts of the country. Being outsiders, they have been allotted the poorest land and have been given the poorest conditions to live under. Reservoir refugees are often resettled in places which are so poor that it is difficult to eke out an existence, or they are removed from place to place because the areas they occupy are designated for further developments. The Chinese government has done little to alleviate the enormous poverty problems in these fragile communities.

The Three Gorges Dam Project, which is presently being carried out in Sichuan, will flood a huge area along the Yangtze River between Chongqing and the dam. Approximately 1.3 million people are in the process of being removed. They are being relocated partly within the same counties, but to steeply sloping, almost infertile land (as opposed to the rich land along the river bank which they had before), thus depriving the peasants there of the opportunity to expand their arable area. It is widely known that the calculations used to justify this move have been systematically manipulated to hide the fact that there is not sufficient land for them.

The Three Gorges area has been held back in development for about three decades, awaiting decisions on the dam project, and therefore the local population is not in the least equipped to cope with the transfer to other places. While Chinese poverty policy is carried out in one part of the political system, other policies generate additional problems.

However, it is important to consider that the 6–7 per cent of the Chinese population who live in poverty *are* the objects of concerted and partly successful poverty alleviation policies.

CONCLUSIONS

Since the early and mid-1970s development policy has emerged as a field of politics which dynamically integrates poverty alleviation, restructuring of agricultural production, and environmental and family planning in cross-sectoral initiatives.

In spite of a general tendency of political segmentation in different, competing ministries, departments and local governments, the Chinese leadership seems determined to overcome the structural problems by encouraging inter-departmental cooperation and comprehensive approaches. This is not likely to be an out and out success. On the contrary, there are many obstacles to be overcome, and many difficulties in achieving genuine cooperation. However, the integration of development issues, and the fact that the central leadership presses for solutions to the poverty and environmental problems, means that ministries and local governments must follow suit.

Most importantly, China participates effectively and firmly in the inter-national cooperation on these issues, and is less and less likely to view development as an entirely domestic affair. While it is unlikely that China will have abolished poverty by the year 2000, or that it will be able to solve all environmental problems or keep the population growth within a low level, China is making major efforts to address these problems.

FURTHER READING

On China's environment, Edmonds (1994b) and Smil (1993) give the most comprehensive and up-to-date coverage. For a summary of the problems, see Edmonds (1994a). An excellent work which is somewhat out of date is Smil's, *The Bad Earth. Environmental Degradation in China* (1984). Also see Ross (1988), Kane (1987), Banister (1987) and Qu and Li (1994). A historical perspective is found in the excellent *Studies on the Population in China* by Ho (1959, 1967).

12   Women and gender issues in China

This chapter provides an overview of the way in which the People's Republic of China has dealt with the 'woman question'. It is argued that a materialistic analysis of the position of women, combined with an understanding of the social contradictions that gave primacy to the ideology — of nationalism and socialism — and to overarching projects of the Party and the state — revolution, reconstruction and modernization — have meant that, though women's position has improved, issues of gender have not been confronted by the Chinese leadership.

THE 'WOMAN QUESTION' AND MARXISM

The Chinese communists were acutely aware of the oppression of women in their society, and were committed to the cause of women's equality. From the start the communist revolutionaries were insistent that China's modernization could not be complete without the inclusion of women in the public sphere. Like most other socialist state countries, at the time of the setting up of the Chinese state, the 'woman question' was debated within the materialistic framework set out in Engels' book *The Family, Private Property and the State* (1978). The key feature of this position is that the roots of women's oppression lie in the denial to them of property and, through that, access to the public sphere as independent actors. The question of the private/public dichotomy has particular significance in Marxist politics. The division between the two is regarded as signifying the alienation of individuals in society. The obliteration of the private/public dichotomy is one of the goals of communism.

Women, the public and the private in political discourse

In China, while the elimination of the private/public dichotomy was considered as a goal only in very limited radical political phases like during the Great Leap Forward, there was a conscious reinterpretation of these arenas. 'Public' work came to mean work for the state and 'private' work encompassed the rest (Jacka, 1992: 119). This analysis of women's oppression had the great advantage of simplicity, which allowed socialist revolutionaries to have immediate concrete policies that would encourage inclusion of women into the public sphere. The mobilization of women into waged work became the central plank of the Chinese revolutionary state's policies on women.

An equally significant result of the above analysis of women's position in society was the critique that the communists developed concerning existing Chinese social relations. Marxism in this context represented the traditions of modernism which were endorsed by the CCP in opposition to the traditional society in China. Together with the ideological framework of Marxism, the communists were influenced in their formulaton of the position of women by the changes taking place in Chinese society. The young professional classes in treaty ports had lifestyles in marked contrast to the traditional Chinese patterns of family – with polygamy and arranged marriages. The 'modern' and 'progressive' Chinese professionals were celebrated in the popular media in the 1920s and 1930s. Journals like the *Life Weekly* (*Shenghuo Zhoukan*) published by Zou Taofen were influential and promoted the nuclear family, together with ideas of monogamy, and equality between men and women. Women were encouraged to participate in social life and to pursue professional careers. The Chinese communists, who saw themselves breaking with traditional China and creating a new modern society, accepted this new pattern of nuclear families as the basis of future policy (Yeh, 1992).

In a reversal of the traditional liberal understanding of civil society as a site for individual protection, action and struggles, civil society came to be cast as the arena where the oppression of women was perpetrated, tolerated and sanctioned. Civil society was the repository of 'feudal values', of backward social ideas, and was thus inherently oppressive. The revolutionary state, in this context, became the transformative hand changing the balance of power in the old civil society. The attack upon civil society was therefore legitimized as the communists set about creating a new socialist society. This attack, of course, very soon became a generalized attack upon all forms of social relations and organizations unacceptable to the communist regime and led to a virtual freezing of civil society itself. The consequences of this freeze for women were significant and particular.

CHANGING LIVES: WOMEN UNDER THE REVOLUTIONARY STATE

The first initiatives: Rights and education

This materialistic analysis of women's oppression led to a huge mobilization of women in areas of waged work in China after 1949. The other most significant area of reform was the family. The Marriage Law of 1950 prohibited concubinage, introduced monogamous marriage, and gave a woman the right to marry the person of her own choice, and the right to divorce and maintenance (Box 12.1).

Box 12.1 *The Marriage Law of the People's Republic of China: Excerpts*

Chapter I
General Principles

Article 1

The feudal marriage system based on arbitrary and compulsory arrangements and the supremacy of man over woman, and in disregard of the interests of the children, is abolished.

The New Democratic marriage system which is based on the free choice of partners, on monogamy, on equal rights for both sexes, and on the protection of the lawful interests of women and children, is put into effect.

Article 2

Bigamy, concubinage, child betrothal, interference in the re-marriage of widows, and the exaction of money or gifts in connection with marriages, are prohibited.

Chapter II
The Marriage Contract

Article 3

Marriage is based upon the complete willingness of the two parties. Neither party shall use compulsion and no third party is allowed to interfere.

Article 4

A marriage can be contracted only after the man has reached 20 years of age and the woman 18 years of age.

Chapter III
Rights and Duties of Husband and Wife

Article 8

Husband and wife are in duty bound to love, respect, assist and look after each other, to live in harmony, to engage in productive work, to care for their children, and to strive jointly for the welfare of the family and for the building up of the new society.

Article 9

Both husband and wife have equal rights in the possession and management of family property.

Chapter V

Article 17

Divorce is granted when husband and wife both desire it. In the event of either the

Continued over

Box 12.1 *Continued*
husband or the wife alone insisting upon divorce it may be granted only when
mediation by the district people's government and the judicial organ has failed to
bring about a reconciliation.

Article 19
In the case of a member of the revolutionary army on active service who maintains
correspondence with his or her family, that army member's consent must be
obtained before his or her spouse can apply for divorce.

The Land Law, which was passed in 1950, allowed women to hold property
in their own name and a right to a share in the family inheritance. These legal
rights were seen as the foundations upon which to build a better life for women
in the new Chinese society. In 1958 the Great Leap Forward was launched to
speed up China's progress towards communism, and this led to the
communization of agricultural cooperatives and the setting up of communal
eating places, launderettes and crèches. By 1959, an estimated 4,980,000
nurseries and kindergartens and more than 3,600,000 dining halls were set up
in the rural areas (Croll, 1978: 268) Women entered commune production as
individuals in their own right and earned their own 'work points', giving them
economic independence within the male-headed family. The emphasis on the
mobilization of people to serve the cause of state communism allowed women
to participate in public-centred activities, supported by the increased social
provision of services like crèches and launderettes. The Great Leap Forward
failed and was followed by a disastrous famine which claimed millions of lives.
As a result of the failure there was a greater emphasis on social stability and
economic recovery. The Party/state decided to withdraw from the more radical
social measures which could be construed as an attack upon the traditional
family. This led to the closure of public dining halls, launderettes, etc. The
family-based social provision was back on the rails. One can speculate that one
of the reasons for peasant non-cooperation with the communists during this
period was the perceived attack upon the family. The challenge posed to the
patriarchal family by community provision of domestic services and the crossing
of the private/public boundary by the state could not have been palatable to the
male heads of family, a group that also provided the Party/state with most of
its rural cadres. Indeed, the communists had once before experienced peasant
hostility when they had tried to alter the balance of power within the family
during the Jiangxi Soviet period, 1929–1934 (see Johnson, 1983: Chapter 4).

Education was always regarded by Mao and the Communist Party as crucial
to building a new China. The debates concerning education have been intense
and sometimes bitter, as evidenced during the Cultural Revolution. However,
whether seen as a tool of ideological or materialistic transformation of the

Chinese society, education for women was regarded as an important means of granting them access to better jobs and a more independent life. While no special measures were taken to ensure that women were equally represented at all levels of the educational pyramid, the emphasis on flexible patterns of education in the countryside during the Cultural Revolution did allow vast numbers of girls and women to get some formal education. It is no surprise that the expansion of female education in China occurred mainly in two periods: 1950–1958, and 1966–1976, both periods of high mobilization of women into the public sphere (Table 12.1).

Table 12.1   *Number of female students as a percentage of total enrolment*

Year	Higher education	Regular secondary schools	Primary schools	Teacher training
1949	19.8	—	—	—
1951	22.5	25.6	28.0	26.0
1955	25.9	26.9	33.4	27.1
1958	23.3	31.3	38.5	31.5
1973	30.8	33.0	40.7	—
1975	32.6	39.3	45.2	—
1976	33.0	40.4	45.5	—
1978	24.1	41.5	44.9	29.8
1983	26.9	39.5	43.7	37.2
1987	33.0	40.8	45.4	—
1989	33.7	41.4	—	45.9

Sources: State Education Commission (1984: 40); *Chinese Education* (1989: 7); 'Statistical yearbook of China', China Statistical Information Service Centre (1990: 675)

At a more informal level, the chaos of the Cultural Revolution also allowed many women to leave their villages, counties or towns and travel all over China as Red Guards (Box 12.2). For many this was an exciting and liberating experience (Honig and Hershatter, 1988: 4). The campaign against the Chinese philosopher Confucius, launched in 1972, also focused on his derogatory attitude towards women and criticized it (see Johnson, 1983: Chapter 13).

In sketching out the various initiatives that were taken to improve the position of Chinese women by the Party/state we can observe the real difference that was made to the lives of millions of women in China. The critique that follows of the way the 'woman question' was addressed in China cannot in any way take away from the material improvements in women's lives. However, a closer look at the issue shows not only the limitations of the materialistic approach to the question of women's status in society, but also reveals how the nature of the state that developed in China did not allow the autonomous assessment and

---

Box 12.2 *Militia women*
How bright and brave they look, shouldering five-foot rifles
On the parade ground lit up by the first gleams of day.
China's daughters have high-aspiring minds,
They love their battle array, not silks and satins.

[Poem by Mao, February 1961] (Mao, 1976)

---

articulation of women's needs in their own voice. A paternalistic state *gave* women rights it thought appropriate; self-affirmation and an independent setting of agendas was not allowed.

Patriarchy, paternalism, and the Party

One of the reasons why the Chinese Party/state did not allow independent women's organizations and movements political space was their own politics. The class struggle analysis of historical movements meant that Marxists had always been suspicious of separatist organizations. Special interests were considered not only divisive of class solidarity, but also somehow inherently selfish. Lenin, in creating the monolithic party apparatus, further strengthened this opposition to independent organizations. An hierarchical and disciplined organization could not function as a unity if distracted by autonomous interests wanting a separate space within the organization. 'The leadership of the party' was to be the golden rule of communist organization; so much more so, if the transformative role of the Party/state is seen in the light of the above discussion about the state and civil society relations. If the Party was cast as the repository of the 'most advanced ideas' in society, it *knew* what was best for the people. It could, of course, ask for advice and help but could not allow its legitimate position as *the* organization of social transformation to be eroded in any way by competing organizations that could be considered more genuine in their representation of specific interests. While, in China, there was no debate about whether there should be an All-China Women's Federation, as there had been in the Soviet Union in 1917/1918, its constitution makes clear that the federation's role is to help implement the Party/state policies on women, and that it functions under the 'leadership of the Chinese Communist Party' (Croll, 1983: 123) The importance of this lack of autonomy becomes clear when we examine the record of the Chinese Party/state on the 'woman question' in greater depth.

Judith Stacey (1983), Kay Ann Johnson (1983), Margery Wolfe (1985) and many other critics of the Chinese policies on women have contended that the CCP colluded with the patriarchal system in China to get peasant support for the revolution. They argue that as Marxism lacks a conceptual framework within which to analyze the nature of an autonomous 'sex-gender system' (Stacey, 1983: 263), the Chinese leaders of all political convictions labelled discrimination against women in socialist China as a remnant of a 'feudal ideology' (Johnson, 1983: 214). This allowed the use of the 'woman question' to attack what were labelled as 'feudal elements' by the dominant faction within the CCP. It also meant that the debate about women's equality did not leave the confines of communist ideology. It did not become a gender issue challenging the various modes of power within Chinese society. Women were not allowed the public political space they needed to debate and frame their own demands in their own voice.

A final point needs to be made about how the 'woman question' has been considered in China. In August 1937 Mao had written, 'whatever happens, there is no doubt at all that at every stage in the development of a process, there is only one principal contradiction that plays the leading role . . . while the rest occupy a secondary and subordinate position' (Mao, 1977: 332). And it was only the Communist Party which could decide which the principal contradiction was. In grading social contradictions in this way it becomes clear that the issue of gender inequalities could not be given the status of a primary contradiction. Apart from the fact that the leadership of the CCP was predominantly male, they were operating with no clear ideas on patriarchy other than the famous Engels' text (1978). The gender-blindness of the CCP leadership combined with the organizational pre-eminence of the Party itself meant that the marginalization of issues of gender was almost a foregone conclusion. Further, 'universal priorities' – whether the making of the revolution, or the reconstruction of the economic system or its modernization – had to take priority over 'partial interests'. Engendering these 'universal' agendas was never attempted; the specificity of women's needs was not taken on board. An examination of the Chinese policies on women in the context of the above discussion reveals a complex picture of Chinese women's lives under communist rule.

Marriage, monogamy and mortality

Though the Chinese communists presented the introduction of monogamous marriage under the Marriage Law of 1950 as a protection for women against concubinage, such a restricted explanation of the law did not allow for a more general debate about gender relations within marriage.

> The contradictory aspects of monogamous marriage noted by Marx and Engels, were omitted from Chinese discussions about family and marriage reform in this period; its progressive contribution to extending freedom of individual choice to both sexes dominated all other possible representations. (Evans, 1992: 149)

By inference, any form of sexual relations between men and women that did not follow a monogamous pattern were normatively flawed. The Marriage Law of 1950, for example, refers only to 'husbands' and 'wives'. While there is provision to prevent discrimination against 'children out of wedlock' the strong presupposition is that marital boundary frames sexual relations between men and women, and that marital family is the site for construction of social relations. The attack upon the nuclear bourgeois family, institutonalized through marriage, which formed the core of Marx's and Engels' analysis of women's position in capitalist society was completely disregarded.

The only distinction that was made within the framework of monogamy as a social relationship was between the bourgeois and socialist monogamy, the latter being naturally superior to the former because of the more independent economic position of women under socialism (Evans, 1992: 151). As a consequence of this emphasis on monogamy, social stability came to be linked to social morality which in turn was made dependent on the monogamous family. 'The implications for women were striking . . . women's interests were no longer to be served by prioritising their new marital rights, but by making concessions to conservative opinion in order to preserve family and marital stability', writes Evans (1992; also see Box 12.1: Article 19). As the family was not challenged as a site of women's oppression but only modified to embody 'proletarian values', the question of family property also remained unresolved. Exogamous marriages remained the norm, and there was no systematic challenge to the male-headed family and/or gender relations within it. This emphasis on monogamy and sexual morality continues to be emphasized ever more strongly today as a bulwark against social instability that might result from the dramatic changes in the Chinese economy.

CHANGING LIVES: WOMEN UNDER THE MODERNIZING STATE

'Four Modernizations': A new context for women

The continuing withdrawal of the post-Mao state from a controlled economy and a transformative agenda in social relations, and the rise of a civil society, have created a complex set of realities and options for Chinese women. Among the Chinese and foreign observers of the modernization and marketization of the Chinese economy, and its impact on women's lives, there seem to be emerging two different responses. The first is a critical re-evaluation of the past and blames the Maoist/authoritarian regime for the subordinate position of women. The emphasis is on the political oppression and the compromises with patriarchy, and the economic deprivation and cultural starvation that are regarded as the by-products of the Maoist era (Link, 1984; Dai, 1987). The other tendency that is emerging among women writing about Chinese women in the era of reform is one we can call 'revisionist'. There is a growing concern among women about the newly emerging social and economic relations in China and the role of the Party/state in that context. Here, the aim is to go back and re-examine the real gains that Chinese women made during the Maoist period, and also the negative consequences for women living under the emerging social and political relations in the post-Mao era (Zhang, 1992; Evans, 1992; Honig and Hershatter, 1988). The weakening of the economic monopoly of the state and the introduction of the market are the focus of study for analysts representing both these tendencies. The market represents choice, mobility, and a functioning civil society for one group, and insecurity, lack of social support, unfair competition, and a threat to participation of women in the public domain for the other. The picture, of course, is very complex. The impact of the introduction of the market in the Chinese ecconomy has not been the same on all social groups. Even within groups, the reforms have touched the lives of members in different ways. Furthermore, the 'evolving pattern of social interests . . . has an important impact on the course and content of the reforms' themselves (White, 1993: 198).

Modernization, markets and work

The reforms have focused primarily on the 'modernization' of the Chinese economy. Productivity, efficiency, competition and marketization are terms of most use in explaining the thrust of the reforms. This is done without any examination of the many layered meanings that these concepts can have. The gender-blind approach to waged work, and economic and political mobilization, that we saw under the earlier regime continues. Employment is an area that has been fundamentally affected by the new reforms. The division of labour in the public sphere has never been problematized by the Chinese state. Women have generally been concentrated in low-skilled and low-paid jobs. Whenever the question of women's work and women at work has been discussed it has been by taking the man as the reference point: what men can do, women can do too. Here, we examine two different sections of women at work in the public sphere to illustrate the different ways in which the reforms are affecting their lives. The first set is employment for women graduates; the second, women's work in rural areas.

China's graduate women are privileged in many ways. These are women with education, and, increasingly, educated family backgrounds. Until the mid-1980s, graduates were allocated jobs according to a central plan drawn up by the Ministry of Planning with the help of the State Education Commission (see Rai, 1991: 174–8). Under this system women students tended to be allocated schools teaching jobs that were low-status and low-paid. Competition for jobs, introduced slowly and cautiously, was to allow all students to compete in the 'free' market for the jobs that they wanted. Things have not worked out quite as expected.

The paternalistic state in the Maoist period set about liberating Chinese women by mobilizing them into the workforce of the country. The modernizing state in the post-Mao period is giving women a choice – allowing them to go back to being mothers and wives if they wish to do so. While the massive task of Chinese economic reconstruction in the 1950s needed the labour of women, growing urban unemployment in the 1980s means that the state is allowing a huge waste of education and training in order to ensure the status quo in gender relations that is seen as necessary for the country's social stability. *Zhongguo Funübao* reported that in 1986, 'among the unemployed young people in the country, the proportion of women rose to 61.5 percent' (*Chinese Education*, Summer, 1989: 28). On the shop-floor, pressures of profitability and economic efficiency, and a lack of any gendered analysis of the division of labour in the private sphere, is forcing women out of jobs. Crèches have been closed down and managers do not want to give maternity benefits to their women employees. 'The losses *caused by women* bearing children for the regeneration of the human race should not be borne by factories . . .' (ibid.: 86, [italics added]). In many areas women are being 'encouraged' to take retirement at the age of 45. As contractual work begins to replace tenured employment, the managers can refuse to renew their contracts, and are doing so. The ethics of the market are also used by managers to 'prove' the unsuitability of women in the public sphere – they are not competitive, and are plagued by divided loyalties. Women, under these conditions, are finding the market a hostile place. In Henan, of the 66 women surveyed, 90 per cent wanted to work in state-owned enterprises (ibid.: 41).

The response of the state to this attack upon women's right to work has been muted. As a protector of women's social position, the state has exhorted industrial enterprises to recruit women, but without confronting in any way the question of the sexual division of labour. On the contrary it has acceded to the demands of the managers that the state subsidizes maternity benefit. Delivery and Child-Bearing Funds have been set up in many cities, contributed to by both the enterprises and local governments, to support women workers during their maternity leave (*Women of China*, September, 1990: 22–4).

In rural China, the situation is different. The decollectivization of agriculture and the introduction of the 'family contract system' have resulted in a significant expansion of both cash crop production and the non-agricultural sector. Between '1978 and 1984 grain acreage decreased by 8 percent and the acerage sown to economic crops increased by 47 percent. At the same time, the proportion of the total rural labour force used in crop farming declined from 75.2 percent to 62.7 percent' (Jacka, 1992: 124). Further, the new system of production has formalized family-based production. Even under the commune system, while a woman's wages were merged with her husband's or father's at the time of distribution, the accounting of individual wages was generally practised. Now the male-headed family is the only economic unit recognized, other than in exceptional circumstances. Another feature of rural reforms has been the increasing concentration of middle-aged women in the area of food production (see Rai and Zhang, 1994). Food production is a notoriously labour-intensive, low-paid area of work and has traditionally been women's work. As in the case of urban women, the state in the countryside is responding to this shift in women's work by encouraging and 'enabling' them to do better and earn more. For example, in 1989 a campaign called 'Competing and Learning' was launched, under the auspices of the All-China Federation of Women, to improve the productivity of rural women workers engaged in food production. During this campaign there has been no questioning of the gender division of labour and its consequences for women's lives; the emphasis remains on enabling women to produce more in their traditional area of work. However, younger women are not so bound to the land as the middle-aged family women. The informal relaxation of the *hukou* system has allowed young women to travel to the cities in search for better-paid work, or to travel as traders. This migration of rural women to the cities has created other problems for them – sexual and economic exploitation in a largely unregulated market.

In both the above cases of women's employment under the reforms we can see an important shift in the political rhetoric of the post-Mao state. As the state retreats from its transformative role in society and by default lays that responsibility with the operations of the market, the individual is beginning to separate out from the collective; the individual who now carries responsibility for her situation and social status in society. A new liberal rhetoric underlies state initiatives to enable women to do better for themselves. The language of social transformation and responsibility is being replaced by individual initiative and opportunity. As the experience of women in other market societies shows, this new ethos is a mixed blessing.

Modernization and family planning

The state is not continuing to retreat from the public sphere in a uniform manner. Indeed, in one particular area affecting women, the state has been extremely interventionist. The one-child policy of the Deng leadership has become an important issue for Chinese women. The constraints on Chinese development are considerable, and made worse by a huge population. There is, thus, a need to address the issue of population growth. However, as in most other countries, the issue of development and planning have been disassociated from the gender question. The tension between the needs of the economy – a smaller population – and the rights of women to be able to make decisions about their own bodies, has not been addressed. The result is that the imposition of the one-child family policy has been implemented at the cost of further erosion of choices for women. Linked to the issue of the right to choose is also the need for greater information, better medical services and trained personnel to provide the infrastructure that would allow informed choices to be made. In a context where the state is cutting back on such infrastructural services, the implementation of the one-child family policy leads to added pressures on women. While women have limited access to educational and information services, the state continues to wield its political power to implement its policies. While there was no official campaign launched in pursuance of this policy; a campaign style was adopted, and very heavy social and financial pressures were used, together with a complex set of incentives, to ensure its implementation. The policy has been largely successful in the cities, where families are more dependent on state provision of services, but less so in the countryside, where the peasants have subverted the policy quite successfully by using their increased incomes to pay the fines imposed.

Women have suffered in different ways from the one-child family policy. Within the family, they are often blamed, and sometimes ill-treated, for producing unwanted daughters. The main burden of contraception falls on women, as the IUD and the pill are the major contraceptives used. Female sterilizations far out number male sterilizations. Abortions take both a physical and emotional toll on the women. The system of surveillance is extremely intrusive on women's privacy. While practices vary, there are areas where women's menstrual cycles are recorded on wall-charts in their workplaces. Another issue that has arisen as a result of this policy is the status of girl children in the family. Sex ratios favour boys (106.32:100, boy:girl) to a worrying degree (Davin, 1992). While the cases of reported female infanticide are not significant, the neglect of baby girls is more widespread, resulting in higher mortality rates among girl children. There has also been a negative impact on girls' education; 70 per cent of the illiterates in China are female.

THE PUBLIC AND THE POLITICAL SPHERES: NEW AGENDAS FOR WOMEN

The institutionalization of participatory processes, the validation of oppositional organizations, the formalization of procedures by which the state and civil society relate with each other, and, most critically, the opening up of the public space needed for the civil society to flourish, are crucial issues affecting the social and political position of women, among others, as an interest group.

Women organizing women?

The current situation in China is an evolving one, and one full of promise as well as conflict. On the one hand, there is clearly much greater independence given to the already-established mass organizations, like the All-China Women's Federation, to set up their own agenda, which might not always be conducive to the Party/state policies. On the other hand, the Party's continued refusal to consider significant power sharing does not allow the deepening of political reforms. However, in the last decade the resistance to particular features of state policies has been tolerated. Further, the 'opening up' of China to the rest of the world has meant the influx of new ideas and vocabulary. Chinese women, for example, are beginning to examine theories other than the materialist explanations of women's social oppression. In this political context Chinese women have been protesting against the new inequalities and discrimination that they are facing.

Zhongguo Funü and *Zhongguo Funü Bao*, the publications of the All-China Women's Federation, have been inundated with angry letters written by women who feel that they are being forced out of their jobs, or discriminated against at the time of promotions. One contributor asked: 'in today's attempt to build the Chinese economy and implement the Four Moderizations, do we or don't we need knowledge? Do we or don't we need talent? If the answer is yes, then female university graduates should be respected and utilised' (Honig and Hershatter, 1988: 250). Such articles make clear that the Chinese women do not want to leave work, but that it is the values of society that are pushing them in that direction: 'Most women are worried that having no job may jeopardise their position' (see *Chinese Education*, Summer, 1989: 51). A survey of 500 married couples in Shanghai by the Shanghai Academy of Social Sciences found that only '23.7 percent of married women are willing to return home to concentrate on household matters', and most of them saw this as a contingency measure rather than choice (ibid.: 50). Significantly, the language of rights is also emerging in this evolving political context, as is one of equal opportunity.

However, what is more difficult to judge is how much independence the All-China Women's Federation will be allowed in voicing the opposition of its members in the public sphere. As the study of the campaign to 'compete and learn' has shown, the federation is very much part of the Party/state agenda for furthering economic reform, but has not challenged the gendered biases operating in constructing policies on women. The role of mass organizations as transmitters of state policies under the Maoist regime has not fundamentally altered in the post-Mao era. Further, the history of these organizations does not allow their members to trust them. While the greater leeway that the mass organizations are now allowed in dissenting from the Party line is clear to most, the trust and confidence will take a long time to develop. The political waters are even more uncharted and therefore dangerous where autonomous organizations are concerned. These are beginning to form at various levels – from academic women's networks to informal associations protecting the material interests of their members, like the Beijing Association of Domestic Workers.

Women in public life

In the area of public life under the post-Mao leadership, women are not only facing pressure to retreat from the economic sphere, but also from the limited role they played in political life. With disappearing crèches, and women stepping out of the networks of organized employment, avenues for political participation have become far more constrained than they were. Rural women have been particularly hit by the changes in agricultural production. The commune system included women on its various committees to give them a representative character; the same was the case with the various revolutionary committees that managed the factories. With the dissolution of the commune system and the disbanding of the revolutionary committees, women are being slowly pushed out of the public political sphere. Changes in the system of agricultural production have meant family- and house-based work for women – a 'courtyard economy' is now being encouraged. This has taken away the public space in which they encountered each other and exchanged views. In the cities, too, the pressures on women to leave their jobs are forcing them into leading more 'private' lives. The political activism is no longer simply confined to working within the state-endorsed mass organizations. However, because of the very limited political reforms allowed by the Party/state, there has not yet developed a free public space within which women can organize their own interests.

An article in *Zhongguo Funü* on public and private responsibilities of women concluded, 'Men taking part in politics requires opportunity and ability; women taking part in politics requires opportunity, ability and family support. The unfairness of this situation demands our consideration' (*Women of China*, April, 1990: 3). An editorial in *Beijing Review* commented on the declining numbers of women in public life: 'in the 1987 re-election of leading bodies at the county and township levels, the number of women representatives was found to be down in 12 provinces and municipalities. In some areas there was not a single woman in county and township government' (Zhang, 1992: 41). The view that the Women's Federation is taking on this matter is illustrative of the way the question is being approached in China today. As Zhang notes, 'Women's political participation is not regarded as an independent activity; it must be based on economic participation'. An official of the federation made it clear that 'the increase in women's *participatory capability* [in economic production is] central to improving the status and role of women in social production' (Zhang, 1992: 51). The materialist construction of the 'woman question' remains the framework within which the federation continues to consider issues of women's social and political position.

CONCLUSIONS

Gender relations in China have been considered by both the Maoist and the post-Maoist regimes as subsidiary to the more urgent agendas set by a largely gender-blind Party/state. Secondly, neither the Maoist nor the post-Maoist regimes have challenged the patriarchal foundations of gender-based discrimination against women. In our study of monogamy and the politics of women's employment in the urban and the rural areas, it becomes clear that the communists have failed to confront the traditional patriarchal social arrangements, and, indeed, have built upon them for achieving more 'urgent' economic and political goals.

Liberal theorists have insisted on the 'integral relationship between a realm of protected privacy and the quality of political participation' (Bachrach and Botwinick, 1992: 132–6). Feminists have argued to the contrary that the protection provided by the private sphere is a gendered protection. 'Personal is political' is a feminist slogan that challenges a gender-blind approach to the question of the public/private dichotomy. It disputes the assumption that the private sphere provides equal protection to the woman and the man. Feminists have argued that the family, which provides the social foundations of the 'private' sphere, needs to be 'opened up' to critical scrutiny to reveal the silences imposed upon women within the confines of the 'private' sphere. In her critique of patriarchal liberalism, Carole Pateman argues for making family relations a testing ground for the concept of equality. Unless family relations are conceived of and lived equally between genders, whatever the differences that might characterize the sexes, public equality will be gravely undermined (see Pateman, 1989: 118–40). If we were to regard the position of the Chinese women in the context of this debate, their situation is doubly difficult.

The Maoist state did not respect the boundaries between the private and the public spheres and mobilized women into the public sphere through the waged economy, but did not challenge the patriarchal assumptions of a traditional civil society other than within a narrow materialistic framework. Thus, while the private sphere came under attack, it was primarily to bring women into employment and as part of the Party/state attack upon the civil society. Neither the nature of work and the sexual division of labour, nor patriarchal family relations themselves, were challenged other than to support the socio-economic agenda of the state. An emphasis on class politics also refused women the liberty of organizing in the public political sphere in their own interests. In the post-Mao era Chinese women are again caught in a dichotomous position. The emerging civil society is making the private sphere more of an autonomous space, but the protection from the gaze of the omnipresent state is being bought at a significant cost by women. Without contesting patriarchal family relations the 'protection' given by the private sphere to women can only be partial, and conditional upon conformity with the norms set by a largely patriarchal society. While the emerging civil society does potentially allow women the space to contest these patriarchal norms, that potential has yet to be realized in any significant measure. The continued refusal of the Party/state to give up its monopoly of political power, and its insistence upon monitoring the public sphere on its own terms, makes it difficult for women to organize in their own interests' other than at peripheral levels.

FURTHER READING

For an overview of the 'woman question' in China before the impact of the economic reforms see Croll (1978), Johnson (1983), Stacey (1983) and Wolfe (1985).

For post-Mao perspectives see Croll (1983), Davin (1992), Evans (1992), Gilmartin *et al.* (1994), Honig and Hershatter (1988), Jacka (1992), Rai *et al.* (1992) and Rai and Zhang (1994).

13 Ethnicity, the nation and the state

China is the home of many nationalities. How can one talk about *Chinese* nationalism (as opposed to 50-odd different nationalisms)? Is nationalism a threat to Chinese unity? The largest Chinese ethnic group, the dominant Han nationality, speaks many different dialects and is internally divided in sub-groups; how can it be that such a heterogeneous part of the population can be considered as one nationality? Does China hold together as a nation and as a state? How does the political system deal with the underlying, potential ethnic ruptures in Chinese society?

INTRODUCTION

There are two roots of the Chinese nationality issue, one belongs to the Marxist–Leninist heritage, and the other belongs to the origin of China as a modern state in 1911 and the imperial legacy.

THE MARXIST–LENINIST HERITAGE

Marxism is a radically internationalist school of thought, advocating a world revolution, intending to sweep away the artificial differences of class and nation which divide humankind. The internationalism of the *Communist Manifesto* and early Marxism was tempered and eventually lost during the Russian Revolution and eventually Stalin's rise to power. While Stalin never explicitly gave up the ultimate, utopian internationalism inherent in Marxism, he argued for revolution in one country, thereby placing national statehood above the revolution: each nation-state would go through a revolution rather than be engulfed in a world revolution. This idea became prominent in the Chinese version of Marxism–Leninism; consequently the Chinese Communist Party had a positive dogma on which it could base its claim for national sovereignty. Following the logic of the Marxist–Leninist perception, the CCP carried out a revolution in a territorial unit which was perceived as a nation-state, with its own national interests. The distinction is between: (a) fighting a revolution against encroachment by imperialism, using the national bourgeoisie as natural allies and seeing a nationalist discourse as a strategic stepping-stone towards international unity of the proletariat; and (b) fighting a revolution within China's borders to attain national independence and realize socialism and communism within these borders. The former understanding of the revolution was effectively discarded in the 1930s through Stalin's repression of the Trotskyites, both in the Soviet Union and in China. The latter goal was upheld by the Chinese Communist Party throughout, and involved the forced perception of the Han Chinese as one unitary nation.

With regard to other peoples living in the vast Chinese territory (who were distinctly different from the Han in terms of history, culture and language), Stalinist-inspired Marxism–Leninism also offered a set of norms for handling ethnic affairs. The idea was that each ethnic group should be allowed internal self-rule within the community of the Marxist state.

THE IMPERIAL LEGACY

The modern Chinese state was born as a multi-ethnic state. One of the main factors which legitimates the Chinese state is this multi-ethnic heritage.

The Qing empire (1644–1911) was the outcome of the Manchu conquest of China, and the official administration of China in the following 250 years or more was in the hands of officials from this non-Han Chinese tribe, and it was conducted both in Manchu and in Chinese. Administration in different parts of the empire reflected the different statuses of the nationalities. The Manchu 'homelands' in the north-east were out of bounds for Chinese settlers (until the 1870s) and were segregated administratively from the Chinese provinces. The empire also included Tibet and Mongolia. All these regions outside the Great Wall were administrated through separate offices in the imperial administration, and were controlled by military governors.

The 1911 Revolution, which forced the last emperor, the infant Pu Yi, to abdicate in 1911, was inspired by a growing Han-Chinese nationalism, and resentment among Chinese bureaucrats that the imperial government (which had been reformed between 1906 and 1911) was still dominated by Manchu princes. Ironically, it was the 1911 Revolution which established China as a multi-national state. There were two reasons for this:

1. In the negotiations between Yuan Shikai (the Han-Chinese governor who represented the imperial throne) and the revolutionaries, it was agreed that the Manchu court and the Manchu nation should receive the protection of the new government. Also, it was established that the Five Nations should form the basis of the new state: the Han, the Manchu, the Mongolian, the Tibetan and the Moslem. Guarantees for respecting their culture and territories were issued in declarations in 1911.
2. The revolutionaries realized that a nationalist programme based on the Han nation would add to the fermentation along the northern borders and would

jeopardize the territorial integrity. In particular, the Mongolian nobility tended towards independence; they stood to gain due to their great indebtedness, and with the collapse of Qing military presence, they were able to assert their own influence. Manchuria, at the same time, was being infiltrated by Russians, who among other things controlled the railway line through Manchuria. It was essential for the revolutionaries to emphatically include the border nationalities in the nationhood of the new republic.

The Moslems (Hui) as a category included a number of Islamic ethnic groups in China, some more sinicized (assimilated into the Han nationality, especially by adopting Han-Chinese dialects and cultural traditions) than others. Although Moslems were spread all over China, their inclusion among the Five Nations was because of their link to central Asia, which the Russian empire sought to subjugate, and the large number of Moslems living in Xinjiang, Ningxia, Gansu and other Chinese regions in the north-west.

The Mongolians had been subjugated by the Qing and included in the Chinese empire. The Mongolians were heavily indebted to Han-Chinese traders. Their territory was ruled partly by Qing generals and partly by a distant nobility permanently settled in the northern parts of Beijing. They had, with a lethargic attitude, seen their territory taken over little-by-little by Chinese settlers. In spite of the Qing empire's ruthless divide-and-rule policy towards them, they formed an ethnically and linguistically rather homogeneous group.

The Tibetans lived in remote areas in the Himalayas and formed a scattered yet ethnically relatively homogeneous people. Pressure from Great Britain (especially an expedition by Younghusband in 1902/1903 to Lhasa) and the Russian empire caused the early Chinese Republic to regard Tibet as strategically important. However, in spite of the Five Nations' rhetoric and the historical Chinese claims to sovereignty in Tibet, the 1911 Revolution meant that China lost its actual influence over Tibet.

The Manchus formed a dwindling, and highly sinicized group, who claimed their ancestral lands in the north-eastern provinces. The sole fact that the Qing empire had been under the rule of the Manchu dynasty made them important.

The Han were the most important and by far the largest of the Five Nations, constituting between 90 and 95 per cent of the total population. They were a rather heterogeneous ethnic group, which shared a common cultural heritage, a history as a nation, and a common written language, but were very different in terms of spoken language and popular culture. From the latter part of the nineteenth century, a 'modern' nationalism, based on a mixture of racial, cultural, historical and territorial concepts, had started emerging among the Han Chinese, very much inspired by opposition to the Qing, and strongly contributing to the downfall of the dynasty in 1911.

As we shall see later, the reduction of the multi-ethnic basis of the Chinese Republic to the Five Nations did not reflect the real ethnic composition of China. It was a construct of political expediency and of hardly more than cosmetic significance. But it did constitute a fundamental legitimation of the national and territorial unity of the Chinese Republic.

The early republicans, the various warlord regimes, and the Guomindang government, all failed to honour the equal status and rights of the non-Han nations. It can be argued that in long periods between 1911 and 1949, large territories were not actually controlled by any Chinese government. But to the extent, and in the periods, that governments were able to have a military presence and civil administration in the north-east, Mongolia, the north-west and Tibet, the main concerns were directed at supporting Han-Chinese settlements (especially in Mongolia and the north-east) and curbing any trends towards establishing separatist political bodies. In particular, Chiang Kai-shek's nationalists ruthlessly pursued Han-chauvinist policies, and saw the regions of other ethnic groups as potential areas for settlement of Han people.

The republican government divided the Mongolian regions into different 'special zones', and established a separate administration in the eastern part of Tibet, called Xikang Province (literally Western Sichuan), thus dividing Tibetan territory into two parts. In reality, Xikang was the only Tibetan territory where there was actual Chinese government control during most of the period before the Chinese communists regained sovereignty in Tibet in 1950.

THE PEOPLE'S REPUBLIC

The policy of the Chinese Communists towards the question of ethnicity was inspired by many factors:

● The most prominent factor was the legacy of the national and territorial integrity of China which had been claimed during the 1911 Revolution. The five stars of the Chinese flag each represents one of the Five Nations. The most simple explanation of this is that any serious claim to rule China must reflect the Chinese territory as it was established by the early republic. Any claim for less would be considered unacceptable by most Chinese. The full territorial claim must recognize the unity of the Five Nations.
● The liberation of China during the Civil War of 1945–1949 was gradual, based on a series of victories. Inner Mongolia was among the first regions to be liberated; instead of the previous division of Mongolia into small administrative zones, the communists made a point of uniting the Chinese-controlled Mongolian areas (Outer Mongolia had been *de facto* independent since 1911, and had formally formed a separate state in 1923) into a large administrative region called Inner Mongolia. The communist alliance with the Mongolians and Moslems during the Civil War was important.
● The Leninist state, as represented by the only existing role model, the Soviet Union, was multi-national, and Lenin and Stalin had devised organizational structures for dealing with national minorities. The Chinese Communist

Party, therefore, could use this as a point of departure for the way in which China could accommodate its national minorities.

The People's Republic of China, since its founding, has dealt with national minorities by giving substantial minority populations nominal self-rule at a relevant level of authority (see Table 13.1). This means that if a majority of a township's inhabitants belong to one national minority, the township will be given the status of an 'autonomous township', with more internal decision-making power than normal townships. If the majority of the population in a district-level jurisdiction is from one nationality, it is designated as an 'autonomous *zhou*', and a similar provincial-level jurisdiction is called an 'autonomous region'. These jurisdictions do not necessarily follow ethnic and cultural borders, and neither are they comprehensively reviewed to reflect changes in the ethnic composition due to migration and population growth.

Table 13.1   *National minority jurisdictions*

Provincial level	Autonomous region	Ningxia (Hui), Xinjiang (Uygur), Guangxi (Zhuang), Inner Mongolia, Tibet
District/city level	Autonomous *zhou*	31 nationwide
County level	Autonomous county (called banners in Mongolian areas)	96 nationwide
Township/town level	Autonomous township	
Village	Autonomous village	

The terminology of 'autonomy' does not mean that there is real independence in all fields of policy, but it means that there is more scope for local decisions on education, finances, culture, religious affairs, etc.

China has a total of 56 national minorities, which have gained official recognition, and a total of 91 million people or 7.5 per cent of the total population belonged to these at the end of the 1980s, according to the 1990 census. The largest national minorities are: *Zhuangzu* (in Guangxi Zhuang Autonomous Region, 15 million); *Manchu* (Manzu, north-east China, 9.8 million); *Moslems* (Huizu, in all parts of China, 8.6 million); *Uygur* (Weiwuerzu, in Xinjiang Province, 7.2 million); *Tujiazu* (in Hunan, 5.7 million); *Mongolian* (Mengzu, in Inner Mongolia, 4.8 million); *Tibetan* (Zangzu, in Tibet, Qinghai and Sichuan, 4.6 million). The smallest national minorities number a few hundred members.

The problem in China is that there is no such thing as a general Chinese citizenship. It is assumed that a Chinese citizen is also always a member of an ethnic group, be it Han, one of the 56 official national minorities, or a foreign person who has been naturalized; and the ethnic category is always expected to be officially registered and has to be accounted for administratively. Official, administrative procedures discriminate between minorities. For the individual person, it means that the ethnic identity, and its official recognition, are significant personal attributes (Box 13.1).

This may be understood in several ways: (a) there may exist a claim from those belonging to national minorities to be positively recognized in order to be able to practise their own social and cultural life, their traditions and religions, and to use their own language; (b) it may be that the Chinese state wants to classify all nationalities in order to control them, treat them according to their needs, and to be able to favour their official representation within the political system; and (c) it may reflect an attempt by the Han majority to draw a line between them and the national minorities.

The three sets of arguments which can be developed from the above are relevant and plausible explanations, and they are mutually related. According to Dru C. Gladney (1994), many different (more than 350) ethnic groups in China seek official recognition; he mentions that at least 15 groups (other than the already-recognized 56) were being considered officially, and he lists nine of them. To claim positive recognition reflects the wish to gain identity in a context where national identity counts – to be particular in relation to other groups; but it also is a wish to gain from special policies directed towards national minorities (including different family planning policy, different financial

---

Box 13.1 *The Constitution on national minorities*

The People's Republic of China is a unitary multinational state built up jointly by the people of all its nationalities. Socialist relations of equality, unity and mutual assistance have been established among them and will continue to be strengthened. In the struggle to safeguard the unity of the nationalities, it is necessary to combat big-nation chauvinism, mainly Han chauvinism, and also necessary to combat local–national chauvinism. The state does its utmost to promote the common prosperity of all nationalities in the country.

This Constitution affirms the achievements of the struggles of the Chinese people of all nationalities and defines the basic system and basic tasks of the state in legal form; it is the fundamental law of the state and has supreme authority. The people of all nationalities, all state organs, the armed forces, all political parties and public organizations and all enterprises and undertakings in the country must take the Constitution as the basic norm of conduct, and they have the duty to uphold the dignity of the Constitution and ensure its implementation.

(Source: the Preamble of the Constitution of the People's Republic of China, 1982)

arrangements, etc.). The state has set up an apparatus for registering and administrating official ethnic differences – a system which allots different rights to different ethnic groups. This enables selective social control and formal structures for political inclusion or co-optation of groups, some of which might otherwise alienate themselves from the political system. If they were not officially classified, explicit political inclusion and co-optation would be impossible. In a political system where minority peoples are given special treatment, including a licence of moral, cultural, religious and social liberties which the leadership does not wish to extend to the majority of the population, it is essential to demarcate the border between the majority and the recognized minorities. The official, positive recognition of non-Han ethnic groups thus reflects the wish to allow national minorities a family planning policy with no restrictions on the number of children, to allow certain ethnic groups to retain their marriage patterns and traditions of conducting their sexual life, and to allow various forms of religious practices which are otherwise considered 'superstitious' to be realized by national minorities, without extending these freedoms to the Han. To distinguish between Han and non-Han in official structures also makes it easier to claim a unity of the Han nationality despite the fact that the Han internally is a very heterogeneous ethnic group.

POLITICAL CO-OPTATION

How are national minorities included in the political system? To what extent can they participate in politics? In order to assure the representation of minority interest, there is a practice that the government in all minority areas is in the hands of members of the predominant nationality (Box 13.2).

There is a system of double posting, so that the head of a nationality area (autonomous region, autonomous *zhou*, etc.) belongs to the national minority in question, while the secretary of the Party branch at the same level is a Han Chinese. A number of vice-heads of government are likely to be Han, and deputy-secretaries of the Party branch are likely to be from the national minority.

THE HAN – DIVERSITY AND IDEOLOGICAL UNITY

The divisions between different groups of Han Chinese are huge and very manifest. The most conspicuous is the difference in dialects and sub-dialects. There are eight large dialect groups of Han-Chinese language, which are mutually unintelligible.

The largest group is North Chinese, from the stock of which *Modern Standard Chinese* or *Mandarin* (called *Putonghua* or *Guoyu* in Chinese) has been extracted. Approximately 40 per cent of all speakers of Han-Chinese

---

Box 13.2 *The Constitution and nationality self-rule*

Article 95   ...Organs of self-government are established in autonomous regions, autonomous *zhou*, and autonomous counties. The organization and working procedures of organs of self-government are prescribed by law in accordance with the basic principles laid down in ...the Constitution.

Article 99   ...The people's congresses of nationality townships may, within the limits of their authority as prescribed by law, take specific measures suited to the peculiarities of the nationalities concerned.

Article 112   The organs of self-government of national autonomous areas are the people's congresses and people's governments of autonomous regions, autonomous *zhou* and autonomous counties.

Article 113   In the people's congress of an autonomous region, *zhou* or county, in addition to the deputies of the nationality or nationalities exercising regional autonomy in the administrative area, the other nationalities inhabiting the area are also entitled to appropriate representation.

   The chairmanship and vice-chairmanship of the Standing Committee of the People's Congress of an autonomous region, *zhou* or county shall include a citizen or citizens of the nationality or nationalities exercising regional autonomy in the area concerned.

Article 115   The organs of self-government of autonomous regions, *zhou* and counties exercise the functions and powers of local organs of state as specified in ...the Constitution. At the same time, they exercise the power of autonomy within the limits of authority as prescribed by the Constitution, the law of regional autonomy and other laws, and implement the laws and policies of the state in the light of the existing local situation.

(Source: the Constitution of the People's Republic of China, 1982)

---

language speak a North Chinese dialect or Mandarin as their mother tongue. Most North Chinese dialects are mutually intelligible, albeit with some difficulty. Mandarin is mainly based on the Beijing, Shandong and Tianjin sub-dialects, but has received some distinct influences from Shanghainese (the Wu dialect group). Mandarin was formed as a national language from the 1920s. The old guanhua used by bureaucrats in Beijing during the Qing dynasty had been the spoken language of administration at the court, and elements of this language spilled over into Mandarin. The impetus to form a national standard language came from the the New Culture Movement that arose around 1916, and which daringly introduced a new written language (to replace Classical

Chinese). The new written language, *new baihua*, combined the characters in ways which came close to the practice of spoken language in terms of word formation and grammatical structure. The writers of this generation used the existing structures of the spoken language in Northern Chinese to gradually create a written standard language. In the 1920s, the emerging standard was accepted by the Guomindang government in Guangzhou, despite the facts that the new standard language was not spoken in south China, and that the most prominent people in the Guomindang were not primarily Mandarin speakers themselves. The aspirations to rule all China, the perception of Beijing (at that time called Beiping) as the conventional capital of the nation, and the fact that the *new baihua* of the New Culture movement had become the written language of the new educated classes, swayed the Guomindang towards Mandarin rather than Cantonese. Similarly, the communists *de facto* recognized the new standard language and used it in their publications. In the 1950s a Language Reform Commission was set up to simplify the Chinese characters, so, since the end of the 1950s, the written language in the mainland has been different from the written language in other parts of China (Hong Kong, Taiwan, Singapore and Macau), but this has not affected the great similarity, almost identity, between Mandarin as spoken in Taiwan and in the mainland as a national standard. Mandarin is taught in schools all over the country, and is the only language which is allowed in the electronic media (apart from Cantonese and Shanghainese).

The second-most influential dialect group is the *Yue* dialect, which includes *Cantonese* (Guangdonghua). This dialect group covers a number of dialects spoken in Guangdong Province, Hong Kong and Macau. The most important of the sub-dialects is Cantonese, which has an unofficial 'standard' form, spoken in Guangzhou, Macau, Hong Kong, Nanhai, Zhuhai, Foshan, urban Jiangmen and Shenzhen. The other main sub-dialect is *Taishanhua*, a cluster of dialects in Taishan, rural Jiangmen, Xinhui, Taiping (an area of out-migration often referred to as *Wuyi*), and in Heshan and Gaoming, which is mutually almost unintelligible with Cantonese. A number of Cantonese sub-dialects in Zhongshan, Zhaoqing and Luoding can be partly understood by speakers of 'standard' Cantonese. The distribution of so many dialects and sub-dialects in a small area like the Pearl River delta is rather unique. In addition to the complexity of the Yue dialect and its sub-dialects, the use of other dialects like Minnanhua and Hakka in large parts of Guangdong, as well as the recent rise of Mandarin in Shenzhen, and the use of entirely different languages spoken by national minorities like the *Lizu*, makes Guangdong look like a linguistic patchwork. It has, however, given rise to Cantonese as a 'standard' language, used for inter-local communication. This development has been supported by the fact that Cantonese became the *de facto* language of the British colony in Hong Kong, and was used in the official administration dealing with the Chinese population. Although Cantonese is not as well underpinned as Mandarin as a standard language (there is a lack of systematic descriptions of the language, poor dictionaries, lack of officially recognized standards for transcription, etc.), its use in the electronic media in Hong Kong and Guangdong, as well as its wide use among overseas Chinese as the most important lingua franca, mean it is a language which is gaining importance and wider acceptance. Even without formal teaching it is becoming a popular non-Mandarin language skill acquired by Chinese living in other parts of the country. Chinese written in Guangdong and Hong Kong is mainly based on Mandarin, but some informal writings and the odd novel, as well as Hong Kongese popular magazines and advertisements, are written in Cantonese, using a number of characters not found in Mandarin; written Cantonese is almost unintelligible for Mandarin speakers.

The third-most important dialect group is *Wu* (Shanghainese). This dialect is spoken in Shanghai and the southern part of Jiangsu Province, i.e. Wuxi, Suzhou and Changzhou. During the mid-1900s it developed into the cultivated language of the industrial and intellectual upper classes of Shanghai, and has so acquired a certain social status for public communication in Shanghai, while other dialects used among Shanghai's population, especially non-Wu dialects from northern Jiangsu are stigmatized as primitive. Shanghainese is used in local electronic media, and with Shanghai's rise as an affluent commercial centre, the status of Shanghainese is presently on the ascent.

The fourth dialect group is *Hakka (Kejia)*, spoken by groups of people spread over large parts of China, especially in Jiangxi, Hunan, Guangdong and Sichuan. The Hakka people have a history of exclusion and prosecution which in the common lore has caused their migration from the northern parts of China to the South, and from there towards Sichuan. As outcasts they have been pushed into the hills and mountains and the most infertile areas. Their plight has given rise to a huge mythology about their character and history. Many of those who took part in the Long March and in the other communist struggles were Hakka, since the communist base areas were situated in those uninhabitable mountain regions which were predominantly the homes of the Hakka.

The fifth dialect group is Minnanhua, or Southern Min, and covers dialects spoken in southern Fujian and in Taiwan. Although Mandarin has become the official language in Taiwan, the majority of the Han-Chinese population on the island are Minnanhua speakers, and Minnanhua is used in the electronic media alongside Mandarin.

Minbeihua is a dialect group in northern Fujian, covering several dialects. The Xiang (Hunanese) and Gan (Jiangxi dialect) are dialect groups, covering a number of sub-dialects in Hunan and Jiangxi, respectively.

There are other strong lines of division between sub-groups of the Han. One of the main issues is the high degree of local chauvinism, especially the classical triangle of mutual distrust and resentment between: (a) Beijing bureaucrats and intellectuals, (b) Shanghai merchants, industrialists and avant-garde artists, and (c) Guangzhou traders. Northerners tend to regard southerners as treacherous and dangerous, while Cantonese regard northerners as rude and violent.

Beijingers regard Shanghai people as arrogant, while Shanghaiers look at people from Beijing as slow and without style. These and more crude stereotypes are still very much alive and create cleavages of distrust and mutual exclusion down through the Han nationality. As people from Guangzhou say: 'The Sichuanese always praise their province loudly. The funny thing is, they always come to Guangdong to make a buck'.

Similarly, there is a tendency to prefer contacts with, or rely on people of, the same local origin. In Chinese politics, the phenomenon is referred to as 'gangs' – the persons in the top leadership who hail from or represent interests in Shanghai (Jiang Zemin, Zhu Rongji, etc.) are referred to as the Shanghai Gang. The Shanghai Gang's increasing power has been observed with great animosity by the Beijing Gang.

There are many other, mainly cultural divisions among the Han. Different food cultures, which are very distinct and based on different interpretations of traditional concepts of food and health, give each region its own distinct features which accentuate linguistic differences and character stereotypes. Traditions, popular religion and behavioural patterns are also distinctly different from one region to another.

The fact that the Han of the northern and southern parts of China may be as different as any nations in Europe does not mean that they are not, or should not be, considered as one nationality. The differences can be understood as different versions of the same cultural heritage, and this is exactly what happens. The Han nationality is a political and social construct which postulates common historical roots of the Han. The 'modern' type of nationalism promoted by Liang Qichao during the late Qing dynasty and by Sun Yat-sen around the 1911 Revolution was aimed at generating unity among the majority of the Chinese, first against the Qing and then against the foreign forces encroaching on China. Sun Yat-sen's nationalist programme was aimed at creating political unity against all political odds, and so the construction of a common Han root for all Chinese was just as important as awarding equal rights to the Five Nations.

FORGING NATIONAL UNITY

To make all 56 national individual minorities become one Chinese nation, while retaining their own characteristics, has been a difficult task for the Chinese leadership.

As mentioned, co-optation of minority interests is one important factor. The written Constitution insists that each national minority, no matter how small, must be represented by at least one delegate at the National People's Congress (Box 13.3).

Similarly important has been the education of cadres from each national minority. A special university – the Central Institute for Nationalities – was established, which gave training in a wide range of subjects, but whose most

---

Box 13.3 *The Constitution and representation of nationalities*

Article 59   The National People's Congress is composed of deputies elected by the provinces, autonomous regions and municipalities directly under the Central Government, and by the armed forces. *All the minority nationalities are entitled to appropriate representation* ...

Article 70   The National People's Congress establishes a *Nationalities Committee* ...

(Source: the Constitution of the People's Republic of China, 1982)

---

important contributions were: (a) to educate administrators at various levels, and (b) to educate outstanding artists in the traditional arts of the minorities. This arrangement is rather peculiar, since it concentrates people from all nationalities in an artificial course structure, teaching stereotypic ways of dealing with management and ethnic differences. Alumni networks (one of the most important assets of Chinese administrators) were mainly within the field of national minority administration, not within the general ministries. The graduates, therefore, were more limited than if they had received relevant training at the People's University, Beijing University or any of the other central-level universities. However, people from national minorities could also gain access to general universities, and many were educated there.

So why have the Central Institute for Nationalities? Precisely because the Chinese state wanted to create a framework for nationalities affairs, and wanted to generate and refine nationalities' artistic expressions in a comprehensive way.

The best and most pliable elements of nationality culture were presented in terms of Chinese national unity. In the media, national dances, music and songs are woven together in a mixture which implies national unity at the same time as individual characteristics of each nationality are given emphasis. At the same time, administrators educated at the Central Institute for Nationalities were trained in the art of combining a stereotypic understanding of their own culture with the unity of the Chinese nation.

To sum up, the Chinese Communist Party early on adopted a style of political co-optation of the various nationalities by forging a national unity, which prescribed centrally cultivated types of cultural diversity by educating administrators from national minorities in the administration of national minority affairs, and by guaranteeing formal political representation of all recognized nationalities (Box 13.4).

Box 13.4 *Autonomous nationality powers*

Article 116   People's congresses of national autonomous areas have the power to enact autonomy regulations and specific regulations in the light of the political, economic and cultural characteristics of the nationality or nationalities in the areas concerned. The autonomy regulations and specific regulations of autonomous regions shall be submitted to the Standing Committee of the National People's Congress for approval before they go into effect. Those of autonomous *zhou* and counties shall be submitted to the standing committee of the people's congresses of provinces or autonomous regions for approval before they go into effect, and they shall be reported to the Standing Committee of the National People's Congress for the record.

Article 117   The organs of self-government of the national autonomous areas have the power of autonomy in administering the finances of their areas. All revenues accruing to the national autonomous areas under the financial system of the state shall be managed and used by the organs of self-government of those areas on their own.

Article 118   The organs of self-government of the national autonomous areas independently arrange for and administer local economic development under the guidance of state plans.

  In exploiting natural resources and building enterprises in the national autonomous areas, the state shall give due consideration to the interest of those areas.

Article 119   The organs of self-government of the national autonomous areas independently administer education, scientific, cultural, public health and physical culture affairs in their respective areas, protect and cull through the cultural heritage of the nationalities and work for the development and flourishing of their cultures.

Article 120   The organs of self-government of the national autonomous areas may, in accordance with the military system of the state and concrete local needs and with the approval of the State Council, organize local public security forces for the maintenance of public order.

Article 121   In performing their functions, the organs of self-government of the national autonomous areas, in accordance with the autonomy regulations of the respective areas, employ the spoken and written language or languages in common use in the locality.

Article 122   The state gives financial, material and technical assistance to the minority nationalities to accelerate their economic and cultural development.

  The state helps the national autonomous areas train large numbers of cadres at different levels and specialized personnel and skilled workers of different professions and trades from among the nationality or nationalities in the area.

(Source: the Constitution of the People's Republic of China, 1982)

CONFLICTS AND PROBLEMS

The history of Han and minority contacts abound in frictions and problems of racism. Han attitudes in daily contacts often emerge as petty forms of racist abuse, and occasionally officials have aroused protest from minorities by violating the sanctity of places.

Tibet

The greatest conflict is related to Tibet, which poses an intractable problem for the Chinese government. The exiled Dalai Lama, who lives in India, insists on Tibetan independence, a demand also voiced by some groups within Tibet. The religious authorities in Lhasa are normally very close to Beijing's policies, but the successful scrutiny from the outside by the exiled community seeks to widen any discord between Beijing and Lhasa. For fear of the rise of a strong independence movement, the Chinese government holds an iron grip on Tibet, while at the same time trying to modernize the economy and open up natural resources in the region.

The case of Tibet is very complex. Tibet is a sparsely populated area with large uninhabitable areas, difficult communication lines and a poorly developed economy. The area's character means that it cannot easily sustain itself, and that it is likely to fall prey to dominant neighbouring powers. The British in the early part of the twentieth century sought to expand their imperial interests into Tibet, which bordered on British India; and Tsarist Russia also sought to gain influence in Lhasa. The *de facto* collapse of Chinese authority in Tibet between 1911 and 1950 did not give Tibet a status of real independence or sovereignty. Apart from a small number of scientific expeditions, and visits by a few travellers, Tibet remained virtually closed to foreign influence due to its inhospitable terrain and climate. It was with the Chinese resumption of sovereignty in 1950 that the opening up of Tibet began.

The dilemma that faced the Chinese was that the appalling poverty and inhuman conditions in Tibet were directly attributable to serfdom upheld by a theocratic elite. 'Liberating' the Tibetan people therefore involved active encouragement to let the suppressed people 'settle accounts' with their rulers. The Chinese resumption of sovereignty was thus a social revolution to the benefit of the oppressed, and at the same time an attempt at gaining political control.

However, the Chinese and Tibetans in 1950/1951 negotiated an agreement on the 'Peaceful Liberation of Tibet', which involved direct negotiations between the central government in Beijing and the theocratic leaders in Lhasa. The principles were internal self-rule and maintenance of the cultural, religious and economic organization of the region. The Dalai Lama in 1959 instigated an uprising against Chinese rule, which was effectively quelled by Chinese troops. The Dalai Lama fled to India. Helped by the Chinese, the Tibetan serfs started a social revolution which gave them freedom and power. The new political structures established between 1959 and 1961 gave voting rights to all adult Tibetans, including women. In 1965, Tibet's status within China was formalized by the establishment of the Tibetan Autonomous Region.

Tibet, like many other peripheral societies in the world, relies on substantial financial support from the central government and on a large and growing trade. The development of Tibet is based on investment in infrastructure, tourism, industry and the exploitation of natural resources, including improvement of agriculture. The problems of economic development are that, although development is intended to be benign, it bears the stamp of a non-native culture, outside aid and economic dominance. As opposed to fully endogenous development, exogenous development is felt to be intrusive and alien. The threat to the cultural and religious heritage is seen, by a large part of the Tibetan population, to come from the outside, from China. This causes resentment and frictions to emerge, while at the same time increasing the material standards of living.

The problem of Tibet is very much a foreign policy issue. The exiled Tibetans in India have led a vociferous campaign for a separation of Tibet from China, and have been able to exploit China's dependency on foreign powers to promote their own interests. Some conservative powers in the United States, who opposed Nixon's and Kissinger's China policy, and saw the admission of China to the UN Security Council as a 'betrayal of Taiwan', have been very receptive to exiled Tibetans' propaganda, which has been mixed up with a highly loaded human rights crusade against China. These issues have been utilized to argue against China's 'most favoured nation' status in trade with the United States, and to argue against almost any Sino-American official contact. Chinese-led modernization of Tibet is seen as heavy-handed, and as a political measure designed to undermine Tibetan culture. The deployment of Chinese technicians, specialists and scientists in Tibet is construed to be aimed at changing the ethnic composition of Tibet. The opening up of natural resources in Tibet is seen as exploiting the Tibetan people. The exiled Tibetans' propaganda surrounding these issues is successful in inciting unrest in Tibet, which provokes heavy-handed suppression by the Chinese authorities in Tibet, thus escalating the conflict potential.

Moslems

Historically, the most intense conflicts have been between the Han and the Moslems, with serious uprisings and massacres as late as the 1960s and 1970s, and many incidents in the 1980s and 1990s. The Moslem communities are well organized and successful. Most historical incidents have been due to racist behaviour from Han officials.

In China's north-western regions, the Islamic minorities are asserting a greater degree of national independence and a large potential for separatism has emerged, to a great extent fuelled by the independence of ethnically close groups in central Asia after the collapse of the Soviet Union. Border trade has enhanced the cross-border contacts, and have given various Islamic communities more self-confidence in dealing with Beijing.

The central government conducts a very cautious policy towards the various nationalities in Xinjiang, Ningxia and Gansu, extending many economic and political concessions to the region. However, one policy is still pursued, which is damaging and likely to cause long-term problems: the encouragement of Han-Chinese migration to the north-west. This policy has its roots in Sun Yat-sen's ideas for China's development, which were formulated in the 1920s. One of his slogans was 'Open Up the North West' (*Kaifa Xibei*); in spite of contemporary criticism, it gained great weight and was tacitly taken over by the communists. The semi-arid and arid zones in the Chinese north-west are, considering their resource base, overpopulated. However, the Chinese central authorities settled millions of (mainly Han) people in the north-west between 1949 and the present. Resettlement of 'reservoir migrants' from large construction projects like the Three Gorges Dam Project partly takes place in the north-west. This, in spite of the fact that some presently fertile areas in the north-west only have a time horizon of 10–20 years before their water dries out. One aim of pursuing a migration policy may be to dilute the non-Han element of the population, in the pursuit of divide-and-rule tactics.

Environmental constraints

A new and very painful problem has arisen during the late 1980s and early 1990s. Some of the regions which are populated by national minorities are so lacking in natural resources and possibilities for development that the Chinese government has difficulties in helping improve their living standard. In almost inaccessible mountainous areas in Guangxi and Guizhou, and in some very arid areas in Ningxia and Gansu, the situation is critical. The Chinese government has some experience in resettling people from one place in another, but in most cases this has only affected Han people. Solutions will have to be found in this dilemma, for both a responsible attitude to poverty and development (providing clean drinking-water, acceptable living standards and the wherewithals for self-sustenance) and respect for the integrity of an ethnic group.

CONCLUSIONS

The Chinese concepts of ethnicity are based on simple Stalinist principles which were utilized in the early Soviet Union to define the different groups which were made eligible for separate status as nations. They are used to set an official framework of distinction, which is normative and constantly regenerates differences. The policy of segregation is pursued to create an overall unity for all Chinese of all nations; a unity which has the task of keeping together the Chinese territory and maintaining internal peace.

The reforms in 1978 and the fall of the Soviet Union in the early 1990s have created a new situation. One main difference is that all spontaneous popular and economic activities have become easier. Relatively remote border regions with large groups of national minorities in Xinjiang, Inner Mongolia and Heilongjiang, as well as in Yunnan, have been able to profit from direct border trade, and often have an advantage since they cooperate with people of the same cultural and linguistic extraction across the border. Some national minorities have taken advantage of various business opportunities that opened up during the reforms, and in the mid-1980s, for example, a nationwide network of Uygurs were involved in semi-illegal dealings in foreign currency.

It is precisely the lack of reliable market mechanisms, open channels of information and other factors, which increase trust and reduce risk, that has given ethnic and linguistic divisions a new significance. Mutual trust is constructed, based on the myth of common background, and so we see long lines of trade and industrial cooperation which are based on ethnic affinity between the participants. However, the growth of a more anonymous market and more effective structures in the market place are likely to push aside ethnic-based alliances in the longer term.

The cross-border contacts of ethnic minorities have given rise to government fears of segregationist tendencies, e.g. fears that Mongolians and Kazakhs may seek national unity across the border, rather than within China, and fears that Islamic fundamentalism will challenge the unity of China.

Can China exist as a multi-ethnic state in a world where ethnic difference is gradually splintering the large empires? While the Soviet Union with its internal Russian chauvinism had a Russian population of less than 50 per cent, the Han population is more than 90 per cent of the total population in China. The Han population is the dominant demographic element in the population, even in the areas belonging to national minorities. This means that the likelihood of secessionism is very small.

The real question then is whether Han nationhood has a future. Has the myth of a common Han identity gelled together the Chinese from the south and north? Will the inter-regional resentment tear China apart? Will the people from Guangzhou become so angry with the Shanghai Gang in the leadership that they want to seek independence? We believe that the Han identity has been very successful, and that the inter-regional controversies are only to be expected in such a large country: every regional entity wishes to position itself in the best possible bargaining position.

Migration upsets the existing patterns of regionalism, and will continue to create social exclusion. The Sichuanese and people from Guangxi, Hunan and Jiangxi form an important element in the labour market in Guangdong, but they are regarded in negative terms by the local population (like the Gastarbeiter – foreign workers – in Europe). The immigration of northerners to the special economic zone in Shenzhen has turned that city into a predominantly Mandarin-speaking city, and Hong Kong is poised to follow suit after 1997: the Hong Kong Chinese are already eagerly acquiring Mandarin skills. The rise of Shanghai to a regional power centre in finance and commerce may reinforce Shanghainese temporarily, but the broader trend, the greater immigration of blue- and white-collar workers from other parts of China and the international importance of that city, will gradually nudge Shanghai towards adopting Mandarin as a lingua franca.

Increased independence and the assertion of local interest may give a reinforced push towards the use of local dialects in daily life, and Chinese all over China may want to hear their own dialect on the radio and television, and may be in defiance of state policy by adopting dialects in certain official and semi-official contexts. This is only understandable when the use of dialects even for *private* conversations are officially banned at colleges and universities. Against this trend towards local self-assertion, the greater market-based interaction will increase the role of Mandarin, Cantonese and English, and a growing proportion of Chinese will be able to converse fluently in Mandarin, and to use the two other lingua francas.

FURTHER READING

The two best and most recent accounts of national minorities in China are Gladney (1994) and Heberer (1989).

An excellent case study of Han ethnicity in China is Honig (1991).

For a long historical perspective and a comprehensive analysis of Han identity and Han perceptions of race, see Dikötter (1992).

14 Conclusions

At the end of the twentieth century China finds itself in a very different position to that at the start of the century. It is politically stable and powerful, and able to deal with other nations of the world in an independent and self-confident way. This self-confidence is based on the history of the success of the CCP in pursuing, gaining and maintaining its power, and on China's economic success in recent years. Based on a political and economic infrastructure that was put in place during the first 40 years of the People's Republic, China is today able to build on this legacy to further its interests. Here, we discuss the major issues before the Chinese leadership today and speculate on how these issues might affect China in the next decade or so.

ECONOMIC MODERNIZATION

The Chinese economy has grown rapidly, a growth which does not show any signs of subsiding yet. Of course, high growth rates can be sustained if the start level was low and the gap between the Chinese and other major economies is still large. The low age profile of the Chinese population means that the large majority of the population is in the working age groups (this will remain so until well into the twenty-first century) so that the burden of the non-productive population on the economy is relatively light. The political management which has led to this growth has shrewdly used the imbalances and barriers in the economy to promote rapid sectoral growth, which has invigorated other parts of the economy. Reforms of the state-owned enterprises seem to be being carried out, reforms which will probably increase productivity and profitability of the state sector, while at the same time necessitating a degree of urban unemployment. The continued absence of proper social security frameworks may lead to some destitution among urban residents; this will affect the least-productive and most frail elements who had an existence within the *danweis*, but who are likely to form a destitute sub-stratum of urban poor if their relation with the *danwei* system is broken. The more-productive elements will, if they are forced to leave state employment, be able to find other legal sources of income.

In the long term, however, the Chinese state will have to establish a social security, unemployment benefit and health insurance system. The cost of such a system would initially be an insignificant burden on the economy, because the young, predominantly healthy workforce would draw very little upon such a system, and even the inclusion of the existing generations of pensioners in a new system would not be problematic. However, it will be interesting to see how large public funds, amassed as premiums for social insurance schemes, will be controlled. Will they be used to bolster the state's finances by investment in state bonds, or will they be invested in productive assets through the financial markets? New dominant, corporate investors in the Chinese stockmarkets may give the state interesting new control over the private and semi-private enterprises.

The Chinese economy in the 1980s went through a period of inflation which had both a destabilizing effect and a sobering effect on the economy: destabilizing, in the sense that it caused people to lose faith in the Chinese economy, and sobering in the sense that it cleaned out unproductive savings and gravely devalued the fixed wages in state-owned enterprises. The result was that real income increments had to be earned by increased productivity. In the 1990s inflation has been reduced to more moderate levels than in the 1980s. The state has, in 1993–1995, gained such control with the banking system that it can in theory reduce the risk of inflation. However, the removal of some major consumer subsidies and the increasing autonomy of state-owned enterprises (especially with regard to the wage bills) in the early 1990s have increased the intrinsic pressures for consumer price inflation. It is likely that China will continue to experience moderate consumer price inflation for a long time.

The dual-track price system and the foreign currency exchange system which were in use in the 1980s have been abolished in the 1990s. This means that two major sources of petty corruption have disappeared. A third source of daily corruption was related to low prices for public services which were in short supply; with official price levels now more or less reflecting the demand, petty corruption has been reduced in many parts of daily life, and has been replaced by higher prices. However, corruption continues to be an issue for the Chinese economy; it is difficult to eradicate, and is impossible to distinguish clearly from legal and socially accepted practice. Anti-corruption campaigns by the Chinese leadership have been used for political reasons to attack political enemies. It is impossible to expect corruption to disappear easily: the campaigns are not broad enough nor sufficiently neutral in a political sense to gain general public acclamation. In the immediate future there is no prospect for doing away with large-scale corruption, but a gradual development of a non-corrupt business culture, supported by the need for efficient administration and for fair and open competition; the institution of a professional, better-salaried civil service (as opposed to the political control with appointments in the present cadre system); and increasing professionalization and independence of the judicial system, are all likely to gradually reduce corruption. However, as long as certain rights, services and commodities are either subsidized or allocated politically, the root cause of corruption will continue to exist.

Economic development in China has been harmful to the ecological environment. The expansion of industry and the increased demand for transport have increased pollution levels drastically. Non-renewable resources are being depleted, and land is turned from rice fields into concrete jungles. This process is likely to continue. However, it is important to note that the inland provinces which produce the major part of China's fossil energy supplies are likely to increase the price for energy consumption in all of China. The low prices presently paid for coal and oil are not sustainable in the long term, and will have to be compensated for by financial transfers or price increases. Higher energy prices are likely to increase the efficiency of energy consumption and to reduce pollution. The 1982 boiler regulation and the ban on small coal stoves in many large cities have already had remarkable results, while pollution from vehicle emissions has increased. There is no likelihood of sudden changes in China's air pollution problems. In the long term, low-pollution urban mass-transport systems and better combustion technology may alleviate the problems. The worst-case scenario is urban degradation due to overpopulation, collapse of public infrastructure, and depletion of urban regulation due to lack of finances; in such a scenario pollution will almost certainly be unstoppable.

China has a high level of technology, and is able to mobilize enormous expertise among Chinese scientists abroad. Recent changes in the domestic management of scientific research and the highly competitive higher education system ensure China has access to the most advanced technology in the world. The ability of the state to control large scale investment and policy coordination have been utilized to ensure rapid introduction of advanced communication technology, computer networks in higher education, etc. The rate of technology introduction has been too rapid in some areas. The main problem is that large parts of the country do not have skilled personnel and technological infrastructures to deal with high-level technology. The top-level structures are well equipped and well staffed, but intermediate levels still face serious problems due to lack of funding and skilled staff. The Chinese state is likely to develop high-level technology through joint central–local investment projects and large-scale training programmes, which will enable the major parts of China to make a 30–50 year technological leap in about one decade. Market competition and increasing raw material prices, combined with greater consumer selectivity, will force the early rural enterprises to adopt more capital-intensive equipment during the two first decades of the twenty-first century; their demands for labour will change, and better skills will be needed. The rural enterprise sector, therefore, is likely to divide into a highly sophisticated, modern structure, and a dynamic undergrowth of low-skill, low-investment enterprises which will cater for the rural poor in terms of employment and consumption.

General levels of education in China are of a good standard if compared with other Third World countries. However, for a rapidly modernizing country like

China, a semi-educated workforce will become a liability after the smaller cohorts (resulting from the one-child policy) start entering the labour market in the last years of the 1990s. In the 2020s and 2030s China's economy will have to rely on even higher technical sophistication and increased productivity per labourer to meet the needs of large cohorts of pensioners. The modernization and further improvement of the educational system and supplementing it with life-long training seem essential for successful economic development. In spite of China's laws on universal compulsory education, many rural children (especially girls) do not attend school due to high school fees and the loss of the child's labour. The Hope Programme, helping poor children to an education may have some limited effect, but the real issue of education as a motor for future economic development has not yet been coined as a policy.

Economic development has in, the 1980s and 1990s, created an enormous social mobility. Social strata have been turned upside down, and a large portion of the population is on the move, or rather lives and works in a place different from the place of permanent residence. The social mobility has been essential for economic development. At a very practical level, the new economic elites have replaced the old economic elites without any battle: they became rich without ostensibly challenging on the powers of the old elites and gradually gained influence; they represented a new, dynamic stratum in the population. Although there is room for further growth in the new entrepreneurial class, the social turnover of the early 1980s is now history, and the new rural class divisions are likely to remain basically as they are now for a long time to come.

Migration, conversely, is likely to increase during the next few decades. The differences in economic development in different parts of China will continue to lure people away from poor areas with the prospects of better earning in richer areas. Migration will, for example, continue to contribute cheap labour to the urban construction and to major infrastructural projects. It will continue to supply cheap labour to factories and agriculture in coastal areas, and it is likely to contribute a not-insignificant part of the population in all major cities. Although this mobility creates tensions (and allegedly more criminality), it is fundamentally sound. The Chinese state will need to find a structure which can deal with the new social realities, and will need to provide adequate social, educational and medical services to these new groups; they will also need to find ways of policing their activities more effectively. Migration creates many new opportunities for economic development due to the inter-regional trade links and market information structure they entail. Highly educated migrants in Shenzhen have already changed the status of that city, and they will do the same to Shanghai and Hong Kong very soon. But one should not forget the other end of the scale: the workers from Jiangxi, Anhui and Henan who built the Kowloon–Beijing Railway which is due to open in 1997, or the workers from poor areas in Guangxi, Sichuan, etc., who have built high-rise buildings in Guangzhou and Shenzhen. Further urban and infrastructural development in China can only take place with the advantage of cheap supplies of labour.

There is some urgency about this: China needs to have a fully developed modern infrastructure by 2030 and will need to have completed the structures of the urban areas by the same time, making them suitable for housing the rural–urban migrants permanently, and being able to cater for them when they go on pension. By that time, the supply of cheap labour will have dried up, and large infrastructural projects will become prohibitively expensive.

Poverty in China is a field that economic policy has not been able to cope with. The state seeks to eradicate poverty by the year 2000, but is likely to fail in its general (much too ambitious) aim. The relative deprivation is likely to increase, so the poorer will become poorer in relation to the other parts of the population, but, following the overall increase in living standards, their life quality will gradually improve. The poorest and most fragile parts of the population face resettlement in other parts of the country, due to depletion of resources. The state will have success in beating poverty in many parts of the country, but in the short and medium term, the widespread existence of poverty will remain a distressing, sore point for the Chinese leadership.

NATIONAL SECURITY

Over the last 40 years China has been more or less able to secure its international borders and resolve most disputes with its neighbours. However, with the collapse of the Soviet Union, the post-Cold War period poses important and difficult questions to the Chinese leadership. A new balance of power, unmediated by the superpower rivalry, has to emerge in the immediate vicinity of China and this will have important consequences for China's future direction. There are two views as to what might happen in the future as far as China's regional security is concerned. One view, based on the realist theory, suggests a 'back to the future' scenario with instability in the region and a classical balance of power with China isolated because of the suspicions of the smaller nations. The realists point to the unresolved rivalries between Taiwan and China, and India and China, and to the almost complete absence of effective multi-lateral political organizations or a military bloc, to suggest that a period of instability lies ahead. The other view, based on liberal theory, points to the new realities and discourses and suggests that going back is not an option for China and the region as a whole The liberals argue that the logic of the economic success of the East Asian nations, which is based on interdependence in trade and technology, and finance, works against any escalation of tensions in the region (see Buzan and Segal, 1994).

Will China see instability and chaos in the years to come? Or will its growing economic position be a bulwark against political unravelling? The signals are mixed. On the positive side, China is becoming increasingly tied to the international economy and becoming a member of international organizations which underpin the global economic system. As such, it would benefit from the stabilizing impact of these organizations. The internal political dynamics is also not entirely adverse to stability – China continues to have a strong central authority and a highly structured organizational framework. Its leadership, despite some divisions, is largely committed to economic reform of the country. The economic direction for China does not seem undecided, which has encouraged continuing foreign investment in the country, enhancing its economic standing and further improving its chances to build upon its economic success. In terms of China's relations with its neighbours, there have been some positive developments too. The Soviet Union has disintegrated and the direct threat it posed to China has gone with it. Even before the dissolution of the Soviet Union, the two countries had agreed to scale down the military build up on their borders. While the Sino-Indian border dispute has not been resolved, the two countries have decided to continue developing trade and cultural relations in the period since the re-establishment of diplomatic relations in 1976. The strains between Pakistan and India have not affected this new low-key but stable building of relations between India and China. Hong Kong is another issue that has been resolved to the Chinese satisfaction in the last 10 years, despite constant irritants on both the British and the Chinese sides. China has also been building relations with Japan, who is a major investor in China. If the international economic system is important to stability in China, it is also dependent on China's growth for its own stability. It is this mutual interdependence that the liberal theorists point to as a positive indication of things to come as far as China is concerned.

There are some severe strains within the Chinese system, however, that might belie this sanguine interpretation of future developments in China. There are several flashpoints that might spark conflagration in the region of East Asia, and have an impact on Chinese politics. For China the most important potential conflict lies in Taiwan. Both the government in Beijing and the government in Taibei have always claimed the undivided sovereignty over the whole of the Chinese territory, maintaining the status of Taiwan as a part of China. However, increasingly, local Taiwanese population and leaders are seeking independence from China. A declaration of independence by Taiwan will pose serious political questions for China. On the one hand, there is the massive Taiwanese economic investment in China, but, on the other, there is the question of Chinese sovereignty. If China intervenes militarily to resolve the Taiwanese issue, it will meet with opposition, not only from regional states but also from the USA and other Western powers. Another issue for China's security is internal – there is already considerable concern about the weakening power of the central government in China, and the growing influence of regional governments of the successful southern provinces. Conflicts about resource allocation, central taxation, and autonomy in decision-making processes lie ahead. The question to answer here is: how flexible is the Chinese political system in making new arrangements within the old political framework? The breakup of China in the face of new 'warlords' is unduly pessimistic; the tensions arising from uneven development and unequal benefit from the marketization of the Chinese economy are, however, significant.

The scenario that we witness, however, may not be that of a breaking up of China, but that of the economic pressures gradually forcing about new political structures and regional power relations within China. The present political structures of central–local relations may be inadequate in a situation where the inland provinces in China become increasingly dependent upon the coastal provinces for their subsistence, and where coastal provinces more than ever need the raw materials, fossil fuels and unskilled labourers which the inland provinces can provide. What appear to be secessionist or centrifugal forces, may in reality be realignment of economic interests in the political sphere within the unitary state. The Taiwan issue can also be understood in this context. Taiwanese investment and manufacturing and trading interests in the Chinese mainland are huge. The mainland needs Taiwanese capital investment, and Taiwan needs cheap labour and large markets. Taiwan, therefore, is already so closely knit into the economy of the Chinese mainland that approachability in the political sphere is likely. The Taiwan independence movement, oddly enough, gives credibility to this observation: political approachability has become so potentially real that elements of the Taiwanese society have begun to express opposition.

POLITICAL CHANGE

Crucial to China's future development is the viability of its political system. The major question here is of course whether the Chinese political system will in the long run be able to absorb the pressures generated by the marketization of the Chinese economy? While there is an assumption in liberal political theory that economic and political markets go together, the evidence from many East Asian countries is contrary to this assumption. Very often we find that a strong, corporatist state is a precondition for the success of economic reform, and for the rapid growth of an economic system. The examples of Japan, South Korea, Singapore and Taiwan are clear in this regard. In the long run, however, we see that there is a propensity for economic and political systems to come closer together, as we are witnessing in South Korea and Taiwan. However, there seems no simple correlation between marketization and democratization.

In China the CCP, while promoting marketization, has continued to refuse to share political power. The legacy of the warlord period, and a general acknowledgement that a weak state might lead to political instability, has meant that internal opposition to this monopoly of power has been rather weak. Unlike other Third World states, China has benefited from external investment, but has rebuffed any pressures to give ground on political reform. The size of the country, its economic strength and the political control exercised by the CCP has allowed it to do so even after periods of crisis, such as the June Fourth

Incident. The pressures that challenge the political system are therefore not predictable. It is in this unpredictability that lies a serious challenge to China's future stability.

The marketization of the economy has had significant unintended results – the rise of new social groups; the weakening of important control mechanisms like the *hukou* system; the movement of populations resulting in unforeseen pressures on resources and the consequent breakdown of the welfare system for many; the rise of internal and international crime; and corruption within society and also the CCP. All these pressures create a problem of management for the CCP; they are also potentially explosive political issues. An authoritarian state system can legitimize itself through its efficiency in delivering the social and economic goods that it has promised. If there is a sense that the state is unable to deliver these goods, in particular unable to use its political authority to redistribute the newly generated wealth without prejudicing incentives to further growth, the breakdown in legitimacy can become severe. There are several options that the political leadership has in such a situation. The first is suppression, which in a country as big as China, and as visible as it is now, can be of only limited value. There is also a second option, which would be to open up the political system to a multi-party system. Neither of the above options suit the Chinese leadership. This is not to say that the Chinese state does not use violence against its citizens, or that it does not restrict their right to freedom of speech and expression; it does. It suggests that suppression by itself is not the most viable option for the Chinese leadership. Reaction to the Tiananmen Incident gave a clear signal to the Chinese leaders that the economic consequences of political suppression can be severe. However, it was also an important lesson to the international community that the Chinese leadership will not be pushed into making concessions in a way that weaker states might. Another option before the Chinese leadership is that of manoeuvring between conciliation of peak interest groups and suppression of other oppositional groups. The peak interest groups in any society are the most articulate and influential; these also change over a period of time, and they are both economic and cultural elites. We have some evidence of this strategy already being used – the attempted co-optation of the intellectuals into providing input into state policy through think-tanks and other inducements. However, the problem here is the unwieldy nature of the CCP. No longer the disciplined cadre party of the early years, the CCP is deeply implicated in corruption in China, and has lost its lustre ideologically. The disciplining of the Party and its cadres is therefore an urgent task if China's authoritarian model is to survive.

In the last decade, political power has been dispersed downwards in the political system. In spite of the political power monopoly of the CCP, it is evident that increasing numbers of people are included in policy making, and are able to express their views and preferences within certain limits. The emergence of non-governmental organizations and the popularity of critical consumer institutions indicate that the public is approaching political participation in a gradual, circumspect process. While independent political opposition is not likely to appear, a slow process of empowerment has already begun, from below, which may result in a gradual reform of the political system. Rural political power is very problematic; the disenfranchised peasants are still given no opportunity to organize themselves, and they are poorly represented in the political system of the state; the result has been eruptions of spontaneous local violence in the countryside. Strata of newly rich peasant entrepreneurs have already emerged, who are instinctively anti-statist and intent on broadening local patronage links and gaining indirect political influence; there do not exist any structures which may disband repressive local power centres that are made up of rich entrepreneurs and local Party cadres. However, the CCP is at the moment changing basic-level structures in rural areas, including elections for villagers' committees and the expansion of the CCP presence at the village level. One can only hope that Chinese peasants will in the future be able to participate more actively and productively in political life.

One of the features of Chinese politics in the last 45 years has been the problems associated with the succession of leadership. The succession to Mao was both unseemly and unpredictable and led to great blood-letting within the Party. China took an entirely new direction after the death of Mao. Therefore, the question that teases China-watchers constantly is whether the post-Deng leadership will change direction once again. China-watchers look for indications that aspirants are manoeuvring for position, and that alliances and counter-alliances are being made for a succession battle. It is important to note that in 1994/1995, Deng Xiaoping's role as supreme arbiter has declined drastically. While he is still officially revered, there is no indication that he actually performs a function in political life any more. A succession struggle, therefore, is no longer a question of Deng Xiaoping's health or death. A new, administratively professional structure of the leadership is likely to assert itself in the coming years, a leadership which does not derive its legitimacy from the Long March, but from the ethos of political management in the post-Liberation state and Party organs. The succession, thus, may be difficult: the political system will have to cope with structures for policy making and conflict resolution which hitherto depended on a supreme arbiter and a dominant figurehead. The ability of the present Chinese leadership to reform the political system so that it becomes adequate for a more open, more collective governance, and more perceptive of popular demands, is the main concern relating to the political stability of the future. In spite of media hyperbole, succession struggles are an issue of the past.

Political stability is the major issue before China today. Its programme of modernization depends on how successfully it resolves this issue.

Bibliography

Adelman, J. R. (1980) *The Revolutionary Armies: The Historical Development of the Soviet and the Chinese People's Liberation Armies*, Westport, CT: Greenwood Press.

Almond, G. and Verba, S. (1963) *The Civic Culture: Political Attitudes and Democracy in Five Nations*, Princeton, NJ: Princeton University Press.

Anon. (1957) *Socialist Upsurge in the Chinese Countryside*, Peking: Foreign Languages Press.

Anon. (1966) *Carry the Great Proleterian Cultural Revolution Through to the End*, Peking: Foreign Languages Press.

Bachman, David and Yang, Dali L. (eds) (1991) *Yan Jiaqi and China's Struggle for Democracy*, Armonk, New York: M. E. Sharpe.

Bachrach, Peter and Botwinick, Aryeh (1992) *Power and Empowerment: A Radical Theory of Participatory Democracy*, Philadelphia, PA: Temple University Press.

Banister, Judith (1987) *China's Changing Population*, Stanford, CA: Stanford University Press.

Barnett, Doak A. (1964) *Communist China: The Early Years 1949–55*, London: Pall Mall Press.

Baum, Richard (1994) *Burying Mao: Chinese Politics in the Age of Deng Xiaoping*, Princeton, NJ: Princeton University Press.

Benewick, Robert (1995) 'Tiananmen Crackdown and its Legacy' in *China in the 1990s* R. Benewick and P. Wingrove (eds), Basingstoke: Macmillan.

Bergere, M. C. and Chesneaux, J. (eds) (1977) *China from the Opium Wars to the 1911 Revolution*, Hassocks: Harvester Press.

Bettelheim, Charles (1974) *Cultural Revolution and Industrial Organization in China*, New York: Monthly Review Press.

Bianco, Lucien (1971) *The Origins of the Chinese Revolution 1915–1949*, Stanford, CA: Stanford University Press.

Bickford, T. J. (1994) 'The Chinese Military and its Business Operations: The PLA as Entrepreneur' *Asian Survey* XXXIV (5), pp. 460–74.

Burns, John P. (ed.) (1989) *The Chinese Communist Party's Nomenclatura System. A Documentary Study of Party Control of Leadership Selection 1979–1984*, Armonk, New York: M. E. Sharpe.

Buzan, B. and Segal, G. (1994) 'Rethinking East Asian Security' *Survival* (Summer) 36(2), pp. 3–21.

Chatterjee, P. (1986) *Nationalist Thought and the Colonial World: A Derivative Discourse?*, London: Zed Books.

Chen Erjin (1984) *Crossroads Socialism. An Unofficial Manifesto for Proletarian Democracy*, London: Verso Editions.

Chen Nai-Ruenn and Galenson, Walter (1969) *The Chinese Economy under Communism*, Edinburgh: Edinburgh University Press.

Chesneaux, J. (1968) *The Chinese Labor Movement, 1919–1927*, Stanford, CA: Stanford University Press.

Chesneaux, J. (1973) *Peasant Revolts in China 1840–1949*, London: Thames & Hudson.

Chesneaux, J. (1978) *China from the 1911 Revolution to Liberation*, Hassocks: Harvester Press.

Chow Tse-tung (1960) *The May Fourth Movement*, Cambridge, MA: Harvard University Press.

Christiansen, Flemming (1990) 'Social Division and Peasant Mobility in Mainland China: The Implications of the Hu-k'ou System' *Issues and Studies* 26 (4), pp. 23–42.

Christiansen, F. (1994) 'Democratization in China: Structural Constraints' in *Democracy and Democratization* G. Parry and M. Moran (eds), London: Routledge.

Croll, Elizabeth (1978) *Feminism and Socialism*, London: Routledge & Kegan Paul.

Croll, Elizabeth (1983) *Chinese Women Since Mao*, London: Zed Books.

Crook, Isabel and Crook, David (1979) *Revolution in a Chinese Village: Ten Mile Inn*, London: Routledge & Kegan Paul.

Dahl, R. A. (1961) *Who Governs? Democracy and Power in America*, New Haven: Yale University Press.

Dai Youqing (1987) *Stones of the Wall*, London: Sceptre.

Davin, Delia (1992) 'Population Policy and Reform: The Soviet Union, Eastern Europe and China' in *Women in the Face of Change: The Soviet Union, Eastern Europe and China* Shirin Rai, Hilary Pilkington and Annie Phizacklea (eds), London: Routledge.

Deng Xiaoping (1984a) 'A New Approach Towards Stabilizing the World Situation' and 'Safeguard World Peace and Ensure Domestic Development' in *Build Socialism with Chinese Characteristics*, Beijing: Foreign Languages Press.

Deng Xiaoping (1984b) *Selected Works of Deng Xiaoping (1975–1982)*, Beijing: Foreign Languages Press.

Deng Xiaoping (1984c) 'Uphold the Four Cardinal Principles' in *Selected Works of Deng Xiaoping (1975–1982)*, Beijing: Foreign Languages Press.

Dikötter, Frank (1992) *The Discourse of Race in Modern China*, London: Hurst.

Donnithorne, Audrey (1969) *China's Economic System*, London: Allen & Unwin.

Dreyer, J. T. (1993) *China's Political System: Modernisation and Tradition*, Basingstoke: Macmillan.

Eckstein, Alexander, Galenson, Walter and Liu, Ta-chung (1968) *Economic Trends in Communist China*, Edinburgh: Edinburgh University Press.

Editorial Departments of Hongqi and Renmin Ribao (1963) *The Origin and Diffences of the CSPU and Ourselves: Comment on the Open Letter of the Central Committee of the CPSU*, Peking: Foreign Languages Press.

Editorial Departments of Hongqi and Renmin Ribao (1967) *Circular of the Central Committee of the Chinese Communist Party (May 16 1966)*, Peking: Foreign Languages Press.

Edmonds, Richard Louis (1994a) 'China's Environment' in *China Briefing 1994* William A. Joseph (ed.), Boulder, CO: Westview Press, 143–70.

Edmonds, Richard Louis (1994b) *Patterns of China's Lost Harmony. A Survey of the Country's Environmental Degradation and Protection*, London: Routledge.

Engels, Fredrick (1978) *The Family, Private Property and the State*, Beijing: Foreign Languages Press.

Evans, Harriet (1992) 'Monogamy and Female Sexuality in the People's Republic of China' in *Women in the Face of Change: The Soviet Union, Eastern Europe and China* Shirin Rai, Hilary Pilkington and Annie Phizacklea (eds), London: Routledge.

Fairbank, J. K. (ed.) (1968) *The Chinese World Order: Traditional China's Foreign Relations*, Cambridge, MA: Harvard University Press.

Fairbank, J. K. (1987) *The Great Chinese Revolution 1800–1985*, London: Picador.

Fitzgerald, Charles Patrick (1952) *Revolution in China*, London: Cresset Press.

Fitzgerald, Charles Patrick (1964) *The Chinese View of Their Place in the World*, London: Oxford University Press.

Friedrich, Carl J. and Brzezinski, Zbigniewk (1956) *Totalitarian Dictatorship and Autocracy*, Cambridge, MA: Harvard University Press.

Gilmartin, Christina K. *et al.* (eds) (1994) *Engendering China: Women, Culture and the State*, Cambridge, MA: Harvard University Press.

Gittings, J. (1967) *Role of the Chinese Army*, London: Oxford University Press.

Gladney, Dru C. (1994) 'Ethnic Identity in China: The New Politics of Difference' in *China Briefing 1994* William A. Joseph (ed.), Boulder, CO: Westview Press, pp. 171–92.

Goodman, David S. G. (ed.) (1984) *Groups and Politics in the People's Republic of China*, Armonk, New York: M. E. Sharpe.

Goodman, D. (1994) *Corruption in the People's Liberation Army*, Working Paper no. 40, Australia: Asia Research Centre, Murdoch University.

Gray, Jack (1990) *Rebellions and Revolutions*, Oxford: Oxford University Press.

Guillermaz, J. (1972) *A History of the Chinese Communist Party, 1921–1949*, London: Methuen.

Harding, Harry (1981) *Organizing China. The Problem of Bureaucracy 1949–1976*, Stanford, CA: Stanford University Press.

Harding, H. (ed.) (1984) *China's Foreign Relations in the 1980s*, New Haven, CT: Yale University Press.

Harding, Harry (1987) *China's Second Revolution. Reform after Mao*, Washington, DC: Brookings Institution.

Hartford, Kathleen and Goldstein, Steven M. (eds) (1989) *Single Sparks: China's Rural Revolutions*, Armonk, New York: M. E. Sharpe.

Heberer, Thomas (1989) *China and its National Minorities: Autonomy or Assimilation*, Armonk, New York: M. E. Sharpe.

Hinton, William (1972a) *Fanshen. A Documentary of Revolution in a Chinese Village*, Harmondsworth: Penguin.

Hinton, William (1972b) *Hundred Days War: The Cultural Revolution at Tsinghua University*, New York: Monthly Review Press.

Hinton, Harold C. (ed.) (1980) *The People's Republic of China 1947–1979. A Documentary Survey*, Wilmington, DE: Scholarly Resources.

Ho Ping-ti (1959) *Studies on the Population in China*, Cambridge, MA: Harvard University Press.

Honig, Emily (1991) *Creating Chinese Ethnicity: Subei People in Shanghai, 1850–1980*, New Haven, CT: Yale University Press.

Honig, Emily and Hershatter, Gail (1988) *Personal Voices: Chinese Women in the 1980s*, Stanford, CA: Stanford University Press.

Howe, Christopher (1971) *Employment and Economic Growth in Urban China 1949–1957*, Cambridge: Cambridge University Press.

Howe, Christopher (1978) *China's Economy. A Basic Guide*, London: Paul Elek.

Howe, Christopher and Walker, Kenneth (1989) *The Foundations of the Chinese Planned Economy. A Documentary Survey, 1953–65*, Basingstoke: Macmillan.

Howell, J. (1995) 'Civil Society' in *China in the 1990s* R. Benewick and P. Wingrove (eds), Basingstoke: Macmillan.

Hu Chiao-mu (1978) Observe economic laws, speed up the four modernizations, *Peking Review*, nos. 45–7 (Nov. 10, 17 and 24).

Hua Guofeng (1977) *Peking Review* 20 (1), pp. 31–44.

Huntington, S. (1968) *Political Order in Changing Societies*, New Haven, CT: Yale University Press.

Huntington, S. and Nelson, J. M. (1976) *No Easy Choice: Political Participation in Developing Countries*, Cambridge, MA: Harvard University Press.

Isaacs, H. J. (1961) *The Tragedy of the Chinese Revolution*, Stanford, CA: Stanford University Press.

Jacka, Tamara (1992) 'The Public/Private Dichotomy and the Gender Division of Rural China' in *Economic Reform and Social Change in China* Andrew Watson (ed.), London: Routledge.

Jencks, H. W. (1982) *From Muskets to Missiles: Politics and Professionalism in the Chinese Army, 1945–81*, Boulder, CO: Westview Press.

Joffe, E. (1967) *Party and Army: Professionalism and Political Control in the Chinese Officer Corps, 1949–1964*, Cambridge, MA: East Asian Research Center, Harvard University.

Joffe, E. (1984) 'Civil–Military Relations' in *Chinese Defence Policy* G. Segal and W. T. Tow (eds), Basingstoke: Macmillan.

Joffe, E. (1987) *The Chinese Army after Mao*, London: Weidenfeld & Nicolson.

Johnson, Chalmers (1971) *Peasant Nationalism and Communist Power: The Emergence of Revolutionary China*, Stanford, CA: Stanford University Press.

Johnson, Kay Ann (1983) *Women, The Family, and Peasant Revolution in China*, London: University of Chicago Press.

Joint Economic Committee of the US Congress (1968) *An Economic Profile of Mainland China*, New York: Frederick A. Praeger.

Kane, Penny (1987) *The Second Billion. Population and Family Planning in China*, Harmondsworth: Penguin.

Kim, S. S. (ed.) (1984) *China and the World: Chinese Foreign Policy in the Post-Mao Era*, Epping: Bowker.

Ladany, Lazlo (1988) *The Communist Party of China and Marxism 1921–1985*, London: Hirst.

Lampton, David M. (1987) 'Chinese Politics: The Bargaining Treadmill' *Issues and Studies* 23 (3), pp. 11–41.

Li, C. and Bachman, David (1989) 'Localism, Elitism, and Immobilism. Elite Formation and Social Change in Post-Mao China' *World Politics* 42 (1), pp. 64–94.

Lieberthal, Kenneth (1976) *A Research Guide to Central Party and Government Meetings in China 1949–1975*, White Plains: International Arts and Sciences Press, 321 pp.

Lieberthal, Kenneth (1995) *Governing China*, New York: W. W. Norton.

Lieberthal, Kenneth and Dickson, Bruce (1989) *A Research Guide to Central Party and Government Meetings in China 1976–1986*, New York–London: M. E. Sharpe, 339 pp.

Lieberthal, Kenneth and Oksenberg, Michel (1988) *Policy Making in China. Leaders, Structures, and Processes,* Princeton, NJ: Princeton University Press.

Link, Perry (1984) *Roses and Thorns: The Second Blooming of the Hundred Flowers in Chinese Fiction 1979–80,* Berkeley, CA: University of California Press.

Lipset, S. M. (1960) *Political Man: The Social Bases of Politics,* London: Heinemann.

Loewe, M. (1990) *The Pride that was China,* London: Sidgwick & Jackson.

Long, S. (1991) *Taiwan, China's Long Frontier,* London: Macmillan.

Lovejoy, C. D and Watson, B. W. (1986) *China's Military Reforms* Special Studies in Military Affairs, London: Westview Press.

MacFarquhar, R. (1974a) *The Hundred Flowers Campaign and the Chinese Intellectuals,* New York: Octagon Books.

MacFarquhar, R. (1974b) *The Origins of the Cultural Revolution: Contradictions Among the People,* Oxford: Oxford University Press.

Maitan, L. (1976) *Party, Army and Masses in China,* New York: Monthly Review Press.

Manion, Melanie (1991) 'Policy Implementation in the People's Republic of China: Authoritative Decisions versus Individual Interests' *Journal of Asian Studies* 50 (2), pp. 83–105.

Mao Zedong [1927] 'Report on an Investigation of the Peasant Movement in Hunan' in *Selected Works of Mao Tsetung* vol. I, Peking: Foreign Languages Press (1965), pp. 23–62.

Mao Zedong [1929] 'On Correcting Mistaken Ideas in the Party' in *Selected Works of Mao Tsetung* vol. I, Peking: Foreign Languages Press (1965), pp. 105–16.

Mao Zedong [1936] 'Problems of Strategy in China's Revolutionary War' in *Selected Works of Mao Tsetung* vol. I, Peking: Foreign Languages Press (1965), pp. 179–254.

Mao Zedong [1937a] 'On Practice' in *Selected Readings from the Works of Mao Tsetung,* Peking: Foreign Languages Press (1971), pp. 65–84.

Mao Zedong [1937b] 'On Contradiction' in *Selected Readings from the Works of Mao Tsetung,* Peking: Foreign Languages Press (1971), pp. 85–133.

Mao Zedong [1938] 'Problems of Strategy in Guerrilla War Against Japan' in *Selected Works of Mao Tsetung* vol. II, Peking: Foreign Languages Press (1965), pp. 79–112.

Mao Zedong [1939] 'The Chinese Revolution and the Chinese Communist Party', in *Selected Works of Mao Tsetung* vol. II, Peking: Foreign Languages Press (1969), pp. 305–34.

Mao Zedong [1940] 'On New Democracy' in *Selected Works of Mao Tsetung* vol. II, Peking: Foreign Languages Press (1965), pp. 339–84.

Mao Zedong [1942] 'Talks at the Yan'an Forum on Literature and Art' (May 1942) in *Selected Works of Mao* vol. III, Peking: Foreign Languages Press (1965).

Mao Zedong [1943a] 'Some Questions Concerning Methods of Leadership' in *Selected Works of Mao Tsetung* vol. III, Peking: Foreign Languages Press (1965), pp. 287–94.

Mao Zedong [1943b] 'Get Organized!' in *Selected Works of Mao Tsetung* vol. III, Peking: Foreign Languages Press (19??), pp. 153–61; in *Selected Readings from the Works of Mao Zedong,* Peking: Foreign Languages Press (1971), pp. 295–305.

Mao Zedong [1945] 'The Foolish Old Man Who Removed the Mountains' in *Selected Works of Mao Tsetung* vol. III, Peking: Foreign Languages Press (1965), pp. 321–4; in *Selected Readings from the Works of Mao Zedong,* Peking: Foreign Languages Press (1971), pp. 320–3.

Mao Zedong [1956] 'On the Ten Major Relationships', in *Selected Works of Mao Tsetung* vol. V, Peking: Foreign Languages Press (1977), pp. 284–307.

Mao Zedong [1957] 'On the Correct Handling of Contradictions Among the People' in *Selected Works of Mao Tsetung* vol. V, Peking: Foreign Languages Press (1965), pp. 384–421; in *Selected Readings from the Works of Mao Zedong*, Peking: Foreign Languages Press (1971), pp. 432–79.

Mao Zedong (1972) *Quotations from Chairman Mao Zedong*, Peking: Foreign Languages Press.

Mao Zedong (1976) *Mao: Poems*, Beijing, Foreign Languages Press.

Marx, K. (1968) *Marx on China 1853–1860*, London: Lawrence & Wishart.

Maxwell, N. (1971) *India's China War*, New York: Pantheon.

Maxwell, Neville (ed.) (1979) *China's Road to Development*, Oxford: Pergamon Press.

Medvedev, R. (1986) *China and the Superpowers*, Oxford: Blackwell.

Mehnert, H. (1963) *Peking and Moscow*, Weidenfeld & Nicolson.

Meisner, Maurice (1986) *Mao's China and After. A History of the People's Republic*, New York: Macmillan/The Free Press.

Nathan, Andrew (1973) 'A Factionalism Model for CCP Politics' *China Quarterly* 53 January/March, pp. 34–66.

Nathan, A. (1990) *China's Crisis: Dilemmas of Reform and Prospects for Democracy*, New York: Columbia University Press.

Naughton, B. (1988) 'The Third Front: Defense Industrialization in the Chinese Interior' *China Quarterly* 115 (September), pp. 351–86.

Needham, J. (1970) *Clerks and Craftsmen in China in the West*, Cambridge: Cambridge University Press.

Nelsen, H. W. (1981) *The Chinese Military System: An Organizational Study of the Chinese People's Liberation Army* 2nd edn, Boulder, CO: Westview Press.

North, R. C. (1963) *Moscow and the Chinese Communists*, Stanford, CA: Stanford University Press.

Oi, Jean C. (1989) *State and Peasant in Contemporary China. The Political Economy of Village Government*, Berkeley, CA: University of California Press.

Oksenberg, Michel (1969) 'Sources and Methodological Problems in the Study of Contemporary China' in *Chinese Communist Politics in Action* Doak A. Barnett (ed.), Seattle, WA: University of Washington Press, pp. 155–215.

Pateman, C. (1970) *Participation and Democratic Theory*, Cambridge: Cambridge University Press.

Pateman, Carole (1989) *The Disorder of Women*, Cambridge: Polity Press.

Perry, E. (1980) *Rebels and Revolutionaries in North China 1845–1945*, Stanford, CA: Stanford University Press.

Pieke, Frank (1995) *The Ordinary and the Extraordinary: An Anthropological Study of Chinese Reform and the 1989 People's Movement in Beijing*, London: Kegan Paul International.

Pye, Lucien W. (1971) *Warlord Politics, Conflict and Coalition in the Modernization of Republican China 1912–1949*, London: Collier Macmillan.

Pye, Lucien W. (1991) *China: An Introduction*, New York: Harper Collins, 418 pp.

Qu Geping and Li Jinchang (1994) *Population and Environment in China*, Boulder, CO: Lynne Rienner.

Rai, Shirin (1991) *Resistance and Reaction: University Politics in Post-Mao China*, Hemel Hempstead: Harvester Wheatsheaf.

Rai, Shirin M. (1994) 'Gender and Democratisation or What Does Democracy Mean for Women in the Third World?' *Democratization* 1 (2) pp. 209–28.

Rai, Shirin M. and Zhang Junzuo (1994) 'Competing and Learning: Women and the State in Contemporary Rural Mainland China' *Issues and Studies* 30 (3), pp. 51–66.

Rai, Shirin, Pilkington, Hilary and Phizacklea, Annie (1992) *Women in the Face of Change: The Soviet Union, Eastern Europe and China*, London: Routledge.

Riskin, Carl (1987) *China's Political Economy: The Quest for Development Since 1949*, Oxford: Oxford University Press.

Ross, Lester (1988) *Environmental Policy in China*, Bloomington/Indianapolis, IN: Indiana University Press.

Said, E. (1995) *Orientalism*, Harmondsworth: Penguin.

Schifrin, Harold Z. (1968) *Sun Yat-sen*, Berkeley, CA: University of California Press.

Schram, S. (1973) *Authority, Participation and Cultural Change in China*, Cambridge: Cambridge University Press.

Schram, S. (ed) (1987) *Foundations and Limits of State Power in China*, London: School of Oriental and African Studies, University of London.

Schumpeter, J. A. (1947) *Capitalism, Socialism and Democracy* 3rd edn, New York: Harper Torchbooks.

Schurmann, Franz (1966–1968) *Ideology and Organization in Communist China*, Berkeley, CA: University of California Press.

Schurmann, F. and Schell, O. (1967) *Imperial China*, Harmondsworth: Penguin.

Schurmann, F. and Schell, O. (1968) *Republican China, Nationalism, War and the Rise of Communism 1911–1949*, Harmondsworth: Penguin.

Schurmann, F. and Schell, O. (eds) (1977) *Communist China: Revolutionary Reconstruction and International Confrontation 1949–66*, Harmondsworth: Penguin Books.

Schwartz, Benjamin (1968) 'The Chinese Perception of World Order' in *The Chinese World Order: Traditional China's Foreign Relations* J. K. Fairbank (ed.), Cambridge, MA: Harvard University Press.

Sckocpol, T. (1979) *States and Social Revolutions: A Comparative Analysis of France, Russia and China*, Cambridge: Cambridge University Press.

Selden, Mark (1971) *The Yenan Way in Revolutionary China*, Cambridge, MA: Harvard University Press.

Sheridan, J. F. (1975) *China in Disintegration: the Republican Era in Chinese History 1912–1949*, London: Collier Macmillan.

Shih Chih-yu (1990) *The Spirit of Chinese Foreign Policy*, London: Macmillan.

Shirk, Susan L. (1993) *The Political Logic of Economic Reform in China*, Berkeley, CA: University of California Press.

Shue, Vivienne (1988) *The Reach of the State*, Stanford, CA: Stanford University Press.

Skilling, H. Gordon (1966) 'Interest Groups and Communist Politics' *World Politics* 18 (3), pp. 435–51.

Smil, Vaclav (1984) *The Bad Earth. Environmental Degradation in China*, London: ZED Press.

Smil, Vaclav (1993) *China's Environmental Crisis: An Inquiry into the Limits of National Development*, Armonk, New York: M. E. Sharpe.

Snow, Edgar (1937) *Red Star Over China*, London: Gollancz.

Stacey, Judith (1983) *Patriarchy and Socialist Revolution in China*, Berkeley, CA: University of California Press.

State Education Commission (1984) *Achievement of Education in China: Statistics 1949–1983*, Beijing: People's Education Press.

Statistical Yearbook of China (1990) *Chung-kuo t'ung-chi nien-chien 1990*, Peking.

Strand, D. (1989) *Political Participation and Political Reform in Post-Mao China*, Copenhagen Discussion Papers no. 6, Copenhagen: University of Copenhagen.

Su Shaozhi (1988) *Democratization and Reform*, Nottingham: Spokesman.

Sutter, R. G. (1978) *China Watch: Sino-American Reconciliation*, Baltimore, MD: Johns Hopkins University Press.

Teng Ssu-yu and Fairbank, J. K. (1981) *China's Response to the West: A Documentary Survey 1839–1923*, Cambridge, MA: Harvard University Press.

Treadgold, D. W. (ed.) (1967) *Soviet and Chinese Communism: Similarities and Differences*, Seattle, WA: University of Washington Press.

Unger, Jonathan (1987) 'The Struggle to Dictate China's Administration' *Australian Journal of Chinese Affairs* 18 (July), pp. 15–45.

Walder, Andrew G. (1986) *Communist Neo-Traditionalism: Work and Authority in Chinese Industry*, Berkeley, CA: University of California Press.

Wei Ching-sheng [Wei Jingsheng] (1979) 'Human Rights, Equality, Democracy. On to the "Fifth Modernisation"' *Issues and Studies* 15 (11), pp. 86–101.

White, G. W. (1994) *Markets and Civil Society in China* Discussion Paper, Sussex: IDS.

White, Gordon (1993) *Riding the Tiger: The Politics of Economic Reform in Post-Mao China*, London: Macmillan.

Whitson, W. W. and Huang Chen-hsia (1973) *The Chinese High Command: History of Communist Military Politics*, London: Macmillan.

Wich, R. (1980) *Sino-Soviet Crisis Politics*, Cambridge, MA: Harvard University Council on East Asian Studies.

Wolfe, Margery (1985) *Revolution Postponed: Women in Contemporary China*, London: Methuen.

Womack, Brantley (1991) 'Review Essay: Transfigured Community: Neo-Traditionalism and Work Unit Socialism in China' *China Quarterly* 126 (June), pp. 313–39.

Wong, Christine P. W. (1994) *Economic Reform in the People's Republic of China*, New York: Oxford University Press.

World Commission on Environment and Development (WCED) (1987) *Our Common Future*, London: Oxford University Press.

Wright, Mary C. (ed.) (1968) *China in Revolution: The First Phase, 1900–1913*, New Haven, CT: Yale University Press.

Yahuda, M. (1978) *China's Role in World Affairs*, London: Croom Helm.

Yahuda, M. (1983) *Towards the End of Isolationism: China's Foreign Policy after Mao*, London: Macmillan.

Yang, Mayfair Mei-hui (1989) 'Between State and Society: The Construction of Corporativeness in a Chinese Socialist Factory' *Australian Journal of Chinese Affairs* 22 (July), pp. 31–60.

Yeh Wen-hsin (1992) 'Progressive Journalism and Shanghai's Petty Urbanites: Zhou Taofen and the Shenghuo Weekly, 1926–1945' in *Shanghai Sojourns* Fr. Wakeman Jr. and Wen-hsin Yeh (eds), China Research Monograph no. 40, Berkeley, CA: Center for Chinese Studies, pp. 186–238.

Young, J. R. (1987) *The Dragon's Teeth: Inside China's Armed Forces*, London: Hutchison.

Yu Guangyuan (ed.) (1984) *China's Socialist Modernization*, Beijing: Foreign Languages Press.

Zagoria, D. (1962) *The Sino-Soviet Conflict 1956–61*, Princeton, NJ: Princeton University Press.

Zhang Junzuo (1992) 'Gender and Political Participation in Rural China' in *Women in the Face of Change: The Soviet Union, Eastern Europe and China* Shirin Rai, Hilary Pilkington and Annie Phizacklea (eds), London: Routledge.

Zhao Ziyang (1987) 'Advance along the Road of Socialism with Chinese Characteristics' *Beijing Review* 30 (45) 9–15.

Index